THE RUSSIAN REVOLUTION

THE RUSSIAN REVOLUTION

Marcel Liebman

PREFACE BY ISAAC DEUTSCHER

TRANSLATED BY ARNOLD J. POMERANS

RANDOM HOUSE   NEW YORK

To the memory of my brother Henri

(1927–43)

who died at Auschwitz

Contents

Foreword

WHAT merit this book may have can only spring from the triple task its author has set himself: to outline the main stages of the Russian Revolution; to reconstruct the climate in which it took place; and to examine the ideological preoccupations – and hence the ideals – of its main protagonists. Few books in the abundant literature devoted to this subject have combined these aims, and yet the full meaning of the 1917 Revolution cannot be grasped in any other way. The reader must judge for himself if my attempt has been successful, but even if it is, it does not pretend to be more than an introduction to a deeper study of one of the most fateful events in modern history – an event, we may be certain, that has by no means exhausted its effects.

Among the many sources on which I have drawn – all of which are listed in the Bibliography – some deserve special mention because of their general interest and scope. These are Sukhanov's *The Russian Revolution, 1917 – A Personal Record* (Oxford University Press, 1955), E. H. Carr's *The Bolshevik Revolution* (Penguin, 1966), John Reed's *Ten Days that Shook the World* (Vintage, 1960), and above all Trotsky's *History of the Russian Revolution* (University of Michigan 1967) which, irrespective of its author's personal involvement, offers a remarkably living and well-documented survey of the period February–October 1917.

I shall be well content if I succeed in convincing the reader of the magnitude of the subject under review and also of the limitations of the present work. If I have been able to stimulate further interest, to provoke questions and to pose some of the major problems, I shall have done quite enough in a field where dogma continues to hold sway and to distort the historical truth – by uncritical praise no less than by blind hatred.

It is most unusual for an author to pay homage to the writer of his Preface, but the sudden death of Isaac Deutscher, a few days after he had finished his introduction to this book, imposes this sad duty upon me. Let me first of all acknowledge the great debt my present work owes to that great historian, whose countless

9

suggestions, reflecting his unrivalled knowledge of the subject, have proved invaluable.

However, there is a much wider debt that I, like so many of my contemporaries, owe to Isaac Deutscher. At a time when everything bearing upon the Russian Revolution tended to degenerate into invective or blind adulation, Deutscher, more than anyone else, distinguished himself by his efforts to analyse the events with sympathy, yet without prejudice. Deutscher never pretended to an impossible degree of neutrality; on the contrary, his extraordinary grasp of the communist phenomenon sprang from his deep personal involvement in one of the most important problems of our time. His gifts, moreover, transcended those of the historian—his writings present us with an authentic Marxist interpretation of the modern world, an interpretation that differs completely from its official caricature. To historians and sociologists alike he serves as a model of objectivity coupled with keen intelligence and great learning, and with what C. Wright Mills has called the 'sociological imagination'—which is nothing but the desire to understand man's destiny, the better to speed his emancipation.

M.L.

Brussels
August 20th, 1967

Preface

As the Russian Revolution passes into its second half-century few are those, even among its bitter enemies and opponents, who would still deny its world-historical impact and significance. This has clearly been the greatest formative event of the century, indeed the most momentous social-political upheaval since the French Revolution; in scope, vitality, and in the global range of its consequences it surpasses its French predecessor. Yet when a young worker or a student wants to find out how the Revolution happened, by what stages it developed, what were the factors that determined its outcome, who were the men and what were the ideas that inspired it, he is not able to find any brief, intelligible and reliable History that contains the answers to his questions. This is a curious circumstance which requires a few words of comment.

That the enemies of the Revolution have been unable to produce a coherent account of the events that shook Russia and the world in 1917 is hardly surprising. They have not yet recovered from the shock. Most often class prejudice, resentment and ignorance colour their views. And indeed if one does assume that a social order based on capitalist property is the natural order of things, or that reason and human nature alike require that mankind be ruled in the traditional way, if not by fascist dictators then by great generals or by 'democratic' elites, monarchical or republican, then of necessity one views the events of 1917 as an outrage against reason or human nature, an outrage committed by monstrous people and devils incarnate. In the stultifying atmosphere of the Cold War this view has indeed been assiduously advocated or insinuated in the West by innumerable writers and propagandists who see the upheaval of 1917 as the still active source of almost all the evils that have afflicted humanity ever since. In a way these writers and propagandists pay their unwitting tribute to the Revolution and testify that its challenge is still alive. Yet what they offer the public is never the actual story of the Revolution but merely a demonological travesty.

Unfortunately, our young intelligent reader does not find much help when he turns for enlightenment to writers of the Left, those whom he regards as friends of the Russian Revolution. He will find these too strangely uninformative and uninstructive, and their accounts of the Revolution cliché-ridden and lifeless, devoid of sociological depth and psychological truth and so producing a kind of Byzantine effect. M. Louis Aragon's recent *History of the U.S.S.R.* is a striking example of this kind of literature. What is it, one may ask, that paralyses the imagination, understanding and power of expression of a writer of this calibre when he tries to cope with a theme which should, and on the face of it does, inspire him? The situation would be simple if one could merely say that M. Aragon shares the lot of so many authors of Lives of Saints, authors among whom there were quite a few talented poets. The point is that the failure of M. Aragon and of authors of his school of thought is not due merely to an innocent excess of devotion or to *trop de zèle*. The writers of official Communism have for so long purveyed the historical forgeries and myths produced by the Stalinist school of falsification that even when they have been free to jettison some of these, they have not been able to recapture and grasp the historical truth of the Revolution. Even in the era of the so-called de-Stalinization they have still had to observe so many prohibitions and taboos, to slide over so many of the crucial events and to cover with silence the roles and even the names of so many leading actors, that the history of the Revolution has in fact been forbidden ground for them, forbidden and unknown ground. Even in this glorious jubilee year most of the revolutionary leaders of 1917 — Trotsky and Bukharin, Zinoviev and Kamenev, Rykov and Tomsky, and many, many others — are still unmentionable in Moscow or are mentioned only as evil influences; and now it is a requirement of *bon ton* to ignore even Stalin. What would we say of 'historians' who tried to relate to us the French Revolution without describing the roles or even mentioning the names of Danton and St Just, of Desmoulins, Hébert, Cloots, and most other prominent Jacobins, and were content to speak only of Marat and occasionally to drop a hint about Robespierre?

History written in this manner not only does a terrible injustice to historical personalities. It blots out important groups of men who were inspired or guided by them. It obliterates or distorts their ideas, initiatives and deeds. It leaves out of account such large and vital parts of the story that what is left is of necessity fragmentary, inorganic, and incomprehensible. In effect, the Party of the Revolution appears in the writings of Stalinist and Khrushchevite historians not as it was in 1917, but as a shadow of the Communist Party of today incongruously projected back, in all its grotesquely bureaucratic respectability, upon the screen of 1917. What vanishes in the process is the heaven-storming defiance and courage and the warm humanity of the revolutionaries of 1917, their broad and open-minded intelligence, their world-embracing ideas and ideals, their fearless strategy, their supple tactics and their great inner-Party freedom. Small wonder that a story and an image so sadly impoverished is incredible, offers little inspiration and teaches no lesson relevant to our present problems and preoccupations.

Yet despite this sad state of contemporary writing on the origins of the Soviet regime, the history of the Russian Revolution is no *tabula rasa*. In the first decade after their victory the Bolsheviks themselves brought out an immense amount of objective historical documentation, and many actors and eye-witnesses, Russian and foreign, friendly and hostile, described their experiences. Trotsky's large *History of the Russian Revolution* stands out as a magnificent and unique monument to the Russia of 1917 — no other great revolution was as fortunate as the Russian to find a historian of genius in one of its supreme leaders. And in recent years a complete outsider, Professor E. H. Carr, a British historian, has chronicled in many cool, detached and detailed volumes an account of the first years of the Soviet regime. What has been lacking, however, is a work of more modest dimensions that would offer readers of the young generation a reliable introduction to the events of 1917 and enable them to grasp the significance of the Bolshevik upheaval.

Marcel Liebman's book fills this gap very ably. The author has managed to condense in a short space an enormous amount of vital information about almost every aspect of the historical background and of the Revolution itself; and he has produced a coherent, vivid and exciting narrative. He tells his story with the seriousness it deserves, but also forcefully and with admirable verve. He has succeeded indeed in summarizing in an easy and intelligible manner the present state of our historical knowledge in this field. He is popular but he does not talk down to his readers and does not oversimplify the complex issues with which he has had to deal. And while he leaves the reader in no doubt as to where his own sympathies lie — M. Liebman writes as a Marxist and a socialist passionately interested in the significance of the Revolution for our epoch –he narrates and analyses the revolutionary process with exemplary truthfulness and objectivity. One might argue with him about this or that point of his interpretation. I personally, for example, would question some of Liebman's conclusions in his last chapter ('The Fate of the Russian Revolution'), where it seems to me that he underrates certain negative aspects of Stalin's policy in the aftermath of the Second World War, and that he has not sufficiently gauged the whole depth of the moral-political crisis in the post-Stalinist U.S.S.R. But these are bound to be debatable issues in any case; and I find the book as a whole so good and valuable that I have no hesitation in recommending it most warmly and expressing the hope that it will find a very wide and appreciative readership.

August 14th, 1967   Isaac Deutscher

I

The Russia of the Tsars

A S EUROPE entered the twentieth century, scientific discoveries
came in quick succession, industrialization and urbanization
proceeded apace, communications were greatly improved,
public education spread far afield and old traditions crumbled
under the blows of technological progress. Suddenly, everything
seemed quite new, and nothing seemed impossible. On the political
plane, the working class had begun to challenge the bourgeoisie
more and more openly, wondering whether capitalism might not
be in its death-throes at last. Humanity was about to throw off its
ancient shackles, to move forward to a greater future in a spirit of
unprecedented hope.

It was the twentieth century, but at the far side of Europe,
Russia was still in many respects in the Middle Ages; poverty and
ignorance continued unchecked, even though industry, still in its
infancy, was beginning to make rapid strides. This immense
country, run by an outdated autocracy, was in itself an anachronism, surrounded on all sides by the germs of a new world. At its
head, an obsolete and weak monarchy tried to disguise the empti-
ness of its existence behind a magnificent, if badly cracked, façade
of pomp and splendour. In the twentieth century, it set out to
remain what it had been since its inception: omnipotent, unchallenged and divinely appointed. In 1896, at his coronation, the
last Tsar of the Russias, Nicholas II, heard the Metropolitan
Archbishop of Moscow say that 'this visible ornament is symbolic
of the invisible crown set upon thee as head of all the Russian
peoples by our Lord, Jesus Christ, King of Glory.' True, such
invocations were not limited to Russia, but nowhere else did
monarchs greet them with the conviction, the unshakeable certainty, that they represented not so much a useful social ritual as a
living reality. For as far as Nicholas II was concerned, he was
indeed a divine ruler, or rather the embodiment of divine authority.
Leo Tolstoy was perfectly right to affirm in 1901 that 'autocracy is
a form of government that may meet the needs of some Central

African tribe cut off from the rest of the world, but certainly not
those of the Russian people ... ' Tolstoy—like so many other
Russians, from the intelligentsia down to the angry industrial
proletariat—was protesting against the inertia of a whole system
and the blindness of a single man.

The Russian autocracy

From its very inception, the Russian state had been based on
arbitrary rule and tyranny. Ivan the Terrible (1553–84) stamped
his country indelibly with the twin marks of absolutism and terror,
originally in order to crush the selfish and anarchic power of the
boyars. Their suppression—we shall see by what methods—
enabled the former Muscovite prince to proclaim himself 'Tsar'
(Caesar) and to contend that 'all Russian sovereigns are supreme
kings and as such beyond reproach.' This Byzantine conception of
political authority did, in fact, have some justification while the
country preserved the Oriental characteristics that stemmed from
its peculiar origins, Mongol influences and complete isolation from
the West; but it lost all sense once the windows towards Europe
were opened. Peter the Great, in particular, made absolutism even
more absolute when he turned the Orthodox Church into his docile
instrument and humble servant.

After his death, the nobility succeeded to some extent in limiting
the powers of the monarchy by vesting certain prerogatives in a
Privy Council composed of high officials who enjoyed the confidence of the nobility. However, the Council was not nearly as
important as it might have been. On the ruins of boyar rule, the
Tsars had created a nobility of service: only those serving the state
as officers or administrators were raised to the nobility. Depen-
dence on the Tsars was thus a permanent characteristic of the
Russian nobility, preventing it from becoming an independent
agent in the running of the state. Its privileges were numerous, its
powers derisory. Even under Catherine II (1762–96), when the
nobility was put in charge of local government and relieved of
service obligations by a special charter, it still failed to wield any
real influence in the state at large. The autocratic power of the
Tsars remained unchallenged, and if, in the eighteenth and nineteenth centuries, Their Imperial Majesties failed to act against the
interests and wishes of the nobility, it was less because of resistance
on the part of the latter than because of the inertia of the machinery

of state. This may be gathered from the fact that when Alexander II decided, somewhat belatedly, in 1861, to emancipate the serfs, their noble owners offered him little opposition, despite their obvious resentment and fears. In fact, the nobility ceased to play any kind of independent role in the sixteenth century. Subsequently, Alexander III (1881–94) was able to limit its competence to 'the direction of petty affairs.

The nobility was politically sterile, the bourgeoisie utterly impotent. The entire history of Russia was moulded by this negative factor, by the absence of vigorous or even viable institutions capable of representing the views of the various social classes and so counterbalancing the weight of the autocracy. True, until the middle of the seventeenth century, the *Zemsky Sobor* ('National Assembly') used to forgather regularly—it even met in permanent session from 1613 to 1622 after choosing Michael I, the founder of the Romanov dynasty, as the new Tsar. But in reality this assembly, in which the peasants, making up 95 per cent of the population, were not represented at all, was no more than a temporary—and ineffective – stopgap; having existed for a century, it vanished into oblivion, once again leaving the monarchy in full control. Clearly, Tsarism was unable and unwilling to reform itself; it could only be toppled by force.

If, negatively speaking, Tsarism owed its survival to the absence of a powerful challenge within or without, it could, on the positive side, count on the absolute support of a bureaucratic caste, however inefficient. All Russian society was constricted in the straitjacket of the hierarchized *chin*,[1] a highly disciplined company of men who, like their Prussian counterparts, strutted about in splendid uniforms. The bureaucratic nature of the country may also be gathered from the official role assigned to the Russian universities when they first appeared in 1804. One of their objects was the advancement of knowledge, but, in the views of the Russian legislators, this was a secondary function; the main one was to select and train officials for the administration.

---

[1] The *chin* was a network of grades covering the entire administration and army. It was divided into fourteen levels, ranging from College Registrar to Imperial Chancellor in the civil branch, and from ensign to field marshal in the army. Everyone from the eighth rank upwards was automatically raised to the nobility. It was characteristic of Russia that State service was thought to be a reason for ennoblement.

As Boris Nolde[1] has put it, before the Revolution all Russian statemen were state officials first and foremost.

All in all, the Tsar himself was only a supreme bureaucrat. In the middle of the nineteenth century, he emerged as the tip of an administrative pyramid, as one who wielded divine prerogatives through an ever more powerful and all-embracing network of state officials. However, his personal whims remained absolute law; he could appoint and dismiss ministers and other officials at will. He might decide to listen to his counsellors, or then again he might not; in either case, he himself was answerable to nobody. Military and diplomatic questions, in particular, were his exclusive province, and so were most political decisions of any consequence, so much so that the Minister of the Interior was generally considered the Tsar's public mouthpiece. The Council of Ministers, moreover, lacked the sort of corporate existence that might have ensured it some standing or authority –the sovereign dealt individually with every minister in turn, and even when, at long last, the function of the President of the Council was officially recognized (1905), the Tsar continued to treat his chief minister as a subaltern unworthy of any real confidence.

This political subordination, which often degenerated into abject servility, fully reflected the mediocrity of the Russian bureaucratic machine. State officials did not constitute the social elite of the country. Badly paid, they sought solace in the bottle or the greased palm. Every rank had its own price, and it was common knowledge what colour bank bill went with what kind of stripe on the uniform. The level of education among the bureaucracy was deplorable: at the end of the nineteenth century, 80 per cent of all provincial officials had not even finished primary school.

Neither efficiency nor authority could be expected from so defective a body of men. They were mere tools of the autocracy, and poor tools at that. Their best representatives, aware of the urgency with which changes were needed, or at least feeling the need for some independent action, proved quite incapable of gaining the Tsar's ear. The most moderate reforms met with his blank refusal. Until the eve of the Revolution, the regime remained utterly complacent; capriciousness was the rule of office, incompetence paved the way for ultimate downfall.

To these defects of the system must be added the incapacity and

[1] B. Nolde, *L'ancien régime et la Révolution russe*, p. 98.

mediocrity of the Tsars themselves. Throughout the nineteenth
century they were men without vision, courage or imagination.
Their hatred of the intelligentsia was but a reflection of their own
intellectual incapacity. Brute force had become a substitute for
vigour, and the most hidebound conservatism served them all for
a political creed and a programme.

The nineteenth century began with the reign of Paul I (1796–
1801), whose mental health was doubtful, and though his successor, Alexander I (1801–25), enjoyed the respect of Europe for some
time and came to the throne with liberal intentions, he too ended
as a failure, an incoherent mystic.

With Nicholas I (1825–55) Russia was given her autocrat *par
excellence*. He became known as 'The Knout' and, not content
with oppressing his own subjects, turned himself into the 'gen-
darme of Europe', helping reactionaries of whatever variety, and
suppressing the Polish and Hungarian revolutions with brute force.
Fear of change was an obsession with him, love of secrecy a mania.
When he was finally convinced that reforms had to be introduced,
he insisted that they must be so gradual, indeed imperceptible, as
not to upset the system in any way. He accordingly entrusted them
to secret committees and, lest anyone guess his real intention, gave
these committees the most preposterous titles. In 1839, for instance, he called the commission studying peasant conditions a
'Committee for the Normalization of the Contributions and Local
Taxes in the Western Provinces'.

Alexander II (1855–81) may appear to have been an exception to
the general rule, to have been that *rara avis*, a liberal Tsar. But
appearances are deceptive. True, he introduced important reforms
—the emancipation of the serfs, the modernization of the judicial
apparatus, and at the end of his life he even dreamed of setting up a
representative assembly, albeit with consultative functions only.
But in all these plans he never considered the slightest diminution
of his autocratic powers; indeed, he sometimes caused those who
so much as suggested such a thing to be deported.

Alexander III (1881–94), for his part, reverted to the old form.
When he came to the throne, this despot, to whom one of his
nobles referred repeatedly as 'crowned idiot' or 'august imbecile',
declared in his famous manifesto of April 28th, 1881, that henceforth he would not discuss the destiny of his empire with anyone
but God. When this dialogue failed to produce all the expected

results, the Tsar chose as his additional confidant his former tutor, Constantine Pobiedonostsev, a reactionary of a diehard stamp rare even in Russia. It was this, his favourite adviser, who confided to Alexander III the prophetic thought that, in Russia, a revolution and even the bloodiest of upheavals was preferable to a Constitution. Not surprisingly, oppression, which had previously been no more than an arm of the autocracy, now became its very raison d'être.

Nicholas II, the last of the Tsars

One of the drawbacks of hereditary and personal rule is that it cannot ensure the quality of its representatives. Thus while Russia was undoubtedly an autocracy under her last Tsar, no one would have guessed it from the person of her lacklustre and eccentric ruler. Rarely can a decadent regime resist the effect of involuntary but systematic destruction wrought by this kind of man.

Clinging to power and unwilling to share it with anyone else, Nicholas II lacked all the qualities that go into the making of a statesman. On his coronation, he confided to a friend that he was utterly unprepared to tackle the business of government. 'I understand absolutely nothing about matters of state. I have not the least idea of how to address my ministers.' And, during the twenty-three years of his reign (1894–1917), he never acquired the skill.

But then, his real interests did not lie with men and politics. The diary he left tells us at length about his real preoccupations: apart from the audiences he granted and the visits he paid, he mentions a great many details of his family life, and describes his favourite pastimes—riding, skating and, above all, hunting. We are given a precise list of the quarry he bagged on successive chases. And this was the man who until the end of his reign thought himself fit to preside over the destiny of a great power.

Contributing further to his downfall were his weakness of character and extreme political myopia. 'A lamentable lack of will-power is the Emperor's greatest fault,' declared Count Witte, one of his chief ministers. Add to this his dissimulation and duplicity— the Tsar was loath to impart disagreeable decisions to even his closest confidants—his obtuseness and lack of foresight, and one begins to realize why he held intelligence in such low regard, why he wanted the very word 'intellectual' to be dropped from the language. It would seem that the advice he accepted most freely—

and with the most enduring effects—was that of Pobiedonostsev, Procurator of the Holy Synod and his former tutor. It was from this man that he absorbed his political credo, to wit, that popular representation is 'the greatest fraud of our time'; that liberty and political rights are alien to the Russian soul and as such pernicious; that education must be limited to the Scriptures and elementary arithmetic—'all the rest is superfluous and even dangerous.' In fact, there was no reactionary tenet that Nicholas II failed to make his own. Hence the choice of his other advisers, among them Prince Vladimir Meshchersy, whose extreme right-wing opinions no doubt made up for his scandalous reputation. Another was Rasputin, to whom we shall be returning. For the rest, the Tsar made no secret of his sympathy with such ultra-conservative organizations as the Union of Russian Peoples (which had close links with the terrorist Black Hundreds). Moreover, if we are to believe Count Witte—who, admittedly had no great love for him—Nicholas II despised all those he thought less stupid than himself.

When dealing with such men, historians generally wax lyrical on their generosity of heart and high morality. And, indeed, Nicholas II was a loving father and an ideal husband. Nor was his sincerity in doubt; for it may be considered a corollary of all his misjudgments and anachronistic political views. As for his morality, we cannot pass in silence over the dogged determination and often quite brazen cruelty with which he persecuted political prisoners and, more generally, political opponents. He bore personal responsibility for the many acts of terror perpetrated by his administration, and he systematically refused to exercise his right to commute the many death sentences handed out by Tsarist tribunals after the revolutionary upsurge of 1905 to 1906. Indeed, when General Trepov declared that he did not intend to spare his bullets, thus provoking a wave of public indignation, he received the warm support of his sovereign.[1]

No account of Nicholas II would be complete without reference to his shadowy and unbalanced queen, the Tsarina Alexandra. The mystical, and sometimes downright pathological, ravings of this

---

[1] When Nicholas II received a report from the Governor of the Baltic provinces about an officer who 'carried out summary executions even of people who had offered no resistance', the Tsar jotted in the margin of the document 'Good fellow.'

woman would be of no more than passing interest, were it not that
she exerted the most nefarious pressure on her husband. Authori-
tarian in outlook, hysterical in temperament, she believed that she,
too, had a divine mission: to preserve the autocratic patrimony for
her son, the hapless Alexis, whose fatal haemophilia rendered him
all the more precious to her. Over the years, Alexandra's piety
degenerated into the morbid superstition that laid her open to the
machinations of a host of charlatans, from Philippe Encausse, a
prophet from Lyons, to Rasputin, that living symbol of the
absurdity and decadence of the Tsar's regime.

Alexandra who, as we shall see, finished up by running Russia on
her husband's behalf, was so conservative as to make Nicholas II
look a progressive by comparison. This pious woman abhorred not
only all revolutionaries—that went without saying—but also anyone with the slightest desire for reform. Her correspondence with
the Tsar, particularly during the war, when military operations
removed Nicholas from his court and she ruled on his behalf,
bears full witness to her political frenzy. 'Be more autocratic,'
Alexandra pleaded, 'never forget that you are an autocratic ruler
and that you must remain one.' And she added that 'Russia loves to
be caressed with a horse-whip—such is the nature of these people.'
She was thinking of Russia in general and, it seems, of liberals in
particular. In the same vein, she implored her husband, 'Be an
Emperor, be Peter the Great, be Ivan the Terrible, be the Emperor
Paul. Crush them all ... No, don't laugh at me, you wicked man ...
Send Lvov to Siberia ... Miliukov, Guchkov and Polivanov to
Siberia as well.' All her letters were a curious mixture of near-
hysterical savagery, of demented political ideas and mad protesta-
tions of love.

Such, in brief, was the character of Russia's despots on the eve
of the Revolution. Their historical failure was highlighted further
by the scandalous intrigues of Rasputin, 'the debauched monk',
who was at one stage the power behind the throne.[1]

In pre-revolutionary Russia, autocracy was thus maintained by
brute force and often by sheer terror. The Tsarist regime was
permanently identified with the negation of all liberties. A few
years before its downfall, Peter Stolypin, the President of the
Council, told a petitioner who had come to plead on behalf of the

[1] See Chapter 3.

peasants in his region, 'You don't know for whom you are inter-
ceding. All of them are mad brutes and can only be ruled by fear.
If we gave them liberty, they would massacre all of us—you, and
anyone wearing a suit.'

Indeed, very little in Russia had changed since Ivan the Terrible
imposed his will with the help of a special police force, the
notorious *oprichniki*, who turned terror into a systematic technique,
as for instance when they destroyed Novgorod and killed sixty
thousand of its inhabitants. And if Ivan the Terrible may be called
the embodiment of Oriental despotism, then it is equally true to
say that Peter the Great, whose name has come to stand for
westernization, proved no less tyrannical a hundred and fifty years
later. Thus, during October 1698 alone, he sentenced close on
seven hundred people to death for their alleged participation in a
rebellion. He may be remembered in history books for his great
military victories and for having founded St Petersburg, but his
delight in inflicting torture revealed another side of this Tsar. He
ordered his own son, the heir presumptive, to be tortured for his
alleged part in a conspiracy. The charge was never proved, but the
Tsarevich died of his injuries, inflicted in the Tsar's presence.

This type of barbarism abated with time, but the system of
terror imposed by the secret police became a fixed institution.
True, Alexander I thought for a short spell that he could abolish it,
but he quickly changed his mind. Reborn with new vigour in 1807,
police terror reached its peak under the reign of Nicholas I, and
continued to hold its own until the end of the old regime.

In fact the very notion of freedom seemed incompatible with
Tsarism. None of the political liberties that had long since been
written into Western law existed in Russia before the 1905 Revolution. No opposition of any form was tolerated and the conspiracy
with which Dostoevsky was charged, and for which he was sentenced to death,[1] was a conspiracy in name only. The only crime
these men had committed was to join intellectual groups for the
purpose of discussing reforms or such vague Utopian ideals as
Fourier's theories. But then, the very idea of private discussion
aroused the fury of a regime whose Minister of Public Education

---

[1] Dostoevsky's sentence was commuted to deportation at the very last minute.
On that occasion, Nicholas I withheld his pardon until the prisoners were standing on the scaffold. Dostoevsky recalled the four years spent among political
prisoners and criminals in his *Memoirs from the House of the Dead*.

was heard to declare that he would not sleep peacefully in his bed until the publication of all literary works was proscribed by law.

Until 1865, no books or papers could be published without prior approval by the authorities; that year, Alexander II decided to introduce a more subtle system of censorship by special tribunals. In the event, the new censors were all puppets and invariably abused their authority. An official document dating from 1819 asserted that 'private persons are not allowed to approve or disapprove of political decisions in writing,' and a professional censor by the name of Nikitenko explained that 'if one counted all the officials involved in censorship, their number would greatly exceed the list of titles published every year.'

The peasants

At the end of the nineteenth century, less than 13 per cent of Russians lived in towns;[1] the rest was made up of a vast and miserable mass of peasants for whom, as an old Russian saw had it, God was too high and the Tsar too far away, and who, watching their geographically closer but physically no less inaccessible masters, sighed bitterly that 'we look at the same sun but do not eat the same dinner.'

The Russian peasants had only just emerged from serfdom; not until 1861 did Alexander II deign to emancipate them—two centuries after his more enlightened subjects and clear-sighted officials had begun to clamour for the removal of this anachronism. Nicholas I admitted in 1842 that 'serfdom in its present form is, without doubt and by common consent, a terrible evil,' but one that 'it would be far worse to remedy'. Alexander II, for his part, considered that 'it is better to get rid of serfdom from on high than wait for its abolition from below.'

Serfdom, in fact, was as old as Tsarism itself. It first appeared in the fifteenth century and—significantly—grew ever more widespread in Russia while tending to disappear from the rest of Europe. Its chief cause was the grinding poverty of the rural population. Indebted to the prosperous landowners and harassed by tax collectors, Russia's peasants had to choose between two evils: they could either renounce their freedom of tenure, or else

[1] At the time, the corresponding figures were 33 per cent in the United States, 54 per cent in Germany and 77 per cent in Great Britain.

abandon the land and go elsewhere in search of better fortune. The majority chose the first alternative, but for all that, massive peasant migrations became a characteristic feature of life in the Russian countryside.

Originally distinct from slaves in that they were attached to the land on which they lived, the Russian serfs were gradually reduced to a state of slavery, in fact if not in law. Only serfs attached to Crown estates fared slightly better than the rest. The vast majority were abandoned to the whims of the landed gentry, who by a law of 1649 were granted the most sweeping powers. In the next century, Catherine II—the 'enlightened despot'—merely stepped up the repression: no matter how great her cultural achievements, the peasants had little reason to rejoice in her reign. Let the reader judge for himself: the owners of serfs were given the right to deport their hapless charges to Siberia,[1] to sell them individually or by the family on the open market or otherwise, and to sentence them to death. A French traveller, crossing Russia in the eighteenth century, recorded that he could hear the cries of tortured peasants wherever he went. And when it came to awarding her favourites with 'souls', Catherine II was more generous than most—one nobleman alone is said to have come by 120,000 serfs in that way.

This situation continued well into the nineteenth century. At the beginning of his reign, Alexander I issued an edict against the arbitrary deportation of serfs to Siberia, but in 1822 he had second thoughts and revoked it. Thus the peasantry continued to eke out a living under intolerable conditions—so much so that they came to pose an increasing threat to the Tsarist regime. In a police document dating from 1839, it was conceded that 'serfdom is like a powder-keg under the State.'

Morally indefensible, serfdom was also economically harmful. The emancipation of the serfs was a necessary, though not a sufficient, condition for the modernization and improvement of agriculture. While serfdom persisted, an indifferent and lazy nobility, relying on near-unpaid labour, was able to put off every attempt to increase the yield of the land and to survive on near-medieval farming methods. At the same time, nascent capitalism was crying out for the emancipation of the peasants. Indeed, how

[1] From 1760 to 1772, 20,000 Russian peasants actually settled in Siberia; some authorities claim that they represented no more than 25 per cent of all deportees; the rest are said to have perished on the way.

could industry obtain the factory hands it so urgently needed if country folk remained tied to the soil?

It was in these circumstances that Alexander II abolished serfdom in 1861. Overnight, the serf became a free man, was able to marry whom he pleased, own property, go to law, choose between agriculture and industry or commerce. However—and this was the reverse of the coin—he had to pay a large price for his new-found freedom: the land he tilled did not become his own until he had handed over a large indemnity to the state (which straight away advanced the full sum to the former owners) by instalments spread over forty-nine years, with a fixed interest rate of 6·5 per cent.[1] Even then, the serfs did not so much become owners as usufructuaries—the land itself was made over to the traditional peasant commune, whose rights were vested in the village assembly, or *mir*. In many respects, therefore, the peasant did not do more than change masters, for he remained tied to a highly traditionalist institution that was, by and large, deaf to any claims for agrarian reform.

This was not their only disappointment; in most cases the value of the land was considerably inflated, doubtless because the authors of the reform bill felt that the serfs should be made to pay not only for their land but for their freedom as well. Moreover, the new distribution reduced the size of the average peasant holding, which in most cases already provided no more than the bare minimum for existence. An inquiry held in 1878 showed that half of the twenty-one million serfs formerly owned by the *pomeshchiki* (rich landlords) lived below the minimum subsistence level. In the years following the emancipation act, their condition deteriorated further still.

In these circumstances, the bitterness of the Russian peasants is only too understandable. Their fondest hopes had all come to nothing. Convinced that the Tsar, in whom they continued to put blind trust, had been misled by his nobles, they continued to wait desperately but vainly for the '*ukase* writ in gold' by which Father Tsar would finally liberate them from their yoke. Their disappointment, however, did not always take passive forms: in various parts of the country the publication of the Imperial edict

---

[1] The peasants could buy their freedom in yet another way; namely, by agreeing to work the land of their former masters for 30–40 days a year without pay. The majority opted for the indemnity.

marking the end of serfdom was followed by grave disorders. In the year 1861 alone, there were close on five hundred serious incidents, followed by bloody repression.

In any case, on the eve of the First World War, the Russian countryside was a picture of direst poverty. Only a small minority of rich landowners, the *kulaks*, escaped the common fate. These *kulaks* had first appeared in the wake of Stolypin's great two-stage reforms of 1906–10. His chief object had been the dissolution of the old *mir*, in whose deliberations all male inhabitants had a voice. The *mir* dealt with problems of farm management, the collection of taxes, and the administration of justice in minor offences, and so traditional was it in outlook and constitution that it acted as a brake on the reforming zeal of the most enterprising peasants. That is why Stolypin believed that the creation of a peasant middle class, in other words the introduction of modern capitalism into the countryside, called for the abolition of the *mir*.

And in this he succeeded. However, the rise of that class merely served to accentuate the sharp contrast between the life of a small privileged minority and the lamentable condition of the great mass of peasants, whose hatred of the *kulaks* survived the upheavals of the Revolution.

The housing conditions of most peasants remained barbarous, their ignorance legendary and their food entirely inadequate. While Russia figured among the world's chief grain exporters, her peasants lived in a state of permanent malnutrition. 'We ourselves shall go without food, but we shall export,' declared Vishnegradsky, Minister of Finances under Alexander III. Thus, while upper-class Russians were renowned for their remarkable appetites, the *moujik*, in about 1910, consumed less wheat than most other people: 203·1 kilogrammes per year compared with 838·6 in the United States, 345·6 in Belgium and 311·2 in France. Nor did he eat meat, except on very special occasions. 'Bread and water, that's all we've got,' as a popular saying put it. Large population increases served to aggravate the situation further, as did the archaic agricultural methods.[1] The burden of taxes did the rest. Towards the end of the nineteenth century, the total amount raised by direct taxation was 208 million roubles, of which the starving peasantry contributed 195 million.

[1] In 1904 a mere 82,000 tons of fertilizer was used in the whole of Russia, when more modern methods would have called for at least 6,000,000 tons.

This fact alone is enough to condemn the regime out of hand, and while the authorities could generally rely on the ignorance and apathy of the countryside, so many injustices and humiliations were bound to lead to successive waves of unrest. No wonder that, throughout Russian history, peasant revolts have followed one another, always suppressed, always to recur.

Here lay one of the fundamental differences between Russia and Western Europe. In 1848, the French bourgeoisie was able to crush the working class because it could muster support among the peasantry who feared the Revolution even more than the forces of reaction. The Russian *moujiks*, for their part, lacked organization and class-consciousness; their outbursts had the brute force and incoherence of instinctive explosions, but in the coming struggle between the working class and the autocracy there was nothing to guarantee that the famished peasants would not grasp the hand which the industrial proletariat was eagerly holding out to them. And the peasants, that immense section of the nation, also represented the immense majority in the army. It was crystal clear that if the countryside once rose up, and if the urban proletariat infused it with enough political cohesion, Tsarist Russia would topple, never to rise again.

The working class

Now it was precisely in that immense country, with its vast peasant majority, that the proletariat first began to flex its muscles, taking stock of its true strength and mustering its forces. Modern capitalism was a recent innovation in Russia, but at the turn of the century industrialization had begun to make rapid strides, thanks chiefly to the expansion of the railway system. Industrial growth was spectacular in the last decade of the nineteenth century. It slowed down between 1900 and 1909, only to redouble from 1910 to the beginning of the First World War. By then, Russia was producing 36 million tons of coal (which was a tremendous advance on previous figures, but meagre enough when compared with Germany's 190 million or America's 517 million), and 4·6 million tons of cast iron (Germany: 16·8 million; U.S.A.: 31·5 million). The chemical industry was in a less favourable position, and the machine-tool industry practically non-existent.

The most characteristic feature of Russian industry was its high degree of concentration. In 1914, 76 per cent of Russian workers were employed in factories with more than 100 employees, 56 per cent in factories with more than 500 employees and 40 per cent in factories with more than 1,000 employees—the last percentage had been 31 per cent in 1901. The concentration of industry was therefore an extremely rapid development, as we may also gather from the fact that, whereas Russian industrial enterprises employed an average of 43 workers in 1887, the figure had risen to 157 by 1908. The concentration of labour in highly developed industrial complexes was one of the chief factors in heightening the class-consciousness of the Russian proletariat.

A second feature of Russian industry was the relative youthfulness of the workers, and a third the relatively close links that bound the proletariat to the countryside. An appreciable number of Russian workers had only recently left their rural homes, and there were some six million seasonal workers who returned to the country at harvest time and worked in the factories only during the 'dead' season. Whenever there was a slump, moreover, there was a mass exodus of workers from the urban areas. While this trend tended to militate against the growth of working-class solidarity, it was countered by the gradual emergence and growth of a permanent urban proletariat. Thus, while in 1905 only 2,700,000 industrial workers had settled in the towns for good, their ranks had swollen to three million in 1914. This was still a relatively small number, but high concentration acted as a spur to concerted action.

These three million workers were the spearhead of a revolutionary mass movement which, from the 1880s onwards, organized innumerable strikes and in 1905 showed beyond a shadow of a doubt that it was no longer prepared to put up with its inferior condition. Thus the historical importance of the Russian working class was quite disproportionate to its numerical strength. To begin with, the economic situation of many Russian workers was one of continuous deterioration. Between 1860 and 1890, nominal wages rose slightly but real wages fell by some 20 per cent. Most observers agree that they dropped even further from 1890 to 1899. From 1905 to 1910, nominal wages as well as real wages were whittled down once again, and from then until the outbreak of the war, wages only just kept up with rising prices: analyses of working-class family budgets therefore reveal, not surprisingly, that the entire wage packet was devoted to the satisfaction of the most elementary needs.

Moreover, not even these could be satisfied in the majority of cases. Housing conditions, in particular, were appalling. The large factories in which most industrial workers were employed were flanked by barrack-like tenements, with dozens of people to each insalubrious dormitory. Most families had to share tiny rooms, often with unmarried people, occupying the beds in shifts. Even so, these conditions were better than those of people employed in the smaller factories. In a number of them, the workers had in fact to bed down on the floor, sometimes with their entire family. Here they would eat, work, sleep and procreate. An official report in 1897 speaks of women giving birth in such workshops, and of sick people lying down beside the machines. In the province of Moscow —which held the unenviable record in this field—60 per cent of all workers lived and laboured under such conditions.

For the rest, the workers' tenements were desolate wastes, with unpaved and unlit alleyways and a total lack of sewers. Here the Russian proletariat tried to regain its strength after each murderous day; for, until the end of the nineteenth century, the working day was rarely less than twelve and very often fourteen, fifteen, sixteen and even eighteen hours long. Indeed, in a number of carpet factories, people had to slave away for twenty-one hours at a stretch.[1] In 1896 and again in 1897, the workers of St Petersburg struck for a shorter working day, which, in most cases, still exceeded fourteen and even fifteen hours per day. This strike, and also the industrial action of provincial workers, forced the authorities to lay down a maximum working day of eleven and a half hours for adults and nine hours for children. The same law also made Sunday a rest day for all. However, the new laws were widely ignored. The Minister of Finance himself published a circular in 1898 by which a whole series of enterprises was authorized to increase the normal working day. By a new law of 1906, the maximum working day was officially reduced to ten hours, but as the state did not always extend this law to its own employees, it was in no position to force private enterprise to observe it.

The same was true of all other legislation aimed at improving the workers' lot. A law of 1882 prohibited the employment of children under twelve, and limited the working day of all children under

[1] M. Florinsky, *Russia, a history and an interpretation* (New York, 1955), vol. 2, p. 932.

fifteen to eight hours. The enforcement of this law was entrusted to a body of newly created inspectors who did little to make it respected. In 1885 came a law prohibiting women and children under seventeen from working night shifts. A year later came legislation prohibiting payment in kind and fixing various other relations between workers and employers. At the same time, the penalties for participating in or fostering strikes were increased. Before 1903, there was no workman's compensation of any kind, and employers could not be held responsible for any accidents on their premises. But the large-scale employment of raw recruits from the country made industrial accidents inevitable, and cried out for state intervention. As a general rule, all concessions had to be wrung by the working class itself from a state whose hesitations, vacillations and tendency to go back on its word did little to increase its prestige. Moreover, the achievement of these social advantages in the face of state resistance persuaded the industrial proletariat that salvation lay in better organization and struggle.

However, the working class had no legal means of fighting for better conditions. Trade unions were not officially recognized until 1906, following the first successes of the Revolution; before then, all trade union activity was systematically repressed. The only workers' organizations sanctioned by the state were the Zubatov Unions, so called after the chief of the Moscow security police who was responsible for setting them up. This type of 'police socialism', which was meant to keep the workers in check, often went much further than its sponsors intended — many strikes were, in fact, inspired by its more militant leaders.

Trade union activities in Russia, as we have said, were systematically frustrated until the end of the old regime. Even when, at long last, the unions were legally recognized, they continued to be harassed by a system to which, in social matters as in politics, any form of liberalism was tantamount to suicide.

The impossibility of liberalism

Russia had two possible means of meeting the demands of the twentieth century: reforms leading to increased popular representation and participation or political and social upheavals, the historical answer to anachronistic structures piously enshrined and savagely defended. But the first alternative was never feasible in

Russia, where conditions were unpropitious to the emergence of bourgeois democracy based on parliamentarianism in politics and liberalism in the economic sphere.

In the West, the rise and expansion of democracy was made possible by the existence of a deeply rooted, enterprising and dynamic bourgeois class. It was the bourgeoisie—chiefly in England, the cradle of liberalism—that had brought about the accumulation of capital and the transformation of society. And no matter what we may think of the sacrifices this transformation imposed upon the disinherited classes, of the suffering and dehumanization it brought to the proletariat, we cannot deny that it represented a considerable historical advance.

In Russia there were many people who hoped that their country might follow the same path.[1] Tsarism was clearly creaking in all its hinges, and the first steps towards industrialization merely served to feed the prevailing liberal illusion—for that was all it was. Those who hoped that Russia might step into the shoes of the West were, in fact, overlooking an essential difference: the weakness, or rather the absence, of a Russian bourgeoisie with anything like the energy, spirit of enterprise and determination possessed by its Western peers.

One of the classes officially recognized by the Russian state was the so-called 'urban class', consisting of merchants and artisans. But it was of relatively small economic importance, for the simple reason that urban industry was a poor and late upstart in Tsarist Russia, which, as we have seen, was a predominantly rural country.[2] There was another factor as well. Until the eighteenth century, the distinction between urban and rural inhabitants, between town and village, was vague, since most of the more highly populated centres were administrative and military concentrations rather than commercial centres. The most typical case was St Petersburg, a purely artificial creation, built for reasons of prestige and political considerations and certainly not for commercial or economic reasons. The bourgeoisie, here as elsewhere, remained numerically weak to the very end of the old regime: there was no one able or willing to bridge the wide gulf between the exclusive social elite and the immense majority of the population.

[1] See Chapter 2.
[2] In 1913, the population of towns with upward of 100,000 inhabitants accounted for only 6 per cent of the nation.

It should also be stressed that the Russian bourgeoisie had an entirely different composition from its Western counterpart. In particular its subjection to the State contrasted sharply with the high degree of independence enjoyed by the Western middle classes. While the latter were chiefly made up of entrepreneurs playing an active, and later a decisive, role in the economic revolution of their age, a large proportion of the Russian middle class consisted of state officials and professionals who in no way provided a firm foundation for a liberal system. They were weakened by their lack of economic and social independence which went hand in hand with pernicious political anaemia. They at no time formed a pressure group strong enough to threaten the worm-eaten structure of the Tsarist autocracy, or to act as a general focus of opposition. Russia never had anything to compare with the powerful thrust of the French Third Estate; indeed, it was not until 1905 that a Russian Liberal Party, the Constitutional Democrats (Cadets) saw the light of day. In fact, many more bourgeois elements were found in the ranks of the revolutionary workers' and peasants' parties—the Social Democrats and Social Revolutionaries[1]—than in political organizations reflecting the aspirations of their own class.

The belated entry into politics of a middle class lacking strong social foundations had decisive repercussions on the course of political events during the last years of the Tsarist regime. Russian liberals proved incapable of taking a coherent and realistic line. During and after the 1905 Revolution, they did adopt an intransigent attitude to the government, but that attitude could only have borne fruit with mass support. However, the Russian bourgeoisie was not a large class, and if, on the whole, it felt hostility towards the authorities, it had neither the power nor the drive to translate this feeling into mass action. This was not, moreover, a phenomenon peculiar to Russia: even when the bourgeoisie succeeds in giving a political movement the direction and the enthusiasm for action without which no success is possible, it is rare for the bourgeoisie itself to 'take to the streets'. It prefers to leave this thankless task to the less individualistic and poorer classes, whose misery drives them on to desperate acts, who know that they have nothing to lose but their chains. Also, the bourgeoisie increasingly realizes, in countries where it has not yet come to power, that its

[1] See Chapter 2.

struggle against the authorities may benefit the proletariat as well. An onslaught by the disinherited masses strikes greater terror in the bourgeois heart than all the despotic muddlings of a repressive government which, after all, does not endanger the very survival of the bourgeoisie as a class.

In these circumstances, one might have expected the Russian middle classes to reach a mutually beneficial understanding with Tsarism. But nothing of the kind happened. Tsarism itself was largely at fault here; it was far too tied to the landed aristocracy, far too steeped in reaction, to lend itself to any sort of compromise. But the liberals, too, lacked the kind of subtlety and shrewdness in negotiation that is normally associated with their class. This was possibly because, in Russia, revolutionary methods appealed even to those who were least capable of wielding them. Here we have a further difference between Western Europe and Russia—while Western labour parties were increasingly swayed by bourgeois ideas and practices, in Russia the bourgeoisie was influenced by the revolutionary proletariat and tried vainly to copy its methods of struggle.

In any case, Tsarism did not disappear before it had demonstrated that the middle class was totally incapable of stepping into its shoes. The very basis of liberalism was lacking in Russia. The events of 1905 were to show that the only force capable of challenging the autocracy was the urban proletariat, which, despite its youth, inexperience and lack of organization, was brimming over with revolutionary spontaneity. It—and it alone—during the 'second' 1905 offered itself as a candidate for state power.

'Liberal Tsarism'

The revolutionary wave that swept through Russia in 1905–6 produced a radically new constitutional situation. For decades the autocracy had resisted the clamour for reforms raised by the intelligentsia and by the more enlightened section of the bureaucracy. In other European countries, these demands had resulted in a constitution that put an end to arbitrary rule, but Russian reactionaries loathed and feared the very idea of the kind of constitution to which the European liberal movement had rallied throughout the nineteenth century. 'The mad clamour for a constitution spells the ruin of Russia,' wrote Minister Pobiedonostsev, one of Nicholas II's chief advisers, as late as 1901.

It was in this sense that the 1905 Revolution, though crushed in the end, did not constitute a defeat. Previously the authorities had responded to all constitutional demands with stiffer measures and systematic recourse to terror. This is how Catherine had reacted to the Pugachev revolt, and, if she needed a further lesson, the French Revolution had convinced her that force alone could preserve her empire. Nicholas I took much the same line with the Decembrists[1] and with the Polish and Hungarian insurrectionists of 1830 and 1848, so much so that a conservative observer exclaimed that 'whenever they [the European revolutionaries] blunder in the West, it is their Russian brethren who pay for it.' But 'blunders' in Russia herself were treated in much the same way. Every outburst of popular wrath was answered with increasing police brutality,[2] when, without prejudice to its security, the state ought to have, and could have, treated these outbursts as clear signs that the system was in need of greater elasticity and that new strata of the population must increasingly be associated with the function of government. But it was characteristic of the basic weakness of Tsarism that it could never think up any alternative to blind repression.

Then came the Revolution of 1905, which not only forced the Tsar to grant a constitution but also persuaded him to act the liberal. The very first revolutionary wave, in August 1905, caused him to set up a. representative assembly, the Duma—a purely consultative body whose members were to be elected indirectly, on the basis of heavily weighted class representation. This measure, far from appeasing discontent, merely served to strengthen it, for it proved the Tsar's lack of goodwill no less than his basic weakness. And so, at long last, Nicholas was forced to grant his country a constitution, in October 1905. Was this the beginning of a new era, the first step towards the establishment of a constitutional monarchy, the first move towards a parliamentary and bourgeois democracy, a move that might have spared him the cost of a revolution?

The chief innovation of the new measure was to establish the principle of universal suffrage and to grant the Duma more than

---

[1] See Chapter 2.

[2] Thus Alexander III reacted most brutally to the assassination of Alexander II, and Nicholas II to the assassination of Sipiagin, the Minister of the Interior, and to the general increase in popular unrest.

purely consultative powers. This might have looked like parliamentary democracy, but it was nothing of the kind. To begin with, the Duma lacked control over ministerial decisions. Thus when, soon after its inception, the Duma passed an almost unanimous vote of no confidence in the government, no one was noticeably affected. In fact, the Council of Ministers remained responsible to the Tsar and to him alone, and the Tsar continued to appoint and dismiss ministers without the slightest reference to the assembly.

The Duma was left to deal with minor legislation and budgetary matters, but even here its powers were strictly limited. Not only did the sovereign have to approve every legislative act, but he also had the right to govern by decrees (*ukazes*) whenever the Duma was not in session. Moreover, an important part of the budget was withheld from the scrutiny of the assembly, the government retaining sole control over all matters pertaining to the army, the navy, the diplomatic service, the Church, and the vast expenditure of the court.[1] Significantly enough, one of the most important legislative steps taken during the reign of Nicholas II, the Stolypin reforms of the agrarian economy, were the work of the government itself, acting by decree and without the collaboration of the Duma. The authority of the Duma was further undermined by the fact that its powers were divided between the lower chamber, or Imperial Duma, and the upper chamber, or Imperial Council, composed of a number of members appointed by the Tsar, and an equal number elected by various privileged institutions. In these circumstances, granting the upper chamber the same powers as the lower meant depriving the Duma of any real political influence, and ensuring that it could never become a counterweight to the autocracy. Moreover, many categories of citizens were excluded from the franchise, among them women, workers in factories with less than fifty employees, migrant workers and landless peasants. The rest were divided into a series of electoral colleges according to social

---

[1] On the eve of the World War the royal family, consisting of some sixty members, still drew heavily on public funds. All Grand Dukes (sons and grandsons of Tsars) received an annuity of 280,000 roubles (£35,000 at the then prevailing rate of exchange), Princes of the Blood (great-grandsons of Tsars) received one million roubles on attaining their majority, as did Grand Duchesses on getting married. These vast sums notwithstanding, members of the imperial family were in the habit of leaving their bills unpaid for years. All claims had to be submitted to the Tsar and no court had jurisdiction over them.

status; there was one college for landowners, another for townsmen, a third for peasants and Cossacks, a fourth for workers. Not
all were equally represented in the Duma: the landowners
appointed one deputy for every 2,000 voters; the townsmen one
deputy for every 7,000 voters; the peasants one deputy for every
30,000 voters and the workers one deputy for every 90,000
voters.

The results of the elections to the first Duma, which began its
work in 1906, persuaded the government that these arrangements,
conservative though they were, were still far too liberal. The Duma
included a powerful contingent of Cadets—some 170 to 180
deputies—supported by a 'workers' group' of 100 deputies, all of
them to the Left of the Cadets. The national minorities (Poles,
Ukrainians, Lithuanians, Latvians, etc.) could muster a further
60 to 70 deputies. On the extreme Left were 18 Social Democratic
deputies, and to the Right of the Cadets were some 30 to 40
'moderate' liberals. Finally, there were some 100 deputies without
precise political affiliations, but influenced by the radicals. As for
the conservatives, they failed to obtain a single seat. In these
circumstances, any collaboration between the Duma and the
government proved impossible. The assembly was dissolved, and
to ensure that new elections would not prove equally embarrassing
to the Tsar, the government, violating its own Constitution,
changed the electoral law without reference to the Duma. These
changes turned the Duma into a caricature of a representative
assembly: popular and national minority representation was reduced to a mere 15 per cent, and the people of Central Asia were
completely deprived of the vote. In addition, the strength of the
various voting colleges was 'adjusted': one 'grand elector' each was
to be nominated by 230 landowners, by 1,000 monied townsmen,
by 15,000 lower-middle-class voters, by 60,000 peasants and by
125,000 workers. In this strange ballot, the vote of a worker thus
weighed some 500 times less than that of a nobleman. Since the
results of the new election pleased the government no more than
those of the first, the police were instructed to implicate the
socialist deputies in an imaginary plot that provided an excuse for
dissolving the Second Duma. The docility of the Third Duma,
which met in November 1907, saved the Tsar the trouble of a
further dissolution.

'Liberal' Russia thus lacked a legislative assembly with even a minimum of independence, and the Tsar continued to rule supreme and unchecked. The Council of Ministers had no real powers; the Tsar could, and often did, ignore the advice of its President, and continued to treat individually with each of his ministers.

Very little, indeed, had therefore been changed by the constitutional reforms, and still the Tsar was not content, trying time and again by coups d'état to whittle away what little authority was still vested in the 'constitutional assembly'. In 1913, V. A. Maklakov, the Minister of the Interior, known for his reactionary opinions, presented a plan that was aimed at achieving this end. Nicholas II declared himself 'pleasantly surprised', but on July 1st, 1914, had to shelve the Maklakov project in the face of unanimous opposition by the rest of his government.

In view of all these intrigues, and the determination of the ruler of 'all the Russias' to hang on to his powers and frustrate any attempt to infuse the new institutions with any life of their own, only the most naive observer could speak of a liberal wind of change. Nicholas II merely pretended to accept the idea of a constitution, and that, as it were, at the point of a gun. Only when Count Witte, his minister, had urged him to avoid fresh upheavals by this measure; when some of the leading members of the imperial family came out in support of Witte; and when the Grand Duke Nicholas threatened to shoot himself unless a constitution were granted, did the Tsar finally relent, or rather pretend to do so. And once the immediate danger was past, and the Revolution had been crushed by the most brutal methods,[1] the Tsar had but one wish: to revoke the concessions he had been forced to make against his own will and the better judgment of many of his closest advisers.[2]

What then remained of all these liberal pretensions?

Freedom of the press had been proclaimed and the powers of the censor limited, but the Tsar himself decreed, just before the war, that no newspaper must mention the name of Rasputin, which was then on everyone's lips. According to a circular which Stolypin sent to all provincial governors on September 15th, 1906, political parties whose existence was officially recognized could be banned 'if their aims, although formally in accordance with the law, were

[1] These methods earned the then Prime Minister the nickname of 'Stolypin the Hangman': 1,100 people were executed from September 1906 to May 1907.
[2] Returning from the first session of the Duma, Count Fredericks, the Tsar's confidant, declared that he would never again be seen with 'these brigands ready to assassinate us all'.

not defined with sufficient clarity', or if they 'evinced hostility to the government'.

Only in religious matters did the Tsar soften his attitude, declaring that he would henceforth be far more tolerant of Catholics in Poland, Protestants in the Baltic provinces, Muslims in Asia, and Uniates and 'Old Believers' at home.[1] As for the Jews, who had been subjected to the harshest and most humiliating treatment, Nicholas did nothing at all to improve their lot. Jew-baiting was, in fact, a hallowed Tsarist institution, one that reached its peak in the nineteenth century when Jews were relegated to special 'residential provinces' in Poland and in White Russia. In 1886 they were barred from the administration and the legal profession. At about the same time, the government introduced the *numerus clausus* by which the number of Jewish places in the universities and high schools was severely restricted. Forced conversions of Jews were reported from all parts of the country, and in the 1880s came the first of hundreds of pogroms, vicious raids on a defenceless people organized with the connivance of the authorities. The most notorious pogrom, which caused bitter indignation throughout Western Europe, took place in Kishinev in April 1903. On that occasion 130 people were murdered or grievously injured while the police, acting on the orders of the Minister of the Interior, stood by with folded arms.

Religious persecution in Tsarist Russia had always gone hand in hand with open discrimination against Russia's subject nationalities who made up the great majority of the Tsar's peoples. The crushing of the Poles—after the national uprisings of 1830 and 1863—was roundly condemned by the rest of the world, but the Tsarist authorities merely stepped up their discrimination against Polish patriots, even proscribing the use of the Polish language in the administration and the schools. The emergence of 'liberal' Tsarism in no way lessened the plight of the Poles, though elsewhere, in Finland for instance, Nicholas II was forced, in 1906, to grant a new constitution. As for the Ukrainians, the Latvians, and

---

[1] The Uniates, who were mainly concentrated in the Ukraine and in White Russia, accepted union with Rome while yet observing the Orthodox rites; the 'Old Believers' or 'Old Ritualists' refused to accept the reforms introduced by the Patriarch Nikon in the seventeenth century (changes in the number of prostrations during the reading of a certain prayer; the number of fingers used in making the sign of the cross).

notably the national minorities in the Caucasus and Asia, they continued to be treated as inferior races to the bitter end; the Tsar felt that only by opposing all their ethnic and cultural claims could he keep them in continued subjection.

Darkest Russia

Such was Imperial Russia on the eve of her collapse. Despite all its hollow pretences, autocratic and obsolete Tsarism continued to crush every striving for freedom. It not only suppressed all attempts to liberalize political and social life, it also stifled all cultural stirrings. Tsarism became identified not only with despotism, but also, increasingly, with the worst form of obscurantism.

In his distrust of the intelligentsia, his hatred of culture, Nicholas II was following a long reactionary tradition. Even Catherine II, the friend of philosophers, the patron of Voltaire, was not free from this taint. Not that she was indifferent to intellectual matters; but she, too, felt strongly that 'as soon as our peasants develop a taste for learning neither you [she was addressing the Governor of Moscow] nor I will remain in our places.'

This attitude was clearly reflected in the realm of public education. At the beginning of the eighteenth century, Russia still lacked primary schools, and when Peter the Great established the Russian Academy of Sciences, secondary education was still unknown. Even at the end of his enlightened reign, the whole country could boast no more than four thousand schoolchildren. It was not until the nineteenth century that a Ministry of Education was set up with orders to devise a national school system. It was not by chance that Alexander I chose as his first Minister of Education an old courtier whom the Tsar himself declared to be a mere nobody. In about 1825, when some 1,200 students were enrolled in the four universities[1] and some 7,700 pupils were attending secondary schools, primary schools were still few and far between, and non-existent in the countryside. In any case, there could hardly be any talk of public education in a country where, according to an official memorandum of 1845, the authorities contended that 'Young people in the lower strata of society have no use for [secondary and higher] education ... which simply helps to alienate them from

[1] The University of Moscow was founded in 1755 (but during the thirty-four years of her reign Catherine II granted only a single medical degree); the University of St Petersburg was established in 1819.

their natural habits and in no way profits the state.'[1] It was not until about 1857 that children of classes other than the nobility were first admitted to the universities. And while public instruction did make some progress during the late nineteenth century, there were still many glaring gaps, especially at the lower end of the scale: in 1881, only 9 per cent of all children in the age-group of seven to fourteen were attending schools (one boy in six and one girl in thirty-two), and peasant children were not expected to waste their time at school for more than one or two years at the most. A primary school system was first set up at the beginning of the twentieth century, not so much by the government as by the local *zemstvos*.[2] Need we add that this development, praiseworthy though it was, did not appreciably raise the intellectual potential of a country which still had an illiteracy rate of 76 per cent on the eve of the First World War?

But such statistics, however telling, fail to give a true picture of the cultural climate fostered by the Tsars. What few schools and colleges there were dispensed obscurantist ideas rather than true knowledge. In 1828, it was decreed that textbooks of physiology and anatomy must not contain terms likely to 'offend against instinctive decency'. In 1849, the universities were ordered to discontinue lectures on philosophy and European constitutional law, both of which were declared subversive. At the same time, the government decided that the chairs of logic and psychology must henceforth be held by professors of theology, who alone could ensure that the teaching would not offend against the canons of religious orthodoxy. In 1871, the Minister of Public Education — of whom it was commonly said that his post was created to restrict rather than encourage learning—thought up a new project: all secondary schools must give pride of place to the teaching of dead

[1] Forty years later, the official attitude was still much the same. Thus in 1882, Delianov, the then Minister of Public Education, included in one of his ukases the immortal sentence: 'The children of coachmen, servants, cooks, washerwomen, small shopkeepers and others of the same type must not be encouraged to aspire above the condition to which they were born.'

[2] The *zemstvos* were local assemblies, mainly of nobles, founded during the reign of Alexander II. They enjoyed a large measure of autonomy in social and administrative matters, and fostered public instruction and the improvement of hygiene. In time, they came to play an increasingly important political role, and despite numerous rebuffs from the central government, helped to protect the peasants from the worst autocratic excesses. At the beginning of the twentieth century, they contributed to the rise of liberalism and the foundation of the Constitutional Democratic Party.

languages. Apart from mathematics, these subjects were the only ones to find favour in the eyes of the authorities: they were unlikely to give rise to arguments that could detract from respect for public institutions. Moreover, the Minister took care to stipulate that the study of Greek and Latin must not degenerate into the study of ancient civilizations; only the soothing virtues of grammar must be instilled into Russian pupils. And familiarity with the rules of syntax remained the exclusive passport to the universities until 1902. This was in full accord with the principle defined by Alexander II —the 'liberal' Tsar—namely, that 'all education must conform with the principles of true religion, and with respect for private property and public order.'

Not surprisingly, therefore, school life was conducted in a parade-ground atmosphere. All schoolboys and students had to wear uniform, and this was but one aspect of the rigid discipline with which the authorities tried to regiment school activities and teaching methods. Throughout the nineteenth century there was a constant effort to militarize the universities and to anaesthetize all forms of academic life. The university authorities had no autonomy at all, and except for a very brief period during the 1860s, professors, and particularly rectors, were expected to act as mouthpieces of the government rather than as men of science and learning.

In this field, Tsarism demonstrated to what extremes disregard for even the most elementary aspects of intellectual liberty can lead. Let us content ourselves with quoting this tragi-comic anecdote: when Uvarov, the arch-reactionary Minister of Public Education (1833–49) published a book on ancient Greek civilization, he felt impelled to omit the word *demos* (people), and in a book on history, he deliberately refrained from telling his readers that some Roman emperors had been assassinated—they simply 'perished' for unspecified reasons.[1]

If only all these measures had, at least, produced the desired effect! Instead, state repression served increasingly to identify intellectual activity with revolutionary agitation. Nothing, not even the law preventing students and professors from going abroad, could stop the ferment of ideas. Despite all the ukases, the militarization, the arrests and the deportations, the Russian universities remained perpetual foci of rebellion, and supplied the

[1] It was the same Uvarov who declared that the aim of his policies was to 'delay the progress of Russia by 50 years'.

opposition with an ever-growing number of militant supporters: Tsarism itself had convinced the intelligentsia that the attainment of even the most elementary liberties called for the complete over-throw of the prevailing system of government.

So degenerate had Tsarism become[1] that it lost the support of its last remaining allies: the feeble nobility and the incompetent administration. On the eve of its collapse, Tsarism was thrown back on the pathetic loyalty of the Russian Church, a body entirely subservient to the state and increasingly afflicted by senility. Russia had been the last refuge of the Eastern Orthodox Church after it had been subdued by Islam, and the Church had paid for this privilege by surrendering every vestige of its former independence. In the eighteenth century the office of patriarch was abolished, and control of the Church and its possessions passed into the hands of the state. Unlike the Catholic Church as it was, for instance, in France before the Revolution of 1789, the Russian Orthodox Church had never been very powerful. Its only strength was the dead weight of blind faith, in which ritual was far more important than dogma; and so dogma degenerated into pure superstition. No wonder, then, that the Russian Church lost much of its hold on the more thoughtful section of the population—no sooner had religious tolerance been proclaimed than a vast number departed the fold, 300,000 defecting in 1905–8. In 1905, the government[2] decided to set up a special commission for reforming the Orthodox Church, but when Tsarism disappeared twelve years later, the Church was still much as it always had been.

It would not, however, be true to say that religion as such was dead in Russia—far from it. But the State fostered Christian ideas simply as a means of ensuring humility and submission together with utter contempt for rational argument. In fact, since religious devotion was equated with mere ritual, its essence usurped by ceremonials and public spectacles, the flock was prevented from grasping the true message of the Gospel—the more so as the Orthodox Church never thought fit to establish a catechism. The dispensation of religious knowledge was not one of the numerous

---

[1] See Chapter 3.

[2] In 1721, when Peter the Great replaced the patriarchate with the Holy Synod—which was no more than an administrative college run by a Procurator-General with ministerial rank—the Church was turned into just another branch of the administration.

duties devolving upon the clergy, who, in this as in so many other spheres, were completely at one with the authorities.

In December 1916, three months before the monarchy was overthrown, the Empress Alexandra wrote to Nicholas II that 'a great and magnificent epoch is dawning for your reign.' Only so utterly short-sighted a woman could have imagined that it was still possible to preserve the Tsar's discredited rule. Soon afterwards, a revolutionary movement that had resolutely turned its back on the past struck Tsarism a body blow from which it was never to recover.

2

The Russia of the Revolutionaries

THE obstinate determination of the Tsars to preserve their anachronistic regime was rivalled only by the equally un-flinching will of the revolutionaries, in the face of the most brutal reprisals, to tear down the crumbling walls of the state edifice. The last fifty years of Tsarism may be described as a permanent confrontation between the forces of reaction and thousands, later tens and hundreds of thousands, of men determined to defeat them.

Before then, the absolute monarchy, bloody though its excesses were, had met with very little effective opposition; except for sporadic peasant revolts, the stability of the regime was shaken only by criminal and scandalous events and not by political attack. Thus the seventeenth and eighteenth centuries had witnessed quite a few palace revolutions set off by dynastic quarrels and repressed with great ferocity. They were partly caused by Peter the Great's decision to put an end to the feudal custom of electing the Tsar by an assembly of nobles. By laying it down that all future Tsars could appoint their own successors, he opened wide the door to court intrigue and violence. This continued until 1796, when the Emperor Paul established the principle of inheritance of the throne in the direct descending male line.

In the early nineteenth century, the Marquis de Custine still had good reason to assert that the Russian autocracy was a form of 'absolutism tempered by assassination'. The amorphous mass of the people, cut off from the rest of the world, continued to stand impotent on the side-lines while the autocracy waxed strong, and obscurantism reigned supreme. It was only when she finally emerged from her age-old isolation that Russia took stock of the full measure of her backwardness and enslavement—during, and immediately after, the Napoleonic wars, when thousands of young Russian aristocrats serving in the armies of Alexander I suddenly discovered Europe, and the need for progress and liberty. The patriotic fervour of the entire nation in 1812 and 1813 had driven it home to these young men that the privileged classes owed the vast mass of starving and exploited Russian peasants an immense debt of gratitude, and to repay it they and the best of their successors laboured with might and main throughout the nineteenth century.

Having tasted, if not true liberty, at least the promise of liberation, numerous officers joined clandestine organizations on their return to Russia and began to forge revolutionary plans. In this, Russia resembled the rest of Europe, where a host of secret revolutionary societies modelled on the Italian *carbonari* had sprung up. In St Petersburg alone, there now appeared the 'Order of Russian Knights', the 'Union of Salvation', the 'Union of Welfare', and many other groups, all of them representing the first concerted attempts to oppose Tsarist absolutism and to obtain a liberal constitution.

The main challenge came from a group of officers who had originally banded together in the 'Southern Society' and the 'Northern Society' but later split up for political reasons. In December 1825, the most radical of them, under the leadership of Paul Pestel, decided to take advantage of the latest dynastic crisis[1] and seize power. Thirty officers supported by three thousand soldiers tried to prevent the senators from taking an oath of allegiance to Nicholas I. The insurgents, relying more on their natural enthusiasm than on any great organizational skill, had hoped that they might win over the rest of the garrison, but instead they were dispersed by their own comrades-in-arms, leaving behind dozens of dead. This was the end of the Decembrist revolt. Its epilogue was played out on the scaffold; all the leading conspirators, including Pestel, were hanged.

But though it had failed pitiably in its attempt to overthrow the Tsar, the Decembrist uprising marked a turning-point in the history of Russia. For the first time violence had been used in an attempt to wrest specific reforms from the reluctant regime, and although the movement adopted techniques reminiscent of the palace revolutions of former years, its ideals were democratic, and its spirit of sacrifice called forth new efforts and fresh struggles. The Decembrists became an example to future generations—the

[1] Alexander I had died without a male descendant. He left two brothers, but one of them contracted a morganatic marriage, thus renouncing his right of succession.

historian Pokrovsky called theirs a 'non-revolutionary revolution'. Their very failure drove home to their successors that the only way of modernizing Russia was to make a 'revolutionary revolution'.

The failure of the Populist movement

Nicholas I, for his part, concluded from the Decembrist uprising that the best way of preserving his throne and absolute powers was to increase repression. The autocracy became more autocratic, the police more ubiquitous. At first it looked as if this method was producing the desired effects: the revolution was held in check, particularly since there was no class capable or even desirous of leading the resistance. Protests against autocratic abuses were deflected into literature, which came to express the full fury, the desperation and the frustration of whole generations of Russian intellectuals. It was the latter who, for years to come, constituted the only serious opposition to the regime, the only group united in the refusal to put up with the oppressor. They were known as the 'intelligentsia', a term that described them far better than the word 'intellectuals', which tends to ignore one of the most important characteristics of the phenomenon we are discussing. What united the members of the Russian intelligentsia was not simply, or even chiefly, the fact that they belonged to a particular economic class, but that all of them were swayed by a powerful ideological current: by solidarity born of common resistance, and often fed by common oppression. Their refusal tended the more readily towards radicalism and revolution because the Russian intelligentsia was not drawn from the socially conservative bourgeoisie; most of its members were the enlightened sons of state officials and noblemen. Unable to give expression to their resentment in the political arena, many of them took to the pen, chief amongst them the great literary critic Vissarion Bielinsky, who was to have a decisive influence on the Russian revolutionary movement.

Universities were the chosen arena of all this intellectual and political ferment. In addition to the motives that drove most intellectuals into opposition, students suffered from a special disability: they were the direct butts of government attempts to regiment education and to stifle all forms of independent thought. Student opposition to Tsarism, and direct links between the students and the revolutionary movement, were a characteristic feature of intellectual life in late nineteenth-century Russia. Even when the working class took direct charge of the revolutionary struggle and gave it a far more vigorous spirit, Russian students continued to fight by the workers' side and often supplied their leaders. Whenever the authorities force them to choose between abject submission and revolt, the most dynamic and noblest of the growing generation will unhesitatingly take the second path, feeling nothing but disgust for the state, nothing but hatred for the common oppressor.

For many decades, the political struggle against Tsarism thus remained the monopoly of small, isolated and hence impotent groups. The first of these appeared in the early 1860s – 'Young Russia', founded in 1861, and 'Land and Freedom' (*Zemlia i Volia*) founded in 1862. Influenced by the ideas of Nicolai Chernyshevsky, of Bielinsky and increasingly of Michael Bakunin, the great revolutionary thinker and anarchist, these organizations decided to overthrow the regime by terror. This decision was forced upon them by the prevailing social conditions. They could not count on the support of the masses: most peasants were apathetic and totally indifferent to politics; the working class had not yet come into existence; and the bourgeoisie was still far too weak to press political claims of its own. In short, the revolutionaries were forced to do battle not only against the absolutist state but also against the inertia of its victims.

How could the masses be shaken out of their apathy? Two methods seemed possible, and both were tried by Russian revolutionaries. The first was violence—the assassination of leading statesmen might convince the masses that the state was not as strong as it appeared and hence encourage them to side with the revolution. This was the attitude adopted by Young Russia, The People's Will (*Narodnaia Volia*) and, a few years later, by Hell, a Muscovite organization—no less ephemeral than the rest.

The other method called for more patience. One of its chief advocates was Peter L. Lavrov, the great systematizer of Populist ideas. Lavrov believed firmly that education and propaganda would bring home to the masses that theirs was an intolerable condition and convince them that it was both right and possible to shake it off. Such, in brief, were the two poles of the revolutionary movement in Russia: terror and propaganda; and there were many militants who, in varying degrees, tried to reconcile the two.

In fact, the entire history of the Russian revolutionary movement was marked by the successive predominance of one or the other of these two trends, whose vogue at any particular point depended on its recent successes or failures.

Both parties, however, were at all times united in the firm conviction that, in the last resort, the people themselves must take their destiny into their own hands, and in this respect they differed markedly from the Decembrists and the reformist bureaucrats. Their trust in the masses reflected their democratic faith and provided the Russian revolutionary movement with its inspiration and banner between 1860 and 1890, the so-called 'Populist' phase of the struggle.

The term 'Populist' was coined in 1861, a year that in many respects marked a milestone in the history of modern Russia. That year, Alexander II, the 'liberal Tsar', having just emancipated the serfs, took a series of repressive measures against the universities, thus causing Alexander Herzen, the famous revolutionary writer who had fled to London, to compose his appeal to Russian students in his Russian-language émigré paper *Kolokol* (*The Bell*): 'Go to the people,' he told them. 'That is where you belong, exiles from science, soldiers of the Russian nation!' His cry was taken up by an entire generation of angry young men.

The early 1860s were given over to badly planned and poorly organized conspiracies. In 1866, a member of the Hell group failed in his attempt to assassinate Alexander II, and this failure helped to convince many terrorists of the error of their ways. As a result, the Populist movement entered a new phase. Study circles were set up, and their members—mostly students—were encouraged to make ever closer contact with 'the people'. When their appeals to the workers in near-by factories fell on deaf ears, they turned instead to the 'true Russian masses', that is to the peasants, whose terrible condition had been highlighted by the famine of 1873–4. In the spring, some two to three thousand student and other agitators, many of them women, abandoned their studies, their families, their home comforts, and went to 'the people', serving them as teachers, mechanics, agricultural experts, veterinary surgeons, nurses, doctors and sometimes even as entertainers. All of them wanted to mix with the peasants, to live like them and to be accepted by them without reserve. The 'mad summer' of 1874 was entirely given over to this extraordinary display of devotion, idealism and

naivety—naivety because the *moujiks* responded very badly to this
invasion by peaceful revolutionaries whose motives they failed to
understand. In some cases they even denounced the intruders to
the police, with the result that hundreds of students were arrested.
This did not prevent the volunteers from returning, with renewed
fervour, in 1875. The experiences of the second wave were no less
disappointing than those of the first, police repression no less
savage. Several thousand young people were thrown into gaol and
some of them were not brought up for trial until 1877. Scores of
them died in Tsarist dungeons; many more became insane. Their
persecution culminated in the 'trial of the 193' in 1878, and the
sentences meted out to them were so savage as to provoke indignation throughout Russia.

The 'go to the people' movement had, in any case, failed to
achieve its objectives. Bielinsky had said that 'the people need
potatoes, not a constitution' and, unable to provide them with
either, the Populists once again looked for new paths to liberation.

In 1876, they set up a new organization, again called Land and
Freedom. Its emergence marked a double turning-point. Not only
did it help to transform the Russian revolutionary movement from
a mass of splinter groups into one that came to draw in a very large
section of the intelligentsia, inviting them to more or less direct
participation, but it also led to the elaboration of a clearly defined
theoretical and practical programme. To begin with, the new
movement demanded that the large estates be split up and divided
among the peasants, and called for more power for the village
assemblies and greater local autonomy. It said very little about
specific political action, its members believing that the peasants
would not respond; they did, however, point out that their programme could never be realized except by a violent revolution.

To that end, Land and Freedom hastened to turn itself into a
militant force—police repression made the conspiratorial method
seem more appropriate than ever before, and recourse to terror no
less essential. All this called for a clandestine and disciplined party,
divided into regional groups, each with up to two hundred members but supported by a much larger number of sympathizers. An
illegal press would be set up to keep all members informed of
activities in other parts, and a special 'disorganization group' would
act as a defence corps against the police.

Since the original programme struck many as being far too

moderate, it was revised and given a far more radical tenor. In particular, the 'disorganization group' was charged with agitation among the army and with 'the systematic extermination of the most dangerous or the most eminent members of the government'. It was also instructed to carry terror into the countryside, notably by setting fire to the manors of the most hated landowners.

The new programme led to a rupture between those who put most of their trust in terror, and the rest who, while not ruling out the use of violence, stressed the importance of education, propaganda and agitation among the masses. In 1879, the more peaceful wing banded together to form the *Chernyi Perediel* (Black [Earth] Redistribution),[1] led by George Plekhanov. However, the majority opted for violence and joined The People's Will, whose exploits were to give the Populist movement its most tragic aspect.

Between 1879 and 1881, a wave of terror shook Russia, as The People's Will, under the leadership of Sophia Perovskaia and A. I. Zheliabov, set to work. In February 1879, Prince Kropotkin, the Governor-General of Kharkov, was assassinated; a month later, an (unsuccessful) attempt was made on the life of General Drenten, head of the Third Section (Security Police); in April of the same year, the revolutionaries tried to assassinate the Governor of Kiev; in May, the Arkhangelsk Chief of Police was stabbed. But the chief target of the revolutionaries was Tsar Alexander II himself, whom they sentenced to death in September 1879. To their mind, regicide was the best means of capturing the popular imagination and of eliciting a response from the people. In November 1879, they tried to derail the royal train, and the Tsar was only saved by a last-minute change of route. On February 5th, 1880, the banqueting hall of the Winter Palace was blown up just as the royal family was about to sit down to a gala dinner; the Tsar himself was spared, but sixty guardsmen were killed. Finally, on March 1st, 1881, the Tsar was killed by one of two bombs hurled at his sledge.

This apparent triumph of The People's Will was to prove its eventual downfall—far from being shaken by the death of this autocrat, the government clamped down on the terrorists and destroyed their party in 1883. Moreover, Alexander III proved far more intransigent, reactionary and implacable than his predecessor,

[1] The *Chernyi Perediel* reflected the will of the revolutionaries to transfer all landed estates to the peasant communes, possibly through the *mir*.

and his reign merely served to emphasize the intrinsic weaknesses of the Russian Populists (*narodniki*). Their determination and heroism may have earned them the admiration—and sometimes the fear—of the bourgeois opposition, but the peasantry, whom they were trying to win over, remained quite apathetic. For all that, terrorist attacks continued apace. In 1887, a plan to assassinate Alexander III was discovered before it could be put into practice, and scores of young people directly or indirectly implicated in the affair were arrested. Among them was a nineteen-year-old student who, after volunteering to shoulder the entire blame, told his judges, 'There is no better way of dying than to lay down one's life for one's country. Such death does not fill honest and sincere men with any fear. I have had only one aim, to serve the unfortunate Russian people.'

A few days later, the young man was hanged. He was Alexander Ilyich Ulianov, and his younger brother, Vladimir, was to achieve world renown under the name of Lenin.

Meanwhile, terrorism and Populism kept losing ground; the former because, while it admittedly wiped out some of the tyrants, nevertheless left the tyrannical institutions intact, and the latter because it failed to keep up with social and economic developments.

What was the precise nature of this Populist movement, a movement that aroused so many passionate hopes and engendered so much fear and hatred? It was a specifically Russian form of socialism, and as such tried to hasten the emancipation of the masses by means that were completely alien to Western Europe. Russia in the nineteenth century was torn by two irreconcilable modes of thought, reflecting two distinct conceptions of social progress. On the one hand there were those who, like Alexander Herzen, sought freedom in copying the West, who felt that only after passing through a capitalist phase could Russia catch up with her more advanced neighbours and go on to socialism, the ultimate goal. To them, Europe represented both economic and intellectual progress and the promise of social democracy. However, after 1848, when the French proletariat was crushed by the bourgeoisie, many Populists came to look upon Western Europe as a mercantile jungle, or as Herzen himself put it, a 'syphilitic sore infecting the blood and bones of society'.

Henceforth, they determined to look for the light in the East, and as the Russian middle classes increasingly admired the West, so the revolutionaries became declared Slavophiles. The Slav people, and the Russians in particular, were suddenly endowed with the most wonderful virtues; they embodied vitality, solidarity, idealism, sincerity, and—above all—socialism, while the West was full of vice, selfishness and capitalist greed. Even the Russian *moujik*, who had previously inspired nothing but contempt or pity, was suddenly idealized. 'Our peasants represent Russia's future,' Herzen proclaimed, and Bakunin, echoing this remark, declared that the Russian peasants were 'born socialists'—one had only to look at their traditional institutions and particularly at the *mir*, the communal body in charge of village affairs, to realize that. These and similar traditional manifestations of the collectivist spirit among the Russian peasantry encouraged the Populist hope that Russia might yet by-pass the Western road to socialism which led through exploitative capitalism and had been built on the ruin of the small peasantry. Neglecting the economic factors, and simply rejecting competitive capitalism as alien to the Russian soul, these men refused to see that the *mir* was a backward institution, responsible for low agricultural productivity and at least partly to blame for the abject poverty of the Russian peasant, and for the glaring contrasts between the landless and proletarianized *moujiks* and the petty landowners. The Populists also failed to appreciate that the *mir* had become a mere instrument in the hands of the authorities, who used it chiefly as a collector of taxes. But then the *mir* was the only voice, however muffled, the peasants had, and that is why the Populists clung to it. As Peter Lavrov put it, 'Our social revolution will come from the country, not the towns.'

This illusion was partly due to the social origins of the Populists, many of whom were of aristocratic extraction and hence much closer to the peasants than to the urban bourgeoisie. For all that, the *moujiks*, inured to misery, refused to heed their call, and the struggle of the Populists was as vain as it was heroic. Worse still, their admired peasants were so primitive that during the famine of 1891–2, for instance, hosts of them invaded the Volga towns, sacking hospitals and setting upon the doctors who had come to fight the cholera epidemic, and whom they accused of poisoning wells.

To whom, then, could enemies of Tsarism turn for support? Capitalism, which the more romantic Populists refused to consider as a step towards progress, had begun to take root in Russia, and as industrialization spread it brought in its wake the classical consequences: the depopulation of the countryside and the emergence of an urban proletariat. In the light of these events, many Populists came to realize that the path to Russian socialism might not, after all, be as unique as they had supposed; that the standard-bearer of progress was not the Russian peasantry, steeped in barbaric conditions, but, as elsewhere in Europe, the working class. This realization, coupled with the spread of Marxist doctrines, led to the rise of the Russian Social Democratic Party and hence of Communism.

The birth of Russian socialism

Having tried terror and propaganda in the countryside for many decades, the Populist movement, and with it all organized opposition to Tsarism, had come to a dead end. No one grasped this fact better or more quickly than George Plekhanov, who soon afterwards came to be looked upon as the father of Russian Marxism. He had never accepted the doctrine of individual terrorism, and in his subsequent disputes with the Populists had come to challenge their other ideas as well. In the end, he wholeheartedly embraced Marxism as the only valid alternative to the romantic reveries of his comrades. In 1883, when living in exile in Geneva, he founded the first Russian social-democratic group, called 'Emancipation of Labour' (*Osvobozhdenie Truda*), and for the next ten years he worked intensely to achieve what had become his main objective: to win the Russian revolutionary movement over to the Marxist cause.

Though he chose a propitious moment, Plekhanov had to overcome a host of formidable obstacles. To begin with, Karl Marx and Friedrich Engels had taught that since the capitalist class was destined to perish from its own contradictions, it was up to the rising class—the industrial proletariat—to destroy it and then step into its shoes. Thus, and only thus, would there arise a new political and economic system heralding a new civilization: socialist at first and then communist. The working class was thus assigned an historic mission: to put an end first to its own exploitation, and then, by the abolition of all classes, to the exploitation of man by man. In looking beyond the immediate potential of the working class, Marxism was a child of its time: its optimistic belief in the impending emancipation of humanity was in full accord with the new horizons opened up by science; its militancy was a fitting response to the misery engendered by capitalist industrialization;

and its paradoxical determination to treat the most oppressed, the most dehumanized class, as the instrument of man's liberation, was based on the recognition of an undeniable social and economic phenomenon: the birth and development of the industrial proletariat, whose interests were diametrically opposed to those of the bourgeoisie and whose number—and hence potential strength— was growing from day to day.

Marx, however, had derived his theories from his studies of Western Europe, where rapid industrialization was leading to the emergence of monopoly capitalism, and hence to an intensification of the class struggle. Did the same analysis apply to backward Russia? Marx himself was doubtful. Thus, in his preface (written in 1882) to a Russian edition of the *Communist Manifesto*, he asked: 'Will the Russian peasant communes (primitive communal holdings that are already in decline) give rise to a higher form of communist land ownership, or will they rather follow the same process of degeneration that we have been observing in the historic development of the West?' Granting the first alternative was tantamount to arguing, with the Populists, that Russia could, as Marx himself put it in 1877, avoid 'all the pitfalls of capitalism'. However, the decline of the *mir*, the weakness of the Populist movement and the growing unrest of the workers convinced early Russian Marxists that their country was no exception to the general rule, and that Russian socialists must choose the same path as their Western comrades: the organization of the working class into an independent revolutionary force.

As a first step, they tried to wean the younger generation from its Populist illusions. To this end, Plekhanov and his circle—Vera Zasulich, Leo Deutsch and Paul Axelrod—now devoted all their energies. The brilliant mind and vast knowledge of Plekhanov stood the movement in excellent stead, but what proved even more crucial was the action of the masses: for the first time in Russian history the opposition to Tsarism spilled over the narrow confines of the intelligentsia, for the first time the people themselves were on the march. And, contrary to expectation, they were not the peasantry, but the urban proletariat.

In the 1870s, the first Workers' Circles and Labour Clubs were born in St Petersburg and the provinces. They were still tiny organizations, with at most two hundred members each, and easy prey for the Tsarist police. Their ephemeral existence, moreover, helped to restrict their influence to a very small proletarian elite. Hence it was not until 1885 that the first mass strike could be organized—in a large textile factory outside Moscow. It involved eight thousand workers and had profound repercussions. A journalist commenting on the event declared that 'Revolutionary propaganda has entered the factories, and the workers are beginning to voice the same demands as the proletariat of Western Europe. The ideas of Marx and the International have begun to infect the Russian proletariat.' This article anticipated the actual course of events in Russia itself by several years, though in Poland and other Western Provinces the workers proved considerably less backward. The Polish Socialist Party was founded in 1888, and in 1897 numerous Jewish workers' organizations banded together into the Union of Jewish Workers of Lithuania, Poland and Russia (*Bund*). In Russia herself, the Social Democratic Society of St Petersburg had succeeded in recruiting an appreciable number of workers by 1890, and on May 1st, 1891, it organized a 'Labour Day' attended by many hundreds of workers. It was, however, the foundation in 1895 of the Militant Union for the Emancipation of Labour—in which the young Lenin, still known as Vladimir Ilyich Ulianov, played a leading part—that gave Russia her first political movement with mass support from the factory workers. Moreover, it served as a model for a large number of similar organizations that sprang up throughout Russia during the next five years.

The Russian socialist movement had at last been launched. In 1886, between thirty and thirty-five thousand workers in St Petersburg went on strike for a shorter working day (ten hours!), and though a thousand or so of the strikers were arrested, the stoppages continued for four weeks. Henceforth, strikes became a permanent feature of Russian life.[1] True, they were mainly for short-term economic objectives, but they also fostered a militant spirit of working-class revolt. This became obvious during the coronation of Nicholas II in May 1896, which the authorities wished to turn into a massive demonstration of pro-Tsarist fervour. In the Khodinsky Fields on the edge of the capital, where hundreds of thousands of people had assembled to be regaled with free food and drink, the crush suddenly gave way to panic, and some three thousand spectators were killed or injured. Foolishly, the

[1] According to official figures there were 60,000 strikers in 1897, 43,000 in 1898, and 97,000 in 1899. Historians are agreed that these figures are far too low.

Imperial couple continued on what was meant to be their triumphal entry into St Petersburg, until street riots forced them to turn back and postpone the procession to the next day. The Tsar himself was no longer safe from the wrath of the people.

Was it then true to say that the urban masses had become a political force in the land? Early socialists had few illusions on this score, thanks largely to the influence of Vladimir Ilyich Ulianov (Lenin). Born in 1870, the son of an inspector of public schools for the province of Simbirsk, Lenin took to revolutionary politics in his youth, perhaps in protest against his brother's execution in 1887. So active was he, in fact, that the authorities expelled him from the University of Kazan, where he was reading law. A few years later, he was graciously given permission to enrol in the University of St Petersburg, but since the authorities saw fit to withhold a residence permit, he could not attend lectures — which, incidentally, did not prevent him from coming top of his graduation class in 1891. Soon afterwards, he left for his native Simbirsk where his law practice brought him into intimate — if rather unremunerative — contact with the poorest classes, and saved him from the snares in which so many revolutionary intellectuals were caught: in his case, theoretical studies of Marxism went hand in hand with a marked concern for the daily problems of the humblest and least class-conscious of his compatriots.

Back in St Petersburg, Ulianov, as a member of the Militant Union for the Emancipation of Labour, began to publish a number of political pamphlets in which he stressed the penury of the workers, their hardships and the need for better labour conditions, rather than dwelling on the wider political problems. These were not forgotten, but Lenin was convinced that only by keeping to the immediate objectives would he make the workers see the connection between their own depressed condition and the political and social regime that far too many of them took for granted and, in the person of the Tsar, even worshipped.

In December 1893, soon after his first stay abroad and his meeting with Plekhanov, Lenin was arrested and sentenced to deportation to Siberia. By then his political work had already borne fruit: the strikers in the capital had made contact with the nascent socialist organization and had followed its advice to maintain solidarity and discipline.

The last few years of the nineteenth century saw the emergence of a host of new socialist groups which, breaking with the old study-circle tradition, transformed themselves into centres of agitation. In 1898, on the initiative of the *Bund*, a first attempt was made to unite all of them into a single national body. The result was the Russian Social Democratic Labour Party, founded at the Congress of Minsk. It had modest beginnings: only six organizations were represented, among them the Militant Unions for the Emancipation of Labour in St Petersburg, Moscow and some other cities. However, since all the members of the Central Committee elected at Minsk were arrested soon afterwards, the party remained an idea rather than a reality—in fact, the only organized Russian socialists at the time were those living in exile. In 1898 Russian émigrés in Switzerland founded the Union of Russian Social Democrats Abroad with Plekhanov as their most prominent member. Their chief aim was to forge the closest possible links with the Russian working class and its early organizations. That this had to be done from abroad was perhaps the clearest sign that there was complete lack of political freedom in Russia herself, as the abortive Minsk attempt made abundantly clear to all who still had any doubts on the subject.

The tactical and organizational work of an émigré group did not at all suit Plekhanov, a theorist first and foremost, and one whose entire career demonstrated to what extent the intellectual in him eclipsed the man of action. It needed a Vladimir Ilyich to tackle this task and give it a decisive impulse.

In July 1900 Lenin, having served his term in Siberia, left Russia for Germany, where he informed Plekhanov that he was anxious to found a paper that would both serve as an organ of political education and help to co-ordinate revolutionary activities at home. The result was *Iskra* (*Spark*), a weekly with Plekhanov, Martov and Lenin as chief editors. It was at this point that Vladimir Ilyich Ulianov first adopted the name of Lenin—from 1901 (the first issue of *Iskra* was published in December 1900) the future leader of the Bolshevik revolution signed all his articles with the pseudonym under which he came to be known. Thanks to his efforts, a new chapter was opened in the history of journalism no less than in the history of the Russian Revolution. *Iskra*, in fact, performed a theoretical task of major importance without ever losing sight of its founder's chief objective: the creation of a genuine socialist party in Russia.

In the purely theoretical sphere the editors of this weekly, published by turns in Germany and Switzerland, analysed the many doctrinal and strategic problems facing the Russian revolutionary movement and, in so doing, carried on a bitter polemic struggle against the ideological adversaries of Russian Marxism. Having demolished the Populist case, *Iskra* concentrated its fire on such 'deviations' as 'legal Marxism' and 'economism', which threatened to deflect socialists from their revolutionary vocation.

When it first filtered through to Russia, Marxism attracted many followers, not only among revolutionaries but also among intellectuals, attracted by its 'Western' outlook and scientific approach. In the old quarrel between the admirers of the West and the Slavophiles, Marxism came down heavily in favour of the former — adopting the doctrine of Marx and Engels meant opting for the West, turning one's back on the kind of romanticism that saw in the 'Russian soul and soil' the basis of true socialist society. No wonder, then, that Marxism was greeted with such acclaim by Russian academic circles, and that the first Marxists were invited to expound their theories before the Imperial Society of Economists in St Petersburg. Moreover, the censors did not object when this society published a Marxist paper, and *inter alia* brought to the notice of the learned members Peter Struve's important *Critical Notes*. 'Let us recognize our lack of education and learn from capitalism,' Struve declared in it. His 'legal Marxism' was not so much a falsification of Marxism — which freely acknowledged that capitalism had ushered in many economic and technical advances — as a mutilation, for it invited Russia to take the path, not of socialism, but of capitalism — and that is precisely what the urban bourgeoisie wanted. Struve's doctrine conveniently forgot Marx's rider that the virtues of capitalism were buried in the past, and that only its vices survived. The *Iskra* attack on the 'legal Marxists' was a constant rebuttal of this distortion.

The 'economism', on which Plekhanov and Lenin next concentrated their fire, was a particularly Russian phenomenon, rooted in the specific social conditions of the Russian class struggle. This theory, which was propounded in the columns of the *Rabocheie Dielo* (*Workers' News*), another émigré paper, was based on the belief that, since the Russian working class was at all times ready to defend its rights against capitalist exploitation, but refused to give political expression to its aspirations, it followed that socialists must concentrate on short-term economic improvements. The 'economists' argued that every attempt to politicize this struggle was premature. Therefore, until such time as the proletariat became more fully class-conscious, it was best to introduce a 'division of labour' into the work of opposition: the workers themselves would fight for the amelioration of their economic conditions, for potatoes, as Bielinsky had put it, while the progressive bourgeoisie, which alone showed any real interest in political and constitutional problems, fought for political democracy.

It was with this view that the editors of *Iskra* now took issue. They too recognized full well that the political awakening of the Russian workers was a difficult task, but they thought it an essential one for all that. They would not, in any case, admit that on the political plane, the working class and its party must take second place to the bourgeoisie. *Iskra*, too, admitted that the spontaneous struggle of the working class was an economic one, but the mission of the revolutionary party was precisely to make the proletariat take the step from spontaneity to political awareness, from purely industrial to revolutionary action.

Hence it behoved a revolutionary party not simply to preach, but also to organize. However, whereas most members of the staff of *Iskra* were formidable in the sphere of theoretical discussion, only one of their number had the additional genius for organization. This man was Lenin. With the help of his wife, Nadezhda Krupskaia, he devised a masterful system of distributing the paper in Russia, as a means of building up a powerful new party: each agent acted as agitator, propagandist, reporter and local party organizer.

While the rest of the brilliant editorial staff—and Plekhanov most of all—showed a well-bred disdain for the humble work of administration and technical organization, Lenin and Krupskaia became specialists in these fields. It was chiefly thanks to their efforts that *Iskra* went from strength to strength, and that, in 1903, the revolutionary groups that had sprung up from among its readers were able to hold a Congress that carried on where the ill-fated Congress of Minsk had been forced to leave off in 1898.

This Congress, which may be called the launching pad of the Russian Social Democratic Labour Party, began its work in Brussels, in July 1903. Soon afterwards, the obvious presence of Tsarist police informers and the rather inhospitable attitude of the local authorities persuaded the Russian revolutionaries to continue in London, where fifty-seven delegates—including fourteen in a purely consultative capacity—represented twenty-five organizations, among them the Jewish *Bund*, which claimed the right to participate as an autonomous ethnic body. Many delegates had come from Russia, and for all of them this was the first gathering of the kind they had ever attended. It inspired more argument than solidarity—in fact, this first Congress of the Russian Social Democratic Party put an end to labour unity. Three questions, in particular, were hotly debated during its thirty-seven sessions: the formulation of a generally acceptable political programme, the adoption of a constitution, and the election of officials. The first point, though the subject of interminable wrangles, was eventually settled by the almost unanimous vote of all the delegates: political revolution was declared the primary goal of the new party, which thus came out clearly against the 'economists'.

It may seem surprising that the chief bone of contention was eligibility for membership in the new party. While Lenin contended that 'Party membership is open to anyone who endorses the programme and helps the party both materially and also by personal *participation*[1] in one of the party organizations,' Martov, who was to be Lenin's chief adversary for many years, proposed that 'Membership of the Russian Social Democratic Labour Party is open to anyone who accepts the Party programme, helps the Party materially and gives it regular personal *support*[1] in accordance with the directives of one of its organizations.'

The difference between the two formulae, though not immediately obvious, was in fact crucial, for it reflected a basic difference of opinion on the structure of revolutionary organizations. Lenin wanted to restrict party membership to a relatively small circle of individuals, all of them ready for active participation in work that, under the prevailing conditions, must necessarily be of a clandestine nature. Martov, for his part, believed that the party must have a far more loosely-knit structure: those who worked on the periphery of the central organization, accepting its directives and leadership, must be treated in the same way as fully paid-up members. Thus, whereas Lenin wanted a rigidly disciplined group, made up of a small number of 'professional revolutionaries', Martov was in favour of a party whose

[1] Our italics.

nucleus would differ little from Lenin's but which, beyond that, would comprise the largest possible number of sympathizers, enjoying the same rights as the rest. Martov's view was carried by 28 votes to 22, with one abstention.

The debates on this subject were extremely heated. 'For me,' Martov declared, 'there is no point in having a conspiratorial organization unless it enjoys the support of a large Social Democratic Party of the working class.' And he added: 'The broader the title of Party member, the better.' To which Lenin replied: 'If hundreds or even thousands of non-party workers are arrested by the police for participating in strikes or public demonstrations, this will prove that our organization has wide influence.' And on another occasion, but in the same spirit, he declared: 'It is far better that ten workers should not be allowed to call themselves Party members, than that one chatterbox should have the right to do so.' In any case, the differences proved so profound that the elections to the Executive Committee, with which the Congress was to close—and which ought to have been a pure formality— gave rise to further acrimonious exchanges and produced a final break: there was disagreement on the composition of the *Iskra* Management Committee, of the Central Party Committee and of the 'Party Council' responsible to the Congress which would meet every two years. This time it was Lenin who carried the day— simply because a number of his opponents had walked out. The 'Leninists' were elected to the Central Committee, and the running of *Iskra* was entrusted to Lenin, Plekhanov (who had sided with Lenin on the membership question) and Martov. When the latter concluded that Lenin had used improper methods to eliminate people from the Central Committee, he refused to serve, and the result was the now historical split between the 'Bolsheviks' (Lenin's majority) and the 'Mensheviks' (Martov's minority). Their quarrel might strike the modern reader as personal and trivial, and hence as a temporary rift that could easily have been bridged. It was, in fact, to have far-reaching repercussions. Much as nascent Russian capitalism engendered socialism, so socialism, in its very birth-pangs, gave rise to its own heir: Lenin's Bolshevism.

Bolsheviks and Mensheviks

Before the collapse of Tsarism, there were several attempts to heal

the breach between Bolshevism and Menshevism. These alternated
with violent phases in which brother rose up against brother. Exile
merely helped to add fuel to the flames. Separated by many hundreds of miles—by a whole world, in fact—from the theatre of
operations, the Bolsheviks and Mensheviks could indulge at length
in theoretical disputes. Worse still, political differences went hand
in hand with personal recriminations. For all that, the differences
between the two factions were real enough; they reflected two
fundamentally opposed conceptions of the nature of political and
revolutionary action.

There was first of all the problem of Party organization and
structure. Until the Congress of July–August 1903, there seemed
little disagreement on this question. Thus when Lenin devoted a
short pamphlet—*What is to be done?*—to the subject in 1902,
many future Mensheviks received it enthusiastically. In fact, their
acclaim was purely superficial, and in any case full of reservations.

Leninism was not only a particular attitude to revolutionary
strategy, an adaptation of Marxism to Russian conditions in particular and to an imperialist world in general; it was also a specific
conception of the role and organization of the revolutionary party.
As we have said, nothing appeared more important to Vladimir
Ilyich than the construction of a party which would put an end to
the disarray and anarchy that had so hampered the Russian revolutionary movement in the late nineteenth century. 'Give us a party
of revolutionaries,' he exclaimed, 'and we shall turn all Russia
upside down.'

Now such a party had clearly to be attuned to its particular setting. In a country torn by a near-continuous hit-and-run struggle
between revolutionary militants and the police, a country teeming
with *agents provocateurs*, a working-class party on the Western
model would have been quickly suppressed. The Russian revolutionary party had, according to Lenin, to be *close-knit, clandestine,
centralized* and *highly disciplined*; otherwise it was bound to suffer
the same fate as its Populist precursors. Only if its ranks were
made up of a small number of utterly devoted professional revolutionaries could it hope to succeed in its task. The nineteenth-
century anarchist Nechaiev had defined such men as follows: 'The
revolutionary is a marked man; he has no personal interests, affairs,
or feelings, no personal connections, nothing that belongs to him,
not even a name. Everything in him is geared to a single and

exclusive goal, to a single thought, a single passion: the Revolution.' This definition applied in full measure to Lenin himself, and went a long way towards explaining his success. Was it not one of his adversaries, the Menshevik Axelrod, who said of him, 'No one else spends twenty-four hours a day immersed in the revolution, thinking and dreaming of it even at night'? And Axelrod asked himself, with stoic resignation, 'What can you do with such a man?' If that question had not been purely rhetorical, the answer would have been: you can make a successful revolution with him.

Now these professional revolutionaries had, almost of necessity, to be recruited from the bourgeoisie. Only a bourgeois, breaking with his class, could have afforded the luxury of devoting his entire life to the revolution. It was, moreover, extremely useful to a party in desperate need of funds to have leaders whose social origins enabled them to enlist financial support from their rich friends. No party was therefore less working-class—in its social composition at least—than the Bolsheviks. However, when circumstances favoured a mass influx of rank-and-file members, as happened during the 1905 Revolution, the Party's social structure was profoundly changed. Thus while only four of the sixty delegates to the 1903 Congress were of proletarian origin, the Congress of 1907, held in London, was made up of 196 intellectuals and professional revolutionaries together with 116 factory workers. Such an increase, however, could only be the result of exceptional circumstances. Normally, political conditions in Russia called for a closed and clandestine revolutionary party. As a report by a Russian socialist to the Second International put it, 'We fall not only in bloody fights, but also while printing our pamphlets, while selling books, distributing journals and tracts, speaking at meetings, holding conferences ... The average life of a committee is one to two months, that of a paper, one to two issues.' Lenin, for his part, did everything he could to make the best of a bad situation. He became a master in the art of preparing invisible inks, of putting messages into code, of scrambling telegrams, and of ferreting out houses for secret meetings and get-togethers.[1]

The logic of his method was clear enough; its democratic nature

---

[1] Writing to Axelrod from Zürich, Lenin advised him to 'add a crystal of bichromate of potassium—$K_2Cr_2O_7$—to the ink. Use the finest paper and a liquid paste made up of no more than a teaspoon of potato starch per glass of water, ordinary sugar being too strong ... '

questionable. Lenin, for one, was not prepared to have the work of his secret committees depend on majority votes at meetings, attendance of which exposed the members to unnecessary risks. 'Those', he declared, 'who, in an absolutist state, clamour for a large workers' organization with elections, minutes, universal suffrage, etc., are all incurable Utopians.' The virtues of democracy had to be sacrificed, willy-nilly, to the imperative needs of central leadership and discipline, the more so as the principle of centralism had been successfully adopted by most European socialist parties, and quite particularly by the German Social Democratic Party, which, in the early twentieth century, enjoyed immense renown among workers in every land. But Lenin gave it an entirely new meaning: centralism, according to him, meant that local groups must take their directives from a central committee and, indeed, must be appointed by the latter. Hence all authority in the party became vested in a small number of 'professional revolutionaries', all of them members of a clandestine 'apparatus'. In 1907, Lenin coined the now classical term *democratic centralism* and used it to define the relationship between the rank and file of the revolutionary party and its leadership. Critics have pointed out, with some justification, that the Party thus became infused with unequal doses of centralism and inner democracy, in which the latter grew increasingly dispensable. Discipline, in any case, was raised to a cardinal virtue in Lenin's party—it became the very embodiment of proletarian courage and a vital necessity.

What is more, with the help of the 1905 revolution, the Bolsheviks had proved that in the struggle with Tsarism they were ready to counter police terror with violence, thus demonstrating that Marxist principles did not prevent them from taking the Populist line. However, they at no time elevated individual terrorism, so dear to the members of The People's Will, into a political principle.[1] Still, the way in which Lenin prepared, from January 1905, for what he believed was an imminent insurrection, showed that he went a long way towards equating political activity with armed struggle. While biding his time in Geneva, he scoured the libraries for books on military strategy and, in particular, familiarized himself with Engels's diverse writings on the subject.

[1] 'As a revolutionary tactic, individual assassination is irrational and harmful,' Lenin wrote in 1916. 'It is only when it is directly and closely linked to a mass movement that individual terrorism can and does prove useful.'

3

In secret letters to Russia, he tendered practical advice on the art of popular insurrection and on a thousand and one ways of encouraging the army to fraternize with the toiling masses. And his advice was heeded so well that, long after the defeat of the 1905 Revolution, the Bolsheviks continued to practise the methods of armed struggle they had perfected during it—helping to swell the depleted Party funds by a series of daring raids. This was the era of 'expropriations', most often of banks—one raid alone bringing in several million roubles. Stalin was to earn great renown in this sphere.

A semi-military spirit, a keen sense of discipline, unquestioned acceptance of directives imposed from on high—all these implied a fixed view on the relationship between the Party and the masses. Lenin always suspected that, left to its own devices, the proletariat would tend to fit into the ideological mould of the ruling class. To prevent this and to rouse them to full class-consciousness, it was essential to subject the workers to a measure of external discipline by a central body, not necessarily of them, but in close contact with them and capable of showing them the way. Such was the mission of the Bolshevik Party, conceived as their sole spokesman and only vanguard. Hence the distrust which Leninists felt for all other labour organizations, for instance the trade unions, which tended to bury revolutionary aspirations beneath a clamour for minor industrial reforms.

The Mensheviks took quite a different view of the political struggle. Although they too appreciated that the lack of political freedom forced socialists to resort to conspiratorial methods, and to prepare for insurrection, they also believed that this did not stand in the way of the creation of a party which, like the socialist models in the West, opened wide its doors to an ever-increasing number of politically conscious workers. These workers, far from standing in need of an all-powerful central committee, ought, as the St Petersburg Menshevik group argued forcefully in about 1912, to have full control of its clandestine section. The Mensheviks claimed that Lenin suffered from a 'siege mentality'. They too were prepared to have recourse to arms, but only as a last resort; meanwhile they would try to engage in all types of open activity that helped to foster and intensify direct contact with the working class. Having become reluctant exponents of the self-same 'spontaneity' they had previously deplored in the 'economists', the

Mensheviks put their trust in the unimpeded growth of workers' organizations and, to begin with, of the trade-union movement.

After the 1905 Revolution, when the authorities were forced to climb down, however slightly, many Mensheviks decided to work exclusively within the framework of Tsarist laws. Lenin sharply denounced this attitude, and Martov, for once, sided with him. In fact, in this sphere, as in so many others, most Mensheviks modelled themselves on Western socialism, trying to copy its organization and sharing its strategic conception.

Nor was Party organization the only bone of contention between Bolsheviks and Mensheviks; they also differed widely in their analyses of the role of the Russian working class. Thus the Mensheviks believed that Russia must perforce follow in the footsteps of the West, as Marx himself had taught. This meant that, all other things being equal, economic power would eventually come down to the bourgeoisie, which would rule by means of parliamentary institutions. It was in the best interests of the proletariat to encourage this process, i.e. to aid the bourgeoisie in its struggle against Tsarism. Once the new regime—comparable to that of Britain and France—had been inaugurated, the workers could go on to consolidate their own position, challenge the employers and eventually seize power on their own behalf. This approach had an obvious weakness: the Russian, unlike the Western, bourgeoisie was far too weak to overthrow the autocracy, let alone establish a democratic regime. Moreover, was it reasonable to ask the workers to support a class of exploiters, and one that had been described as their future enemies? This type of dialectic might have appealed to academic circles and lent itself to a host of intellectual debates, but had little chance of gripping the imagination of the masses to whom the Mensheviks were addressing themselves.

The Bolsheviks—and above all Lenin—took quite a different view. As good Marxists, they too recognized that before the workers could seize power and inaugurate socialism, the country would have to pass through a phase of capitalism and bourgeois democracy. 'Whoever', wrote Lenin in 1905, 'hopes to reach socialism by any path other than political democracy is bound to end up with absurd and reactionary conclusions, both in the economic and also in the political sphere.' In this he was in full agreement with the Mensheviks. Where he differed from them was in denying that the bourgeoisie was either willing or indeed able to make a democratic revolution. It lacked the necessary drive and energy and was, moreover, paralysed by fear of the proletariat. Hence Lenin concluded that the revolution must be the task of the industrial workers, the only truly revolutionary class in contemporary society. He also believed that the bourgeoisie would oppose this development with all its puny strength, and that the Mensheviks were wrong to ally themselves even provisionally with the middle class.

Did this mean that Lenin expected the proletariat, then a small minority, to overthrow Tsarism all by itself? Far from it—but rather than recommend an alliance with bourgeois liberals he preferred to put his trust in the peasantry, in the revolutionary union of town and country workers, in which the industrial proletariat would play the dominant role.

The events of 1905 did much to strengthen Lenin's determination to win over the *moujiks* to the Bolshevik cause. The Revolution had foundered on the attitude of the army, which was, in fact, a peasant force. In December, when the workers of Moscow had risen up in force, they had counted on support from the conscripts recently mobilized for the war with Japan. But the army had failed them—the countryside had refused their proffered hand. Bolsheviks and Mensheviks drew diametrically opposed lessons from this event. For the former, a repetition of 1905 could only be avoided if the socialist movement openly declared its support for the peasant cause, and so drew them into the revolutionary struggle. In any case, if the workers failed to enlist the help of the countryside, they would be defeated time and again. To the Mensheviks, on the other hand, the events of 1905 and 1906 brought confirmation of the 'orthodox' Marxist view that it was no good relying on the peasantry, the most backward political and social stratum of Russian society. Not without a touch of fatal dogmatism, the Mensheviks therefore repeated the old cry: the working class was not yet ripe for power, and must leave the field to the bourgeoisie. This attitude ignored the diffident behaviour, and, from October 1905—when the Tsar granted a new constitution—the somewhat counter-revolutionary role of an important section of that very bourgeoisie on whose support the Mensheviks counted so fervently.

In this respect, at least, the Bolsheviks took a more realistic view of the prevailing Russian conditions and of the real political strength of the various classes. And so, while the Mensheviks continued to work for an alliance with the Constitutional Democrats in the Duma, the Bolsheviks made overtures to the representatives of the democratic peasantry. Outside the Duma, they tried to collaborate with the Social Revolutionaries, a Party founded in 1900 on the old Populist principles, its roots deep in the countryside. This collaboration became much closer still when an intransigent left wing developed within that otherwise moderate and constitutionalist Party.

According to the Bolsheviks, the alliance between the most advanced section of the proletariat and the most class-conscious peasants was bound to lead to the collapse of Tsarism and the birth of bourgeois democracy. Socialism would not come until later, after an interval whose duration no one was rash enough to predict at the time. But while the Menshevik hopes, based on an alliance between the proletariat and the bourgeoisie, were unjustifiably sanguine, the strategic ideas of the Bolsheviks were no less so. Was it conceivable that, once the Russian working class, with the support of the peasantry, had succeeded in overthrowing Tsarism, it would be content to leave social and economic power in the hands of the bourgeoisie, a class incapable of fighting its own battles or of defending its own interests? For that to happen, the proletariat would have to be 'wise' enough not to drive its own advantage home, i.e. to refrain deliberately from continuing the struggle beyond the bourgeois to the socialist phase. This demanded either a profound familiarity with Marxist theories and an unprecedented degree of self-discipline, or else a revolutionary party with enough authority to stop the working class in its tracks.[1]

Such, in short, were the strategic views of the Bolsheviks and the Mensheviks. To the former, the proletariat had an immediate revolutionary mission—it had to make up for the total debility of the bourgeoisie; to the latter, it could only play second fiddle in the struggle against Tsarism, which would be brought down by liberal forces. Hence the proletariat must defer the struggle for its own

---

[1] Trotsky, who until 1917 did not side with either Bolsheviks or Mensheviks, and who made every possible effort to bring them together, put forward a solution of his own, namely the 'Permanent Revolution'. According to him, the proletariat must achieve a democratic *as well as* a socialist revolution in a continuous process. Lenin, who rejected this theory when it was first propounded, became converted to it in 1917.

emancipation until after the establishment of a bourgeois democratic state. Unfortunately for the Mensheviks, revolution was
already in the air, and the bourgeoisie was in no position to take the
lead assigned to it. The working class, on the other hand, was not
only able but willing to engage in battle, the more so as it could
count increasingly on peasant support. Bolshevik impatience truly
reflected the impatience of the masses.

Despite all these differences and all the tensions they produced
among men cooling their heels in exile, it would be wrong to
think of the Bolshevik and Menshevik parties as two monolithic
organizations permanently at war with each other. On the one
hand, not all Bolsheviks were 'hard liners'; on the other hand, not
all Mensheviks had renounced the use of violent methods. Lenin
himself had nothing of the doctrinaire about him—he, whose
intransigence struck his enemies as clear proof of fanaticism
bordering on dementia, was indeed a man of action, but one whose
intellect was so subtle that it helped to transform the former
strategist of destruction into one of the greatest statesmen of our
century, almost overnight.

His flexibility became obvious, for example, during the revolutionary events of 1905–6. Until then, Lenin might well have been
taken for a committee man, anxious above all to impose a rigid line
on his embattled followers, whose every initiative, treated with
suspicion, had to be channelled and submitted to the imperative
demands of a discipline from on high. True, the views he expressed
often suggested that there was something of the Prussian officer in
him, but Lenin would not have been the revolutionary he was had
he not believed that it was the masses themselves who must ulti-
mately decide their own destiny. Hence he fell foul of many of his
comrades when, in 1905, he demanded that the Party committee
bow to the rising revolutionary tide, and when, in a letter to Russia
written in February of that year, he implored the Bolsheviks to
forget their 'habitual hierarchical preoccupations'. 'Drop all that,'
he warned them, 'or you will be buried with all the honours due to
committee men.' He also demanded that new members be asked
to serve on Party committees. He was particularly indignant to
learn that the leaders—future bureaucrats in miniature—should
have deemed simple workers incapable of holding important
positions in the Party.

In fact, such was the pressure of events that even the most rigid Bolshevik dogmas had to be thrown overboard. Lenin himself offered no resistance to this pressure. During the Bolshevik conference held in Finland in 1905, when the Revolution was at its height, important changes were made to the Party constitution. Not surprisingly, Lenin's definition of Party member was substituted for Martov's, but the Bolsheviks also thought fit to introduce more democratic principles—not so much as a concession to their Menshevik rivals as to the demands of the revolutionary struggle. Special guarantees of local autonomy were added; a number of central posts were henceforth to be filled by elections (and no longer by nomination), and members were given the right to criticize the central committee and to protest against possible abuses on its part. The new constitution stipulated, for example, that if one-sixth of the members of any section demanded it, the Party leaders would have to put the complete propaganda machine at the service of their critics. In few parties—even those in which democratic principles are most fully enshrined—are such liberal rules put down on paper, let alone implemented in practice.

Towards the Mensheviks, too, the attitude of the Bolsheviks in general and of Lenin in particular changed profoundly. To begin with, many of the old quarrels had lost their point now that the Revolution had actually started. In most parts of the country, Bolsheviks and Mensheviks joined in the fight against Tsarism and, after the police had confiscated their respective presses, even published a common paper. A unity congress was held in Stockholm in April 1906, and the Bolsheviks proved no less anxious than the Mensheviks to put an end to the fratricidal war. Thus Lenin, describing developments in the Russian Social Democratic Labour Party since 1905, wrote that 'the arguments of the pre-revolutionary period gave way to agreement on all practical questions.'

The honeymoon was of short duration. After the defeat of the Revolution, hundreds of militants had to go back into exile and, as Lenin noted, 'émigré life engenders a host of petty discords.' The second exile was, moreover, far worse than the first, for it followed the exaltation of battle, the rise of a new hope that had not been fulfilled. No wonder, therefore, that Russian socialists in Paris, Geneva and London were filled with greater bitterness than before 1905. In Russia herself, the Stolypin reaction was triumphant, the working class crushed, its party decimated—in 1909 it had ceased to exist, particularly in Moscow, for all practical purposes. 'The life of the émigré is a hundred times harder to bear today than it was before the 1905 Revolution,' Lenin confessed in a letter to Maxim Gorky.

In this climate of defeat, the Bolsheviks and Mensheviks not only resumed their old quarrels but began to split into further factions. The Mensheviks divided into the 'Liquidators' and the 'Anti-Liquidators', i.e. into those who wanted to liquidate all clandestine organizations, and those who wanted to retain them. In the Bolshevik camp there now appeared the 'Boycotters', opposed to socialist participation in *future* Duma elections, and the 'Revokers', who demanded that all sitting socialist deputies be recalled by the Party. Lenin opposed this 'Leftist' trend most vigorously, but he also had to take issue with yet another faction, the 'Conciliators', who wanted to reach agreement with at least one of the Menshevik groups. Often isolated within his own Party, and once again far from the scene of action, Lenin launched a virulent campaign, not always quite honest, against his adversaries. In 1908 he expelled from the Bolshevik faction all those Leftists who, under Bogdanov, had briefly succeeded in gaining the support of the majority.[1]

As the rift between Bolsheviks and Mensheviks deepened, the Mensheviks did little to stop the trend, while many Bolsheviks actively welcomed it. The final break came in January 1912, when a Bolshevik conference in Prague, attended by no more than fourteen voting delegates, decided that the Mensheviks had, by their actions, placed themselves outside the Party. Hence, they claimed, the Bolsheviks were no longer simply a faction of the Russian Social Democratic Labour Party, but the Party's sole representatives. And when the Second International soon afterwards tried to use its good offices to restore peace between Russian socialists, it met with a blunt refusal from Lenin, who had come to appreciate that the international struggle was benefiting the Bolsheviks at home. The circulation figures of the Bolshevik *Pravda*—the first issue appeared in May 1912—were continuously

---

[1] In the event, Lenin was careful to explain that he wanted them expelled from the Bolshevik faction but not from the Social Democratic Labour Party. He added that the Party itself could include a wide spectrum of opinions, some of them diametrically opposed to one another.

outstripping those of its Menshevik rival, and the Bolsheviks were attracting an increasing number of militant workers to their disciplined ranks. Sure of himself and of his small but resolute band of comrades, Lenin, despite all the hardships he had endured in exile, had been able to forge a revolutionary spearhead that was soon afterwards called upon to prove its mettle.

The 'Bolshevik spirit' had become a reality: discipline did not yet exclude discussion; the will to action never degenerated into adventurism; the authority of a great man had not yet made way for the personal dictatorship of a leader. But though Lenin's party held the promise of revolutionary victory, it also contained the germ of more ominous trends. The enthusiasm of 1917 was to herald the first; the recoil, the stagnation and the isolation of the early 1920s accentuated the second.

The essential fact, however, was this: the proletariat had its champion at last, the state its rightful heir. In July 1914 the working class of St Petersburg went on strike, and the people took to the barricades. The war stopped them short, but did not divert them for long; it merely helped the revolutionary movement to get its second wind.

3

1914–17: The End of Tsarism

IN LATE July 1914, while Europe was feverishly mobilizing for war, the Russian working class launched a new offensive recalling the events of 1905. Since June, the government, reacting to a wave of unrest and strikes, had been arresting hundreds of socialists. The proletariat, particularly in St Petersburg, struck back at once: during the state visit of President Poincaré of France they put up barricades, held tumultuous demonstrations and clashed repeatedly with the police.

A few days later all was quiet again — at least on the surface — as feelings of patriotism and national solidarity gripped the entire country. On August 2nd, St Petersburg, which had overnight been re-christened Petrograd,[1] witnessed an extraordinary spectacle. The day before, war had been declared between Russia and Germany, and when Nicholas II and his family, returning from a *Te Deum*, appeared on a balcony of the Winter Palace, some ten thousand people burst into the national anthem and fell upon their knees. In the Duma, almost the entire opposition declared its support for the government. A Jewish deputy felt free to swear in the name of his people that they, the permanent victims of Tsarist oppression, would act as his most loyal subjects and patriots. Only the Social Democrats — Bolsheviks and Mensheviks alike — declared firmly they would support neither the Tsarist regime nor the imperialist war.

Russia was in no position to challenge the Central Powers — influential Russian circles contemplated without horror or disgust the possibility of an international conflagration, but they believed that Russia would not be ready for war until 1917 at the earliest. The railway system, in particular, was no match at all for the German network: in Russia there was one kilometre of railway line per 100 square kilometres of country; in Germany the corresponding figure was 10·6 kilometres. There was an acute shortage of guns

---

[1] St Petersburg was dropped because it sounded too German.

and ammunition, and there were no air force and telecommunications to speak of.

The reason why Russia could nevertheless launch an offensive against the Central Powers in August 1914 was simply that Germany had turned her face to the West, where she was trying to deliver a quick knock-out blow at France and Belgium. Hence the Tsarist armies were able to sweep into East Prussia, and create the legend of the Russian 'steamroller'. On August 30th, however, German reinforcements reached Marshal Hindenburg, who then scored a resounding victory on the eastern front, at Tannenberg. In the course of this campaign, the Tsarist army lost 300,000 men. It was the beginning of mass slaughter, with the Germans concentrating their heaviest guns on a badly equipped host of poor peasants.

But while they had to beat a hasty retreat from East Prussia, the Russians scored a number of major successes against the Austro-Hungarian forces in the south. They occupied most of Galicia, were only just halted outside Cracow, and were able to hang on to Warsaw, on which Hindenburg had set his sights. These relative successes—heavily paid for—were extremely short-lived: in May 1915 the Russians were thrown out of Galicia. In August the Germans took Warsaw and captured vast areas of Poland and Russia. In September Russian territory was invaded once again, and the Tsarist army just managed to hold the Germans off before the gates of Riga. Plans were being made for the evacuation of Petrograd. One year after the beginning of the war, General Brussilov, Commander-in-Chief of the Southern Army, declared that 'the regular army has disappeared and we are left with a band of incompetents,' and, in the same vein, General Yanushkevich, of the Imperial General Staff, admitted that 'no amount of science can tell us how to wage war without ammunition, without rifles and without guns.'

Poor equipment was, in fact, a major cause of Russia's military reverses. The shortage of ammunition and rifles was so acute that infantrymen going into battle had to rely on the weapons of their fallen comrades; in training camps, one rifle was shared by three recruits. Despite the undoubted heroism of the men, General Knox, the British military attaché in Russia, said of the Russians that they were merely playing at war. For all that, the urgent call for army reform fell on deaf ears. In particular, officers continued to be promoted in the good old way—by seniority alone, unless family ties or personal influence intervened, as it did far too often. A committee of the Duma, charged with the study of military problems, had this to say in a report to Nicholas II in September 1915: 'The present system of promotions is fatal to our cause.' And that is how it remained until the end of the war.

If one adds that provisions, scanty at the best of times, often failed to get through to the front for lack of a proper transport system, and that the medical services were in such a state of chaos that most casualties had to be left untended, the reader will be able to form some picture of the morale of the troops once the exalta-tion of the first victories had worn off. Their general dissatisfaction was increased further by the fact that most of their officers treated them with utter contempt, looking down upon them as a miserable and despicable lot. No one, for instance, took the trouble to tell units leaving for the front why they were expected to lay down their lives, or even that war had been declared. No wonder that desertions in the Russian Army assumed massive proportions, and that whole regiments—sometimes on the orders of their officers— surrendered *en masse*. By the end of 1916 the original army had been 'turned over' three times; its losses (killed, injured and prisoners) were estimated at between six and eight million men.

Many Russian attacks were launched prematurely, chiefly in response to urgent appeals by the hard-pressed Western Allies. For example, in 1914 the Russian offensive against East Prussia helped to weaken the Germans in France and thus to save Paris. In 1916, on two occasions, the Russians were again forced to attack both Germans and Austrians in an effort to divert enemy forces from Verdun and Italy. Russians had begun to tell one another that the English and French were prepared to fight to the last drop of Russian blood.

While it is true to say that things became somewhat more stable in 1916, when desperate efforts were made to improve supplies and equipment, the admission was made in an official police document written in October that 'all those who have had any contact with the army are convinced that it is only a step from complete demoralization; while the men have been clamouring for peace all along, they have never before done it so blatantly and with so much determination. The officers quite often refuse to lead them in attack, for fear of being shot in the back.'

The degeneration of Tsarism

But the source of disaster was not at the front. Never before had
Tsarism demonstrated its total incompetence so brazenly, never
had the regime been so debased. 'Disorganization has become
such', Minister Krivoshein declared, 'that one might believe one-
self in a lunatic asylum.' Instead of taking advantage of the sudden
burst of national fervour and the support of the opposition he
enjoyed at the outbreak of war, the Tsar continued to ignore his
people, and later, when general disillusionment set in and the
Duma asked to be associated with the administration in order to
restore national confidence, he haughtily dismissed their patriotic
efforts. His general attitude may be gathered from the reply he
made to the British Ambassador during his last audience in early
January 1917. Public opinion at that point was so incensed, and the
war effort so hampered, that the British diplomat made bold to
appeal to the sovereign in a matter that was not, strictly speaking,
his official concern: he pleaded for new measures to restore public
confidence. Nicholas cut him short; the ambassador, he declared,
had utterly missed the point—the problem was not at all that the
sovereign had lost the confidence of his people, but rather that
the people had ceased to be worthy of the trust of the Tsar of all the
Russias.

With these words he put the final seal on an interminable series
of errors and crimes. 'Chaos now reigns supreme,' the Grand Duke
Nicholas wrote in July 1916. During two and a half years of war,
the regime saw fit to appoint four successive Prime Ministers and
three Ministers of Foreign Affairs; from autumn 1915 to autumn
1916 alone there were three Ministers of War and five Ministers of
the Interior. It was on appointing the sixth and last that the Tsar
himself exclaimed, 'All these changes make my head reel.' And he
added, 'The worst thing is that, unable to tell from one evening to
the next who will be my ministers tomorrow, I am unable to devise
a smooth working routine.' The last of his Ministers of the Interior
was Protopopov, appointed because, according to the Tsarina, he
had the most extraordinary quality of having loved 'our friend [i.e.
Rasputin] for at least four years'. This friend of Rasputin's was a
notoriously unbalanced person, a man who told Kerensky that he
never took any decisions without first consulting one of his icons
and who, after Rasputin's death, preceded his attendances at the

Council of Ministers with long and frequent spiritualist séances, during which he would take political advice from his late spiritual mentor. Before appointing Protopopov on the Tsarina's urgent insistence, Nicholas II himself observed, 'It would seem that but a few years ago he [Protopopov] was not altogether normal, and I was most reluctant to entrust the Ministry of the Interior to such a man.' However, the Empress was able to set his mind at rest by explaining that 'Protopopova himself is not at all unhinged; it is Madame Protopopova who has the weak nerves.'

In fact, mad or otherwise, the Tsar's ministers were if anything more stable than their Imperial Majesties. In August 1915, without consulting anyone and despite ministerial protests, the Tsar let it be known that he would take personal charge of the army. He accordingly transferred his royal presence to army headquarters in Mohilev, where he remained a meddler and a nuisance to everybody. Worse still, during his absence he entrusted the political destiny of his country to the Tsarina's tender mercies. She took her new role very seriously: 'I like to peer into every corner,' she confided to her husband, 'I like to shake people up, restore order everywhere and to harness all our forces.' And Nicholas II told her: 'Be my ears and my eyes in the capital while I am away.'

Alexandra was the last person to run anything, let alone an empire. Her exalted and mystical nature, her reactionary ideas and obscurantist retainers all combined to render her stewardship catastrophic, the more so as her health, both physical and mental, was fast deteriorating. She suffered from all sorts of diseases; she explained that her face was 'electrified with pain'; her dentist would call every day, sometimes more than once. And between these visits she would devote her doubtful talents to organizing food supplies and transport for the front, and to making administrative, political and military appointments.

So much delight did the Empress take in exercising authority that during the last months of their reign, when her husband rejoined her at the imperial palace in Tsarskoe Selo,[1] she continued to run the country. To enable her to maintain control she gave orders that a secret staircase be built, leading to a small chamber next to the Tsar's cabinet room; from here she could overhear all official conversations. In other words, the Tsar had abdicated well before the Revolution put an end to the monarchy by putting his

[1] A suburb of Petrograd, now called Pushkin.

country into the hands of a woman who said of herself, 'They think I am rather abnormal, but they are wrong. It is just that I am closer to heaven than I am to earth.'

Between her and heaven stood Rasputin, a 'debauched monk' according to most people, but a man of God according to Alexandra.[1] She had absolute faith in him and turned a deaf ear to even the most reliable reports of his personal failings, of the scandals in which he had been involved, of the sordid company he kept and of his notorious debaucheries. All that mattered to her was that Rasputin had relieved the condition of her haemophilic son and heir, the Tsarevich Alexis. And when she replaced her husband at the helm, Rasputin's nefarious hold over her became a matter of grave public concern.

Politically, too, he was all the Tsarina desired. Rasputin held ultra-conservative views, and agreed with the Empress that autocracy was the only form of government suited to Old Russia, a country with her roots deep in the countryside. And Rasputin was a man of the earth, a faithful and humble peasant, or so he gave out. Nor was he entirely devoid of shrewd peasant sense: for example, realizing that the war would prove disastrous to Tsarism, he did his utmost to prevent it and later to stop it. Many people accused him—without any real evidence—of being in the Kaiser's pay.

In any case, from 1915 onwards Rasputin was able to give instructions to all the ministers who, in turn, were obliged to submit all military plans for his approval. He worked chiefly through, and often with, the Empress. The appointment of the unbalanced Protopopov was his work entirely, and so was that of a new Prime Minister, Boris Stürmer, in February 1916. Stürmer, who was never more than Rasputin's puppet, stepped into his predecessor's shoes overnight—the former Prime Minister, poor man, was dismissed without a word of warning or explanation. And while everyone knew that Stürmer was another arch-reactionary, there were grave doubts as to his honesty and morals. For the rest, one of his fellow ministers said of Stürmer that 'his gifts were strictly rationed' and that 'he suffered from acute sclerosis due to old age.' This was the man who, in June 1916, was asked to combine the office of Prime Minister with that of Foreign Minister His dealings

---

[1] Rasputin was not really a monk but a *starets*, one of a band of pilgrims who moved from monastery to monastery, living on alms and on their wits.

with Rasputin and his contacts with other unsavoury personalities were notorious. The Allies, moreover, suspected him of pro-German sympathies. In any case, he, the Empress and Rasputin formed the unholy triumvirate that governed Russia at the height of the war.

Not content with governing the country though 'his' ministers, Rasputin decided to take a direct hand in running the war. On July 4th, 1916, the Empress wrote to Nicholas II: 'Our friend asks you not to order an advance on the northern front; the Germans will fall back by themselves once we have consolidated our gains in Galicia.' In November she informed her husband that Rasputin, after direct contact with the Divinity, had recommended an advance on Riga. Exasperated, Nicholas II finally told his wife, 'Sometimes it seems to me that it is not so much he who helps me to govern my country as I who help him to run the government.'[1]

And so the Tsarist regime, steeped in obscurantism, floundered on in an atmosphere of mysticism and superstition bordering on insanity. While the all-powerful Minister of the Interior was con-sulting his icons and spirits, the Empress herself, now the fountainhead of imperial power, advised her husband in a letter dated September 15th, 1915: 'Don't forget, before the cabinet meeting, to hold up our friend's small icon and comb yourself several times with his comb.' On another occasion, she sent Nicholas II an apple which Rasputin had said would 'strengthen his resolve'. On January 15th, 1916, she wrote: 'Please do not think me foolish for sending you this little flask provided by our friend. All of us have taken a sip from it. Pour yourself a small glass and do drink it to his health.' To which the Tsar, ruler of one of the greatest states on earth, replied: 'I have downed it at one gulp.'

On December 17th, 1916, Rasputin was assassinated by leading members of Petrograd society, among them the Grand Duke Dmitry, a nephew of Nicholas II, and Prince Yusupov, husband of the Tsar's niece. They hoped that by ridding the regime of a man who symbolized its decadence[2] they might yet save it. However, the

---

[1] 'Our friend says that Stürmer may remain Prime Minister for some time,' Alexandra had just informed him.

[2] A further proof of this decadence was that none of the people involved in the assassination were arrested by the authorities, though their names were known.

disappearance of the 'debauched monk' and of his crowd of speculators, adventurers and swindlers changed nothing at all. In
January 1917 the Tsar appointed his last Prime Minister, old
Prince Golitsyn, whom the liberal historian Baron Nolde has
called—with more realism than respect or charity—'that old dod-
derer'. This choice and the manner in which it was made afford us
a remarkable glimpse of a society in utter disarray. Having been
appointed, the old aristocrat, 'utterly dumbfounded', observed to
the Tsar that he had never occupied himself with politics. 'I implored the sovereign', he later explained, 'to spare me this bitter
cup. I assured him that I was too old, that I considered myself
incapable, and that my appointment would be a misfortune.' Upon
which he left, convinced that the Tsar would now choose another.
He was wrong—three days later he received the imperial decree
confirming his appointment.

Yet what was needed at that moment was a tower of strength.
More than fifteen million Russians were under arms, and industrial
mobilization had thrown the economy completely out of gear. The
peasants, unable to export their produce, refused to sell food on the
open market—the rouble was near-worthless and there was little
room for barter. To make things worse, the railway system had
collapsed, and what little supplies there were could not get through
to the front or even to the towns.[1] At the end of 1916 certain
regions of the country—and particularly the main industrial towns
—were threatened by famine. The regime was now completely
discredited, and the race for the succession began in earnest.

Rise of the opposition

The patriotic fervour with which aristocratic and bourgeois circles
had united at the outbreak of war failed to ride the tide of the many
military defeats, of continuous administrative muddles and the
blindness of the authorities. With the best will in the world, the
liberal opposition of former years could not consistently ignore the
systematic sabotage of the national effort—not that they did not
try. Self-control, they believed, was the price that had to be paid
for the victory that in their nationalist fervour they so ardently
desired. The behaviour of Miliukov, the great Russian liberal, was

[1] In 1914, Russia had 20,000 locomotives in working order; this figure had
fallen to 17,000 by 1916, and to 9,000 by the beginning of 1917.

a case in point. Before the war, Miliukov had been one of the fiercest bourgeois opponents of Tsarism, but once war was declared he had only one objective: victory, and the fulfilment of Russia's 'great national hope'—the capture of Constantinople. Formerly a republican—albeit a moderate one—Miliukov became a staunch monarchist, convinced that the alternative was social upheaval. At meetings of the Constitutional Democratic Party throughout the summer of 1915, he made no secret of his attitude: 'If the Revolution should come, it will be not so much an uprising as a hateful mutiny. The rabble will be let loose.'

Liberal and reformist circles therefore did their utmost to avert what seemed to them a national and social catastrophe. Despairing of the administration, they encouraged the *zemstvos*, who had been doing invaluable social work throughout the war, to repair the worst defects in the army medical services. Later, and despite the obstacles the authorities put in their way, the *zemstvos* were urged to bring some order into the disorganized war industries, and so boost the flagging morale at the front, which they did successfully in 1916. The Russian Red Cross, too, was increasingly asked to tackle tasks that did not, strictly speaking, fall within its province.

None of these contributions was, however, capable of resolving what was essentially a political problem. Tsarism might perhaps have retained the loyalty of the nation had Russia succeeded on the battlefield; as it was, the autocracy should have done its utmost to strengthen national solidarity by heeding the call for reform that was being sounded from all quarters. But at no time did the Tsar, let alone the Tsarina, feel disposed to make the least concession.[1]

As a result, the liberal opposition, which had rallied so firmly and loyally round the throne, was driven into open hostility. In the Duma a coalition of six moderate parties was formed, ranging from the conservatives to the Constitutional Democrats—only the socialists refusing to join in. This was the 'Progressive Bloc' which while unable to agree on a precise programme, nevertheless called for a new government enjoying 'the confidence of the nation'. What

[1] Letter of the Empress to Nicholas II, dated March 4th, 1916: 'This war must be your war, this peace your peace, redounding to your honour and to that of the fatherland, but under no circumstances to the honour of the Duma. These people have no right to meddle in such matters.'

this meant precisely, no one was prepared to say—according to some, it was a demand for a constitutional monarchy; according to others, it was simply a call for closer collaboration with the Duma in all matters of public concern in general and in the conduct of the war in particular. Everybody was agreed on one point, however: it was both urgent and essential to get rid of the most incompetent and reactionary ministers, those whose every utterance was an affront to public opinion.

It is significant that this programme should have enjoyed the support of even the most conservative sectors of the nation. Thus, at the end of 1916, the Upper Chamber of the Duma, which was heavily weighted in favour of the Establishment, gave public support to the liberal demands.[1] Moreover, even within the government itself the majority of ministers had begun to urge the Tsar to make concessions to the opposition. In August 1915, for example, ten ministers addressed a plea to their sovereign begging him to carry out a number of urgent reforms. In the months that followed, seven of them were relieved of their posts. In September 1915 the political situation deteriorated further, and to put an end to protests from the Duma, Nicholas II ordered the session closed. The workers in the capital struck back at once by downing tools for two days.

All this was, however, no more than a prelude to the wave of fury that was about to engulf the country. No one except Tsarist lackeys and war profiteers could remain indifferent to the spectacle of a system in total confusion—even the ultra-reactionary 'Union of Nobles' felt impelled to protest publicly against the 'dark forces behind the Tsarina'. In October 1916 a report by the Petrograd police referred to a 'threatening crisis that was about to explode'. The same report asserted that the man in the street was convinced that 'we are on the eve of great events compared with which those of 1905 were mere child's play.'

But who would initiate these 'great events'? The bourgeoisie which, fully aware of what was at stake, had begun desperately to jockey for position, or the impoverished masses whose poverty and yearning for peace were about to explode into action? In a remarkable speech to the Duma in November 1916, Miliukov

---

[1] The conservative majority in the Upper Chamber had been strengthened even further during the war by the addition of eighteen new members all appointed by the Tsar.

hinted that the moment of decision was near. Listing the failures of the regime, the innumerable mistakes it had made and the disasters for which it was responsible, he punctuated his indictment with one question, constantly repeated, 'Is this folly or treason?' Next day the Ministers of War and the Navy informed the Duma that the services were solidly behind the opposition. This time Nicholas II and Alexandra were forced to give way. They dismissed Stürmer, but left everything else unchanged. Vainly, the Dowager Empress pleaded with her son, 'Alexandra Feodorovna must be removed. I do not know how, but it simply must be done. She might suddenly go mad, retire to a convent or simply disappear.' The Grand Duke Alexander, the Tsar's cousin and brother-in-law, was less personal but rather more lucid. In a letter to his sovereign he declared that 'strange though it might appear, it is the government itself which is busily paving the way for revolution.' And still the government continued to act as it had always done.

The hour of the Revolution, though imminent, had not yet struck. Meanwhile, Russia was in the throes of intrigue. The Grand-Duchess Maria Pavlovna, widow of the Tsar's uncle, appealed to Rodzianko, President of the Duma, to get rid of the Empress by force, and though Rodzianko himself refused, others were less timid.

The entire Progressive Bloc was up in arms, Miliukov no less than the rest. Meeting Gaston Doumergue, a French minister on a visit to Russia, he told him that the country was on the edge of a precipice. Doumergue advised patience—the war effort must come first. 'We have exhausted our reserves of patience,' Miliukov replied, 'and if we do not act quickly the masses will go ahead without us.' To prevent this disaster, the Progressive Bloc was now considering a revolution at the top: the Tsar would be forced to abdicate in favour of his son, and the Grand-Duke Michael would act as Regent. The list of new ministers was already the subject of animated discussion.

The army command, too, had joined in the general clamour, and General Krimov informed liberal circles that if there were a coup d'état 'the army would greet it with joy'. General Alexeiev, the Chief of Staff, did not stop at mere messages of encouragement. His relations with the Tsar had always been most cordial, but the General was horrified to discover that secret military plans had been confided to the Empress, and hence to Rasputin. So great was his indignation and disquiet that after consultations with Prince Lvov (who was to preside over the Provisional Government after the Revolution) he arranged for the arrest of the Empress on her next appearance at headquarters. He would then force Nicholas II to remove his wife from the centre of government, or else to abdicate.

But as time was pressing, three future ministers of the Provisional Government—Guchkov, Nekrassov and Tereshchenko (who was to hold the portfolio of Foreign Affairs) devised an alternative plan; they would arrest the Emperor himself during one of his numerous journeys between the capital and Mohilev. However, all these conspiratorial plans were overtaken by the Revolution— hardly surprising, since their originators kept blowing hot and cold. Deep down, all of them were far more afraid of the possible consequences of rebellion than of Tsarism with all its short-comings. Miliukov, for one, had little taste for the part of sorcerer's apprentice. The 1905 Revolution had tempered the ardour of many liberals who had come to consider Tsarism as the lesser of two evils. Its continued degeneration might well have driven some of them to action, but the fear of a perhaps more successful repetition of the revolutionary events which they remembered with horror and anguish was enough to dampen their ardour.

In its race for the leadership, the working class started with a considerable handicap: the war had decapitated its organization. This circumstance did not, however, stop the workers from manifesting their growing discontent in a rapidly deteriorating economic situation. The official number of strikers, which had decreased from 1,450,000 during the first seven months of 1914 to 35,000 during the last five months, rose to 550,000 in 1915 and to almost double that again in 1916. This resurgence reflected a revival of militancy which was the more remarkable in that it took place against a background of war hysteria and the complete suppression of all democratic liberties. In the summer of 1916, some of the strikes began to assume spectacular, almost dramatic, proportions, as the exasperated and famished workers in the industrial cities of Ivanovo-Vosnessensk and Kostroma, and also in Moscow, came out into the streets and did battle with the police.

Their violence was largely a response to the fact that throughout the war prices had risen much more quickly than wages. Thus, though nominal wages had practically tripled from 1913 to 1917, they now stretched less than half as far in the shops.[1]

In May 1916 housewives made a host of raids on food shops, only to be beaten back by hastily summoned army contingents. However, when the government tried to use the same method in October of that year to quell the general factory strike in Petrograd, the two regiments they had called in fired on the police and fraternized with the workers. Four Cossack regiments were needed to 're-establish order', and 150 mutinous soldiers were court-martialled and shot. Nevertheless, the workers continued to strike —the struggle had suddenly spilled over from the salons and corridors of power into the factories and streets. But just as the bourgeois opposition was devoid of vigour and popular support, so the exasperated masses lacked the leaders that would carry them to victory.

The workers' parties had, indeed, been forced to pay a disproportionately heavy, and reluctant, tribute to the war. They had had to bear the full brunt of police repression, and none more so than the Bolsheviks. Inside Russia, the Bolshevik Party was now being run by a 'Russian Bureau of the Central Committee', whose existence until the end of 1915 was more symbolic than real. *Pravda* had been banned right at the beginning of the war, the Bolshevik faction in the Duma arrested and deported. In November 1914 the police raided a secret Party meeting just outside Petrograd and arrested another group of prominent Bolsheviks, among them Leon Kamenev who was quickly packed off to join his comrades in Siberia. As the war made any contact with the Bolshevik leaders abroad almost impossible, the Party was left without a head. Worse still, internal dissension at the beginning of the war had weakened the Party further. Not even the Bolsheviks were entirely immune from the general wave of patriotic fervour, and some among them, particularly those living abroad, rallied to the national cause and broke away from the rest.

However, little by little the old clandestine networks were re-established, as was communication with the political centre—in

[1] Mean nominal monthly wages in 1913 for the entire industrial sector: 85·5 roubles; in 1917: 255·6 roubles. Real wages in 1913: 85·5 (gold) roubles; in 1917: 38 (gold) roubles. These figures, moreover, disguise the considerable wage differences between skilled workers whose real income had been slightly increased and the mass of labourers whose situation had become quite intolerable.

other words, with Lenin. In February 1915 a Bolshevik Conference adopted Lenin's theses on war.[1] Although the leading Bolsheviks — Sverdlov, Stalin and Ordzhonikidze — had been deported to Siberia, the Russian Bureau of the Central Committee gradually found its feet and under the leadership of Shliapnikov and of a young student who adopted the nom-de-guerre of Molotov tried to co-ordinate the activities of some ten thousand militants throughout the country. Moreover, by the end of 1915, a Bolshevik committee in Petrograd had begun to function again. There was an evident parallel between this resumption of Bolshevik activity and the growth of mass militancy — much as the skills the Bolsheviks had acquired in their clandestine struggle helped to increase their efficiency, so the growing exasperation of the masses drove the nation towards more militant action. All this did not, it is true, turn the Bolsheviks into a mass party — a statistical survey shows that its effective strength on January 1st, 1917, was a mere twenty-three thousand and its influence was largely restricted to a few industrial pockets. Nevertheless, and despite the setbacks of the war, the party had survived, and was ready to profit wherever it could. In February 1917 no one could have guessed just how favourable the climate was.

As for the Mensheviks, they were beset by problems of quite a different kind. In the Duma their deputies, like the Bolsheviks, had refused to support the government, but their opposition had been far less intransigent. Here the difference between the disciplined and forceful impetus which Lenin gave his party, and the characteristic laxity of the Mensheviks, was revealed in full. The Menshevik attitude to the war and to Tsarism ranged from uncompromising opposition — the position of the minority — to barely-disguised support. An example may serve to illustrate their political confusion. One of the very few reforms the Tsar condescended to introduce during the war was the creation in 1915 of War Industries Committees in which representatives of the employers and workers were expected to devise means of improving social conditions and of increasing production. While the Bolsheviks refused point blank to participate in what they considered a pernicious form of collaboration with the class enemy, the Mensheviks reacted with their habitual vacillations. Some, like the Bolsheviks, recommended a complete boycott of the committees, others wanted to participate

[1] See pp. 91 ff.

in them but only in defence of working-class interests and for purposes of pacifist propaganda; others again, stepping into the shoes of the pre-war 'liquidators', received the new reforms with unreserved enthusiasm. Each of these three trends tried to pull the rest of the Party along behind it, and there was no discipline to impose a majority view.

While there remained the least hope of military victory, the Mensheviks' equivocal position on war and peace was endorsed, if somewhat tepidly, by some sections of the working class. However, in the summer of 1916 when exhaustion and general misery gave way to mass defeatism, and when a new strike wave began to reflect the radical temper of the masses, the workers showed that they had had enough of the moderation and subtlety of the Mensheviks, and opted instead for open struggle and for the clear, firm and unambiguous policies of Lenin's party.

Lenin during the war

What a curious time in his life these war years must have been for Lenin! While all Europe was fighting, the great man of action had to kick his heels in Switzerland, far from the scene of struggle. Not that he had the least desire to fight in a war that he had decried as imperialist, but he felt cut off from the revolutionary tide that was slowly rising in all the belligerent countries. At certain moments the isolation of the future leader of the communist state must have been unbearable, and he suffered bitterly from it: 'Lacking access to the masses, we can do nothing ... if only we could help a *little* (pamphlets, etc.) that would at least be something,' he wrote to a Party comrade in February 1917—just a few days before the outbreak of the Revolution!

But then Lenin had some cause for doubt. All his political ideas had been based on the belief that the workers would rise up as one against capitalism, when in fact they were now drawn up in bloody fratricidal massacres on battlefields throughout Europe. In his fight for the emancipation of the working class and for the socialist revolution, Lenin, like so many socialists, had always acted in the firm conviction that this struggle was historically justified and in full accord with the objective conditions of modern society. But in 1914 he had suddenly been forced to swim against the tide, buffeted not only by the class enemy but also by those who had formerly been his friends and comrades and who had now gone

over to the war camp. Lenin, too, must have been touched by the
disenchantment so many socialists had begun to feel. 'This war
has sapped my strength, has killed me, has undermined my very
being,' said the French socialist Edouard Vaillant who, in fact, died
within a year of the outbreak of war. Lenin was too robust to give
in to such despair, but there is no doubt that his wartime stay in
Switzerland was the most sombre period of his whole life. At
times, his enforced idleness became intolerable and, as he confessed
in a letter to his friend Inessa Armand, he could only shake it off by
engaging 'in struggle after struggle against political stupidities,
vileness, opportunism, etc. And this from 1893 on. There you are,
that's my fate,' he added.

In other letters he spoke of exile as a 'canker', as a 'calamity'. He
advised Inessa to take up skiing, and made the following revealing
remark: 'It is so good up there in the snowy mountains. Quite
delicious, in fact, and it reminds one of Russia.'

And though in Switzerland he at least escaped the horrors of
war, Lenin nevertheless knew great personal hardship. He pleaded
with publishers for work; he gave lectures and asked his friends
to hold collections, however small—he, who set such little store by
material comforts. In January 1916, just before leaving Berne for
Zürich, he begged a friend to try and find him a room, 'the
cheapest, preferably in a worker's home', and asked about the price
of meals in popular canteens. 'I am extremely short of money,' he
wrote in February 1916, and in October he sent this appeal for
help: 'I must say I need an income, otherwise it simply means
perishing. Truly! The fiendishly high cost of living—there is
nothing to live on.' And he kept on asking for editorial and transla-
tion work: 'If that can't be arranged, then, on my word I shall not
be able to hold out. This is very, very serious.'

Here we have Lenin at the trough of the wave. In an address to
young Swiss socialists in January 1917 the man whose whole life
had been one long revolutionary struggle lamented sadly, 'We
of the older generation may not live to see the decisive battles of the
coming Revolution.' At about the same time he complained in a
letter to Inessa Armand that the Revolution was only making
headway with 'extreme slowness and difficulty'.

Oddly enough, during this period of trial and doubt Lenin's
political stature grew to ever larger dimensions. Until 1914, he had
been just one Russian émigré among many, directing another of

those factions whose existence, to the mind of European socialists, simply revealed an inability to pull together and a love for idle polemics. At Congresses of the Second International, Lenin was barely known—the only Russian socialist of repute was Plekhanov. The world-wide Marxist revolutionary opposition to the Party machine had been led by Rosa Luxemburg, not by Lenin. But with the outbreak of war, Lenin became the chief spokesman of revolutionary socialism, the more so as Rosa Luxemburg had been thrown into gaol by the Germans. Another factor, too, contributed to this transformation. He had never been a purely 'local' revolutionary—his political activities no less than his theoretical studies stamped him a true internationalist. But from 1914 to 1917 international affairs had become his main concern: his struggle against the Mensheviks became a struggle against all those European socialists who preferred patriotic dedication to revolutionary action. The collapse of the Second International had left a gaping void, and those who came to fill it seemed more like voices crying in the wilderness than heirs to a great political movement. And yet the rebirth of revolutionary internationalism was the work of this small group of militants who, despite some reservations, answered Lenin's call. The Second International was dead, the Third was still in its cradle, but Lenin was determined to see it grow to full maturity.

The outbreak of war had surprised him in Galicia, then Austrian Crownland. Before he was arrested as an enemy alien, he had time to learn that the German socialist deputies in the Reichstag, far from opposing the war, had readily voted the military credits demanded by the government of Wilhelm II. Lenin's first reaction was to reject this news as war propaganda, but when he had eventually to swallow the bitter pill, his reaction was one of extreme indignation. 'From today,' he declared, 'I shall cease to be a Social Democrat and become a Communist.' Everything he did during the war and after is summed up in that phrase.

To get him released from prison, local socialists informed the Austrian government that although a Russian, Lenin was more implacably hostile to the Tsar than were the Central Powers, and that his activities, far from strengthening Russia, could only serve to weaken her. Lenin was released on August 19th, 1914, and left for Berne immediately. Here he wasted no time—the day after his arrival in the Swiss capital he called a meeting of all Bolshevik exiles and asked them to approve his war theses. In the next few years all his efforts were aimed at having these theses adopted by European socialists. To that end he engaged in incessant discussions and constant polemics, filling thousands of pages in which accusations were mingled with ardent appeals—all in the service of a unique cause: the transformation of the imperialist war into a civil and revolutionary one.

Lenin had first propounded his views on the war—which were later adopted by all those who may be called the founders of the International Communist Movement—in his 'September Theses', published a few weeks after the outbreak of war. The war, according to him, was a 'bourgeois, imperialist and dynastic conflict' inspired by 'the struggle for markets and the robbery of foreign territory', by 'the desire to frustrate the revolutionary movement of the proletariat and democracy within the belligerent countries', and by the wish to 'divide and decimate the proletariat of all countries by throwing the wage slaves of one nation against those of another to the profit of the bourgeoisie'. Now this interpretation ran directly counter to the views of the great majority of the European Left. German Social Democrats contended that the war had been forced on Germany, and that the fatherland had the right to defend itself against French and particularly British encirclement and also against the threat of Tsarist Russia and of Oriental barbarism. French and British socialists, for their part, argued that it was right to defend the cause of democracy against German imperialism and Prussian militarism. Austrian socialists followed the lead of their German comrades. A number of Russian socialists, including Plekhanov, endorsed the French and British view. They found it extremely difficult to explain the presence in the democratic camp of Tsarist Russia, but they were convinced that a victory by the Western Allies was bound to lead to liberalization at home, even against the will of the rulers. Socialists everywhere, forgetting that not so very long ago they had declared that war was the direct consequence of capitalism, had suddenly turned into defenders of their various fatherlands, of territorial integrity and of the sacred rights of national independence, each side denouncing the other with equally high-flown expressions of indignation. For ten years the International Socialist Movement had gathered under the banner, 'Workers of the world, unite!' Now, as Rosa Luxemburg put it, that slogan was expanded into,

'Workers of the world, unite in times of peace but cut each others' throats once war has been declared.'

This piece of sarcasm sprang from deep disappointment. The Second International, born in 1889, had always been a champion of peace; indeed, anti-war propaganda had become its chief raison d'être. The leading socialists — Jaurès in France, Bebel and Kautsky in Germany, Vandervelde in Belgium, Adler in Austria — had declared time and again that the working class would do everything to forestall the outbreak of a new war, a war that could only profit capitalism. Karl Kautsky, in particular, the respected socialist theorist, had explained why justified national wars were a thing of the past in modern Europe. 'Let the governments beware,' Jaurès had added his voice. 'It they cannot avert the threat of war, the people will be quick to see that a revolution on their own behalf will impose fewer sacrifices than a war waged on behalf of others.' And Edouard Vaillant had had this to say: 'Should capitalism be so foolish as to unleash a war, it will only have itself to blame should the workers draw the only correct conclusion and answer with social revolution.'

Nor had the Second International simply left it at that — during a congress held in Stuttgart in 1907, all the delegates had unanimously resolved that 'should war none the less break out [despite the opposition of the workers] it is their duty to intervene in order to bring it promptly to an end, and with all their strength to make use of the economic and political crisis created by the war to stir up the deepest strata of the people and precipitate the fall of capitalist domination.' This resolution, which was apparently binding on every member of the Second International, was endorsed at all subsequent meetings — until the outbreak of war.

Then in August 1914 the International, far from trying to 'make use of the economic and political crisis created by the war' or to 'precipitate the fall of capitalist domination', used what 'stirring up of the people' it engaged in to persuade the workers that the defence of the fatherland merited supreme sacrifices, and that the moment had come to sink all class divisions in the common struggle for the defence of the nation. The collapse of the Second International was patent; it had beaten a hasty and inglorious retreat in its chosen field of battle. Had not its leaders betrayed their most sacred principles? True, they justified their behaviour by reference to other principles of the International, Jaurès, for

instance, declaring in a now famous phrase that 'a little internationalism leads one away from the fatherland, a large dose of
internationalism brings one back to it.' And, in fact, the Second
International had never rejected the principle of the legitimate
defence of nations and people. The whole problem had rather been
glossed over, for if capitalism was, indeed, the sole cause of war—a
general formula that no socialist would have dreamt of challenging
—what was the meaning of the legitimate defence of one nation
against another? It was illogical and even absurd to affirm that the
responsibility for war belonged to capitalism in general, and to
German, or Russian and British imperialism in particular. In fact,
over the years the socialist movement had lumped together
patriotic with internationalist ideas, and while the latter had
predominated before 1914 they had never been able to oust the
former. No wonder, therefore, that the shock of the war should
have so readily suppressed, or rather anaesthetized, feelings of
international solidarity. Worse still, in many stalwart socialists
patriotism quickly degenerated into rank chauvinism, so much so
that it was difficult to distinguish between the former champions of
peace and universal brotherhood and those whose warmongering
they had always denounced. While the entire bourgeoisie applauded
this miracle of national reconciliation, Lenin loudly cried treason.
In his 'September Theses' he did not simply denounce the
imperialist nature of the war, but pilloried all socialist war
supporters as 'rank traitors to socialist principles'. He added that
there could be no question of collaboration with men who had thus
disqualified themselves from being representatives of the international working class. And in the same way that he had formerly
broken with the Mensheviks, he now called for a Third International, to which none of those who had abandoned the class
struggle and their international commitments at the decisive hour
would be admitted. He no doubt recognized that the formation of
a new organization depended on the right conditions, but the need
for one was never in doubt. This brought him into head-on
collision with an important wing of the socialist movement—the
Centrists—who, while opposed to 'social patriotism' and 'social
chauvinism', did not accept the need for a final break with men
they hoped would return to the fold under more favourable
circumstances. Lenin, for his part, though he clearly distinguished
between Centrists and Rightists in the movement, was as vigorous

in his attacks on the former as on the latter. In particular, he blamed the Centrists for their lack of consistency and resolution, for their advocacy of what was in fact a fictitious form of unity, and for their wishy-washy pacifism.

Lenin, though a bitter opponent of the imperialist war, had, in fact, nothing of the pacifist about him. 'The refusal to do military service, the calling of strikes against the war, etc., are so many stupidities; pitiful and craven dreams of unarmed struggle against the armed bourgeoisie,' he wrote, and he advised the working class to be on its guard against 'those sentimental snivellers who dread war' at a time when 'the world is full of things that must be destroyed by iron and fire in the interest of the emancipation of the working class'. Pacifism, according to Lenin, merely deceived the people into thinking that 'in the absence of a revolutionary movement it is possible to have peace without annexations, without the oppression of nations, without robbery, without planting the seed of new wars among the present governments and the ruling classes'. Hence his slogan, 'Turn the imperialist war into civil war.' Could he not justify it by reference to the resolution at the Stuttgart Congress which the whole International had adopted?

But Lenin's formula was thought too extreme by a number of revolutionary Marxists, who felt that he was ignoring the hard facts and, moreover, assigning quite impossible tasks to the proletariat. Nations were tearing each other apart, factory workers were forging the instruments of death that would be used by their brothers in the trenches to kill workers on the other side. Patriotic songs and national anthems were resounding everywhere, and this was clearly not the time to call for civil war and revolution.

Lenin shocked the socialist camp even more when he began to preach defeatism. 'A revolutionary class in a reactionary government', he argued, 'is bound to hope for the defeat of its government.' And again, 'The transformation of the imperialist war into civil war is greatly facilitated by military reverses'; 'revolutionary action in wartime not only means *hoping* for the defeat of one's "own" government but also working unflinchingly towards it.' On a number of occasions Lenin contended that this general thesis applied particularly to Russia, whose military defeat was a 'lesser evil'. Though his defeatist views earned him a great deal of enmity and abuse, he was, in fact, standing on an old Russian-socialist platform. Thus in 1853, during the Crimean War, many Russian progressives had openly favoured the defeat of their own country as a means of weakening the autocracy. Fifty years later, during the Russo-Japanese war, Plekhanov, at the Amsterdam Congress of the Second International, took much the same view when he declared that 'by breaking one leg of the colossus, Japan is avenging the oppressed.' During that war, moreover, the Japanese Government offered direct aid to a number of Russian revolutionaries, and while the Bolsheviks, the Mensheviks and the Cadets had refused the arms and the money promised them, the Georgian and Polish socialists—Pilsudski among them—had felt no such scruples and accepted the Japanese offer. The future head of the Polish state had even gone to Tokyo to solicit further support. In short, defeatism was no innovation of Lenin's.

But what precisely did he want his followers to do? He at no time advocated such adventurous or romantic actions as sabotage or organized incitement to mutiny.[1] Instead, his 'September Theses' advocated a 'vast propaganda campaign in the army and at the front in favour of a socialist revolution, calling upon the masses to turn their guns not on their own brothers … but against their government …' Lenin also stressed the 'absolute necessity of organizing cells and illegal groups in the army', and of supporting 'all revolutionary actions by the masses of the proletariat', and called on 'socialist women in all the belligerent countries to intensify their struggle'. Above all, however, he put his trust in the systematic encouragement of 'fraternization between soldiers of the belligerent nations, even in the trenches'. Every time that a bulletin brought news of such an event, Lenin was utterly delighted.

For the rest, he saw his task as one of education, demystification, agitation and of separating the sheep from the goats in a new International of true revolutionaries. The war had virtually broken all links between socialists in the two armed camps, not only because of government intervention but also because of the refusal of socialists themselves to communicate with their former comrades. Even as disgust at the carnage became world wide, and more

---

[1] According to Bukharin, Lenin one day put forward the view that soldiers had a duty to 'turn their guns against their officers'. However, this is not borne out by any of Lenin's writings. On the contrary, in a letter to Shliapnikov, who was then leading the Bolshevik faction in Russia, he defined his position as follows: 'Not by sabotage of the war effort, nor by isolated interventions, but by propaganda among the masses … It would be mistaken to call for individual acts of resistance, to shoot officers, etc.'

and more voices began to speak up for international conciliation, many socialist leaders continued to preach peace through military victory. To them, all negotiations were premature, all contact with the 'enemy' pernicious.

Other socialists, particularly those in neutral countries, tried from the very beginning of the war to restore the broken links and to act as intermediaries. Their efforts were welcomed by the German Social Democratic Party, and even by some of its most chauvinist members—doubtless because an early peace would have allowed Germany to hold on to much of the territory she had conquered by force of arms. Most French, Belgian and British socialists, on the other hand, were opposed to all such overtures, and it was over their heads that the Italians called the now-famous Zimmerwald Conference, which met in September 1915 in a small village in the Bernese Oberland. Here official Swiss and Italian delegates mingled with Bolsheviks, Mensheviks and members of left wing and internationalist groups from other parts of Europe, none of whom wished to see socialism buried for the duration of the war. They unanimously adopted a resolution (the Zimmerwald Manifesto) in which they publicly and solemnly expressed their abhorrence of the war policy advocated by most Socialist leaders. The manifesto did not, in fact, end with blaming capitalism for the carnage, but added that:

> Socialist Parties and working-class organizations of certain countries ... have disregarded the obligations that followed therefrom [the resolutions adopted at International Socialist Congresses]. Their representatives have invited the workers to suspend the working-class struggle, the only possible and effective means of working-class emancipation. They have voted the ruling classes the credits for carrying on the war. They have put themselves at the disposal of their governments for the most varied services ... They have given to their government socialist ministers as hostages for the observance of the national truce.'

And the manifesto went on to declare that these socialists had thus 'taken on themselves the responsibility for this war, its aims and its methods'.

During the few days that the Conference sat, Lenin, who was one of the delegates, did his utmost to swing the rest further to the Left. In the end, however, he supported the manifesto (drawn up by Trotsky), but his own followers published a minority resolution in which they called for 'ruthless struggle against social imperialism' as 'the first prerequisite of the mobilization of the proletariat and the restoration of the International'. The declaration also inveighed against the Party Centre, which misused the socialist banner and was thus 'apt to mislead the non-class-conscious element of the proletariat'. 'Civil war, not civil peace, between the classes—that is our slogan.'

In April 1916, when the same tendencies, if not the same men, clashed again at Kienthal, Lenin's ideas had made some headway— even internationalists more moderate than he had grown highly critical of what Lenin had continually denounced as that 'vacillating and pusillanimous Party Centre'. And so while many differences remained, the seeds had been sown for the emergence of a new force—the Communist movement, which the Russian Revolution would endow with so much prestige and dynamic force. The Zimmerwald spirit was, in any case, a turning point in the history of the socialist movement. Lenin emerged from it triumphant, and on the evening of April 3rd, 1917, at the Finland Station in Petrograd, when thousands of Russian workers and soldiers welcomed him back home, they were greeting one who, tested by war and full of new hope, was ready to lead them forward on their revolutionary path.

4

The February Revolution

IN FEBRUARY 1917, Tsarism received its coup de grâce. During the past winter, Petrograd and Moscow had recorded temperatures of −40°C, there was neither bread nor coal to ward off the freezing cold, and the price of food had risen suddenly by some 40 to 60 per cent. Meanwhile the rich continued to live in ostentatious splendour as they built up great fortunes out of the war. A French woman visiting Russia during these crucial weeks was taken aback by this glaring contrast between the misery of the masses and the luxury of the rich: 'Never before have I seen so many cars in the streets, so many diamonds glittering on the shoulders of women. All the theatres were crammed. The fashionable restaurants were the scene of incessant orgies; a bottle of champagne fetched a hundred roubles [ten pounds sterling] and people amused themselves by pouring it out by the bucket.'

And as the social crisis became more acute, the political frame began to show ominous cracks. One did not have to belong to the inner circle to appreciate the utter decrepitude of the authorities; the bourgeoisie, that barometer of political storms, was desperate for a change. The masses, for their part, were prepared to contribute to the struggle the energy and fighting spirit which they alone seemed to possess. When February came, people were no longer prepared to be fobbed off with reshuffles at the top. The Tsar counted for next to nothing, and the Empress for even less. The military commanders were ignored, the party chiefs went unheeded, and even the revolutionary leaders dropped into the background. History has recorded other such exceptional moments, when the nameless masses suddenly erupt with intense fury and become transformed from mere subjects into men—and within a few days cause society to take a vast leap ahead. The result is revolution. While its tide flows, the great actors who held the political stage only yesterday are swept away at one mighty stroke and replaced by faces from the anonymous crowd. The historical record rarely preserves their names. Thus in February 1917 a

Sergeant Kirpichnikov and a few others like him appeared at one moment, only to be forgotten the next, representatives of the immense popular swell that engulfed the old regime and what little remained of its former power and glory.

It is often said that the February Revolution was spontaneous, and in fact it was not organized by any party or by any political leader. The liberals did not want it; the revolutionary leaders were in far-away Siberia or in political exile abroad. All alike were taken by surprise. Those who cannot imagine a strike without a leader, or a revolution without men pulling the strings behind the scenes, must find February 1917 a complete enigma; and none were more mystified than those whom the Revolution bore to power in its first wave of victory. The liberals were terrified lest the axe that had felled the Tsar be wielded against them as well, and even moderate socialists trembled at the idea of seizing power. The Menshevik Skobelev, a future minister in the Provisional Government, travelling on a tram with a journalist during the first days of the crisis, expressed the view that the disorders were bound to turn into pillage and arson and that they had best be repressed before it was too late. Most observers—including some who were sympathetic to the Revolution—spoke of dangerous, uncontrolled and 'elemental' forces. However, although it was spontaneous, the Revolution was by no means due to pure chance. In one of his last reports, an agent of the Tsarist Secret Police asserted that the proletariat had been stirred up by 'propaganda'. And he was quite right, of course—this 'propaganda' had been the work of thousands of militants over many long years, had been disseminated in a host of journals, clandestine and otherwise, and had been driven home still further to the masses by their own intolerable economic conditions, by the horrors of war and by the humiliation of military defeat. Last but by no means least, it had been the work of the Tsarist regime itself, apparently so determined to demonstrate its own injustice and bungling. Hence the February Revolution, although spontaneous, was not produced in a void—it was the harvest of a long struggle, of fury too long contained, of immense efforts, of fatal errors, of accumulated crimes, of a seed carefully planted and suddenly come into flower.

The February Days

During January and the first weeks of February 1917,[1] social tension kept increasing in the capital, and so did the number of strikes. However, it was not any initiative on the part of the working class that set the match to the powder keg, but an action taken by the employers—they declared a lock-out in the great Putilov works, thus throwing into the streets tens of thousands of workers, among them some of the most politically conscious and militant in all Petrograd.

This happened on February 22nd (March 7th), just when incensed housewives, driven by hunger and frustration, had started to invade bakeries and other food shops. Soldiers' wives, whose position was particularly difficult, were prominent among them and so were female textile hands, whose wages were far below the national average.

On February 23rd (March 8th) the socialist organizations celebrated 'Women's Day', and in the prevailing atmosphere the demonstrations went much further than the organizers had intended, particularly in Vyborg and other working-class districts of Petrograd. Procession after procession passed through the street to cries of 'Bread ', 'Our children are starving ', 'We have nothing to eat!' Seditious slogans, too, began to be voiced, and a cry of 'Down with the autocracy!' was loudly taken up by the crowd. There were a few clashes with the police, but no serious injuries; though some 90,000 of the city's 400,000 workers had come out on strike, the situation did not seem to worry the authorities. That very day, Nicholas II, after a long reunion with his family, returned to his remote Mohilev headquarters—even the turmoil in the Duma, where Kerensky had launched a violent attack on the government, did not succeed in shaking the sovereign out of his habitual phlegm.

Next day, however, the number of strikers had reached 197,000, and their courage increased with their numbers. Though the bridges across the Neva, which linked the proletarian suburbs to the centre of the capital, were guarded by the police, the Neva itself

[1] For the period from February 1917 to February 1918, the dates given here are according to the 'Julian' (Russian) calendar; the corresponding 'Gregorian' (Western) dates are shown in brackets. The Julian calendar was thirteen days behind the Western. On February 1st, 1918 (by the Julian calendar—February 14th by the Gregorian calendar), Russia adopted the New (Western) Style.

had frozen over, and the workers had little difficulty in rushing into
the residential and administrative quarters shouting their slogans
('Bread!', but increasingly 'Down with the autocracy!', 'Down with
the war!') and showering the police with stones, with pieces of ice
and other projectiles, but taking care not to molest members of the
armed forces. The police guard, 3,500 or so in number and reinforced with thousands of gendarmes, formed the government shock
troops; according to a scheme worked out during the preceding
months, they would, in fact, bear the brunt of any workers' attack
—if the need should arise, Cossack cavalry regiments stationed in
the capital would be brought in as well. The other regiments would
only be called upon as a last resort.

The Petrograd military garrison was made up of an enormous
number of reservists, including fourteen battalions of reserve
Guards. In addition there were tens of thousands of raw recruits
and family men in uniform, who were temporarily exempted from
front-line service, and determined not to be sent. Their officers
were no keener, so that the authorities had only the military cadets
or *Junkers* to fall back on in case of trouble. In any case, the
presence in the capital of so vast a crowd of men in military great-
coats—there were some 160,000 of them at the time—was frowned
upon by some of the Tsar's best-informed advisers. That their
qualms were fully justified became crystal clear during the
February Days—fairly close relations between workers and soldiers
were established from the start, the former explaining their
grievances to the latter; the officers were unable to do anything
about it, and closed their eyes to it. Even the Cossacks showed an
evident lack of zeal when it came to dispersing demonstrations, and
some of them were warmly applauded by the surprised crowd.
Throughout this time the government, meeting at the Mariinsky
Palace, did not waste its time on the situation in the streets, but
continued blithely with 'current business'.

And 'current business' was, indeed, proceeding apace. By
February 25th (March 10th) the strike had become general and
students, leaving their lecture halls, joined the workers in the
streets. Trams had stopped running and no papers appeared.
Petrograd began to look like a besieged town. Vyborg, to all intents
and purposes, was in the hands of the crowd, and the forces of law
and order had to barricade themselves in the commissariat. This
time no one could doubt the gravity of the situation. From his

headquarters in Mohilev, the Tsar sent the following telegram to General Khabalov, the Commander of the Petrograd Military District: 'I command you to suppress from tomorrow all disorders in the streets of the capital.' The police and the soldiers received orders to open fire on the demonstrators.

At that time, the attitude of the soldiers was still an open question, and the fate of Russia hinged on the answer. As for the police—known as the 'Pharaohs'—and particularly the mounted police, their devotion to the Tsar was never in any doubt. That day the workers suffered their first casualties. The dragoons, too, plunged into the demonstrators, but the Cossacks continued to vacillate; at one point, when they threatened to fire on the crowd, a worker took off his cap, moved towards them and said, 'Brothers, Cossacks, help the workers in their struggle for peaceable demands; you see how the Pharaohs treat us hungry workers. Help us!' Then the Cossacks lowered their guns, and some of them opposed the police. Numerous women, too, invaded the soldiers' ranks, seized their arms and implored them not to fire; little more was needed to weaken men whose resolution was in any case faltering. During the night of February 25th–26th (March 10th–11th), the government was still able to arrest some hundred militant workers and seize members of the Petrograd Bolshevik Committee. But that was their last victory, and one they had occasion to regret. The Bolshevik leaders had acted as a brake on the movement, and in their absence the more militant elements in Vyborg assumed greater authority and used less cautious tactics.

The turning point came on Sunday, February 26th (March 11th). That day, scores of people were fired on by policemen armed with machine-guns and posted on strategic rooftops, and though demonstrators continued to pour into the centre of the capital, by the end of the afternoon the police seemed in full control of the situation. Workers' delegates meeting at Vyborg did not hide their deep disappointment and even thought of calling off the general strike. The masses themselves, however, thought otherwise. Their fury had been mounting throughout the day, and they now proceeded to set fire to several public buildings, including the Palace of Justice.

On the political front, too, the situation had become more explosive. On February 26th, Prince Golitsyn decided to implement a signed but undated imperial ukase and suddenly prorogued the

Duma. The meaning was clear: once again the autocracy was refusing to make even the slightest concession, once again it had chosen the path of naked repression. Rodzianko, the President of the Duma, informed the Tsar by telegram that 'there is anarchy in the capital', and implored him to form a new government under a man who 'enjoys the confidence of the country', adding that 'delay is equivalent to death'. When this message went unanswered, Rodzianko sent a second message: 'The situation is growing worse by the hour. Measures must be taken immediately, tomorrow it will be too late. The last hour has struck, the fate of the fatherland and the dynasty is being decided.' After reading this message, Nicholas II remarked typically to his Minister of the Court, 'This fat Rodzianko has written me some nonsense to which I will not even reply.'

Though the prorogation of the Duma added a new dimension to the workers' struggle, they hesitated to take the final step. Until Sunday, February 26th, the movement had grown from strength to strength, each new demonstration proving more fervent, more determined and more courageous than the last. It was time to choose between withdrawal, which would, in fact, have been an admission of defeat, and a new forward leap, that is, armed insurrection. Everything depended on the attitude of the soldiers: if they chose for the Tsar, the workers would be massacred and the Tsar emerge triumphant from the ordeal. Thus, late on February 26th, there was an hour of uncertainty, a last moment pregnant with suspense when victory and defeat hung in the balance. Then, even while the workers were still trying to get their wind back, the issue was suddenly decided for them: the army, the old army of the Tsars, opted for revolt. A company of the Pavlovsky Regiment on duty along the Catherine Canal had seen the police, entrenched on the other bank, open fire on an unarmed crowd. As people fell round them and others fled in panic, the soldiers spontaneously seized their rifles and fired—not on the demonstrators but on the police. They had crossed the Rubicon at last. Back in their barracks their first act of insubordination forced them to commit a second one: they tried to win over the other companies of their regiment. Then shots rang out in the barracks, and as they re-echoed, February 26th drew to an end.

Next morning, at first light, came a further and decisive act of insubordination. Soldiers of the Volinsky Regiment—including the officer cadets—refused to obey their superiors at morning roll call. They had spent the night discussing their impressions of the day's shooting, and several of them declared that they would never again fire on the crowd. When an officer appeared in the barracks and read out the Tsar's telegram to General Khabalov in an attempt to restore discipline, he merely incensed the soldiers and eventually lost his life. The men, having burnt their boats, poured out into the streets and made for other barracks in an effort to gain new recruits. The mutiny now spread rapidly; at 1 p.m., some twenty-five thousand soldiers, defying their officers, made for the Vyborg district where they fraternized with the workers. Crowded into lorries, clenching their machine-guns, they crossed Petrograd spreading enthusiasm on the Left and casting gloom over the Right, particularly when they rushed the prisons and released all political prisoners. For good measure they also freed many imprisoned criminals, who might have been expected to engage in wild excesses. In fact such excesses were few and far between, which was the more astonishing in that the 'forces of law and order' were by then in complete disarray—General Khabalov barely managed to collect between fifteen hundred and two thousand men whom he posted round the Admiralty and the Imperial Palace. There they stayed for the next twenty-four hours, hoping desperately for reinforcements from the front. By the evening of February 27th (March 12th), almost the entire Petrograd garrison had joined the insurrection, while their officers took to their heels or locked themselves in their quarters.

However, the essential events were being acted out elsewhere: on the morning of the 27th, hearing that the Tsar had prorogued the Duma, many deputies were tempted to defy him, but being too timid for this they hit upon a compromise: they would comply with the ukase by moving from their customary Assembly Hall into another chamber of the Tauride Palace. There they asked the Council of Elders to appoint a Temporary Committee presided over by Rodzianko and including representatives from all parties, with the exception of the extreme Right and the Bolsheviks who, ever since the arrest and deportation of their deputies in 1914, had been without representation in the Duma. The Temporary Committee defined its function as 'the restoration of order in the capital and collaboration with public organizations and institutions'. This was anything but revolutionary, but Rodzianko was still hoping that his aristocratic and military intermediaries might persuade Nicholas II to make what political concessions the liberals had been demanding. In the early afternoon the Duma did not, in any case, evince the least desire to seize power.

In fact, the deputies had no idea of what was happening in the streets. The Tauride Palace had remained an island of peace; so much so that one might have thought the workers were deliberately displaying indifference to what they considered a poor offshoot of the old regime. At 2 p.m., when Tsarism had already capitulated in Petrograd—without having given battle—and Miliukov, the leader of the Cadet Party and the leading liberal of the day, was asked about the intentions of his party, he still saw fit to reply, 'For the moment we cannot take any decisions ... We must first gather accurate information ... and examine the situation; it is early days yet.' Soon afterwards, the masses, swollen by ranks of mutinous soldiers, appeared outside the Tauride Palace. The Duma could no longer hang fire, the less so as they were suddenly informed of the rebirth of the Soviet or Workers' Council. As spontaneous creations of the proletariat, such Councils had first sprung up during the 1905 Revolution, when factory workers in all parts of Russia had followed the example of the industrial region of Ivanovo-Vosnessensk, electing delegates from among their own ranks and in their own factories. But it was particularly the Soviet of Petrograd that had succeeded in giving the action of the masses a coherent direction and expression. No wonder, then, that now, in the first upsurge of revolutionary fervour, they decided to resurrect it: on Friday, February 24th, militant workers, socialist deputies and representatives of the cooperatives had passed a resolution to that effect. Three days later, when the masses had stormed the prisons, freeing a host of Bolshevik and Menshevik militants, the former immediately joined the workers' ranks while the latter made straight for the Tauride Palace, where they met factory delegates and decided to form a 'Provisional Executive Committee' and to call a plenary session of the Petrograd Soviet for that very evening.

At this meeting, presided over by the Menshevik deputy Chkheidze, the victory of the Revolution was proclaimed. Some 250 workers' delegates listened to improvised reports about the events of the day by soldiers from the various regiments stationed in the capital; according to an eye-witness they hung on the

speakers' words 'like children being told a fairy tale'. Their enthusiasm was boundless, and they decided there and then to
commemorate the miraculous alliance between workers and soldiers
by renaming the Soviet of Workers the 'Soviet of Workers' and
Soldiers' Deputies'; henceforth delegates from the factory and the
army would take their seats side by side. The meeting then proceeded to the election of an executive committee and a series of
sub-committees, each charged with the reorganization of particular
aspects of public life in the capital. The working class had found its
mouthpiece at last.

Would the bourgeoisie bow to the will of the working class?
During the entire course of the insurrection it had waited in fear
and trembling. At 2 p.m. Miliukov was still wavering, but in the
course of the evening, after a dramatic meeting with Rodzianko, he
told the excited crowd which had meanwhile invaded the Duma, 'A
decision has been taken. We shall seize power.' Recalling this
historic hour, Rodzianko later wrote that if the Duma had refused
to take this step 'it would have been arrested by the mutinous
soldiers and cut down to the last man'. The Provisional Committee
of the Duma, set up in the morning, would stay on and see to the
'restoration of order and the creation of a government in accordance with the desire of the people and capable of obtaining their
confidence'. Once this decision was taken, Russia found herself
saddled with two representative bodies whose collaboration or
rivalry was to determine the course of events until the seizure of
power by the Bolsheviks: on the one hand the Soviet, representing
the proletariat, and on the other hand the embryonic Provisional
Government which the Allies were to recognize as the legitimate
successor to the Tsar and to which the bourgeoisie delegated the
defence of its class interests.

February 28th (March 13th) brought the final collapse of the
Tsarist forces: the last remaining 'loyal' troops surrendered or dispersed; the Fortress of Peter and Paul capitulated without firing a
single shot; and the Tsar's ministers were either arrested or, like
Protopopov, surrendered to the new authorities. The Provisional
Committee of the Duma proceeded to appoint commissars and to
put them in charge of the various ministerial departments, and also
used its good offices to restore the authority of the officers' corps
which, once the storm had abated, gradually crept out of hiding.
In Petrograd, at any rate, the insurrection was over. The official

records showed that 1,315 persons had been killed or wounded: 53 officers, 602 soldiers, 73 policemen and 587 civilians.[1]

That same day, Moscow joined in the fight. A general strike was the prelude to a seizure of power that proved a mere formality: not a single life was lost in the city. In the provinces, the Revolution was accomplished by telegram, as Trotsky put it: when news of the events in Petrograd filtered into the villages, the provincial authorities took the path of least resistance—they meekly handed over to the newly-formed soviets, or to the Provisional Government. Trotsky tells us that 'in Kharkov, the chief of police, having gone to the railroad station to get news of the revolution, stood up in his carriage before an excited crowd and, lifting his hat, shouted at the top of his lungs: "Long live the Revolution! Hurrah!"' In the first flush of victory sudden conversion to the cause of the Revolution was, in fact, the general rule. According to the French journalist Claude Anet, who was in Russia at the time, red flags appeared in all the streets, and buttonholes and hats—not only caps—were bright with scarlet ribbons. 'You could recognize the reactionaries of yesterday by the ostentatious dimensions of their ribbons,' he added.

On February 28th, therefore, Tsarism was quite dead, but still the Tsar clung to his crown. The history of February 1917 passes over him in almost complete silence—and with good reason. This time, geography adding its weight to politics, he found himself without any influence over the course of events—he was far away from Petrograd, and quite unable to intervene with any effect. On February 27th, Petrograd was in the hands of the revolutionaries, but it was only on March 1st (March 14th) that Nicholas II at long last consented to 'appoint' a government, thus exercising royal prerogatives that were no longer his own. All that day his military train had been shunted from station to station, as he made desperate attempts to rejoin his family in Tsarskoe Selo. When his hopeless situation was finally brought home to him, he ordered a number of front-line regiments into Petrograd. Unfortunately for him the army no longer obeyed his orders, and even the supreme command deserted him. Late on March 1st, the Emperor found himself at Pskov, General Ruszky's northern front. On the morning of March 2nd, General Alexeiev held a plebiscite among his commanders on

[1] In his *History of the Russian Revolution*, Trotsky quotes the figures of 1,443 killed and injured, 869 of them soldiers.

whether or not the Tsar should abdicate. At 2.30 p.m. next day Nicholas was informed of their reply—all were in favour of his abdication; not one proposed resistance, not even Alexeiev himself, who had declared only two days earlier that 'all of us have a sacred duty to remain loyal to our sovereign and fatherland'. Deserted by his commanders, Nicholas had no choice: he would renounce his throne. But just as he was about to make this decision public in a telegram to General Ruszky, he learned of the impending arrival at army headquarters of two Duma leaders, Guchkov and Shulgin, anxious to have an audience with him. Nicholas hastily decided not to send the fatal telegram after all—there might still be a chance of averting final disaster. The two visitors quickly disabused him: they could do nothing for the Tsar himself; they had come to see whether the monarchy could not be preserved without him.

The Tsar had originally wanted to abdicate in favour of his son, but when his physician informed him that the Tsarevich was suffering from an incurable disease, Nicholas decided to make way for the Grand Duke Michael, his brother. In the presence of the two Duma representatives, he now drafted the official text of his abdication. In it, he declared that he had taken his momentous decision so as to enable the nation to recover that unity without which victory over Germany was impossible. The proclamation was signed and dated March 2nd, 1917, 3 p.m. The two deputies readily lent themselves to this fraud—by antedating the document they helped to create the fiction that the Tsar had taken his decision quite spontaneously. In the event these shabby manoeuvres came to nothing, for when Nicholas II decided to hand the crown to his brother the monarchy was already destroyed —he had once again been confusing dreams with reality. He, like his liberal friends, was no longer in a position to bestow royal favours on anyone. At the beginning of March 1917 Nicholas had not simply lost his title—Tsarist Russia as such had ceased to exist.

The role of the liberals

The monarchy, a lifeless body now, a rotting corpse, had died the most pitiable of deaths. It was not so much the Revolution that had killed Tsarism, as its own anaemia; in fact, had the authorities in Petrograd acted with any sort of determination on February 22nd they might yet have stopped the revolutionaries in their tracks. Sukhanov, the leader of the Menshevik Left and a member of the

Soviet Executive Committee, was quick to recognize this fact. If, even on February 28th, 'a single Cossack or other organized unit, however numerically weak, had had the courage to attack us, we should not have known which way to turn, and would surely have been beaten down by the enemies of the Revolution'. The disorganization of the victors was only equalled by the signal weakness of the vanquished, and if we wish to grasp the full import of the 'February miracle', that miracle by which a regime was toppled by a mere show of popular resentment in the streets of Petrograd, we must seek the explanation outside the capital. True, the workers won a great victory there, but had Tsarism preserved only a modicum of its former power it could easily have mobilized the countryside against the capital, the peasantry against the working class, the army against the insurrectionists. However, the Tsar's chief allies of yesterday had abandoned him overnight—generals and aristocrats no less than Cossacks and *moujiks*. From the top to the bottom of the ladder, throughout the worm-eaten edifice of society, there was nothing but what Nicholas II himself called 'treachery, cowardice and knavery'. In France, during the Revolution, the monarchy could rely on the devotion and fanaticism not only of numerous aristocrats and a great part of the clergy but also of the peasants of the Vendée. Nicholas II did not even have his Vendeéns, and it was not by chance that during the civil war that split Russia between 1918 and 1921 few were the counter-revolutionaries who raised the banner of monarchist restoration.

But though the monarchy had been crushed, nothing else had been settled. The peasantry was lying low in the countryside, the aristocracy was stricken with total apathy, so that only two social classes—the bourgeoisie and the urban proletariat—were left holding the political stage. The major problem Russia had to solve during the early days of March was the precise power-relationship between these two groups. This was not a feature peculiar to the Russian Revolution—in all great political and social upheavals of modern history, the ruin of the old régime was the work of an alliance between the bourgeoisie and the popular masses, the latter acting as shock troops and the former as strategists. Outwardly, events in Russia fitted into the same pattern—the Provisional Government, bourgeois in composition, was carried to power by the insurgent masses. However, there was never a real alliance between the two, neither in the days that preceded the insurrection nor afterwards. And one of the chief reasons for this was that in Russia the bourgeoisie had never succeeded in becoming the powerful class it was in Western Europe.

To appreciate the truth of this remark we have only to consider the behaviour of the principal bourgeois representatives during the crucial days of February, and above all of Miliukov, their leader. With his somewhat dry spirit and dogmatic approach, he alone had the kind of intelligence of which Russian liberals were so inordinately proud. Miliukov, in some respects, towered far above the rest of his colleagues. For one thing he appreciated all the advantages and weaknesses of his class and saw, or thought he could see, how the game must be played to best advantage. Let us look more closely at the man himself. Miliukov had long ceased to flirt with revolutionary ideas; during the war he had unreservedly espoused the cause of national defence and the fatherland. However, though he was a firm advocate of the seizure of the Dardanelles and of Constantinople, he was quick to realize that these sacred treasures would have to be paid for with social upheavals at home, and this struck him as too high a price. In fact, by the time the war had started he had come to fear the Revolution as much as the national enemy; so much so that shortly before February 1917 he was heard to declare that every strike, every popular uprising, was nothing but the work of German provocateurs.

No wonder, then, that the events of February threw him into a state of utter confusion, and confirmed his resolve not to lead a government that symbolized everything he detested and feared: the blind power of the masses, their social demands, their desire for total emancipation. During the morning and afternoon of February 27th, when the corridors of the Duma were teeming with intruders and the frightened deputies were faced with a rough crowd in caps and army coats, Miliukov perhaps more than any of those present was torn by anguish and uncertainty. Then he summoned up all the mental resources at his command and made a last-ditch effort to save the old system. Not that he was sentimentally attached to the dynasty, which he himself had fought vigorously in the past; but this Professor of History at the University of Moscow, with his profound understanding of social and political phenomena, was convinced that in this period of social unrest a monarchy was the best safety rail available to the conservative forces.

Accordingly, during the night of March 1st–2nd (March 14th–15th) he intervened in the negotiations between representatives of the Petrograd Soviet and the Provisional Committee of the Duma, and put forward his plan for a constitutional monarchy. When the Soviet delegates treated this suggestion with disdain, and both delegations agreed that the monarchy must not be restored, at least for the present, Miliukov refused to be put off. Next day he went out among the crowd filling the corridors of the Tauride Palace and tried to play a part for which he was singularly unfitted —that of the popular tribune. Though he began with a fierce attack on the old regime in general and on Nicholas II in particular, his plebeian audience remained unimpressed, and kept interrupting him. 'Who has elected you!' they shouted, and as he went on to eulogize Prince Lvov as the incarnation of what was best in Russian society, some insolent voices in the crowd added, 'Not of Russian society but of the rich.' Another of his listeners wanted to know how precisely the liberals intended to solve the dynastic problem. This time Miliukov plunged right in: he announced that the Crown would go to the Tsarevich and that the Grand Duke Michael would be appointed Regent—thus flouting the joint decision of the Duma and the Soviet.

This declaration by the Cadet leader caused a furore—all round him the crowd started hurling abuse at the monarchy and its defender. Miliukov was forced to swallow his words: he now declared that it was not up to him but to the Constituent Assembly to decide what form the new state should take. Next day he told the press that the monarchist ideas he had put forward the previous night were only his personal views, yet at almost the same time he was busy pleading with the Grand Duke Michael to answer the Emperor's call. The Grand Duke agreed to meet members of the Provisional Committee of the Duma, but, once on the scene, quickly realized that he had not the least chance of succeeding his brother. All the deputies present tried to convince him of this; only Miliukov kept insisting that he must accept his historic mission. History counting for less in the Duke's eyes than the safety of his person, he decided to 'abdicate' in his turn, first telling the Constituent Assembly that it was their business, not his, to settle the future of the regime.

Later, when Miliukov became Minister of Foreign Affairs in a government that owed its very existence to the popular insurrection, he declared that 'the revolution was made for the sole purpose of clearing all obstacles in the path of Russia's [military] victory.' But throughout these tumultuous days he had done his utmost to temper the success of the masses by nullifying its effects.

By Miliukov's side stood Rodzianko, President of the Duma and another champion of a government that—a most improbable hypothesis—would enjoy the confidence of both Tsar and nation. Less intelligent than the head of the Cadet Party, Rodzianko was the leading spokesman for all those who placed their hopes in very moderate reforms. As late as February 27th he was still trying to persuade the Tsar to place himself at the head of a more representative cabinet. He told General Ruszky that the 'call for the Tsar's abdication was becoming increasingly *threatening*',[1] and that he was communicating this news with unspeakable sadness. One learning that Prince Golitsyn's government had tendered its resignation to Nicholas II, he covered his face with both hands. 'My God,' he cried, 'how horrible ... Without a government ... Anarchy ... Blood.' And the President of the Duma began to sob. Only the night before, less heart-broken, he had advised the authorities to open portfire on the demonstrators. Various eye-witnesses have reported that he used exceedingly strong language during the insurrection, referring to the workers and soldiers as 'swine' and the like. Rodzianko was also the author of a racy pun that revealed both his peculiar sense of humour and his political philosophy—he referred to the Soviet of Workers' Deputies (*soviet rabochii deputati*) as the 'Soviet of Dogs' Deputies' (*soviet sobatchii deputati*).

Another leading bourgeois light was Deputy Shulgin, who became a member of the Provisional Committee of the Duma. More conservative than Miliukov, he nevertheless persuaded the latter on February 27th to get on to the revolutionary bandwagon, since 'if we do not take power, others will take it for us, those rotters who have already elected all sorts of scoundrels in the factories.' It was Shulgin who called the events leading to the fall of the monarchy a real 'nightmare', and who said enviously of a dead colleague that he had been 'spared the calamity and misfortune of having to witness the Revolution'. More temperamental than Rodzianko, Shulgin had wanted to turn machine-guns on the hated crowd—portfire was apparently far too mild.

[1] Our italics.

Or take Maklakov, who when appointed Commissar of Justice by the Provisional Committee of the Duma told his colleagues, 'The enemy is and remains on the Left.' Or note the attitude of Nabokov, a Cadet and Secretary of State to the Provisional Government. On February 27th, he went to work as usual without changing his routine in the least detail, so much so that he did not have the slightest idea of what was happening outside. When he returned home at night he was not unduly perturbed either: 'The telephone was still working and my friends told me what had been happening during the day … ' And the future Minister of the Revolution added, 'We retired at the usual time.'

And it was an observer close to the liberal circle who summed up their attitude during the first days of March 1917 as follows: 'Officially they were elated; they celebrated the Revolution, shouted hurrah in honour of the fighters for liberty, donned red ribbons, marched under red flags … But deep down and in private they were terrified, and felt like prisoners to hostile and dangerous forces.' And the witness went on to say that on February 27th and 28th, 1917, many liberals 'started sobbing as soon as they got back home, had fits of hysteria caused by despair and impotence'.[1]

And in fact their hostility to the Revolution and to the revolutionaries was matched only by their utter impotence. During the night of March 1st–2nd (14th–15th), representatives of the Duma and of the Soviet arrived at a compromise; from the Minutes of their discussions we gain the impression that the two sides acted as equal partners, but in fact there was a considerable gap between the real strength of the Soviet and the signal weakness of the Provisional Committee of the Duma. From the start, the Soviet was able to take charge of all aspects of public life in the capital; the authority vested in it by workers' organizations and the *de facto* powers the latter wielded were such that in the economic field, and particularly when it came to provisioning the city, the Soviet and the Soviet alone took the real decisions. It was the Soviet, moreover, that issued permits for the publication of journals and papers and decided which banks were to be opened or reopened. The liberals were fully aware of their weakness and, trembling with fear, readily submitted to an authority whose reality they felt but whose legitimacy they questioned. When Rodzianko, for example, wanted to leave for his meeting with the

[1] Quoted by G. Comte in *La Révolution russe par ses témoins*, p. 111.

Tsar in Pskov, it was the Executive Committee of the Petrograd
Soviet to which he had to apply for a passport. Similarly, the
Grand Duke Michael, unhappy candidate to the throne, had to
ask the Petrograd Soviet to provide him with a train for his visit
to the capital. 'The Executive Committee', he was told, 'will not
authorize a train because of the high cost of coal. However,
Citizen Romanov can go to the station, buy a ticket and travel on
a public train.'

It followed naturally that the Soviet wielded political power as
well. It was they, for instance, who prevented Miliukov and other
monarchist representatives of the bourgeoisie from proclaiming a
constitutional monarchy. The fate of the imperial family gave rise
to another clash between the Soviet and the Provisional Government. The latter had decided to allow the ex-Emperor to accept
the asylum offered by the King of England—official negotiations
with the British authorities were about to be concluded when the
Executive Committee of the Petrograd Soviet first heard of the
affair. Loath to provide the reactionaries with an exiled figurehead, the Soviet protested that the imperial family must be
interned in Russia, and the Provisional Government immediately
climbed down. Some members of the latter, moreover, were doing
their duty like so many reluctant virgins. Thus Guchkov, who
ended up as Minister of War, at first refused his appointment on
the ground that he had no wish to sit in a cabinet whose powers
were purely formal. On March 6th (19th), Prince Lvov, President
of the Provisional Government, admitted publicly that he 'was
not master in his own house', and the Minister of War, in a letter
addressed to General Alexeiev, declared that

> the Provisional Government has no real powers: its orders
> are not obeyed unless they happen to fall in with the wishes
> of the Soviet of Workers' and Soldiers' Deputies. It is the
> latter who control the most important aspects of real power:
> the army, the railways, the postal and telegraph services. One
> might put it quite simply that the Provisional Government
> only exists inasmuch as the Soviet accepts and authorizes its
> existence.

The dual power

Thus in the first days of the Revolution, the Soviet—and it alone
—was in real control of Petrograd. Its representatives were by no

means ignorant of the liberals' attitude to the Revolution. They knew that bourgeois politicians were closer to the defunct administration, to the aristocracy, than to the working masses. Why then did these men fail to hang on to their own power, why did they see fit to negotiate with a weak adversary, why, above all, did they fail to lay down the law and why did they recognize a form of legality that was based neither on moral law, on moral right nor on the telling argument of force?

The conciliatory attitude of the leaders of the Petrograd Soviet in February and March 1917 is, in fact, less surprising than it seems at first sight. To begin with, the Mensheviks and Social Revolutionaries were in the majority, and if the moderation of the former was legendary, it was equalled by that of the latter—the Social Revolutionary Party had for a long time been recruiting its leaders from among the petit-bourgeois intelligentsia which was much closer to the liberal than to the socialist camp. Both factions, in any case, shared the conviction that the proletariat was in no position to seize power, to hold on to it, or to run the state. This was not simply an assessment of the current strength of the working class, or the humble belief that the bourgeoisie had some sort of natural gift or call for governing—in addition to these sentiments, shared by numerous moderate socialists in Russia and elsewhere, respectful in their own way of the most orthodox canons of the social hierarchy, these men, and particularly the Menshevik leaders, were handicapped by the full weight of their particular ideological luggage.

Had they not, in fact, declared that Russia must perforce pass through a capitalist phase, i.e. become a bourgeois democracy? Did they not accordingly believe that it would be wrong to challenge the social supremacy of the bourgeoisie? The controversy between Bolsheviks and Mensheviks had led to the crystallization of two viewpoints that were almost irreconcilable: while the revolutionary militants in Lenin's party looked on the proletariat as the principal agent of political change, the Mensheviks, for their part, saw the bourgeoisie as the only candidate, fitted by vocation and competence, for the office vacated by the Tsar.

The February insurrection certainly did not bear out the Menshevik view. The uprising in Petrograd took place without the participation of the bourgeoisie, indeed, without its support—

passive or otherwise. The bourgeoisie had neither led nor even followed a movement that it treated with a deep distrust compounded of fear and hostility. The insurrection had given the lie to the solidly entrenched Menshevik belief in the revolutionary role of the bourgeoisie, but not enough, apparently, to shake their doctrinal rigidity. After a Revolution which they had failed to anticipate, let alone encourage, they suddenly found themselves in power by a kind of miracle that many of them would gladly have done without. And looking upon themselves as mere usurpers, it was only natural that they should have decided to transfer this power to the bourgeoisie. What seemed even more paradoxical was that some of the shrewdest leaders of the Petrograd Soviet should have wondered whether the representatives of the bourgeoisie would not reject the gift that was being placed in their laps. They were terrified lest the liberals preferred the open arms of the conservatives, and to prevent this from happening they were prepared to make large-scale concessions, particularly on the all-important question of war and peace.

Among the Menshevik and Social Revolutionary leaders there were many who, while rejecting Lenin's radical defeatism, had been opposed to the war all along and who longed for a quick 'democratic peace'. When the pacifist slogans shouted by the Petrograd crowd in February helped to silence the voices of these men, it was not because they had suddenly turned chauvinist— it was simply that they felt all such manifestations were likely to drive the bourgeois nationalists into the reactionary camp. And so men who for years had clung to pacifism in the face of public opprobrium and official repression, overnight shelved their deepest convictions, and this at a time when they were at last given a real chance of translating them into action. They were not insensible of the absurdity of the situation; they fully realized that the masses would look upon their metamorphosis as treachery, but they lacked the courage to break their links with the past and to come out as defenders of the revolution. It was thus that during the night of March 1st–2nd, 1917, the Russian bourgeoisie was given—though not for very long—an unexpected new lease of life.

During the late hours of that night, members of the Soviet Executive Committee met the Provisional Committee of the Duma in the Tauride Palace. Was it purely by chance that the Duma occupied the right wing while the Soviet occupied the left wing of that building? What a difference in atmosphere there was between the two! On the Soviet side everything was in feverish turmoil, in revolutionary disorder, and there were many signs of poverty among those assembled there. But as one passed into the part of the palace assigned to the Duma, one seemed to step into a different world. Having recovered from their first shock, officers had reappeared in strength wearing their glittering uniforms; ushers moved about in traditional livery; everything reeked of distinction, and if there was any disquiet in the deputies' hearts they did their best to disguise it. And when the Soviet delegates, worn out by days of constant labour and by gnawing hunger — they had had neither the time nor the means to procure food — quitted the 'left wing', invaded by crowds of demonstrators and blocked by a mass of gloomy and unshaven prisoners under guard, to enter the sumptuous chambers of the Duma, they came upon massive tables decked out with costly foods and choice drinks in cut-glass-and-silver decanters. Two societies, two worlds, were confronting each other.

As one of the Soviet 'negotiators' was putting forward his case, another, the Menshevik writer Sukhanov, was free to observe Miliukov's expression and saw the liberal professor 'show signs of a keen satisfaction'. Miliukov said straight away that 'in general the conditions of the Soviet of Workers' and Soldiers' Deputies are acceptable.' In fact he could hardly have hoped for better terms: the representatives of the working class, which held sole power in the capital, had declared their willingness to let the Provisional Committee of the Duma form a government, provided only that the Committee declared an amnesty for all political prisoners, guaranteed freedom of agitation and propaganda to all parties, and did not take any steps to predetermine the future form of government. These demands, which surprised everyone by their moderation, were remarkable for what they left unsaid no less than for what they stated overtly. Thus they completely ignored such fundamental problems as the continuation of the war — now horrible and bloody beyond description — the social conditions of the workers and the fate of the peasantry. And was it not ridiculous to ask the future Provisional Government to *grant* political liberty to the people, when the people controlled the streets and held the political destiny of the country in their hands? Small wonder, then, that Miliukov, whom Shulgin had only just informed that all was up with them, should have felt so obviously relieved.

But for the sake of appearances, Miliukov nevertheless felt obliged to raise a number of objections. In particular, he called for a constitutional monarchy—a plea that his own colleagues failed to endorse—and insisted that the Soviet delegates use all their authority to re-establish order, particularly in the army. Finally, he demanded that the agreement between the working class and the bourgeoisie be set out in a common proclamation, stating that the government enjoyed the full support of the Soviet of Workers' and Soldiers' Deputies. At this point the proceedings were cut short by an incident, unimportant in itself but nevertheless casting a chill over the assembly and revealing the true balance of forces: an officer came in and said that Nicholas II was asking to speak to Rodzianko from his headquarters in Pskov, but the President of the Duma refused to go to the telephone unless the Soviet leaders gave him express permission to do so. 'You have the power and the authority,' he exclaimed. 'You can, of course, arrest me ... Perhaps you will arrest us all, who knows!' The Soviet delegates thereupon calmed Rodzianko and the negotiations between the 'partners' were continued and ended that night in general agreement, at least in principle.

The precise terms were published two days later, on March 3rd (16th), when the Provisional Government was officially installed. In its first public declaration, it gave a detailed account of the points of agreement reached during the night of March 1st–2nd, and promised, besides the abolition of all forms of national and religious discrimination, the replacement of the police by a popular militia, and the election by universal suffrage of 'local organs of government'. Finally, it promised that none of the troops stationed in the capital—from which the Petrograd Soviet derived at least part of its power—would be transferred to other parts of the country or to the front. At the same time, the Soviet Executive published a declaration of its own in which it defined its attitude to the Provisional Government. The latter was described as representing the 'moderate strata' of the population. The document ended with the following phrase: 'We suppose that inasmuch as the new government fulfils its promises and effectively combats the old regime, the democratic forces must give it their full support.'

This proclamation did not express profound trust in the new

team, and there were other signs of suspicion on the part of the
Soviet. To begin with, they were struck by the fact that with one
exception the Provisional Government was purely bourgeois in
composition. The new cabinet was led by Prince Lvov who,
during the war, had played a prominent part as President of the
Zemstvo Union. A man without great depth, he stood politically
to the right of the Constitutional Democrats, and had been specially
chosen by the government because his weakness was thought to
reassure the Soviet 'partner'. Miliukov, the real leader and
intellectual fountainhead of the new Government, became Minister
of Foreign Affairs, a field in which he was a specialist and where he
had long ago appeared as a staunch defender of territorial expansion. Guchkov, a man who was notorious for originality rather
than democratic conviction, became Minister of War. At the turn
of the century, he had fought the English on the side of the Boers,
and ten years later he had been involved in the revolt of the
Young Turks. As leader of the 'Octobrist' Party he, too, was well
to the right of the liberals, some of whom had been shocked to
see him unveil a monument to Stolypin the Hangman, the man
who had so mercilessly beaten down the Revolution of 1905. The
Minister of Finance, Tereshchenko, was a new arrival on the political stage: his only claim to fame was that he was a sugar king
with a private fortune of eighty million gold roubles. The Ministry
of Agriculture, an extremely important department during the
acute food shortage, was entrusted to the Cadet Shingarev, of
whom his colleague, Nabokov, said that he was 'a provincial
Russian intellectual tailored to the needs, not of a great state, but
of a provincial or a district administration'.

What was even more striking was the almost total absence in
the cabinet of even the mildest left-wing voices. The only member
with any socialist tendencies at all, and then only with strong
reservations, was the young Minister of Justice, Alexander
Kerensky, who was destined to rise into great prominence only
to become discredited soon afterwards. Kerensky, a thirty-six-
year-old advocate, had made his name as defence counsel before
the Tsarist tribunals. When he first became a Duma deputy he
had leaned towards the Trudoviks, a rather woolly petit-bourgeois
party with vague affinities to the right wing of the Social
Revolutionaries. After the February Revolution, Kerensky joined
the Trudoviks officially, but only as a pure formality—to the end

of his political career he kept aloof from party politics, convinced that he was cut out to be the leader and arbiter of the entire nation. His youth, his fire and his eloquence, the charm which his friends found so disarming, gave rise to the legend that Kerensky was the embodiment of all that was best, purest and most democratic in the Revolution. In reality, his speeches were so full of pathos that many critics came to ask themselves whether he was not an actor first and foremost and a politician only by chance. During moments of great national enthusiasm he undoubtedly knew how to express the patriotic feelings caused by the first flush of victory, but when it came to singing the praises of the Revolution he often made himself quite ridiculous. Not that his fervour was assumed for the occasion; indeed it often bordered on hysteria. But he was a man in whom exaltation would quickly alternate with depression, and whose speeches revealed a morbid propensity for sentimental blackmail. On March 1st (15th), 1917, when he wanted to persuade the Petrograd Soviet that he was the best, indeed the only fit, candidate for the Ministry of Justice, he produced this flight of oratory—in doubtful style but of calculated effect: 'I speak, comrades, with all my soul, from the bottom of my heart, and if it is necessary to prove this, if you do not trust me, here and now—before your eyes—I am ready to die.' No one put him to the proof on that occasion, and his political death soon afterwards made any further show of sacrifice unnecessary.

Kerensky was not only an individualist, he was also highly egocentric, and firmly believed that he was cut out for historical greatness. The call of Destiny, in fact, became his chief political platform, and he constantly referred to the esteem owing to him, held up his great authority and invoked the prestige which apparently surrounded his personality. It was thanks to this prestige that he had reached ministerial rank so early in the Revolution. His nomination for the post had not, in fact, gone forward automatically—the Executive Committee of the Petrograd Soviet had previously decided that none of its members could join the Provisional Government. True, a minority on the Right had expressed the view that a ministerial coalition between the two classes was indispensible, but the great majority of Mensheviks and Social Revolutionaries had favoured a system of external control of the Provisional Government by the Soviet.

Kerensky was a member of the Soviet Executive, and though his functions were not yet clearly defined, by the beginning of March he had risen to be Vice-President. His entire attitude left no doubt as to how anxious he was to obtain a ministerial post, and the liberal leaders were quick to offer him one. He was a godsend to the liberals—apart from the Menshevik Chkheidze, he was the only Duma deputy who had a foot in the Soviet Committee and as such was a most valuable link. And finding itself in such difficult circumstances, the bourgeois government quite rightly thought that two safeguards were better than one: the cautious recognition of the authority of the Provisional Government by the Soviet was one guarantee, but more physical and tangible would be Kerensky's presence in the Cabinet. Kerensky himself welcomed the liberal offer so eagerly that his colleagues in the Soviet reluctantly decided to let him go. However, they insisted that he surrender his responsibilities in the Soviet for which he had, in any case, never shown any great enthusiasm. Kerensky refused to accept this proposal; he was determined to keep one foot in each camp, and in the confused state of the Soviet—and thanks also to the inexperience of its members—he was able to win his point after remarkable feats of eloquence. For all that, his entry into the cabinet in no way solved the crucial problem of the precise relationship between the Provisional Government and the Soviet; it did not answer that all-important question of how dual power was to be exercised.

The term 'dual power', which has since become a standard term in the political dictionary, accurately describes conditions in Russia in February to October 1917, when the country was being pulled in two directions by two irreconcilable forces. 'Dual power' was the existence, side by side, of one institution representing the bourgeoisie, the Provisional Government, and another thrown up by the masses, the Soviet. At the beginning of the Revolution, both arrived at a kind of *modus vivendi*, but while patriotic discourses and delight at the downfall of the old regime may have succeeded in masking the basic conflict during the early euphoric hours, the most lucid members of both camps fully recognized its reality. Thus Sukhanov, who had played a leading part in the negotiations culminating in the agreement between the Soviet and the Provisional Government, called it an 'agreement on the conditions of a duel'.

No doubt not everyone saw matters in this light, least of all those closest to the Soviet camp. The more moderate among them looked upon the Soviet Government as a purely auxiliary body and favoured a joint cabinet. However, in addition to the Bolsheviks—whose attitude was in any case radically transformed by Lenin's return[1]—there were many Mensheviks who thought that the interests of the bourgeoisie and the workers were far too divergent to justify anything but the most ephemeral of relationships. Political manoeuvres, the ambitions of the various leaders, but above all the pressures of the class struggle, were bound to get in the way and threaten what agreement had been reached by leaders whom neither the events nor the masses were disposed to treat with blind respect.

And, in fact, clashes were not long in coming. To end them, the Soviet Executive set up a Liaison Commission whose proposed function highlighted the difficulties of the situation: the Commission was assigned the task of 'informing the Soviet about the intentions and activities of the Provisional Government; of informing the latter about the claims of the revolutionary masses; of exerting pressure on the Provisional Government so as to ensure the fulfilment of these demands and to supervise the implementation of measures demanded by the situation'. In other words, it would determine whether dual power meant collaboration or explosive rivalry.

As soon as the effects of the first shock abated and the bourgeoisie found its second breath, friction with the Soviet became inevitable. A few days after the Provisional Government was officially formed, the Soviet authorized the reopening of the conservative press. By way of thanks, right-wing journalists immediately concentrated all their fire on the Soviet whose legality they challenged, on the soldiers whose lack of discipline they deplored, and on the working class whose claims they dismissed as irresponsible. At the same time, a host of conservative organizations re-formed, and while ostensibly offering support for the Provisional Government did all they could to put systematic pressure upon it. On March 2nd (15th), the Industrial and Commercial Council promised its unreserved support to the Provisional Committee of the Duma—one day before the latter became the Provisional Government. On March 10th (23rd), the

[1] See Chapter 5.

Council of Nobles invited the nation 'to close ranks behind the Provisional Government, now the sole legal authority in Russia'. The liberal press began to clamour for single power and there is no need to specify which particular institution they thought was best qualified to wield authority.

During March 1917, social problems, which had remained unsolved by the insurrection, came to the fore again and in an extremely tense atmosphere. On March 6th (19th), a Plenary Session of the Soviet voted by an immense majority (1,170 to 30) for the immediate cessation of all strikes in Petrograd—a resolution the working class was loath to obey since some of their most pressing claims had still not been met. Numerous workers' organizations, far more radical than their official representatives, made it clear that they would only go back once the length of the working day had been officially reduced. And of those who did go back, many downed tools the moment their eight hours a day were up. As social tension mounted, the Soviet, without great enthusiasm, took up the cry for the eight-hour day, whereupon the conservative and liberal press launched an attack on what they described as a threat to the cause of national defence, and even managed to incite part of the garrison against the workers. The soldiers were told that while their comrades at the front were defending the fatherland and getting killed in the trenches, the strikers were sabotaging the war effort and thus betraying the country. The Soviet and a series of workers' organizations immediately mounted a counter-propaganda campaign, showing soldiers round the factories and telling the garrison about the intolerable conditions of factory life. At the same time the Provisional Government was officially asked by the Soviet to grant the demand for the eight-hour day even before the meeting of the Constituent Assembly in which the liberals wanted to discuss the whole problem. Only then—and despite the resistance of ministers and employers' organizations—did the workers of several industrial centres, including Petrograd and Moscow, gain some satisfaction: but not without having discovered that direct action was a more effective method than negotiation.

Procrastination about the decision on the length of the working day had succeeded in fraying tempers; the problem of peace did the rest—if any single factor had been responsible for leading the masses into insurrection, this was it. During the first demonstrations in February, pacifist slogans had been wildly cheered by the masses. But gradually patriotism, or rather chauvinism, had reared its head again, particularly among the army, so much so that a Bolshevik militant is said to have been lynched towards the end of February for shouting 'Down with the war.' This resurgence of patriotic fervour was reflected on the political plane by vacillation among the Mensheviks, who resolved to mute their pacifist demands lest they embarrass the bourgeoisie. It was, however, idle to hope that they would be able to preserve silence on a question of such burning urgency, especially as the conduct of the war had been entrusted to one of the most unbending nationalists, Professor Miliukov. The new Minister of Foreign Affairs and the circles he represented felt strongly that the new regime must in no way alter the old foreign policy of Russia; the country must not only remain loyal to its allies and continue to fight side by side with France and Britain until final victory, but it must also publicly declare its full support for the Tsarist war aims.

At the very beginning of the war, Russian diplomats had agreed with their British and French colleagues to support one another's territorial claims to the hilt, and Russia had demanded and obtained the promise of new territory in Poland. Then, after Turkey had joined in, Russia had put in further claims, and the Allies had been quick to promise that, in case of victory, she would obtain the Dardanelles, Constantinople and a series of Turkish possessions in Asia. These agreements had been duly enshrined in a host of secret diplomatic treaties.

When he became Foreign Minister, Miliukov informed his colleagues of the contents of these secret pacts, with which he personally was in full agreement. However, not all the members of the Provisional Government were equally enthusiastic, and one of them, the Procurator of the Holy Synod, declared without much respect for diplomatic usage that these secret treaties were the work of 'bankers and thieves'. It was, in any case, difficult to reconcile their existence with professions of faith in a purely defensive war waged for purely democratic motives. Such motives —peace without annexation or indemnities—were, in fact, part of the current baggage of the Left, and reflected the aspirations of even the least radical pacifists, of whom there were many among the Soviet leaders.

Imagine their dismay when on March 6th (19th), they read in

the press that Miliukov, speaking in the name of the Provisional Government, had declared that the new Russia 'would unreservedly adhere to her agreements with the Allies'. This clearly meant that Russia, having got rid of Tsarism, would nevertheless hold fast to the Tsar's expansionist dreams, and this the Soviet refused to stomach. True, a handful within the Soviet supported Miliukov's stand, but the great majority, while favouring the continuation of the war against Germany and Austria for purposes of national self-defence, was bitterly opposed to the old imperialist policy. Others argued that once the Russian soldier could be shown that he was fighting for a just cause, he might be inspired with new courage and so bring the struggle with Germany to a speedier close.

This attitude, in which vague feelings of pacifism were compounded with overt patriotism, led the Executive Committee of the Petrograd Soviet to launch an 'Appeal to the Peoples of the Entire World' in March 1917. It described the war as 'monstrous', said that the moment had come to 'launch a decisive battle against the expansionist ambitions of all governments', and called upon democratic forces in Russia to 'use every means to oppose the annexionist plans of the old ruling classes'. However, the crucial part of the manifesto was an appeal to the workers of Germany and Austria-Hungary to get rid of their semi-autocratic governments, and contained the warning that 'the Russian Revolution will not recoil before the conquerors' bayonets, will not allow itself to be wiped out by any foreign military power'.

When it became clear that the Provisional Government was determined to stick to its traditionalist platform, the left wing in the Soviet began to press for a declaration in favour of 'peace without annexations or indemnities', and the Liaison Committee was instructed to inform the responsible ministers that the time had come for the Provisional Government to renounce all but purely defensive war aims. Miliukov rejected this demand out of hand and told his visitors that as far as he was concerned he would never sign any document embodying this viewpoint. However, when it appeared that most of his cabinet ministers were far less intransigent, he agreed to provide the Soviet with a draft declaration on the war aims of the New Russia.

This text stated, *inter alia*, that the 'Provisional Government considers it to be its right and duty to declare that the aim of

Russia is not to rule over other nations ... but the establishment of a stable peace on the basis of the self-determination of peoples ... But the Russian people will not permit their fatherland to emerge from this great struggle humiliated and sapped in its vital forces.' The declaration added that the Russian Government would 'observe fully all obligations assumed towards our Allies'.

After reading this document, the Soviet Executive declared itself dissatisfied. It particularly objected to the promise to 'observe fully all obligations assumed towards our Allies', which seemed to uphold the validity of the secret treaties and their imperialist clauses. The Government was forced to rephrase its original draft, and the amended text was once again submitted to the Soviet: while reaffirming the needs of defence against foreign aggression and recalling the 'obligation toward our Allies', it stated that 'the aim of free Russia is not domination over other nations or seizure of any foreign territories by force of arms.' Although some members of the Executive Committee deemed this concession quite inadequate, the majority now declared themselves content.

Thus the first sharp clash between the government and the Soviet ended in a compromise which served to shift Russia's foreign policy very slightly towards the Left. The incident had a double significance: it revealed that international politics could not be ignored for long and that the solution of the war problem was a matter of pressing urgency; it also showed that dual power was based on precarious foundations, with both sides pulling increasingly in opposite directions. But worse would follow. In April, the Soviet Executive was refused financial aid by the Provisional Government on the grounds that it was 'a private institution' and as such not entitled to subsidies. Now while patience was one of the Soviet's principal virtues, constant pressure by the masses prevented it from making resignation another.

And even while their leaders wrangled and compromised, two hostile classes—the bourgeoisie and the proletariat—were preparing to make a more resolute stand in defence of their respective claims.

5

Springtide

IT WAS barely a month since the Provisional Government had been officially inaugurated, and already the spirit seemed to have gone out of the revolutionary movement. No one came forward to challenge the agreement between the government and the Soviet, and what opposition it did arouse remained subdued, respectful and, for lack of proper channels, utterly futile. All this was suddenly changed by an event that gave the morale of the revolutionaries a tremendous boost: on April 3rd, 1917, Lenin arrived in Petrograd.

Before he reached the capital, Lenin had had to clear a thousand obstacles. When news of the Revolution surprised him in Zürich he decided to return home at once, but was, of course, without the necessary papers. A telegram to Petrograd remained unanswered, and for the next two weeks Lenin and his companions cooled their heels in Switzerland—the Provisional Government was understandably loath to repatriate men whose intransigent opposition to the war was common knowledge. Attempts to obtain travel documents through Britain proved equally abortive. On March 15th,[1] the impatient Lenin wrote to Inessa Armand: 'I am beside myself with anger because I cannot travel to Scandinavia. I won't forgive myself for not risking going there in 1915.' And two days later, he added: 'We fear we shan't be able to leave this cursed Switzerland.'

At the end of March he was still in Zürich. 'You can imagine', he lamented, 'what torture it is for us to be stuck here at a time like this.' Meanwhile, he concocted a series of incredible schemes: he would travel home by aeroplane, a plan which his wife dismissed as something 'dreamed up in the semi-delirium of the night'. He also thought of travelling on a forged Swedish passport—to disguise his ignorance of the Swedish language he would pretend to be a deaf-mute. This idea struck Krupskaia as no less preposterous than the first: 'You will fall asleep,' she told him, 'and see Mensheviks in

[1] Western calendar.

127

your dream, and you will start swearing at them and shout, "Scoundrels, scoundrels," and give the whole game away ... '

The solution was found by the Menshevik Martov, no less anxious to return to Russia than Lenin himself: they would ask the Germans for permission to travel home via Germany and Scandinavia. An 'Evacuation Committee' representing twenty-three Russian émigré organizations in Switzerland agreed to deal with the matter, and with the help of Swiss socialists managed, after long negotiations, to persuade the Imperial German Government to allow the passage of thirty-two Russians, including Lenin and eighteen other Bolsheviks. There was to be no inspection of passports or luggage, and it was agreed that nobody should leave the train or communicate with anyone outside while they were passing through Germany, and that nobody should be allowed to enter without the permission of the Swiss socialists who were travelling with them (hence the often-heard allusion to Lenin's 'sealed train'). Officially, the Russians would arrange for the release of an equal number of Germans so that outwardly, at least, the whole thing could be made to look like an official exchange of prisoners. For all that, Lenin and his companions realized full well that they might be providing their political adversaries with a chance to smear them as agents of the Kaiser smuggled into Russia for the sole purpose of weakening the war effort. On the night of their departure, the travellers accordingly made a point of publishing a declaration in which they affirmed their desire to contribute towards 'an uprising of the proletariat in other countries, and especially in Germany and Austria'. And when, during the journey, a number of right-wing German Social Democrats, and as such supporters of their country's war policy, tried to make contact with Lenin, the Russian revolutionaries refused to address a single word to them.

The party reached Stockholm on April 13th,[1] and went on to Finland by sledge. On April 3rd (16th), late in the evening, Petrograd made ready to receive the Bolshevik leader.

The Bolshevik Party, a past master at the art of wedding insurrection to spectacular demonstrations, went to great lengths to turn Lenin's arrival into a major display of popular strength and enthusiasm. Whole regiments were lined up before the Finland Station, their officers once again conspicuous by their absence. This

[1] Western calendar.

defection was more than made good by the vast masses of workers who had poured into the capital for the occasion. A sea of red banners and torches, the headlights of armoured cars and a massed brass band, helped to turn the evening into a riot of light and sound.

In the station itself, workers' delegations stood clasping flags, while members of the Soviet, led by the Menshevik Chkheidze, had assembled in the imperial waiting-room—the bourgeois revolution was preparing to welcome its own gravedigger. The most surprised of all was Lenin himself; he had only just asked some of his comrades whether the Provisional Government would not arrest him as soon as he set foot in the capital. His friends had been able to allay his worst fears, but the spectacular reception at the Finland Station came as a complete surprise. Lenin had barely stepped out of the train when a huge bouquet of flowers was thrust into his arms, and the great orator was suddenly left speechless. Then the band struck up and he was led into the waiting-room formerly reserved for the Tsar and his intimates. Chkheidze, the President of the Petrograd Soviet, was the first to speak:

'Comrade Lenin, in the name of the Petrograd Soviet and the whole Revolution, we welcome you to Russia ... But we consider that the chief task of revolutionary democracy at present is to defend our Revolution against all attacks from within no less than from without. We consider that what this goal requires is not disunity but the closing of the democratic ranks. We hope that you will join us in striving towards this goal.'

Lenin, who had barely recovered from his surprise, completely ignored the homily and even the person of Chkheidze—the first public announcement he made in Russia was addressed directly to his 'dear comrades, soldiers, sailors and workers'. 'I am happy to greet in your persons the victorious Russian Revolution, and salute you as the vanguard of the world-wide proletarian army ... The piratical imperialist war is the beginning of civil war throughout Europe ... The world-wide socialist revolution has already dawned ... Any day now the whole of European capitalism may crash. The Russian Revolution accomplished by you has paved the way and opened a new epoch. Long live the world-wide socialist revolution!'

This was the kind of language no one in Russia had heard since the fall of Tsarism. It represented the revolutionary events as but one spark in a much vaster social conflagration. Now—and this was implicit in Lenin's words, though he did not spell it out—a

5

revolution in Western Europe could only mean an attempt to destroy capitalism, to go beyond democracy to socialism. According to most people, Russia had barely started on the revolutionary path that would help her to shake off her quasi-feudal conditions, but Lenin took a much more sweeping view: by linking the Russian to the world revolution, he bridged what had previously been taken for a wide gap in time—the gap between parliamentary democracy and full socialism. Thus the revolution, barely recovered from its first effort, was to start up all over again.

During that first night, Lenin, now unencumbered by official undertakings, to which in any case he had made the minimum of concessions, made sure that his message reached a wider audience than the Soviet leaders and addressed himself directly to the workers and soldiers of Petrograd. As he drove in triumphal procession to the Bolshevik headquarters in the palace of Kshesinskaia, a ballerina who had once been a favourite of the young Nicholas II, he addressed the crowd continually from the bonnet of his car, endlessly repeating the substance of his address to the President of the Soviet. Was the crowd convinced or merely surprised? Lenin did not have time to wonder. He knew that the most urgent task facing him, even before he could start converting the masses, was to recapture his own party, to vanquish its scepticism, its hesitations, its inertia.

Lenin recaptures his Party

During the revolutionary days of February 1917, the Bolshevik Party had played a far from negligible role. Its militants had organized numerous successful demonstrations but had failed to lead the movement towards coherent strategic objectives. This failure was due not only to the political unpreparedness of the masses but also to the prevailing attitude of the Bolshevik leaders. To begin with, it took those in Petrograd quite some time to recover from their surprise at the February uprising and to grasp its full import. Thus it was not until February 25th (March 7th) that they came out with their first pamphlet calling for a general strike, and by then close on 200,000 workers had already downed tools. That same day, Shliapnikov, the leading Bolshevik in the capital, refused to supply arms to the insistent workers. Was he perhaps afraid of so much responsibility? In any case, the exile and deportation of the best-known Bolshevik militants had left the leadership in the hands of lesser men, who allowed the events to run far ahead of them.

In the Soviet itself, the Bolsheviks had a tendency to align themselves with the moderate majority—even if they did not always share the moderates' views, they were too unsure of themselves to take the risk of straying from the main column. In *Pravda*, a young journalist by the name of Molotov called for the complete transfer of political power to the forces of 'revolutionary democracy', i.e. the Soviet, but his opinion did not represent the majority view in the Party. On March 3rd, the day the Provisional Government published its programme, the Petrograd Bolshevik Committee passed a resolution to the effect that it did not challenge the authority of the Provisional Government so long as its activities were in the interests of the proletariat and of the broad democratic masses. This decision faithfully reflected the very cautious attitude of the leaders of the Petrograd Soviet.

The first Bolshevik leaders of any standing to return to Petrograd were Kamenev and Stalin, both members of the Bolshevik Central Committee. They arrived in the capital on March 12th and immediately seized the Party reins, but far from introducing a more radical note, they merely added to the prevailing moderation. Kamenev, in particular, used the columns of *Pravda* to rally support for the Provisional Government in matters of national defence. True, *Pravda* also called for peace negotiations, but the paper was quick to add that while the German army obeyed its Emperor, the Russian soldier must 'stand firmly at his post, answering bullet with bullet, and shell with shell'. During the next few days, *Pravda*, though careful not to repeat this bit of advice—possibly because of the fury and bewilderment with which it had been greeted in some factories—was equally careful not to voice any serious opposition to the government's war policy. On March 7th the editors declared, 'As far as we are concerned, what matters now is not the overthrow of capitalism but the overthrow of autocracy and feudalism.'

A few days before Lenin's return, the Bolshevik Party held a Regional Conference in Petrograd, during which there was a sharp clash of opinions. Stalin declared that 'the Provisional Government has, in fact, assumed the role of defender of the conquests of the revolutionary people ... At present, it is not in our interest to force events by hastening the eviction of bourgeois strata who, inevitably, will one day detach themselves from us ... ' Stalin then submitted a resolution confirming the Party's conditional support for the government. He also advised reconciliation with all Mensheviks who had given proof of moderate internationalism. Now though these proposals were challenged, some of them quite sharply, by an important section of the Conference, they were approved by the majority, and thus formed the official Bolshevik platform at the moment of Lenin's return. The latter, attributing the policy to 'revolutionary intoxication', made it clear that, as far as he was concerned, it was a retreat from socialism.

There was, in fact, a world of difference between the views of the master and those of his disciples. Even in Switzerland, Lenin had tried to warn his Russian comrades against their illusions. On March 6th he had sent a telegram to the Bolsheviks in Stockholm, whose message was laconic but perfectly clear: 'Our tactics: absolute distrust, no support for the new government. Distrust Kerensky above all. No alliance with other parties. Wire this to Petrograd.' The message was transmitted, but Lenin's warning was ignored, as were his less laconic 'Letters from Afar' written in Zürich. Though all five of these letters had been sent to *Pravda*, the editors saw fit to publish only one—the first—on the day its author arrived in Petrograd. In it Lenin declared that despite the fall of Tsarism, the war continued to be an imperialist one, and that as he saw it the February Revolution must culminate in the transformation of the war between nations into a world-wide civil war between classes. Without mincing his words, he called the Provisional Government an agent of Anglo-French imperialist capital, support of which was rank betrayal of the working class. He went on to argue that the present stage was only a halt on the path towards a socialist revolution. It fell to the proletariat to prepare for the next stage with the help of two allies: the Russian peasantry and above all the world proletariat. In his subsequent letters, Lenin enlarged on the need for a proletarian militia and on its precise function, and called for an end to the imperialist war. In this he differed radically not only from the Provisional Government but also from the Soviet.

Lenin's views were put cogently and succinctly in a document that has come down to us as his 'April Theses'. When it was first published in *Pravda* on April 7th, Kamenev prefaced it with the following remarks: 'As for the general scheme of Comrade Lenin, it seems to us unacceptable in that it starts from the assumption that the bourgeois democratic revolution is *ended*, and counts upon an immediate transformation of this revolution into a socialist revolution.' In fact, as his subsequent explanations and speeches showed quite unmistakably, Lenin's ideas were much subtler than *Pravda* suggested.

His strategy was based on the firm conviction that the situation in Russia must be seen in its international context, i.e. against the background of the war. 'The war dominates and stifles everything else,' Lenin declared. Here he was merely repeating what he had been saying ever since the outbreak of hostilities: that the war was a prelude to a world-wide socialist revolution. No one in the Bolshevik Party challenged this postulate which was, in fact, part of the credo of all revolutionary Marxists, but as the moderate Bolshevik Rykov put it, 'It is not up to us to initiate a socialist revolution. We lack the power to do so, and the objective conditions are not ripe for it.' Socialism must therefore start in countries with more developed industries. To which Lenin replied, 'You can't say who will begin and who will finish. That is not Marxism but a caricature of Marxism.'

Not that Lenin himself had any doubts as to the weaknesses of the Russian proletariat and the backwardness of his country. Thus in the letter he addressed to Swiss workers just before returning to Russia, he conceded quite freely that 'the Russian proletariat is *less* well-organized, *less* prepared and *less* class-conscious than the workers of other countries.' How then could he elevate it into the vanguard of the proletariat? The answer, according to Lenin, had to be sought in the special historical circumstances of the day, and especially in the war. It was the latter which had helped to topple the old regime, which had produced the revolutionary upsurge of the Russian people, and would surely be followed by social and political crises and hence by revolution in other countries. Russia could and must help to hasten this crisis by the psychological effect of her example. Was not the February Revolution a beacon to workers throughout the world, and did not the Russian proletariat offer them full support? This then was the peace policy for which Lenin sought the support, first of his own Party, and later of the Soviet.

Unlike the Bolshevik leaders who had been shaping the Party's attitude towards the Provisional Government during his absence,

Lenin felt that the government was utterly incapable—with or without pressure from the proletariat—of bringing the war to a speedy conclusion or, more generally, of introducing any serious political or social reforms. Bourgeois in social composition, imperialist in its alliances, its territorial claims and its war aims, the Lvov–Miliukov–Kerensky cabinet was in no position to put a stop to the carnage. Only a popular government reflecting the independent will of the Soviet and breaking with the possessing classes would be able to steer the destiny of Russia—and hence of all Europe—along a new course. That government would repudiate the Tsarist treaties, and by publishing them in full reveal their imperialist nature. It would also invite all belligerent countries to make peace on truly democratic terms, granting all people the right to full self-determination and denouncing all conquests and reparations. Peace on these terms would signify not only an end to German rule over part of Poland, to the oppression of a host of nationalities by the Russians and of Ireland by the British, but also the liquidation of the entire colonial system. Short of realizing these objectives, any peace was bound to be illusory and precarious. According to Lenin, no bourgeois government would or could accept such conditions, and its refusal to do so would inevitably lead not only to a revolutionary struggle between it and the proletariat over which it ruled but to an international uprising, to world revolution.

The revolutionary struggle of the Western proletariat would have a socialist character and challenge the *economic* framework of the existing capitalist regimes. When that happened, Russia would cease to be the leader of the revolution and follow in the footsteps of the West. 'The German, French and English workers will complete what the Russian have begun and socialism will triumph,' the leader of the Soviet state wrote in 1918. That was his fundamental belief and dictated his overall strategy and tactics. On leaving Western Europe, he had made it the substance of his message to the Swiss workers; at the Finland Station he had repeated it in a few laconic words, and then at greater length in the streets of the capital. In his opening speech to the all-Russian party conference in April 1917, he professed it once again: 'The great honour of striking the first blow has fallen to the Russian proletariat but it should never forget that its progress and revolution are but part of a world-wide and growing revolutionary movement which is daily becoming more powerful ... We cannot see our task in any other light ... ' A few months later, when his party had seized power and Lenin addressed the Congress of Soviets, he came back to the same theme.

It followed that Lenin would be utterly uncompromising in his opposition to the Provisional Government, whose very existence he considered a brake on the Revolution and a threat to its survival. This brought him into open conflict with those who thought that the bourgeoisie still had a great deal of work to accomplish, and who felt that the Provisional Government was best fitted to consolidate the achievements of February. To these men, Lenin's ideas were so many Utopian pipe dreams, the more so as he put them forward without reserve.

Thus, hardly had he arrived at Kshesinskaia's palace late on April 3rd when he treated the assembled Bolshevik leaders to a long, improvised speech which, according to an eye-witness, startled and amazed all those present. These men were the most radical socialists in all Russia, yet even they were astounded by the radicalism and intransigence of their leader. What would a wider audience feel when Lenin addressed them in such terms? And Lenin did just that a few hours later, at a joint meeting of Petrograd Bolsheviks and Mensheviks in the Tauride Palace.

The meeting had been specially called in order to sound out the possibility of a closer alliance between the two factions and to prepare their unification. As Lenin began to speak, his eyes strayed over the rows of his old adversaries, cautious and moderate to a man. And it was with these time-servers that many good Bolsheviks were trying to forge a close alliance! Lenin, for his part, wanted nothing of the sort, and that morning he put an end to all dreams of reconciliation. He spared no one, and his audience gave as good as it got. In Kshesinskaia's palace his comrades had listened to him with scepticism but great respect. This time his audience kept interrupting and hurling insults from all parts of the hall. Bogdanov, the Secretary of the Soviet Executive Committee, who was sitting a few yards from the platform, shouted at Lenin, 'This is the raving of a madman! It's indecent to applaud this claptrap!' And the old Menshevik leader, I. P. Goldenberg, declared that Lenin's words smacked of the most primitive anarchism: 'You have presented yourself as a candidate for one European throne that has been vacant for thirty years: the throne of Bakunin!'

'The raving of a madman'—this cry was taken up by Plekhanov in the paper he had been editing ever since his return to Russia, in which he still upheld the ultra-patriotic views that the majority of the Soviet had felt impelled to disown. And when Skobelev, of the Soviet Executive Committee and soon afterwards Minister of Labour, reported Lenin's speech to Miliukov later that day, he added that the Minister of Foreign Affairs had little to fear from such 'lunatic ideas'—a view that the left-wing Menshevik Sukhanov, who was present at the interview, was quick to confirm. Zenzinov, a Social Revolutionary leader, recalling Lenin's speech, said that it was greeted 'not so much with indignation as with jeers, so stupid and fantastic did it sound'.

And what about the Bolsheviks? The meeting of their Petrograd Committee provided the answer: Lenin's theses were rejected by thirteen votes to two with one abstention. However, Lenin could console himself with the knowledge that since February 1917 this particular Committee had been notorious for its extreme moderation, and that others would be far more open to persuasion. During the next few weeks he accordingly used all his dialectic powers, all his gifts of persuasion, to infuse his comrades with at least part of the beliefs he held with such unshakeable conviction.

On April 14th, Lenin had his first direct clash with Kamenev, during another Petrograd Party meeting. While Lenin called for the transfer of all power from the Provisional Government to the Soviet, Kamenev, upholding the prevailing Party line, called simply for 'the most vigilant watch' of the government by the Party. When a vote was taken, Kamenev was beaten by twenty votes to six with nine abstentions.

This was, however, no more than a prelude to a far more important meeting: the all-Russian Bolshevik Party Conference, which took place in Petrograd from April 24th–29th (May 8th–12th) and has become famous as the April Conference. On that occasion Lenin's radical ideas were adopted by a far more telling majority, though even then the resistance of Kamenev and his supporters was far from broken; in fact it made itself strongly felt both during and after the Bolshevik seizure of power. But as far as the Party's relationship with the Provisional Government was concerned, Lenin's triumph was nearly complete: severe strictures on the Lvov cabinet were voted almost unanimously. More important still, a resolution calling on the proletariat in town and country to make active preparation for the transfer of state power to the Soviet was carried by 149 votes to 3, with 8 abstentions.

This did not, however, mean that the Conference stood solidly behind Lenin all along the line. Thus his resolution that 'the Russian Revolution is only the first phase of the first of many proletarian revolutions inevitably engendered by the war' was only carried by seventy-one votes to thirty-nine with eight abstentions. Moreover, during the vote on a resolution calling for Bolshevik participation in an International conference of Zimmerwaldists[1] to be held in Stockholm, a single voice spoke out against the motion. It was that of Lenin, who believed that most Zimmerwaldists were far too tolerant of Social Democratic opportunism.

Still, Lenin's star was clearly rising, and the capture of the most revolutionary of all Russian parties by the most revolutionary of its leaders was now only a matter of time. When he finally carried the day, revolutionary Russia was at long last provided with a viable alternative to the incompetence of the bourgeoisie and the pusillanimity of the Soviet. That alternative still looked uncertain in April, but the exacerbation of the class struggle was to turn it into an historical reality within a few months.

The working class in revolt

The new revolutionary upsurge was only a few months ahead, but during the spring of 1917 no one could have told how close it really was. In the prevailing hectic atmosphere, with tempers everywhere raised to boiling point, Russia continued to flounder in a morass. Deploring what it considered to be anarchic conditions, the liberal paper *Rech* wrote in May that 'Russia is being turned into a kind of lunatic asylum', and a few days later compared the country to Texas and the Wild West.

This comparison ignored one crucial difference: in Russia, the political consciousness of the masses was growing sharper by the day. They were loud in their protests against the war, their inferior conditions and the relationship between the Soviet and the Provisional Government. The citizens of Petrograd were treated to an almost continuous series of demonstrations—during the most tumultuous days, some 500,000 people in a population of two million could be seen milling about in the streets, and usually it was not till late at night that they dispersed. On some days it was

[1] See Chapter 3.

the women who were filing past; on others it was patriotic groups calling for war to the bitter end. Bourgeois processions were followed by peasant processions, but more often than not it was soldiers and workers who crowded into the main thoroughfares. In May 1917 came a heart-rending demonstration by wounded and crippled soldiers, human flotsam from the battlefield, anxious to express their tottering support for an equally tottering regime; on another occasion, a procession of veterans, most of them bearded, called on the government to let them get on with the harvest. 'There is no one in the fields', 'Our families are dying of hunger', 'The young to the war', their banners proclaimed in large letters.

These continuous processions contributed towards the tense atmosphere of the capital. Petrograd suddenly became charged with life: everyone became involved in the agitation of politics and the explosion of ideas so characteristic of exceptional periods in history. Not only the masses were on the move; everywhere groups of men and women (whose presence in great numbers has been noticed by all observers) were engaged in a never-ending political debate: in the interminable queues, on the way home and in the courtyards. The long spring evenings made it possible to continue discussions until the early hours.

> At night [Krupskaia wrote in her Memoirs] I amused myself by opening the window and listening to the heated debates in a courtyard across the road from our house. A soldier was sitting there surrounded by cooks, chambermaids and I know not what other young people. At one o'clock in the morning, snatches of their talk reached me: 'Bolsheviks, Mensheviks ... ' At three a.m.: 'Miliukov, Bolsheviks ... ' At 5 a.m., still the same flow: politics, debates.

The bourgeoisie was deeply perturbed. 'In the midst of this terrible war, the country is turning into one great debating society, one great feast,' complained a liberal paper. Debates, perhaps, but a feast ... ? They were sadly out in their calculations.

In fact, throughout the spring the social and economic situation had been fast deteriorating, and there was widespread and increasing misery and poverty. A moderate socialist member of the Soviet Executive Committee reported officially at the end of May that for 'many categories of workers the situation is one of chronic famine'. Soon afterwards, a leading trade union informed the

government that 'patience has come to an end ... We lack the
strength to go on living under such conditions.' The bread ration,
initially fixed at one pound a day per inhabitant, was reduced to
three-quarters and then to half a pound in Petrograd and Moscow.
Food prices in general doubled during the spring, and even then it
was difficult to get hold of provisions except on the black market
which, of course, catered primarily for the well-to-do. The government, in the person of the Minister of Food, could do no better
than invite the labouring masses 'to even more sustained effort
and indispensable sacrifice'. In some regions the soviets began to
requisition food and distribute it fairly among the population, but
such measures were the exception. The situation was exacerbated
further by the mounting chaos on the railways. No grain reached
the capital from the Ukraine, and reserves were practically
exhausted at the beginning of summer. In July things improved a
little, only to deteriorate again in the autumn when crisis turned
into disaster.

Russia in 1917 was gripped by a galloping inflation: as industrial
activity ground slowly to a halt, the amount of money in circulation
increased from nine thousand million roubles in January 1917 to
nineteen thousand millions at the beginning of October. Industrial
pay could not keep up with this mad escalation, and mean real
wages, estimated at 19·3 roubles per month during the first quarter
of 1917, had decreased to 13·8 roubles by the second quarter.

This spectacular fall in wages gives one no more than a partial
idea of the prevailing misery; in fact, wage reduction went hand in
hand with increased unemployment, as factory after factory closed
its doors. In May, 9,000 workers were dismissed; in June, more
than 38,000; in July the figure had gone up to 48,000. In May 1917
the Soviet Executive Committee, renowned for its moderation,
spoke of a 'general collapse of the country's economic life'. The
official organ of the Petrograd Soviet, in its issue of May 6th, laid
the blame squarely at the door of 'those capitalists who cling obstinately to their profits' and who act as 'disrupters and counter-
revolutionaries'. And, in fact, many employers were sorely tempted
to exploit the general poverty by depressing wages and by a
deliberate policy of lock-outs. In the course of one of their
conferences, a leading Moscow industrialist called Riabuchinsky
stated quite bluntly that 'the emaciated hand of hunger will seize
the members of the different [workers'] committees and soviets by

the throat'. According to an informed observer, the general consen-
sus at this employers' meeting was that the working class would be
taught a 'salutary lesson by the inevitable and progressive closure
of our factories'. Nevertheless, the Congress of Industry and Commerce was careful not to call for a general lock-out; instead, it
suggested the more discreet method of closing a specified series of
factories.

According to their official announcement, this measure had been
forced upon them by the workers' excessive claims and general
truculence. And, in fact, the workers were no longer prepared to be
fobbed off with solemn declarations about liberty and democracy;
what they wanted was food in their bellies, higher wages, a shorter
working day, paid leave and the recognition of their trade-union
rights. In addition, as factory after factory closed down many of
them began to call for 'workers' control', for the right to check the
accounts and to propose, indeed impose, the kind of management
that would ensure a return to full production. This was a fundamental challenge to the employers, and one they considered an unwarranted intrusion into their own privileged domain. Many
moderate socialists took the same view, and dismissed the whole
idea of workers' control as so much anarchist nonsense.

To obtain satisfaction the workers naturally and increasingly
used their traditional weapon, the strike, but so tense was the
general social and political climate that many of the strikes or lock-
outs gave rise to violent clashes. These increased as socialist
journals began to publish figures about industrial profits, which
contrasted sharply with the workers' miserable wages. Lock-outs
were decried as attempts at sabotage, the more so as the leaders of
the February uprising were always the first to be sacked. Grievances
nurtured for years, old humiliations, the ever-present exploitation,
now produced their bitter fruit as workers wreaked personal
vengeance on particularly hated employers or brutal foremen.
There were reports of owners and clerks being beaten and even—
under exceptional circumstances—being killed. During many a
lock-out workers occupied their factories, arrested the employers
and handed them over to the local soviet.

The socialist ministers blew alternately hot and cold on this
ferment, though showing a marked preference for appeals for
calmness. Skobelev, the Menshevik Minister of Labour, admitted one day, 'You workers have every right to be indignant

that the possessing classes should be enriching themselves in times of war.' But he went on to express the hope that their indignation would be kept within strict legal bounds. For the rest, the Provisional Government, incapable of organizing production or of stopping the flight of capital abroad, concentrated its fire on the workers, preaching moderation and patience one day and calling for stricter discipline the next. But to make itself heard it needed far greater authority than it actually enjoyed; authority was the one thing it sadly lacked.

The peasantry on the move

The countryside was no less in turmoil than the towns. For a short period in the early days of the Revolution it looked as if the peasants might meekly sit by, while the government-appointed Agricultural Commission did its job of collecting information before drafting new land legislation and other reforms. But if the authorities hoped that they could fob the peasantry off for long they were quickly disappointed.

Slow to start, the peasant revolution was gathering momentum, especially as vague promises to the *moujiks* went hand in hand with fairly precise government pledges to the landowners. Everyone knew or ought to have known that the Revolution in Russia was inconceivable without a profound transformation of the agrarian system, a running sore that was afflicting tens of millions of increasingly rebellious people. And so, faced with official inertia, the *moujiks* decided to look after themselves. Scores of peasant soviets sprang up, together with hundreds or even thousands of peasant committees with badly-defined tasks but growing powers. The authorities greeted this development with growing and barely disguised anxiety, though what worried them even more than the proliferation of these so-called anarchic institutions was the spread of anarchy itself across the entire Russian countryside. It has been estimated that during March, disorders occurred in 34 districts; in April, the figure rose to 174; in May to 236; in June to 280; and in July to 325. And this was only a beginning: of the 930 cases of land seizure reported to the authorities, 686 took place between July and October. Between the February and October revolutions, 350 castles and manors were sacked—271 during the last three months of 1917.

Most of the trouble occurred in the regions with the most

powerful landowners; those who had always worked their lands themselves—as in many parts of the Ukraine and White Russia— were generally left alone. In short, the Russian peasant had begun to settle old accounts with those whom he held chiefly responsible for his misery. Army deserters, who remembered the bloody lessons they had been taught at the front and who greatly preferred to fight the known oppressor at home than the unknown German enemy, played an increasing part in these disturbances, turning, *inter alia*, on those *moujiks* who from 1906 to 1914 had taken advantage of the Stolypin laws[1] to desert the *mir* and declare their independence. This 'treachery' could never be forgiven, still less the recent fortunes some of them had accumulated, and some were forced to return to the village communities they had abandoned. The rebels also reduced or refused to pay the rent agreed with their landlords or the crushing taxes the state tried to extract from them, drove hired labourers from the land, confiscated farm implements and seed, ploughed up pastures, began to clear forests without permission and went in for large-scale thieving.

As the government neither helped nor hindered them, the *moujiks* became less and less inhibited, planting the 'Red Cock'— that symbol of pillage and arson of the French Revolution—in all parts of the country. In late summer and throughout the autumn, castle after castle and manor after manor went up in flames, and so did a host of artistic treasures, including many irreplaceable books and icons. Worst of all was the destruction of human lives.

Here, too, the Provisional Government bore a grave responsibility. While peasant unrest grew apace and the backward state of the countryside continued to be one of the greatest evils dominating and poisoning the whole of Russian society, they refused to do anything until a Constituent Assembly had been duly elected and had passed the appropriate legislation. It is difficult to tell whether in this decision they were swayed by respect for the legal formalities or acted under pressure from the bourgeoisie, which did not hide its wish to postpone social reforms indefinitely; in any case, while they sat back with folded arms many landowners took the precaution of assigning their estates to foreigners or other persons who seemed unlikely to suffer expropriation. And when the incensed peasants protested to the government, they were met with the usual excuses, inertia and prevarications.

[1] See Chapter 1.

Thus in May, when Kerensky deigned to receive a peasant delegation he cut short their protest with, 'The Provisional Government has the whole matter in hand. Tell your friends that there is no cause for disquiet, that the government and I are doing what we can.' And when one of the peasants had the temerity to point out that they had been promised a ban on all land sales, and that this promise had been broken, Kerensky went red in the face. 'I have said that we shall take all the necessary measures,' he screamed, 'and that is precisely what we shall do.' And seeing that the peasants looked sceptical, he added furiously, 'You can wipe those sneers off your faces.'

All in all, if the government did anything at all, it merely added fuel to the flames. Apart from setting up an Agricultural Com-mission whose—highly confidential—work proceeded at a snail's pace, it contented itself with passing one law entitling agricultural committees (which did not, in any case, wait for this authorization) to requisition non-cultivated lands and abandoned farm instru-ments, and another law banning the sale of land without prior sanction by rural commissions. The last measure, moreover, was not promulgated until late July, when countless estates had already changed hands.

For the rest, the government saw fit to restrict the scope of the agricultural committees to conciliation, and to forbid the seizure of land and all other 'excesses' by the peasants. Addressing local government officers, the Menshevik Minister of the Interior, Tseretelli, ordered them peremptorily to 'suppress with the utmost energy any attempt to sow disorder and anarchy, any arbitrary seizure of lands, any act of violence … ' This penchant for purely repressive measures was the more ominous in that it was not even coupled with efficiency—the authorities lacked the means of implementing them.

As a result, the Provisional Government not only lost face with the peasants, but also aroused the wrath of the landowners whose estates continued to be confiscated. The peasants, for their part, could not even turn to those who had previously championed their cause, chief among them the Social Revolutionary Party and the Congress of the Peasant Deputies. The Social Revolutionaries had long since ceased to be true to their name—well before the Revolution, they had attracted numerous petit-bourgeois elements, vaguely tinged with radicalism, of whom Kerensky was the most striking example. After February, their ranks were reinforced by a considerable influx of men to whom socialist ideas were absolutely alien—intellectuals, lawyers, officers and even convinced Tsarists. The Party was led by Chernov, its original founder, who at the turn of the century had tried to infuse it with radical ideas. When he returned from exile, a few days before Lenin, he still struck a leftist pose but soon afterwards, as Minister of Agriculture, he meekly began to toe the official line. Thus, in June he treated the National Congress of Peasant Deputies to the following harangue: 'The settlement of agricultural disputes by local measures cannot be tolerated. In the absence of a law for the whole of the country, such arbitrary acts are bound to lead to national disaster.' He added that all conflicts between peasants and landowners must be settled lawfully by the appropriate 'Conciliation Boards'.

Even so, the peasants by and large remained loyal to the Social Revolutionaries—in principle if not in practice. But no matter how often and how loudly the Party leaders appealed for calm and discipline or how often they repeated that land reform was the exclusive business of the future Constituent Assembly, when it came to restoring calm in the countryside, their appeals fell on deaf ears.

In the Congress of Peasant Deputies, too, ominous cracks had begun to appear. At an All-Russian Conference convoked in Petrograd on May 4th, a new executive committee was elected, Chernov and Kerensky obtaining more than eight hundred votes, Lenin barely twenty. The general policy of the Provisional Government was endorsed by the vast majority, a result that suggested the Russian *moujik* stood firmly behind the cabinet. In fact, the Congress had also passed a far more radical resolution, namely the immediate 'conversion of all land into national property for equal working use, without any indemnity'. This was an outright rejection of the wait-and-see philosophy and the conservative policy of the self-same Provisional Government in which the Congress had just voted its confidence; it was also a tacit endorsement of the Bolshevik platform to which the great majority of Congress members was ostensibly opposed.

When Lenin was given permission to address the assembly, he found himself before an audience that felt little goodwill towards him and was hardly inclined to pay attention. But the Bolshevik leader, no doubt recalling his dealings with Russian peasants during his early days as an advocate, demonstrated once again how greatly he excelled in the difficult art of expounding even the most compli-cated ideas in clear and simple language. When his time was up and the Chairman wanted to cut him short, the delegates gave him leave to continue. And when he finally did sit down, though he did not carry the entire audience with him, he had certainly made his mark. Sukhanov heard one of the delegates whisper to his neigh-bour, 'Me, I call that good sense ... '

The future leader of the Soviet state was quite content to leave it at that—while his adversaries had engaged in hollow rhetoric, he had sounded the language of revolution and common sense. A few months later, the harvest he had sown began to be reaped on the land.

Russia at the cross roads: war or peace?

A real solution of the complex agricultural problem would have called for a dynamic and unified central leadership capable of carry-ing the whole country with it. As it was, dual power was responsible for continually widening the gulf between the masses and the state, until the Provisional Government was reduced to a head without a body. This was not surprising: based on a fiction—its sovereignty —it fed on a myth, incessantly repeated and raised to the status of a sacred truth—that the February Revolution had been the result of, and bore witness to, a wave of patriotic enthusiasm. Tsarism had apparently been overthrown for the sole and exalted purpose of pursuing the war with greater determination; the nation was said to be ready, indeed anxious, to die for the fatherland. No politicians had ever been more deluded, and their errors bore more heavily on the destiny of Russia than any diplomatic or military pressure from abroad.

For their article of faith was the exact opposite of the truth. Not the desire for revenge, but sheer war-weariness, had driven the masses into the streets in February 1917. Nor had the changes at the top and the emergence of a new social and political climate, culminating in the establishment of soviets, done anything to revive the taste for military adventure—the Russian people had had more than enough of that after three years of bloody and futile carnage. And while there had been demonstrations of great popular enthusiasm and a sense of national euphoria immediately after the Revolution, only the blind optimism and chronic myopia

that were the distinguishing marks of the new Russian leaders
could have confused these with war fever. Kerensky later saw fit to
claim that it was the Allies who, by insisting on unconditional
German surrender, bore the blame for the fall of the Provisional
Government and the triumph of the Bolsheviks. But in 1917
Kerensky more than anyone else confused national enthusiasm
with chauvinism, and with grandiloquent phrases tried to whip his
country into a state of military frenzy. The masses, for their part,
allowed themselves to be fooled some of the time, but not for long,
and the petty leaders of the February Revolution showed little
historical sense when they failed to appreciate the change.

The behaviour of Miliukov was a case in point. It was he who
formulated the war policies to which the Provisional Government
held fast until the end, with minor variations. Convinced before
February that only German saboteurs wanted a Russian Revolution, after February he loudly proclaimed that this Revolution was
synonymous with patriotism and victory in the field. Small wonder
then that his policies proved such a disaster, to the country no less
than to himself.

With all his faults, Miliukov had one great virtue that in other
circumstances might have proved his saving grace: the new head of
the Foreign Service was a man of obstinate determination. When
his first declaration of Russia's war aims and of her adherence to
the secret treaties was hotly contested by the workers' councils, and
when even his own colleagues called for some compromise,
Miliukov blandly refused to budge. Things came to a head with a
diplomatic note he sent to the Allied powers on May 1st (Western
calendar). The leaders of the Soviet had been clamouring for peace
without annexations and indemnities, and it was as a concession to
them that the Provisional Government had finally decided to
inform the Allies of the text of its appeal to the citizens of Russia of
March 27th (April 9th) which expressly renounced all imperialist
aims. Now Miliukov—who had been reluctant to put his name to
that appeal—agreed to transmit it, but only on condition that he
could write an explanatory note of his own. In it he reaffirmed that
'the Provisional Government, while safeguarding the rights of our
country, will fully observe the obligations assumed toward our
Allies.' He also spoke of Russia's determination to obtain 'what
sanctions and guarantees of firm peace were needed to avoid the
resumption of violent conflicts'. In other words, Miliukov had

gone back on the concessions the Provisional Government had been forced to make to the Soviet—his note refuted the very declaration to which it was meant to serve as an introduction. Miliukov had flung down a challenge to the Soviet leaders, convinced that their conciliatory mood would force them to back down.

They might well have done so had not the masses taken matters into their own hands. Hardly had the text of Miliukov's note become known when there was a storm of popular indignation. On April 20th (May 3rd),[1] some 25,000 to 30,000 armed soldiers descended into the streets in protest, and even the Menshevik press joined in the chorus, describing Miliukov's note as a 'denial of democracy'. The demonstrators moved towards the Mariinsky Palace, where the Provisional Government sat, bearing banners with such slogans as 'Down with the Provisional Government!' 'Down with Miliukov!', 'Down with Imperialist policy!', 'Miliukov, Guchkov, resign!'. Although the leaders of the Soviet were not among the targets of these attacks, they decided to persuade the protesting troops to return to their barracks. They were partly successful, though few demonstrators thanked them for the interference. Meanwhile, the workers in the industrial suburbs had decided to come out in support of their comrades-in-arms, and the bourgeois quarters were said to be preparing a counter manifestation. But there were no further incidents that day.

Next morning the demonstrators were out in full force again, and as working-class columns came up against bourgeois processions on the Nevsky Prospect and were greeted with banners proclaiming support for Miliukov and the Provisional Government, blood was shed on the streets of the capital for the first time since the Tsar's fall. The Commander of the Petrograd garrison, General Kornilov, who had barely been able to contain his impatience, asked the Provisional Government for authorization to open fire on the unruly soldiers and workers, but since that would have meant civil war the ministers demurred. Their prudence was a sign not only of wisdom but also of impotence—once again, the Soviet and not the Provisional Government was in control of the situation, and it was the Soviet Executive Committee which published a declaration that 'anyone calling for armed demonstrations or so much as firing his gun into the air' was a 'traitor to the Revolution'. Moreover, the

[1] The events described here are commonly described as the 'April Days'.

Committee banned all meetings or processions for the next forty-eight hours, and the workers heeded this call.

All that remained to be done was to find a political solution to the Miliukov affair. By thirty-four votes to nineteen, the Soviet Executive Committee decided to accept the Government explanation that by his reference to 'sanctions and guarantees of firm peace', Miliukov had meant nothing more sinister than limitation of armaments, the setting up of international tribunals, etc. This, however, was no solution to an extremely serious crisis, and led to bloody clashes in the street. Officials in the ministries and the Soviet might have opted for conciliation, but the people themselves preferred to show their hand. As a result, there was further bloodshed and the situation became too dangerous for further temporization. The Provisional Government now thought that discretion was the better part of valour, and at long last issued a public repudiation of Miliukov's note. Ten days later, the Foreign Minister resigned his post in the government.

The time had clearly come for closer co-operation between the Provisional Government and the moderates in the Soviet—or so the bourgeoisie thought. The result—the First Coalition Government—was still headed by Prince Lvov, but Kerensky became Minister of War, while five others, directly or indirectly associated with the socialist movement, were offered other portfolios. Miliukov, who had refused the Ministry of Education, was replaced by Tereshchenko, the former Minister of Finance, a man with the most respectable upper-middle-class views.

Though the new government had been born out of dissatisfaction with the war policy of the old, it saw no reason to introduce any radical changes. True, in its first official policy statement it promised to seek peace 'without annexations or indemnities', a phrase very dear to moderate socialists, and to urge the Allies to sign an agreement in accordance with the declaration of March 27th. This had called for the abrogation of the secret treaties and particularly of their imperialist clauses. But having issued this statement, the government took absolutely no steps to implement it; indeed, that was the last thing they wanted. As Miliukov said of his successor, 'The Allied diplomats knew that the "democratic" terminology of his dispatches was a reluctant concession to the demands of the moment, and treated it with indulgence.' They were the more content in that the inaugural manifesto of the

Coalition Government affirmed that its chief aim would be to 'strengthen the democratic character of the army so as to increase its offensive and defensive power'.

For no matter how often the Provisional Government issued bland declarations about the purity of its social intentions, no matter how many promises it made of ambitious economic reforms, no matter how loudly it proclaimed the revolutionary virtues of 'peace without annexations or indemnities', its real concern was with the 'offensive'—the full resumption of hostilities after a lull that struck them as having lasted far too long. The problem was not so much military—in fact, the very idea of a Russian victory at this stage was ludicrous—as political: to the Right an offensive was an absolute necessity, to moderate socialists it was a necessary evil.

Thus it was on Cadet insistence that the phrase about strengthening the 'offensive and defensive power' of the army had been incorporated in the government manifesto; indeed, the liberals had made their participation in the cabinet dependent on its inclusion. Nor was this a mere whim, ever since the outbreak of war the bourgeoisie had been insisting that all policy decisions must be subordinated to the needs of the war. Like their peers in the other belligerent countries, they believed that this objective— an increased war effort in the trenches and in the factories—must take precedence over (and indeed justified the postponement of) all social reforms. Hence the call for national unity, and for alliances with the most conservative and reactionary circles. Last but not least, strengthening 'the offensive and defensive power' of the army meant enhancing the prestige and authority of the military command. In the midst of social upheavals, this approach seemed to make excellent—political rather than strategic—sense.

This was certainly the view of members of the old Duma, meeting in 'private session'. One of them, Maklakov, was heard to declare, 'If we succeed in launching an offensive ... then Russia's cure will be quick and complete.' No one could have put it more plainly.

The Soviet majority and its leading representatives had other reasons for supporting the new offensive. Sentimental pacifists though they were, they felt that a weak Russia would have little chance of imposing her views on the Allied powers—Great Britain and France would only heed the advice of a country with a respected army. And what better way of earning respect than a crushing blow struck at the Germans? Victorious in the field, Russia would make her European partners take notice and force them to sign a negotiated peace.

Despite its basic naivety, this argument was not entirely devoid of common sense: ever since February, the Allies had been urging Russia to redouble her attack on the Central Powers. Indeed, the change of regime had been welcomed by democratic circles in France and Great Britain, for both of whom Tsarism had been an embarrassing partner: its very existence had belied the claim that they were fighting for justice and liberty. True, some British conservatives had expressed dismay at the Revolution, but the rest of the world, sharing the illusions of the Provisional Government, declared itself satisfied that the disappearance of the old regime would boost the flagging morale of the Russian soldier and help the Allied cause. And so they rejoiced that the incompetence of the Tsarist administration and the Germanophilia of influential social circles had come to an end.

Henceforth, the attitude of the Western Powers to the Russian Revolution was overshadowed by two considerations: a desire to step up the Russian war effort and, later, a desire to dam up its social repercussions, which threatened not only the Russian bourgeoisie but Western capitalism as well. In 1917, however, the first consideration was paramount, especially as by keeping Russia in the war it still seemed possible to contain the harmful influence of the Bolsheviks. To that end, French and British diplomats stepped up their pressure on the Russian Government. The French ambassador, Maurice Paléologue, a man of conservative bent, had always maintained the closest contact with high society in general and with Tsarist circles in particular—despite the fact that he thought them purblind. The fall of the empire had filled this representative of the French Republic with little enthusiasm. When he heard of officers proclaiming their support for the Revolution in February he thought it a 'saddening spectacle'. For the rest, he felt nothing but contempt and loathing for the new masters of Russia and the social upstarts who had crawled out of their dirty suburbs to invade the elegant quarters. Passing through the corridors of the Mariinsky Palace one day, Paléologue was horrified at the changes. 'In the vestibule where lackeys used to bustle about dressed in sumptuous court livery, untidy, dirty, impudent soldiers now lounge on the benches and smoke.' And while his diplomatic status prevented him from giving free vent to his feelings, he made no special efforts to hide them either. When a group of students stopped him in the street one day and asked him to salute the Red Flag, Paléologue declared, 'I know no better way of rendering homage to the liberty of Russia than by asking you to cry with me, "Long live the war!" ' He, too, took solace from the fact that the new regime might at least drum up the martial spirit of the Tsar's former subjects. Needless to say, the vaguely pacific proclamations of the Provisional Government did not please him; he declared that the official proclamation of March 27th was proof of an excess of 'timidity and ambiguity', that all this sentimental chatter could only impede military progress. Paléologue was on the very best of terms with Miliukov, and it was not by chance that the French Ambassador left Petrograd for good when his friend was forced to resign.

The British Ambassador, Sir George Buchanan, was much quicker to adapt himself to the new climate. Unlike his French colleague, he chose his friends from liberal rather than aristocratic circles, and he showed far greater sympathy for the peace policy of the government and the Soviet majority. His attitude reflected the greater realism of his government—whereas the French insisted that the secret treaties were inviolable, the British proved infinitely more flexible, and granted their Russian allies the right to renounce their own territorial claims provided only that they did not expect Britain and France—to say nothing of the voracious Italians—to make the same sort of self-sacrifice. Thus in his letter of May 21st[1] to the Foreign Office, Buchanan noted that 'the new socialist ministers will naturally be apprised of the contents of Russia's secret agreements, and if the Russian soldiers are told that they must go on fighting till the objects of those agreements have been realized, they will demand a separate peace.' The ambassador accordingly suggested that Britain issue 'some conciliatory but noncommittal statement on the subject'.

But to attain their ends Britain and France were both prepared to employ fair means or foul, ranging from friendly persuasion to economic blackmail. When it came to the former, they could rely on the services of their own labour leaders who, throughout the spring, descended on Petrograd in droves and also visited various

[1] Western calendar.

sectors of the eastern front. Among them were the French socialists Cachin—who betrayed his master's trust when he ended up as a supporter of the Bolshevik Revolution—Laffont and Thomas, who had been decorated by Nicholas II in person, only a few months earlier. The most illustrious British visitor was Arthur Henderson, the future Foreign Secretary; Belgium sent Henri de Man, Louis de Brouckère and, above all, Emil Vandervelde, the President of the Second International and a wartime minister. Vandervelde had caused quite a furore in August 1914 by writing a letter to Russian socialists in which he implored them to drop their opposition to the Tsar and to concentrate on the defence of their homeland. No wonder then that the Russian workers were somewhat sceptical of him and his felicitations on their Revolution.

In general, all these advocates of war to the bitter end—chosen by their governments for that very reason—received a lukewarm reception in the Russian capital. While English, French and Belgian socialists alike called for the destruction of German imperialism as the only way of hastening the advent of universal democracy, the Russians not only turned a deaf ear to all such arguments, but even managed to convince some of the visitors that the territorial demands of their governments were excessive. Needless to say, the governments in question brushed all such objections aside.

The Allies now played their second and greatest trump: they exerted economic pressure. Over and above the prevailing chaos, Russia had suffered crippling war damage, and the Provisional Government was largely dependent on financial aid from the West, and particularly from the United States whose resources were intact. They were now told that no such aid would be forthcoming unless Russia honoured her 'obligations' and played her full part in the war against Germany and Austria-Hungary. In June an American economic mission led by the former Secretary of State, Elihu Root, arrived in Petrograd. Unaccustomed to the polite equivocations so beloved of European diplomats, the American visitor told the Provisional Government quite bluntly that his government's view could be summed up in the single phrase, 'No war, no loans.' At the same time, France and Britain kept insisting that Russia fulfil the undertaking she had given at an Allied military conference in Petrograd (January 1917) to launch an offensive in Galicia during the coming spring.

It was in the wake of all this pressure that the new-born Lvov-Kerensky coalition issued a declaration ending in the following flight of fancy: 'The country must express its will with all necessary authority and send its army into combat.' The second part of this proposition was, of course, the relevant one.

Preparations for the offensive met with strong resistance not only from the Bolsheviks but more generally from all those who felt that these measures were bound to delay the peace and, on the national plane, strengthen the hand of reaction. Even so, the Coalition Government scored a major victory in June, when the Petrograd Soviet approved its strategic plans by 472 votes to 271 with 39 abstentions. All that now remained was to beat the Germans, and, alas, that called for far more than the brilliant oratory of Kerensky, who now took personal charge of the war propaganda machine. In May, soon after he became Minister of War, he issued the following flamboyant command to the army: 'You will carry peace, truth and justice on the points of your bayonets. Free sons of Russia, you will move forward in serried ranks, united by the discipline of duty and by your supreme love for the Revolution and your homeland'. The future was to reveal the wide gulf that divided Kerensky's eloquence from the sordid reality in the field. Meanwhile, the Minister of War continued to harangue his troops and tried to inspire them with his own enthusiasm.

Rounding on those who argued that the tired Russian Army was in no fit state to wage war, the Supreme Commander (for this was the title he had assumed) addressed his troops with what Paléologue has called his 'habitual mixture of histrionics and delusions'. 'Is it really true that the free Russian state is a state of rebellious slaves?' he asked. 'I am sorry that I did not die two months ago, during the first hours of the Revolution … ' (At this point, however, he preferred the soldiers to lay down their lives.) 'I implore all of you to go forward,' he exclaimed on another occasion, 'forward, in the struggle for liberty. You are not going to a banquet but to your death. We revolutionaries have the right to die.'

While his exalted speeches may have impressed the ranks, the officers were generally unmoved by what they called this 'haranguer-in-chief', a man whose oratory a British diplomat has recently compared with Hitler's.

One day, having addressed a large audience in a Moscow theatre in which simple soldiers sat cheek by jowl with elegant ladies,

Kerensky, after his usual flight of hyperbole on the blessings of the new offensive, sank exhausted into the arms of his aide-de-camp, his face ashen in the limelight. Soldiers assisted him off the stage while according to the British diplomat R. H. Bruce Lockhart, who was an eye-witness, 'in a frenzy of hysteria the whole audience rose and cheered itself hoarse ... A millionaire's wife threw her pearl necklace on the stage. Every woman present followed her example and a hail of jewellery descended from every tier of the huge house.'

The soldiers in the audience, though much poorer, seemed no less enthusiastic. True, on another occasion one of them interrupted Kerensky to say that much as he admired the minister's fine speeches he had no intention of getting his body riddled with bullets, but such down-to-earth reactions were exceptional. In general, the men would give their Supreme Commander a standing ovation before carrying him off in triumph, swearing to fight and die for Russia and the Revolution. Soon afterwards, however, when the effects of his words had worn off, they would revert to their customary attitudes: hatred of the officer caste, indifference to or scepticism of all government declarations and above all an immense longing for peace.

The collapse of the army

The gradual disintegration of the Russian Army in 1917 not only struck a blow at the military hopes of the Allied powers but also left the Provisional Government without the means of imposing its authority at home. Not that the weakness of the Russian Army was the sole cause of the events that, in so brief a time, were to lead to the seizure of power by the Bolsheviks. In fact, it was cause and effect in one; and how could it have been otherwise? With nine million men in uniform, the Russian Army constituted an appreciable and highly representative part of the nation. Most soldiers were peasants: 50 per cent of the able-bodied population in the countryside was mobilized between 1914 and 1917. Old rancours, old grievances, old aspirations, had never been forgotten, and now the old cry for land was coupled to a desperate longing for peace.

Even before the February Revolution, these peasants in uniform had lost their taste for trench warfare; after the fall of Tsarism, they had but one wish: to go home and stake their claim to the big estates. This aspect of the class struggle proved of far greater interest to them than military victory, and they accordingly deserted by the regiment. On January 1st, 1917, Russia could boast some seven million soldiers at the front; in October there were only six million. As they escaped by the trainload, excesses and disorders mounted sharply, and all the hapless government could do was recommend that all those who did not return to the front within a stipulated period should be deprived of their right to receive land during the proposed land reforms. And when this period had elapsed, and the soldiers continued to stay on the land, the government could do absolutely nothing about it.

The army was, in fact, the most important factor on the Russian political scene. The outcome of the February Revolution had largely been determined by the attitude of the soldiers—the active participation of some in the insurrection, and the neutrality of the rest at a time when the Tsar most needed their support had sealed the fate of the monarchy. In short, the new regime owed its very existence to the soldiers' revolt, but once in power, it had immediately tried to restore discipline and respect for the officer caste— with, as we saw, a marked lack of success.

Insubordination was not only the result of poor organization, inadequate supplies and major defeats in battle. These stung the troops to the quick, but it was their continued treatment as mere cattle that probably enraged them most. Autocratic Russia had the military machine she deserved—both had the same shortcomings, and both were far behind the times. The officers' corps was as insolent and haughty as the upper classes from which most of its members had sprung, except that while 'polite' Russian society had always modelled itself on the French court, the military caste sought its inspiration in the old Prussian Army.

As a result, the Russian soldier was subject to constant humiliations and petty restrictions. By a regulation dating back to 1913 he was not allowed to enter tramway carriages or restaurants; he could only travel in third-class railway compartments and had to eat in third-class railway buffets; he had to humble himself before his officers, on and off duty, had to address them as 'Your Excellency' or 'Your Honour', and after 1915 had to endure corporal punishment as well as the more usual forms of bullying.

In the circumstances it was inevitable that the events of February should have led to outbursts against the hated officers. Some of them were shot out of hand, but more generally the soldiers contented themselves with showering insults on their superiors and with tearing off their epaulettes. Discipline, respect for authority and obedience all went by the board, as did many of the old distinctions. At the time the soldiers and workers were still in complete control of the streets, and so were able to force the new regime to pass the famous *Prikaz* No. 1 (Order No. 1)—it was at their dictation that the Menshevik leader Skobelev composed this order in the Tauride Palace on March 1st (14th), 1917. This document, of which Trotsky said that it was 'the only respectable one to come out of the February Revolution', granted all soldiers and sailors in Petrograd the right to proceed immediately to the election not only of delegates to the Soviet of Workers' and Soldiers' Deputies, but also of committees in all their units (companies, battalions, regiments, platoons, etc.). It added that in its political actions the garrison was subordinated to the Soviet and its own committees.

The relationship between soldiers and officers was the subject of several special clauses. Standing to attention and compulsory saluting when not on duty were abolished, as were the titles 'Your Honour' and 'Your Excellency'. Moreover, officers were ordered to discontinue their rudeness to soldiers, particularly to refrain from addressing them as 'thou'. It was further decreed that while soldiers would be expected to observe the strictest military discipline during the performance of their service, off duty they must enjoy the same political, civil and personal freedom as all other citizens. Finally, a particularly revolutionary clause laid down that 'all kinds of arms such as rifles, machine-guns, armoured automobiles and others must be kept at the disposal and under the control of the company and battalion committees and in no case should they be turned over to officers, even at their demand.' This stipulation spoke volumes about the men's attitude to their superiors.

The soldiers themselves would have liked to go much further. Thus, five days after the *Prikaz* was published, their delegates asked the Petrograd Soviet to authorize the election of all officers by the ranks. But by then calm had returned to the capital and the leaders of the Soviet were no longer prepared to take orders from below. They called in Kerensky, who quickly persuaded the delegates to withdraw their request. The Soviet Executive Committee had already decided to pass three additional orders, intended to render *Prikaz* No. 1 more palatable to the protesting officers and to

the liberals. For all that, some principles of the *Prikaz* were later
enshrined in a solemn declaration of soldiers' rights drawn up by
the Petrograd Soviet and eventually adopted by the Provisional
Government. It did so reluctantly—Guchkov, as Minister of War,
had refused to sign it and it was not until he was replaced by
Kerensky that the decree was finally issued, with certain 'modifica-
tions'. In particular, it strengthened the authority of the officer
caste and weakened that of the soldiers' committees. Even so,
General Alexeiev saw fit to describe the 'modified' declaration as
'the last nail in the coffin of our army'.

It goes without saying that as soon as the general offensive against
the Central Powers became the main plank in its platform, the
Provisional Government tried its best to bring back the old disci-
plinary code. But the soldiers, afraid of a return to their intolerable
pre-revolutionary condition—not surprisingly, since their former
officers had all been restored to their commands—refused to comply. 'Discipline declines daily,' General Alexeiev, the Supreme
Commander, declared in April in a letter addressed to Minister
Guchkov. 'The authority of the officers has evaporated and we lack
the means of restoring it,' he added. Alexeiev laid the entire blame
on the soldiers' committees, whose role he judged to be disastrous.
More perspicacious commanders did not share this view. Many had
come to realize that the rank and file generally elected officers and
not ordinary privates to the soldiers' committees—not, admittedly,
members of the old military caste, but rather serving officers drawn
from the liberal professions, and as such enjoying the confidence of
the peasants-in-arms. Their eloquence impressed the men, their
democratic attitudes reassured them. And what else could these
poor men do, when most of them felt that their own ignorance
disqualified them from positions of authority?

In their social composition and general outlook, the soldiers'
committees were therefore anything but representative of the social
status and aspirations of the men. In fact they served as a protective
screen between the rank and file and the army command, so much
so that the President of the Fifth Army Committee asserted that
their chief purpose was the restoration of discipline. He also
believed—though undoubtedly his was an extreme point of view—
that the soldiers had the duty to arrest their committee members if
ordered to do so by an officer. In any case, many officers realized
that they themselves would have been placed under arrest had their

regimental committees not intervened. The generals of the old school conveniently overlooked this fact when they blamed the extreme feebleness of Russia on the spirit of democracy or anarchy the soldiers' committees symbolized in their view. This explanation had the merit of glossing over their own responsibility and the fact that the army had been in turmoil well before the Revolution.

Even so, they were right to think that the prevailing political ferment was unpropitious for army morale. From the outside, German propaganda played some part, though not a crucial one, and the same was true of Bolshevik propaganda from within. The Bolshevik Party, which made no secret of its bitter opposition to the continuation of the war, had set up a 'Military Organization' for the express purpose of winning converts in the army, and at the same time their *Soldatskaia Pravda* kept advising the peasant soldiers to join in the expropriation of the big landowners. The Party also called for fraternization between Russian and German soldiers, now an almost daily occurrence and one that according to Lenin was a 'practical means of hastening the end of the massacre'. He added that fraternization itself was not enough; it must be accompanied by the discussion of a definite political programme among the Russian soldiers themselves and also between them and the Germans.

But Bolshevik propaganda made relatively little impact on the peasantry on the land or in the trenches, and for a very simple reason: the Bolsheviks appealed chiefly to the urban proletariat, from whom most of their members were recruited and who gave their policy the most enthusiastic support. Thus at the end of spring the Bolshevik 'Military Organization' numbered no more than 26,000, little enough for an army of between eight and nine million soldiers. Speaking of the contribution of Bolshevik propaganda to the growing pacifism of the Russian Army, Colonel Raymond Robins, the American Red Cross representative, said it was like a lone man sighing in a hurricane.

Paradoxically enough, the collapse of the Russian Army was due in greater measure to those very Mensheviks and Social Revolutionaries who were loudly beating the martial drum, and whose continuous assertions that Russia was fighting for a democratic peace and not for Tsarist imperialism—though what of Allied imperialism?—were greeted with jeers. Told that the Russian war effort was aimed at a negotiated peace in the shortest possible time, the soldiers asked themselves why, in these circumstances, they should not simply lay down their arms and let their leaders get down to the business of signing the armistice. They heard daily that Russia had been freed at long last, and while they rejoiced at these glad tidings they asked themselves what good all this new-found freedom was if they had to rot in trenches.

No wonder, then, that an official document published in the spring of 1917 declared quite frankly that the Russian Army had become 'an exhausted mass of undernourished men in rags, full of bitterness and united only in their resentment and thirst for peace'. Army commanders endorsed this view. Thus General Alexeiev informed the Minister of War during April that pacifism was growing apace. 'The mass of soldiers does not favour the idea of an offensive nor even preparations for it ... I have read with the utmost astonishment the irresponsible reports as to the "excellent" temper of the army. What good does that do? It will not deceive the Germans, and for us it is fatal self-deception.' And General Dragomirov, Commander of the 5th Army, had this to say: 'The fighting spirit has declined. Not only is there no desire among the soldiers to take the offensive, but even a simple stubbornness on the defensive has decreased to a degree threatening the success of the war. Politics, which have spread through all levels of the army, have made the whole military mass desire but one thing—to end the war and go home.' Or take this report by a commissar[1] of the 7th Army:

> In the 12th Division, the 48th Regiment has marched out at full strength; the 45th and 46th Regiments have marched out at half strength. The 40th Regiment has refused to move. In the 13th Division, the 15th Regiment has marched out at near-full strength, the 51st promises to set out tomorrow; the 49th has not moved on the grounds that it is not on duty; the 52nd has refused to march out and has arrested all its officers.

And this happened at the beginning of June, just before the proposed offensive!

Small wonder that, on March 18th, a conference of staff officers on the condition of the army concluded that 'it is impossible to put

---

[1] These commissars were introduced at Kerensky's behest; they were meant to serve as intermediaries between the army command and the soldiers' committees.

into execution the active operations indicated for the spring.'
Innumerable witnesses tell us that in subsequent weeks the
situation deteriorated even further. True, not all regiments were
equally demoralized: the units farthest from the capital were the
least disaffected; the Black Sea Fleet remained more highly disciplined than the seething Baltic Fleet; the cavalry proved more
loyal than the infantry, and so, by and large, did the artillery. But
these differences were not great enough to affect the overall
situation. The High Command tried to improve matters by derisory and ineffective steps: for instance, by the creation of shock
battalions, which in the event proved of little help, and the formation of purely national divisions, a measure that merely increased
the general confusion. Even more spectacular and less effective was
the formation of a women's battalion, which set off towards the
front after a special blessing in Petrograd's Kazan Cathedral.

Judged by purely military standards, the offensive was sheer
folly. On June 18th, after the most intense artillery bombardment
of the war, the south-western armies went into the attack as part
of a general offensive on all fronts. And in fact the Russian army
scored appreciable successes against the Austrian and Hungarian
forces in Galicia, and took large numbers of prisoners. However,
as soon as the Germans joined battle, the tables were rapidly
turned—the Russian advance was halted and the offensive turned
into a rout from Galicia, even though the generals had given orders
to fire on all men who deserted their posts. Elsewhere, the Russians
fared no better—their army simply evaporated.

The illusion of a victorious offensive had been destroyed, and
history could continue on an even course.

6

The Bolshevik Surge

IF BY some unlikely chance the offensive of June and July had been as successful as its advocates had hoped, it might well have deflected the course of the Russian Revolution. Its failure, however, not only highlighted the bankruptcy of the Provisional Government and of the social and political forces behind it, but also showed up the cracks in the coalition between the bourgeoisie and the Soviet majority.

Here we make a clear distinction between that majority and the soviets as such. For as social contrasts and class tension increased, so the soviets, too, became increasingly divided. Nevertheless, right-wing leaders continued to look upon them as an arm of the revolutionary proletariat and hence treated all factions alike with indiscriminate hostility.

The growing differences within the soviets must, in fact, have struck the uninitiated observer as strange, paradoxical and even absurd: the Bolsheviks kept raising the cry of 'All power to the soviets', when the soviets, made up chiefly of Mensheviks and Social Revolutionaries, resolutely refused to assume power. But illogical though it appeared, the Bolshevik approach simply mirrored the more fundamental contradiction of the soviets themselves—revolutionary in origin, their social composition was anything but revolutionary. In principle, this vast assembly of workers' and soldiers' delegates represented the proletariat of town and country, i.e. the disinherited and discontented masses. In reality, things were very much less clear-cut than that.

Take the Petrograd Soviet, the most powerful of all. When it sprang up it consisted of 1,300 members, soon afterwards growing to 3,000. So vast an assembly could clearly do no more than hold public debates, with the result that real power was vested in a much smaller body, the Executive Committee. The latter consisted originally of thirty members, only eight of whom were elected; the rest, apart from the seven members of the Presidium (the President, Chkheidze, two Vice-Presidents and four Secretaries), were designated by the various socialist organizations in the capital, ranging from Bolsheviks on the extreme left to Trudoviks and Populists at the other end of the workers' and democratic spectrum. Characteristically, the eight elected members formed the left wing of the Executive Committee—while there was only one Bolshevik, namely Shliapnikov, his seven colleagues were either radical socialists or left-wing Mensheviks. Soon afterwards, the Executive Committee was reinforced with nine representatives from the soldiers' section.

During April, a National Conference attended by delegates from 185 regional and local organizations decided to reinforce the Executive Committee of the Petrograd Soviet with sixteen provincial delegates, to be nominated by the various socialist parties, and also with a number of prominent figures—generally exemigrants—and a fresh soldiers' contingent. As a result, the Executive Committee now consisted of some eighty to ninety members, and became too unwieldy. It accordingly delegated much of its work to bodies without official existence and without a precise mandate. One of these was the so-called Bureau; another a small but exceedingly powerful and secret committee that certain wits named the 'Star Chamber'.[1] It included members of the Presidium, together with the most influential leaders of the Soviet majority, though no one knew its exact composition. It often took important decisions without reference to the Executive Committee. This situation did not change even when the first All-Russian Congress of Soviets met in Petrograd on June 3rd and elected the Central All-Russian Executive Committee of the Soviet of Workers' and Soldiers' Deputies—with its three hundred members, this new Committee was once again too unwieldy to take effective decisions.

And so a host of small committees superseded the elected assembly, in violation of two basic Soviet principles: close and permanent contact between the masses and their representatives, and the right of immediate recall. From being the spokesmen of soldiers and factory workers, the Soviet Executive was transformed into a series of select bodies, answerable to no one.

The tensions within the Soviet—many of whose members questioned this shift of authority—were increased further by

[1] Until the seventeenth century, the English Star Chamber wielded considerable political and judicial powers. Its secret deliberations—and also its broad terms of reference—were widely criticized.

marked differences of opinion between the workers' contingent and the soldiers' representatives. The workers—and particularly those from Petrograd—constituted the most revolutionary element of the nation. So militant, in fact, were the industrial districts, and so fervently did they seek social and political change, that no party dared to champion their sweeping demands. Thus Lenin had good reason to complain that 'the workers and peasants ... are a thousand times to the Left of the Chernovs and the Tseretellis, and a hundred times to the Left of us [the Bolsheviks]'.

The soldiers' delegates presented a very different political picture; most of them were of peasant origin and hence far less class-conscious than the industrial workers. Fury had thrown the soldiers into the ranks of the Revolution, but for all that they remained politically backward, and their delegates to the Soviet were chiefly made up of reserve officers and N.C.O.s. The fact that these men, together with lawyers, civil servants and other members of the liberal professions, had been allowed to join the Soviet in the first place, showed clearly how informally it was being run.

The balance of forces between the 'Soldiers' Right' and the 'Workers' Left' in the Soviet was heavily weighted in favour of the former: whereas the workers were entitled to elect one delegate per thousand voters, the soldiers were granted one delegate per company (roughly 250 men). At the end of March 1917, for instance, two thousand out of the three thousand members of the Petrograd Soviet had been elected by regimental vote.

This was but one reason for the rigidity of Russian political institutions. In general, it is true to say that institutions, and particularly legal ones which are inordinately sluggish, act as brakes on historical developments. Revolutionary institutions are no exception, no matter how hard they try to guard against formal straitjackets, or how anxious they are to further historical progress. Thus during the most tumultuous hours of the French Revolution, the Convention was constantly under pressure from the masses, whose fervour far outstripped that of the delegates. The Petrograd Soviet behaved similarly, except that its peculiar organization and composition acted as an even stronger brake.

Paradoxically, it was this very moderation that hastened Russia's progress towards the October Revolution: as the conservative wing in the Soviet became increasingly powerful, so the masses set up an ever more insistent clamour for reform. In the end, the timidity of the first and the impatience of the second could no longer be reconciled, and a violent clash became inevitable.

The 'June Days'

The moderation of the Soviet leaders was revealed in a host of different ways. To begin with, many of them went out of their way to appease the bourgeoisie, justifying their attitude with what they believed were real Marxist arguments. The masses, for their part, were quite unable to follow these intricate theoretical demonstrations and arguments, or to approve the extreme subtlety and shrewdness of these tactics, and hence fought a running battle with their delegates. On one occasion, Steklov—an independent socialist who later joined the Bolsheviks—when seconding a resolution of conditional support for the Provisional Government which had been moved by the Soviet Executive Committee, was advised to draw out his speech so as to leave no time for embarrassing discussions at the end of his address.

Later, such precautions became unnecessary—the Soviet merely did as the 'Star Chamber', in its wisdom, decreed. In the Executive Committee, the less politically conscious and more vacillating elements constantly increased their influence at the expense of the Left; in the Plenary Assembly, the militants who had participated in the pre-revolutionary struggle and in the February events were gradually driven into a corner. A similar process occurred in the Menshevik Party: many of its old leaders made way for men who had joined the Party after the fall of Tsarism, often for purely opportunist motives. Thus when Martov returned to Russia—one month after Lenin and by the same route—he found a Party in which thirst for power and rank pragmatism had become the paramount criteria of political behaviour. Martov, who before the war had dominated the Mensheviks by the sheer weight of his intellectual brilliance, now found himself completely isolated; so much so, in fact, that he played an almost negligible part in what followed.

The swing of the Soviet to the Right was accelerated by the creation of a coalition government in May. The call for a broader cabinet had first been sounded by the liberals. On April 26th, Kerensky had joined in the chorus, brushing aside all Menshevik objections. Some of these were extremely sharp, for though the traditional arguments against a coalition weighed less heavily on the Mensheviks now than they had two months earlier, many Party leaders remained convinced that an open alliance with the bourgeoisie would diminish their hold over the masses. The ferment that had followed the publication of Miliukov's note to the Allies had shown unmistakably that the workers were quick to hit back, and that the best way of containing them was to preserve the independence of the Soviet with respect to the Provisional Government. Moreover, a coalition between the bourgeoisie and the Soviet majority had the unpleasant corollary of leaving the field of opposition to the hated Bolsheviks. On April 28th, the Executive Committee of the Soviet accordingly rejected the coalition principle by twenty-three votes to twenty-two.

Its supporters massed for a counter-attack. The liberals, especially, felt that only the presence of socialists in the cabinet could force the workers to moderate their claims and, in particular, to accept the need for greater military effort. Many workers, too, favoured a coalition, although for quite different reasons: they believed that socialist ministers would tie the hands of the bourgeoisie. So great was the combined pressure of these groups that the Soviet Executive Committee reversed its earlier decision on May 1st, approving the formation of a coalition government by forty-four votes to nineteen. Four days later the new cabinet was installed.

It was headed by Prince Lvov, with Tereshchenko as Minister of Foreign Affairs, and though six socialists or socialist sympathizers were given posts in it, they were heavily outnumbered by the liberals. Kerensky was made Minister of War; the Mensheviks Tseretelli and Skobelev became Ministers of Posts and Telegraphs and of Labour; the Social Revolutionary Chernov became Minister of Agriculture. The Ministry of Justice went to Pereverzev, who counted himself something of a Social Revolutionary; and the Ministry of Food went to a member of the Popular Socialist Party, the extreme right flank of the workers' movement.

Liberal hopes in the new government were not entirely fulfilled: though plans for the military offensive went ahead, the authority of the Provisional Government was in no way enhanced by its socialist reinforcements. On the contrary, the fears of some Soviet leaders were proved justified: mass support swung increasingly away from them to the extreme Left.

For all that, the majority of the Soviet stood solidly behind the

Provisional Government. In the middle of June, at the First All-Russian Congress of Soviets, the Bolsheviks could muster no more than 105 delegates out of a total of 822; the Social Revolutionaries, with 285 delegates, were the largest contingent, followed by the Mensheviks with 248. Apart from the Bolsheviks, the opposition consisted of some 70 left-wing Mensheviks led by Martov and a few independent radicals. There were also close on 200 delegates belonging to small splinter groups or to bodies without precise political affiliation. The Congress expressed its confidence in the new government by 543 votes to 126 with 52 abstentions, thus giving the new ministers a clear mandate and endorsing the subsidiary role the Soviet had accepted on the formation of the coalition—henceforth it would no longer insist on keeping control of government activities. In practice, however, whenever a serious crisis arose, the Soviet could only re-establish calm by appealing to the masses over the head of the government, thus reluctantly reasserting its independence.

This is precisely what had happened during the 'April Days' when the Petrograd Soviet had taken it upon itself to ban all demonstrations for forty-eight hours, thus proving to all the world that when it came to the crunch the Soviet and not the government pulled the strings. Again, while the Mensheviks and the Social Revolutionaries dismissed the Bolshevik call of 'All power to the soviets' as utterly irresponsible, whenever the situation was too grave for subterfuge or procrastination, they too were forced to allow the Soviet to wield the kind of power that, by an excess of caution, it dared not wield in its own name.

The events of June and July 1917 were to provide these moderate socialists with their last taste of office, then as ever in the service of the Provisional Government. The popular agitation and ferment that erupted during these days reflected with particular sharpness the mood of frustration that had possessed the nation ever since the spring. Then, quite suddenly, these dark stirrings were galvanized into mass political protest.

In Petrograd, where the Bolsheviks were daily growing in strength and where the Anarchists, too, had begun to enjoy a large measure of popular support, Lenin's Party summoned all workers and soldiers to a mass street demonstration on June 9th. Plans for it had been laid well in advance, but so as not to give the Mensheviks time for a counter-demonstration, the Bolsheviks did not make their intentions public until the last moment. The official slogan given to the demonstrators was the tested Bolshevik cry of 'All power to the soviets!'. For the rest, the Bolshevik leaders wanted the demonstration to be a peaceful affair; when a small extremist faction suggested that 'the occupation of the Post and Telegraph office and of the Arsenal would not be amiss if a clash should occur', Lenin, supported by the Central Committee, quickly overruled them. Meanwhile several regiments had announced their decision to join the demonstration, and no one could tell whether or not they would be carrying arms.

This question was never answered, for the Soviet Executive Bureau banned all demonstrations for the next three days. The Bolsheviks, at first, declared that they would ignore the ban, but when the All-Russian Congress of Soviets endorsed the Bureau's decision, the Bolsheviks, after due deliberation, decided to bow to the will of the majority. All that remained to be done now was to convince the workers. To that end, scores of Soviet delegates went out into the barracks, the factories and the industrial quarters, haranguing the masses until late into the night. Their mission completed, they went back to report to the Soviet, and as fifteen of them succeeded one another on the platform the assembly was treated to a series of harrowing tales. In the workers' districts, the delegates had been received with catcalls; in the barracks, they had been insulted and accused of being mere hirelings of the capitalist bloodsuckers. The speakers concluded that only the Bolsheviks now enjoyed the support and confidence of the people.

In reality, even this last claim was exaggerated, for the Bolsheviks, too, were roundly condemned when they tried to explain to the workers why they had agreed to call off the demonstrations. Quite a few factories passed votes of censure on the Bolshevik leadership, and a number of incensed workers even tore up their Party cards in protest. For all that, the streets of Petrograd remained empty next day.

Not particularly worried by the attitude of the masses, the Menshevik and Social Revolutionary majority in the Soviet did not disguise their glee at the latest turn of events. Only the night before, they had justified their ban on all demonstrations by conjuring up the vague threat of a counter-revolutionary putsch. Now, they rounded not on the Right but on the Bolsheviks, whom Tseretelli described as evil plotters. The official Menshevik paper declared: 'It is high time to unmask the Leninists as criminals and traitors to the Revolution.' The Bolsheviks had obeyed the will of the Mensheviks, so clearly they must be much weaker than most people had imagined. The time had come to convince the masses of the marked superiority of the constructive and reasonable policies of the government, and at the same time to prove to the bourgeoisie, which for weeks had been terrified by the spectre of Bolshevism, that its lack of confidence in the Soviet majority was completely unfounded. And so the Soviet decided to call a mass demonstration of its own for Sunday, June 18th, at which the working class and the Petrograd garrison would be able to proclaim their enthusiasm for the coalition.

Up to the last moment, Mensheviks and Social Revolutionaries alike were convinced that this was precisely what was going to happen. On June 17th, during a meeting of the Soviet, Minister Tseretelli treated the Bolsheviks to the following homily: 'Now we shall have an honest review of the revolutionary forces. The procession will not bring out divided groups but will represent the Petrograd working class in its entirety; it will not take place against the will of the Soviet but at its invitation. Now we shall see if the majority of the workers is behind us or behind you. Today we are not discussing plots hatched in some back parlour, but a test in the plain light of day. Tomorrow we shall see … '

The results were to be judged by the demonstrators' banners and slogans. The Soviet Executive had given out the slogans 'Universal Peace', 'Immediate Convocation of a Constituent Assembly', 'Democratic Republic'. This choice had been quite simple—the slogans in no way offended Menshevik and Social Revolutionary susceptibilities and were yet designed to appeal to workers and soldiers with Bolshevik sympathies—after all, the Bolsheviks, too, were in favour of universal peace, had called for the convocation of a constituent assembly and a democratic republic. If therefore—as was only to be expected—the great mass of the demonstrators rallied behind the official slogans, the moderate socialists would have clear proof that they enjoyed the support of the proletariat.

On Sunday, June 18th, the people of Petrograd took to the streets in their thousands. Those who had feared that they would boycott a demonstration called by the Mensheviks were greatly relieved. Between 400,000 and 500,000 people came out and, to the further delight of the moderates, behaved with the utmost decorum and with quite unexpected restraint. The night before, when a few Soviet leaders had called on Anarchist headquarters in the industrial suburb of Vyborg to discover whether they intended to arm their supporters, they had received reassuring but somewhat evasive replies. Now the Anarchists had come out and, though armed, walked peacefully enough behind their black banners.

Leaders of the Menshevik and Social Revolutionary Parties, together with socialist members of the Provisional Government, surveyed the teeming masses from a special tribune erected on the Mars Field near the grave of the February martyrs. Imagine their surprise when the wretched workers, instead of shouting the expected slogans, passed by with large banners proclaiming such Bolshevik catchwords as 'Down with the Ten Minister-Capitalists!', 'Down with the Offensive!', 'All Power to the Soviets!', 'No Separate Peace with Germany nor Secret Treaties with the Anglo-French Capitalists!', 'The Right to Life is Higher than the Right of Private Property!', 'Peace to the Hearth, War to the Castle!'. From time to time a few stragglers would pass by with the official banners, but they were so many drops in a huge tidal wave. The men on the tribune looked utterly dumbfounded.

The test was conclusive. In his paper, *Novaia Zhizn*, Maxim Gorky, who was not yet one of Lenin's party, wrote that 'the Sunday demonstration revealed the complete triumph of Bolshevism among the Petrograd proletariat.' Many provincial towns witnessed similar demonstrations, and June 18th must indeed have been a black day for the Provisional Government and for its Menshevik and Social Revolutionary allies. For the Bolsheviks, on the other hand, it was a day of great triumph—intransigence, far from increasing their isolation, had driven the toiling masses into their arms.

The Bolshevik tide

However, not all Bolsheviks were equally enthusiastic about their great success; indeed, some barely succeeded in hiding their embarrassment. What were they to do with this victory? They realized that many of their comrades would now clamour for more radical tactics. And though the Party as a whole had never wavered in its opposition to the Provisional Government, a policy Lenin

had impressed upon it after his return in May, the leadership
had remained extremely cautious and circumspect. Thus they had
meekly accepted the Soviet ban on demonstrations in April, and
had played no part in organizing the subsequent protest movement
against Miliukov and the Provisional Government. True, once the
movement had started, the Bolshevik Party had been quick to jump
on the bandwagon; a small group had even called for the immediate
overthrow of the government. But Lenin and all those who
mattered in the leadership had resolutely attacked such 'leftist'
ideas. In *Pravda*, Lenin wrote that the motto 'Down with the
Provisional Government' was 'an empty phrase that leads to
attempts of an adventurous character'. And he added, 'Our Party
considers the decision ... of the Soviet of Workers' and Soldiers'
Deputies to have been completely correct and as such it must be
accepted without further discussion.'

In June, when the Bureau of the Soviet Executive once again
issued a ban on all demonstrations, Lenin's reaction was very
similar: at first he thought of ignoring the ban, but when the
Congress of Soviets intervened he quickly changed his mind;
despite strong opposition from his own rank and file, he, or rather
the Bolshevik Central Committee, simply published a protest and
left it at that.

This degree of prudence and moderation did not, of course,
reflect Lenin's long-term views; he simply felt that he must cut his
coat according to his cloth. To his mind, the February Revolution
had several achievements to its credit which he was determined to
preserve. Lenin declared on several occasions that though February
had not brought true democracy—far from it—it had nevertheless
turned Russia into 'the freest country in the world'. Thus while
Russia allowed all forms of anti-war agitation, the war had
stifled all democratic liberties elsewhere—even in 'free England'.

Lenin, so quick when it came to denouncing the failures and
obfuscations of liberalism and parliamentary democracy abroad,
was therefore inclined to be much more lenient towards the hybrid
regime born of the February Revolution. 'The transfer of all power
to the real majority of the people, that is to the workers and the
poor peasants, can nowhere be achieved as peacefully as it has been
in Russia,' he wrote. True, by speaking of the 'real majority' he left
himself a great deal of leeway, but his emphasis on peaceful
struggle was nevertheless an essential ingredient of all the strategic

conceptions he elaborated and propagated during the first months of the Revolution. In this, at least, he agreed with the right wing of his Party and with Kamenev in particular—the civil war, he affirmed during the April Conference, was one 'long, peaceful and patient' propaganda campaign.

It would be quite wrong to think that Lenin was simply mincing his words on this all-important question—his entire political career bore witness to his forthrightness, to his refusal to spread illusions. Later, when he judged that peaceful and moderate tactics were no longer appropriate, he made no secret of it, and proclaimed his change of heart in a host of articles and speeches. However, throughout the spring of 1917 he kept insisting on the need for temperance, rounding time and again on his more impatient followers. In April, he rejected the idea of overthrowing the Provisional Government in 'the ordinary [read violent] way', because in his opinion that government enjoyed the support of the Soviet and the 'blind trust of the masses'. In these circumstances it was idle to force the pace; life itself would open the workers' eyes soon enough. Lenin concluded that the 'transfer of power to the soviets ... involves considerable difficulties and calls for a particularly arduous preparation on the part of the forces of the proletariat'.

What, then, were the Bolsheviks to do? Their leader returned constantly to the same theme: they must 'explain the truth to the masses'. 'Here', he asserted, 'is the key to the political situation.' The masses must be freed of their mistakes by 'disintoxication' and by 'fraternal persuasion'. And all this had to be done 'without haste', without 'rushing the fences'. On hearing him, his comrades must often have asked themselves whether Lenin had not suddenly turned reformist. For who but a reformist would have said of the overthrow of capitalism that it must be achieved 'intelligently and gradually by relying only on the consciousness and organizational ability of the immense majority of workers and poor peasants'?

In June, in his speech to the First All-Russian Congress of Soviets, Lenin still insisted that Russia was the exceptional case in which a peaceful revolution was possible.

This possibility, however, was subject to one condition, which Lenin defined on many occasions: 'We must', he wrote in *Pravda* of April 14th, 1917, 'rely *solely* on education, but only so long as no one uses violence against the masses.' He used the term violence in its widest sense, applying it, for instance, to the suppression of democratic liberties. And more plainly still, he told the Bolshevik Conference in April, 'As long as the capitalists do not use violence against the soviets ... our Party will oppose violence and will try to root out the fatal error of the revolutionary chauvinists[1] by fraternal persuasion alone ... '

Not that he believed that the struggle for socialism must invariably be kept within the strict bounds of bourgeois legality or peaceful methods. Violence, albeit hidden beneath certain legal forms, lay at the very heart of bourgeois democracy, and the proletariat was bound to react in kind. However, the Russia of 1917 was an atypical case—the emergence of soviets had liberated the energy of the people, preparing them for the peaceful and gradual seizure of the reins of political power.

Here Lenin was guilty of a double error. First, he underestimated the revolutionary fervour, or at least the impatience, of the most radical sector of society, and also the power of resistance of the bourgeoisie; secondly, he underestimated the latter's ability to influence the Soviet. The masses were, in fact, far less patient than Lenin believed them to be, and the Soviet far too concerned with reassuring the bourgeoisie to pay much heed to the workers' demands. Lenin, who had managed to turn his Party to the Left, now found himself to the Right of the masses. Thus when most militant workers and soldiers were already thinking of overthrowing the Provisional Government, Lenin still deemed this objective impossible, or at least premature; when hundreds and thousands of workers and soldiers rose in protest not only against the 'minister-capitalists' but also against the majority in the Soviet, Lenin once again took a cautious line, wondering whether there might not be too wide a gulf between the revolutionary spirit of Petrograd and the more even temper of the provinces. What good would it do to press the revolutionary claims of workers of the capital when the countryside stood completely aloof?

Nor did the Bolsheviks restrict their relative moderation to the hectic days of April 1917; they reacted likewise even in moments of comparative calm. This is borne out particularly by the temperate tones in which they addressed the peasants. True, unlike the Socialist Party, the Bolsheviks did not call for the restoration of law

---

[1] Lenin was referring to those right-wing socialists who argued that the best way of defending the Russian Revolution was to bring the war against German autocracy to a victorious conclusion.

and order; indeed, they gave public support to the confiscation of big estates. Unlike all the rest, they felt that the peasantry was perfectly right to repair the worst injustices before a Constituent Assembly could be convoked. While freely admitting that the latter alone was fully entitled to take definite decisions about the fate of the land, they saw nothing wrong with the peasants seizing back some of the fields they had forfeited through debt. Any other solution would have struck them as fraudulent, and they objected particularly to the idea, so dear to Chernov, that special Conciliation Commissions consisting of landowners, agricultural workers and peasants might help to settle all differences in the most amicable of ways. As Lenin explained, the very idea of such conciliation, or even of a disinterested dialogue between landowners wielding considerable economic and social power and dispossessed *moujiks*, was quite ludicrous. However, this 'permissive' attitude often went hand in hand with an excess of caution: thus the Bolsheviks opposed individual seizure of land on the ground that only Peasants' Committees should have the right to confiscate estates. Moreover, they stated their strong objections to pillage and destruction. Lenin returned to this theme time and again, before audiences of all sorts. In an article entitled 'The Tasks of the Proletariat in Our Revolution', published in September 1917, at a time when the entire Russian countryside was seething with discontent, he called for the confiscation of all private lands, but added that it was important to 'insist on the need of *increased* food production ... to stress that damage to livestock, tools, machines, buildings, etc., is absolutely impermissible'. An address he delivered to soldiers stationed in Petrograd, which was reprinted by *Pravda*, was in much the same vein: 'The Peasant Committee must confiscate [the land] without delay, but must ensure the safety of all property, no matter of what kind, must prevent all forms of dilapidation, and must help to *increase* the grain output.'

At the April Conference of the Bolshevik Party, Lenin made this view part of an official resolution: 'The Party advises peasants to seize the land in an organized manner, not to damage property, and to increase agricultural production.' And when he addressed the peasants themselves, he kept repeating the same message. This was also the purpose of his 'Open Letter to the All-Russian Peasant Congress' published by *Soldatskaia Pravda* on May 11th, 1917. And he told the delegates to this Congress: 'We favour an immediate transfer of the land to the peasants, *provided*[1] it is done with the highest degree of organization possible. We are absolutely against anarchist seizures.'

And though the situation in the factories was less 'anarchic' than in the countryside, though acts of violence and destruction were much less common, Lenin nevertheless gave the same advice to the workers, urging them, too, to increase rather than impede production. In no way, therefore, did he encourage chaos with a view to creating a power vacuum—if anything encouraged chaos it was the refusal of the Provisional Government to make any real concessions to the demands of the people in general and the peasants in particular.[2]

In any case, during the first few months of the Revolution, Lenin and his Party preached gradual and peaceful progress towards the transfer of power to the soviets. Now this could clearly not take place while the Bolsheviks remained a minority in the soviets. In April 1917, he specifically repudiated the accusation that he 'wanted to seize power with the support of a minority'. 'We are still in the minority', he continued, 'and are fully aware of the need for capturing the majority.' And in May 1917 he repeated much the same thing: 'We do not want to "snatch" power, because revolutionary experience has taught us that the only solid power is that which enjoys the support of the majority of the population. To snatch power is sheer adventurism, and our Party will have no part of it.' Doubtless, what Lenin meant by a 'majority' was an open question—his entire career had shown that he was not encumbered with fine legal scruples. Thus he would sometimes speak of a *true* majority, by which he meant the majority of the workers and peasants. He was not at all concerned about the support of that tiny minority, the owning class, i.e. about parliamentary democracy in the Western manner. Here, his attitude was inconsistent, since he also attacked the Provisional Government for its failure to summon a Constituent Assembly. But what else was this institution, elected by universal suffrage and hence enjoying the support

[1] Our italics.
[2] It can, of course, be argued that by recommending the seizure of land, the Bolsheviks—despite their appeals for order and discipline—were, in fact, advocating a policy that was bound to lead to violence. But as Trotsky has shown in his *History of the Russian Revolution*, violence and destruction during the autumn of 1917 were least common in regions where the Bolshevik influence was strongest.

of all classes, if not an institution of a parliamentary type? In any case, Lenin poured scorn on the Menshevik thesis that only a parliamentary democracy dominated by the bourgeoisie could lead Russia to a better future—to his mind Russia was quite ready to become a 'democratic republic', or rather a 'Soviet republic'. It would be a 'democracy from below', and as such would have a truly democratic administration, and a workers' militia with social as well as military functions.[1]

Where exactly did Lenin want Russia to go then—towards a 'Soviet Republic' or a Constituent Assembly based on the bourgeois model? A policy embracing one of these alternatives while not completely rejecting the other must strike the modern reader as thoroughly confused. However, in the midst of a revolutionary situation these and similar quasi-doctrinal problems are generally ignored. Revolution calls for a great deal of improvisation, a large dose of empiricism. In this matter, as in so many others, the events themselves finally cut the Gordian knot.

Meanwhile, Bolshevik faith in a gradual and peaceful transition to soviet democracy was given a great boost by the Party's growing strength. The February Revolution had caught them in a difficult situation. At the beginning of war they had been driven underground, and the exile or deportation of most of their leaders had driven them further into a corner, so much so that after the Tsarist collapse they were able to send only a relatively small contingent of delegates to the Petrograd Soviet—only a single member of the Executive Committee was a Bolshevik.

The rapid expansion that followed—reflected by the enthusiastic welcome accorded to Lenin on his return—was not entirely unrelated to the reactions of the bourgeoisie, who after a virulent campaign against the soviets had begun to concentrate their fire on the Bolsheviks. In so doing they inevitably enhanced the latter's popularity with the urban working class. The Bolsheviks for their part, in rejecting any form of collaboration with the Provisional Government or alliances with other socialist parties, were counting on their rivals' mistakes; though they, too, had not the least idea

---

[1] According to Lenin, the militia, in which women would serve by the side of men, was expected to act as police and welfare officers. In particular it would make sure that 'every family has enough bread ... that no rich adult consumed milk while poor children have to go without; that the palaces and fine mansions deserted by the Tsar and the aristocracy did not remain unoccupied but served as shelter for the homeless and poor.'

of how quickly the masses would be won over. It happened so fast
not only because of the Bolshevik genius for organization, the
devotion of Party militants and the lucidity of the leaders, but in
equal measure because of the blunders of the Mensheviks and
Social Revolutionaries. The growing discontent of the people, who
as we saw vented their feelings in gigantic demonstrations, was
bound to profit the only Party that came out as a bitter opponent
of the authorities and whose political and economic programme
echoed the claims and aspirations of the most militant workers.
Reduced to the bare essentials and expressed in very simple
language, that programme was: Peace, Land and Bread! In
adopting it, the Bolsheviks took a great gamble, but could console
themselves with the fact that the moderate socialists with their
wishy-washy policies were increasingly out of touch with the
people, who sought neither the military glory nor the promise of a
Constituent Assembly that were constantly being proffered to them.

Demagogues to some, revolutionaries to others, the Bolsheviks
attracted a swelling stream of new recruits and sympathizers
throughout the spring of 1917. Thus, while the Bolshevik faction
of the Russian Social Democratic Party[1] counted no more than
23,600 members on the eve of the February Revolution, by the time
the National Party Conference was held in April, this figure had
risen to 79,000. At the Bolshevik Congress on August 8th, the
Party secretary revealed that the number of members had gone up
to 200,000,[2] including between 22,000 and 25,000 from the industrial centres and mines in the Urals, 50,000 from Moscow and
41,000 from the capital, where the Party had tripled its forces since
April. At the time, the Petrograd branch of the Menshevik Party
numbered a mere 8,000.

Though most of the new recruits had no previous political
affiliations, a number of Mensheviks had begun to join in the
general influx.

What was most striking in this process was its social composition: while the Social Revolutionaries and Mensheviks kept
attracting petit-bourgeois elements, the Bolshevik recruits were
almost exclusively of proletarian origin, and hence gave the Party
a unique aspect.

Its hold on the masses outside was no less spectacular. The

[1] See Prague Conference, p. 72.
[2] Other sources give different figures, varying from 180,000 to 240,000.

soviets of most industrial sectors in Petrograd were captured by the Bolsheviks in April, and informed observers tell us that by May the Party could count on the support of a third of all workers in Petrograd. In June, the workers' section of the Petrograd Soviet, voting on the Bolshevik resolution that all power be transferred to the Soviet, gave Lenin a resounding victory: the motion was carried by 173 votes to 144.

At the same time, the municipal elections in the industrial suburb of Vyborg gave the Bolsheviks 37 seats out of a total of 63. Moreover, at a conference of Petrograd factory delegates, Lenin's and Zinoviev's call for workers' control was supported by 335 delegates out of a total of 421. From that moment the Bolsheviks received constant support from these factory committees, which reflected the will of the proletarian masses much more clearly than the higher institutions of the Soviet. Finally, on June 20th, new elections to the Moscow Soviet gave the Bolsheviks a clear victory: they took 206 seats, the Mensheviks 172, and the Social Revolutionaries 110.

Nor were the Bolshevik successes limited to the working class; the soldiers, too, went over to them in increasing numbers. Thus, in June the Petrograd garrison which had supported the moderates only a few weeks earlier took up the Bolshevik demand for immediate transfer of power to the Soviet. Specific resolutions to that effect were passed by the 1st Machine-Gun Regiment, by the Pavlovsky Regiment, the Artillery School and many other units. This leftward swing was provoked as much by discontent with living conditions as by the growth of political awareness. The boredom of barrack life, the fear of being sent to the front, but also—and increasingly—the desire for peace, opposition to the impending offensive, and the lack of provisions—all these were grist to the Bolshevik mill.

The sailors in the Baltic Fleet, stationed on the small island of Kronstadt to the north of Petrograd, gave the Bolshevik success additional impetus. Kronstadt had first come into the political limelight in 1905, when its sailors had risen up against their officers—more arrogant, repressive and exclusive than even the army command. These sailors had also been in particularly close contact with workers in the naval arsenal, who were the most militant men in all Russia. Last but not least, most sailors were townsmen rather than peasants, and many of them were anxious to emulate the example set by the mutineers on the battleship *Potemkin*. All in all, Kronstadt was in a state of great ferment. This profited the Anarchists no less than the Bolsheviks, so much so that the extreme Left was able to play a considerable role during the events of the summer and autumn.

But to return to the capital: on June 3rd at the All-Russian Congress of Soviets, the Bundist[1] Lieber and the Menshevik Tseretelli opened the debates with eulogies of the Provisional Government; Tseretelli even saw fit to point out that the coalition, with all its faults, was the only political force capable of solving Russia's problems. When he had finished, Lenin rose to reply. 'The Minister of Posts and Telegraphs has declared that no political party in Russia is ready to assume full power. I say to him: Yes, that Party exists! No party can refuse this power, and our Party will not refuse it. It is ready at any moment to take over the government.' As might have been expected, this declaration produced various reactions in the assembly—while the benches on the extreme Left applauded, the rest received it with laughter and sneers. This Party, which had just declared its readiness to assume full power, accounted for a mere 10 per cent of the delegates to the Congress.[2] Lenin was nothing but an idle boaster. Unfortunately for these delegates, the masses were far less sceptical—as the 'July Days' were most convincingly to prove. Oddly enough, July would also bring Bolshevik progress to a halt, so that the moderate socialists and liberals could, for the last time, nurture the illusion that they held the destiny of Russia in their hands.

The July Days

At the beginning of July, tension increased further in Petrograd. Strikes spread and the entire Putilov works, with its 35,000 men, downed tools. When the workers' delegates and those from seventy-three other factories and labour organizations met on June 23rd, they no longer asked for control over production and wage increases, but demanded the immediate transfer of power to the Soviet. Tempers had begun to run high in the streets and barracks as well, so much so that the authorities decided to transfer

[1] The Bund, a Jewish workers' union, shared the moderate views of the Soviet majority.

[2] The delegates to the All-Russian Congress had been elected at a time when the Bolsheviks were much less popular than they were in June.

numerous units to the front—ostensibly in readiness for the impending offensive. This caused another furore. The 1st Machine-Gun Regiment, for example, which had been asked to supply thirty detachments, kept back all but ten; other units refused even that and passed motions of censure on the Provisional Government. The streets once again filled with excited crowds. On June 20th and 21st, war veterans, far more anxious to bring in their crops than to serve on the battlefield, demonstrated in force, demanding to be sent back home. In Kronstadt, the sailors reacted violently to government measures against the Anarchists. In Vyborg, too, the situation had become so explosive that the local Bolsheviks, taken by surprise, declared that they had constantly to stand by as 'firemen'.

In this they were merely carrying out Party orders—the Central Committee, having judged that the people of Petrograd were less anxious for action than they had been during the June Days and that the more militant section of the proletariat was out of step, had decided to preach calm. A member of the Vyborg Bolshevik Committee wrote in the Party paper on June 20th that 'we had to deploy a great deal of energy to calm the ruffled tempers.' A few days later, a conference of Bolshevik leaders, after discussing the situation concluded that it was far better to 'wait until the ruling parties have disgraced themselves completely, for then the game is ours'. At the Putilov works, the Bolshevik delegates asked the workers to 'restrain their legitimate indignation'. Lenin, for his part, writing in *Pravda* on June 21st, warned the workers and soldiers against 'the absurd hopes they might place in such isolated and disorganized actions'.

But tempers remained frayed and the capital continued in a state of acute crisis. The liberals did the rest—on July 2nd, five Cadet ministers resigned in protest against government concessions to the Ukrainians.[1] The road seemed clear at last for a truly socialist government, and hence for the transfer of power to the Soviet for which the most militant sections of the country had been clamouring all along. It looked as if a single shock, just one more tremor, would suffice to give power to the proletariat.

But during the morning of July 3rd the socialist ministers, after due deliberation, let it be known that the departure of their liberal colleagues in no way lessened the need for a coalition, and that the

[1] See Chapter 8.

former ministers would be given time to reconsider their position. Meanwhile, their departments would be run by senior officials. The soldiers, however, thought otherwise. The Machine-Gun Regiment, in particular, decided that the moment had come for a massive demonstration and asked other units to join them and to bring their arms along. At this point, the Bolshevik 'Military Organization' decided to intervene, and sent messengers to the machine-gunners asking them to drop their plan. When these men returned to Kshesinskaia's Palace they were convinced that they had made their point. 'It was an immense surprise to us,' one Bolshevik leader later reported, 'when at seven o'clock in the evening a horseman galloped up to inform us that ... the machine-gunners had again resolved to come out.' The situation was the more critical in that the rebels had made contact not only with a number of other regiments in Petrograd, but also with the sailors and workers of Kronstadt. There the Anarchists had managed to persuade tens of thousands of people that it was time to take action, while the Bolsheviks, following the orders of their leaders, were still calling for patience. But the Anarchists won the day, and even forced the Government Commissar to approve a march on Petrograd.

Meanwhile, workers from the industrial districts of Petrograd were making ready to invade the government quarters and, like the soldiers, they intended to bring their arms with them. (Several weeks earlier, the Soviet Executive had given official recognition to the workers' militia, and only the most naive delegates could have believed that the militia would keep their rifles strictly to themselves.)[1] Moreover, on July 3rd the soldiers handed the workers a number of armoured cars, which made their first appearance in the city centre during the late afternoon. The July Days had begun.

Earlier in the afternoon, the Soviet Executive Committee had decided once again to ban all demonstrations. But who would communicate their decision to the people? Neither the Mensheviks nor the Social Revolutionaries were anxious to go on so delicate a mission, and no Bolsheviks were on hand this time. The Soviet was completely paralysed, and remained so for the next twenty-four hours. As for the Bolsheviks, they had problems of their own, the

[1] By decision of the Executive Committee only 10 per cent of the workers could be armed.

more so as Lenin, who was not in good health, had left Petrograd
a few days earlier and was not expected back until next day. Those
who had stayed behind spent the entire evening and part of the
night in feverish discussions. Ought they to follow the recom-
mendation of their own military organization and keep away from
the demonstrations? At about 7 p.m. Kamenev, addressing a
meeting of the workers' section of the Petrograd Soviet, told them,
'We did not call the demonstration, but the masses themselves
have come into the street, and once they have done so our place is
among them. Our present task is to give the movement an
organized character.' He accordingly proposed the election of a
commission of twenty-five, including representatives from all
parties prepared to lead and organize the demonstration. The
Mensheviks and Social Revolutionaries, now in the minority, left
the hall.

Then Kamenev was attacked by the Bolshevik leaders. One of
them, Tomsky, who was later to play an important part in organizing the Soviet trade unions, went so far as to declare that 'the
regiments that have come out have acted in an uncomradely
fashion', and he proposed that the Central Committee issue an
appeal which, while not explicitly denouncing the demonstrators,
called their action inopportune. During the afternoon, this view
received the support of the majority of party leaders, and an appeal
to the workers was drafted. *Pravda* published it in its edition of
July 4th.

At about 8 p.m., Kshesinskaia's Palace was surrounded by
soldiers, who booed loudly when the Bolshevik leaders, addressing
them from the balcony, urged them to go home. Reports had also
reached the palace that workers and soldiers, defying the ban of
the Soviet Executive and the advice of the Bolshevik Party, were
massing in other parts of the city. In these circumstances the
members of the Petrograd committee had no alternative but to
drop their fruitless attempts to restrain the masses and to fall in
with Kamenev's suggestion instead. Attempts to redraft the *Pravda*
article came too late—next morning the official organ of the Bolshevik Party appeared with a large blank space—proof positive of
Bolshevik vacillation. And so, during a magnificent summer's day
followed by a clear northern night, the capital was turned into a
bastion of Revolution. The Cadet Nabokov had this to say about
the actors in this drama: 'The same insane, dumb, bestial faces

which we all remember from the February Days.' By 9 p.m.
seven regiments had drawn up before the Tauride Palace. Meetings
were improvised, and up rose the customary cries of 'Down with
the capitalist ministers!', 'Down with the Provisional Government!', 'Down with the offensive!' But graver incidents were
reported as well, and shots rang out as workers clashed with
counter-demonstrators. These exchanges continued well into the
night, while workers continued to pour into the city. At 4 a.m.,
some thirty thousand men from the Putilov works arrived at the
Tauride Palace and loudly joined in the demand that the Executive
Committee assume full power. At about the same hour, twenty
thousand sailors and workers in Kronstadt prepared to sail up the
Neva to the capital.

Inside the Tauride Palace, the Central Executive Committee of
the Soviet continued its deliberations for most of the night. A few
hours earlier, the Menshevik and Social Revolutionary deputies
had sent a telegram to the 5th Army calling for reinforcements.
How untenable their position had become may be gathered from
the subsequent declaration by the Menshevik Voitinsky: 'On the
first day of the demonstration', he explained, 'we had at our disposal no more than a hundred men—we had no other forces.' And
so they were reduced to firing verbal broadsides. At 1 a.m.
President Chkheidze rose, while everyone held his breath to hear
what great measures the platform had at last dreamed up. 'This is
an exceptionally grave situation,' he began. 'The Presidium has
taken an exceptional decision. We declare that it must be binding
on everyone. All those present must undertake to carry it out.
Those who refuse this obligation should leave the hall at once.' No
Bolsheviks were present, but all the same some of the more radical
deputies rose and left the meeting, Trotsky among them. Many
others protested loudly against Chkheidze's order. A vote was
taken, and while the President received the necessary majority the
dissenters refused to give the required undertaking, and no one
insisted that they should. The meeting went on to condemn the
demonstration and resolved to send delegates to apprise the men in
the barracks and factories of the 'will of the Soviet'. The effects of
this kind of gesture, which had become traditional by then, were
imperceptible. A few hours later the demonstrations started all
over again, and with greater force and violence.

This time they enjoyed the official support of the Bolsheviks but, for all that, retained the spontaneous character of the previous day—no one came forward to lead the masses towards a specified goal. The twenty thousand sailors and workers of Kronstadt hoped to find such leadership in Kshesinskaia's Palace, where they went on the morning of July 4th, immediately after landing in Petrograd. Lenin, who had cut short his leave of absence, greeted them with obvious embarrassment. He mentioned his poor state of health and apologized for having to be so brief. For the rest he was extremely vague, contenting himself with conveying to the demonstrators the blessings of his party and expressing the conviction that power would be bound to pass into the hands of the Soviet. Finally, he adjured them to remain 'calm, firm and vigilant'. This piece of advice left the demonstrators no wiser than they were before.

As on the 3rd, it was on the Tauride Palace that the demonstrators now converged—all factory workers in the industrial suburbs were on strike and several hundreds of thousands had by now flocked into the city centre. Miliukov called it 'a desperate situation'. Having abandoned the Mariinsky Palace for the safety of General Staff Headquarters, the Provisional Government was completely cut off from the rest of the country—rumour had it that the Minister of Foreign Affairs and another leading personage had taken to their heels. And despite all this, and though the forces of law and order—made up essentially of a few Cossack companies— were unable to keep the situation under any kind of control, the demonstrators failed to press their advantage home—they did not seize a single public building or strategic centre.

What bloody incidents did occur were as sporadic as the demonstrations themselves: the Kronstadt sailors hit back when snipers fired at them from the rooftops, and blood flowed when the demonstrators suddenly came face to face with a Cossack detachment, though most of the victims were innocent bystanders.

During the whole afternoon, the crowds kept pouring into Petrograd, simply to show their numerical strength and to proclaim their desire for change by way of banners and slogans. Towards 5 p.m. the sailors, worn out by debates and skirmishes, moved to the Tauride Palace and demanded a meeting with the Soviet leaders. Though it had rained in the afternoon the atmosphere had remained stifling, and the demonstrators had an easy task of climbing in through the open windows. When they threatened to enter the chamber, Chernov, the Minister of Agriculture, came out to pacify them. He was greeted with catcalls and threats. Someone shouted, 'Search him! See whether he is armed!'

'In that case I won't speak,' declared Chernov. The men desisted, and he was allowed to deliver a brief address which, far from calming the crowd, merely incensed them further. Then there were scuffles, of which various witnesses have given us jumbled accounts. In any case, Chernov ended up in a car and was declared under arrest as a hostage. No one knew who precisely had seized the Minister, but the atmosphere was extremely ominous. Trotsky blamed the incident on *agents provocateurs*, whose presence during those two days was noted by many observers.

A group of workers immediately rushed off to report the incident to the Central Executive Committee. 'Comrades,' cried one of them, 'the crowd is about to hack Comrade Chernov to pieces.' In the ensuing din, Chkheidze asked Kamenev, Martov, Lunacharsky —later Commissar of Education in the Bolshevik Government— and Trotsky to go to the help of the unfortunate minister. Since Trotsky was highly respected among the sailors, it was he who addressed the vast crowd outside. He asked the sailors not to hurt their cause by petty acts of violence against unimportant individuals. 'Let those who are for violence raise their hands!' he concluded. No one did, and Chernov was released.

A little later, Raskolnikov, the Bolshevik leader of Kronstadt, asked the sailors to return to their base now that they had demonstrated their will to the Soviet. Most of them did as they were told, but two or three thousand stayed behind and it was they who, late that day, took the Fortress of Peter and Paul without firing a shot. Next morning they were dislodged again—just as peacefully.

Hardly had the sailors withdrawn from the Tauride Palace when workers from the Putilov factory came to take their place in the square outside—thirty thousand strong. They were joined soon afterwards by the 176th Reserve Regiment from Tsarskoe Selo, the Tsar's former summer residence on the outskirts of Petrograd. These men were known for their Bolshevik sympathies and had hastened to the defence of the Revolution. But such was the confusion in the capital that the soldiers had only just put down their packs and stacked their rifles when the Menshevik Dan approached one of their officers and asked him to organize the protection of the Central Executive Committee. Sentries were immediately posted at various points of the palace. In short, a leader of the anti-

Bolshevik majority could do no better than call upon a Bolshevik regiment to restore order, while that regiment, which had come all the way from Tsarskoe Selo to Petrograd to demonstrate in favour of the Bolsheviks, saw fit to take orders from a completely helpless adversary.

In the evening, the streets emptied and the centre of interest shifted from the square to the chamber in which the Central Executive Committee of the Soviet was forced to interrupt its weighty deliberations to receive a host of workers' delegations. Chief among these were some ninety workers representing fifty-four factories in the Petersburg district. As five of the men mounted the rostrum, they treated the Executive to a series of speeches that were unusually firm and to the point. 'We demand that the power pass to the Soviet!'; 'We have confidence in the Soviet but not in those in whom the Soviet has confidence!'; 'We demand the immediate confiscation of the land and control over industry!'; 'We are not prepared to wait for the convocation of a Constituent Assembly!' Bolshevik propaganda had clearly made its mark.

When the workers had left, the Central Executive Committee returned to its deliberations and resolved to defer any decision on a possible government reshuffle for a fortnight. In other words, the Executive was trying to gain time while avoiding a head-on collision with the incensed workers and sailors. To proclaim their continued faith in the coalition at this point would have amounted to clear provocation, and though a rainstorm in the late afternoon had helped to scatter the crowds, the authorities were as impotent as ever: a handful of determined soldiers and workers could easily have seized power that day—at least provisionally.

The Mensheviks and the Social Revolutionaries were given one further proof, if such proof was still needed, of the seriousness of their predicament. While they were still in session in the Tauride Palace, a large group of Putilov workers, representing the thirty thousand men outside, burst noisily into the hall. One of them, whom Sukhanov has called 'a classic *sans-culotte*, in a cap and a short blue blouse without a belt' leapt on the speaker's platform, shaking with excitement and anger.

'Comrades,' he cried, 'how long must we workers put up with this treachery? All of you here are debating and making deals with the bourgeoisie and the landlords ... You are simply betraying the working class. Well then, let me tell you that the working class

won't put up with it. There are thirty thousand workers all told
here from the Putilov works. We are going to have our way. All
power to the soviets! We have a firm grip on our rifles! Your
Kerenskys and Tseretellis are not going to pull the wool over our
eyes!'

Chkheidze, who presided over the session, showed complete self-
control. He pushed a note into the quivering hands of the speaker
—the text of a resolution the Central Executive Committee had
just adopted. 'I ask you, comrade, take this, read it. It tells you
what you and your Putilov comrades should do. Please read it and
don't interrupt our deliberations.'

The man, dumbfounded, left the platform and walked out of the
hall, followed by the other Putilov men. The Soviet then returned
to its labours, completely ignorant of what was happening in the
town. At one point, the corridors again resounded with the tramp-
ing of heavy boots, and the deputies' faces turned sombre. Was the
mob returning to the charge? And would they be able to soothe
them again?

Suddenly Dan was standing on the platform and his expression
was one of great glee. 'Comrades,' he called, 'be calm! There is no
danger! Loyal regiments have arrived to defend the Central Executive Committee.' At once, most of the deputies were on their feet,
shaking their fists at the benches of the extreme Left. Then a band
struck up the Marseillaise and armed soldiers burst into the
chamber. It was a 'loyal' battalion of the Izmailovsky Regiment.
The joy of the deputies was unbounded.

Martov hissed to his neighbour, 'A classic scene of the beginning
of counter-revolution ... '

In fact, it was far more than a beginning. With the workers back
in their homes, the soldiers back in their barracks, and most of the
sailors back in their Kronstadt base, the government now felt free
to order the immediate arrest of Bolshevik militants. The printing
works and offices of *Pravda* were sacked. Rumour had it that Lenin
had been unmasked as a German spy, and when this reached, or
rather was communicated to, the undecided regiments of the
garrison, they immediately rallied to the defence of the government. The progress of the popular offensive was interrupted and
a new phase in the history of the Russian Revolution had begun.
Though it was brief, it was nevertheless decisive: the Right came
out of hiding and went into attack.

7

The Right Attacks

KERENSKY did not return to Petrograd until late on July 6th, by which time the Right had launched its offensive. On July 5th and 6th, hundreds of Bolsheviks were arrested—Party members as well as sympathizers. Militant workers were beaten up in the streets, and though only one of them was shot 'officially'—he had been caught distributing party literature—there were numerous lynchings. The men responsible for these were chiefly cadet officers, giving vent to their pent-up hatred of the Revolution, and plain thugs, former members of the Black Hundreds or of the Tsarist police. Meanwhile, the government itself saw to the disarming of the workers' militia in the industrial districts. When Martov protested to the Soviet Executive Committee, his fellow Menshevik Tseretelli, the Minister of the Interior, told him quite bluntly that 'irresponsible groups had better hold their tongues now'.

Kerensky, for his part, thought that the new measures, though vigorous, were not nearly as systematic as they could have been, and called for an outright ban of the Bolshevik Party. Only the night before, one of the leaders of the Soviet Executive—the Bundist Lieber—had promised Kamenev that if the Bolsheviks induced the Kronstadt sailors to return to their base, the government would take no steps against the Party and would release the arrested workers. When Kamenev protested that this promise had been broken, Lieber, speaking for the Executive Committee, blandly informed him that the 'correlation of forces has now changed'.

For all that, most Social Revolutionaries and Mensheviks refused to support the ban of the Bolshevik Party. They realized vaguely that though the reaction was chiefly directed against Lenin and his supporters it might easily turn against the entire Left and threaten the very survival of the Soviet. It was this fear—and the future would show how well-founded it was—that persuaded them to content themselves with the declaration that the Party leaders, beginning with Lenin and Zinoviev, would be brought to trial, albeit on grounds that did not stand up to even the most uncritical examination: the Bolshevik leaders were said to have organized an insurrection against the Provisional Government on July 3rd and 4th, and Lenin and his chief supporters were further accused of being German agents.

The first charge, though not supported by the slightest evidence, was at least plausible. In fact there were only two explanations of why hundreds of thousands of workers and soldiers should have come out into the street, ignoring the orders of the Soviet and proclaiming their opposition to the Coalition Government: either the Mensheviks and Social Revolutionaries had become so unpopular that the masses no longer paid the least heed to them, or discontent had been whipped up by destructive Bolshevik conspirators. It is not at all astonishing that the Government should have plumped for the second alternative; to have adopted the first would have forced them to make a radical revision of their entire policy, and they were less than ever disposed to do this at a time when the Bolshevik star was apparently in the descendant.

However, as we saw, the Bolsheviks had if anything been trying to restrain the masses all along, and so it was exceedingly difficult to indict them on that particular count. Could they be blamed for the occupation of the fortress of Peter and Paul? Like all other actions in July it had been completely spontaneous and, what is more, had not caused blood to be shed. The refusal to heed the Soviet ban on all demonstrations? The Bolsheviks had firmly opposed it. There remained only the Bolshevik boast to the All-Russian Congress of Soviets in June that their Party was ready to assume power. But would true 'conspirators' have openly confessed to the existence of a plot? Did not all the evidence rather point to the fact that the events of July 3rd and 4th had been quite chaotic and hence unplanned? Nothing at all had been done to give the demonstrations a clear objective or to exploit the utter and obvious impotence of the authorities. On one occasion at least the intervention of Trotsky—who was closely associated with Lenin and was on the point of joining the Bolshevik Party—had saved Minister Chernov from the fury of the crowd. And it was an established fact that the most prominent Bolshevik leaders, including Lenin, Kamenev, Zinoviev and Raskolnikov, had issued appeals for calm throughout these tumultuous days. The charge of conspiracy was therefore merely proof of the utter disarray of the Mensheviks and the Social Revolutionaries. The second charge—that Lenin was a German spy—was obviously false and even more ridiculous than the other allegation.

The anti-Bolshevik attack

It was not the first time this slander had been uttered. Soon after Lenin's return, a number of bourgeois journals had raised the same cry, whereupon hostile crowds had assembled outside Kshesinskaia's Palace shouting, 'Down with Lenin!' and 'Lenin to Germany!' Krupskaia describes in her memoirs how one day she overheard two gossiping women say to each other, 'What are we to do with this Lenin from Germany?' 'Drown him in a well, that's what.' Miliukov, less prone to take such drastic solutions, told the British Ambassador that the army was ready to arrest Lenin and that the government was waiting for the 'psychological moment'. But his hands were tied: the official paper of the Petrograd Soviet, and hence of the Menshevik and Social Revolutionary majority, kept protesting loudly at what it called 'this campaign against a man who has devoted his entire life to the service of the working class'.

After the 'July Days', however, the psychological moment seemed to have come at last, or rather a number of ministers felt that the very survival of the Provisional Government depended on a frontal attack against Lenin's Party by fair means or foul. This seemed to them the more essential as the July demonstrations had coincided with military failure. By resuscitating the slander that Lenin was a German spy they hoped to kill two birds with one stone: to incite the people of Petrograd against the Bolsheviks at a time when their supporters were in control of the streets, and to blame the military defeat not on the incompetence of the generals and ministers but on the criminal activities of the Bolshevik traitors. This is precisely what Prince Lvov meant when he said, 'It is my firm opinion that our deep breach on the Lenin front has incomparably greater importance for Russia than the breach made by the Germans of the south-western front.' And when Kerensky, then away at the front, learned of the desperate situation of the Provisional Government, he ordered the Prince to 'speed the publication of all the information [on Lenin's alleged spy activities] in your possession'.

Towards the end of May the ministers had been made privy to

the sensational 'revelations' communicated to the General Staff by one Ermolenko, a Tsarist police spy among Russian prisoners-of-war and one who, by his own admission, had taken service with the Germans—for patriotic reasons, of course. According to this great patriot, the German military authorities had informed him that Lenin would be allowed to return to Russia on condition that he acted as their agent. Ermolenko was unable to provide the least shred of evidence to corroborate his slander—not surprisingly when we consider how unlikely it was that the German Intelligence Service should have imparted to one of their least important minions the name of one who must have been among their most illustrious recruits. The Provisional Government had yet another piece of 'evidence': the testimony of the merchant Z. Burstein who, according to Prince Turkestanov, the head of the Intelligence Service of the Russian General Staff, was an unscrupulous villain, not deserving of the slightest confidence. For all that, the government saw fit to give credence to this man's testimony that Lenin had received large sums of money from Germany through Polish revolutionaries. An enquiry by the Russian authorities simply revealed that one of these revolutionaries had been mixed up in drug smuggling, but no proof was advanced to establish a direct or indirect link between the Bolsheviks and him.

All socialist leaders, no matter of what persuasion, and all working-class militants of any importance rejected Burstein's accusation out of hand. The very idea of libelling Lenin—let alone his entire Party—in this way was an insult to common sense. True, the circumstances of his return to Russia could be counted against him, but one could hardly imagine a seasoned spy going out of his way to attract public attention in the way he had done. For the rest, although he was an advocate of 'revolutionary defeatism' and, as such, opposed to the war against Germany, Lenin had never disguised his hostility to the German war machine in general and the Kaiser in particular. Opposing, as we saw, the idea of a separate peace with Germany, he had argued that Wilhelm II was nothing but 'a crowned bandit meriting death no less than Nicholas II', that German capitalists were 'as piratical as Russian, English, French and other capitalists'; and that the war was being 'waged by the German bourgeoisie no less than by the Anglo-French bourgeoisie for the sole purpose of swallowing up other countries ... ' Lenin moreover had opposed Bolshevik participation in the Stockholm Conference[1] on the grounds that it would chiefly serve the interests of Germany, exhausted by the war and anxious to call a truce that would respect her territorial conquests.

On the evening of July 4th, when the leaders of the Soviet learned that the government was preparing to publish the 'evidence' against Lenin, they asked the press not to lend itself to this shabby manoeuvre. One journalist, Alexinsky, a former member of the Bolshevik Party, decided to ignore them. Alexinsky had spent the years 1914–17 in Paris, where he had acquired so bad a reputation that on his return to Russia the Soviet had slammed the door in his face. On July 5th the popular right-wing journal he edited announced that it had clear proof of Lenin's treachery. That same day, acting on his own responsibility—his Social Revolutionary and Menshevik colleagues wanted no part of it—the Minister of Justice decided to order the arrest of Lenin and other Bolshevik leaders. These, as we saw, had already been decried as German spies to the troops, a calumny that had helped to bring the mutinous regiments back 'into line'.

The readiness with which the soldiers swallowed this slander may strike the reader as somewhat surprising. However, there is a general tendency to see a 'foreign hand' behind every social protest movement. Such over-simplified 'explanations' have the great advantage of saving one the bother of prolonged and probing analyses. What is far more surprising is that in his subsequent writings on the Russian Revolution Kerensky should still have repeated the same slander, without advancing any semblance of proof—thus demonstrating that a bad politician is not necessarily a good historian.

The Petrograd Soviet tried first of all to give the lie to the crudest aspects of this anti-Leninist campaign. They appointed an Inquiry Commission charged with discovering the origins of the calumny. But when the government—against the advice of most socialist members and despite strong protests by the bourgeois ministers Tereshchenko and Nekrassov—decided to press charges against the Bolshevik leaders, the Soviet meekly yielded. The charges were the more ridiculous in that Trotsky was included in

[1] The Stockholm Conference was convened in the summer of 1917 by Scandinavian and moderate Russian socialists. It aimed to bring together socialist parties in all the belligerent countries for the purpose of agreeing on a negotiated peace. However, because of opposition on the part of the Western governments the Conference never took place.

them. Trotsky, who had crossed from America to Russia by ship, was said to have stopped over in Germany after collecting ten thousand dollars from pro-German Americans. In repudiating this calumny, Trotsky wrote in Gorky's paper:

> I feel that it is pertinent to state ... that in my entire life I have not only never had at my disposal, at one time, ten thousand dollars, but never even a tenth of that sum. Such a confession, I am afraid, may ruin my reputation among the Cadet public more completely than all the insinuations of M. Miliukov, but I have long since become reconciled to the thought of living without the approval of liberal bourgeois circles.[1]

At the end of July, Trotsky was arrested by the Provisional Government, soon after he had officially entered the Bolshevik ranks—though he had bitterly attacked the latter before the war, he had never joined the Mensheviks. The events of 1917 had helped to overcome what reservations he still had, so much so that when the government clamped down on the Bolsheviks he immediately persuaded the 'Mezhrayontsi', an inter-district organization of which he was a leading member, to make common cause with Lenin's party. The new converts included such leading revolutionary figures as Uritzky, Joffé, Lunacharsky and a host of others who were to achieve prominence in the October Revolution. Henceforth the Bolsheviks could call on the genius of Lenin as well as on the exceptional organizational gifts and the persuasive rhetoric of Trotsky, who became the Party's most brilliant orator.

Meanwhile, Lenin decided to go back into hiding. His arrest was expected on July 7th. That day he waited several hours for the Soviet Inquiry Commission, but when no one arrived the Bolshevik leader gathered that nothing would come of this investigation. What was he to do now? He thought first of all of surrendering to the police, but many of his friends, including Stalin, did their utmost to dissuade him, and he had to admit that his judges were unlikely to dispense impartial justice. 'They are getting ready to shoot us all,' he told Trotsky, and decided to go underground forthwith. For a few weeks he remained on the outskirts of Petro-

---

[1] The charge against Trotsky was the more ludicrous in that a German military tribunal, judging him in his absence in 1915, had sentenced him to several months' imprisonment for revolutionary activities.

grad; then disguised as a railway-driver he left for nearby Finland, where he stayed until the October uprising, writing his chief theoretical work, the *State and Revolution*, and directing his Party from abroad.

The legal inquiry into Lenin's alleged dealings with Germany made no progress whatsoever. Now that the 'Lenin front had been breached' and the authority of the Provisional Government was re-established, the whole slander was conveniently allowed to fall into oblivion. History was to show how insubstantial the case against Lenin really was: after the Second World War, when the official German archives delivered up their secrets, it appeared that though Germany had diverted large funds to Russian and Ukrainian revolutionaries of various persuasions, no one had been asked to render any specified counter services—their general pacifist stand was apparently sufficient reward for the generous donors. The total funds involved exceeded twenty million gold marks. While some of the money may well have found its way to some Bolsheviks, it would appear that none of the Bolshevik leaders, either of major or minor importance, were in any way involved in these arrangements; indeed no document suggests that they even heard of them.[1] The Bolsheviks, moreover, proved exceedingly cautious when offers of financial aid were made to them from other sources. For example, the official minutes of the meetings of the Central Committee show that at the beginning of October 1917 they refused a subsidy offered by a Swiss socialist on the grounds that it was 'impossible to check the real source of these funds'. What sums of money the Bolsheviks did have at their disposal were, in any case, slender in the extreme. Three weeks before the October insurrection, when the Central Committee received a demand from the Petrograd Regional Committee for some 2,500 roubles, the meeting 'approved Comrade Sverdlov's proposal to transfer 1,000 roubles, adding that it would be highly desirable if this sum were reimbursed'.

Lenin once again in exile, several of their leaders imprisoned, their press persecuted,[2] their Party driven underground, the Bolsheviks, after a period of continuous progress now found themselves

[1] See Z. A. B. Zeman, *Germany and the Revolution in Russia (1915–1918). Documents from the Archives of the German Foreign Ministry.*

[2] Once *Pravda* had been banned the Bolsheviks published another official paper, and when this was banned in turn they simply changed its name and thus gained a further breathing space.

7

at bay. True, they had lost very few members, but many of their organizations were in complete disarray—according to the evidence of a member of the Petrograd Bolshevik Committee, official Party activities had ground to a complete halt. Things were no better in Moscow either—a local leader declared that 'panic was rife even among certain members of the Committee'.

The Shift to the Right

In fact, the Bolshevik disarray reflected a much wider process: the failure of July had caused a general swing to the Right and a revival of the conservative forces. While the Left became less pressing, and the Centre more hesitant, the Right, apparently emerging from a long sleep and anxious to demonstrate that it was still a force in the land, made a supreme effort to seize the reins of power back into its own hands. The masses themselves who, until July, had been urging the Bolsheviks forward, had suddenly become discouraged and demoralized. Anti-Bolshevism was the order of the day. Party speakers trying to rally the masses were beaten up, and few Bolshevik meetings now attracted audiences of more than two to three hundred people. Hostility was most pronounced in the army, and especially in those regiments which had been the most active during the July disturbances. Profiting from this climate of opinion, the conservatives, not content with attacks on the Bolsheviks, sacked the Menshevik Party Headquarters in Petrograd and committed a host of similar outrages.

The offensive of the Right made itself felt at every level of social and political life. At the top it was reflected in the behaviour of Kerensky, who suddenly revealed himself in both manner and speech as an arch-reactionary. As the French journalist, Claude Anet, put it, 'He sits in the imperial box, he lives in the Winter Palace or at Tsarskoe Selo. He sleeps in the bed of Russian emperors. A little too much vanity and vanity a little too conspicuous; that is shocking a country which is the simplest in the world.' Addressing delegates to the Moscow State Conference,[1] Kerensky invited them to display a firm 'will to discipline, self-sacrifice and labour'. Speaking on another occasion, he contended that the officers had suffered 'intolerable outrages from the mass of the soldiers'. In his private talks with the British Ambassador, Sir George Buchanan, Kerensky promised that the 'Soviet will die a

[1] See pp. 200 f.

natural death' and that he, for his part, would do his utmost to hasten its demise. From being the idol of moderate socialists and petit-bourgeois democrats, Kerensky had suddenly become the great white hope of the Right. A leading Petrograd Cadet saw fit to proclaim that 'his name will be written in golden letters on the tablets of history.' And Rodzianko, not to be outshone, declaimed that 'this young man ... is reborn each day with redoubled strength for creative labour and the welfare of the fatherland.' Even Nicholas II, with less rancour than political lucidity, looked upon Kerensky with favour: 'This man is definitely in the right place ... the more power he wields the better,' the ex-sovereign confided to his diary. Alas, Kerensky's sudden popularity with the conservatives evaporated as quickly as it had begun once the failure of the military offensive revealed the extreme weakness of his policies.

Kerensky's personal views left a profound impression on the government of which he became the titular head in July. On the 8th of that month Prince Lvov, following the Cadets, had tendered his resignation, and on the 24th, after lengthy negotiations in which the 'Star Chamber' played an important part, a new cabinet was sworn in. The Soviet Executive Committee, consulted afterwards, approved it by 147 votes to 46 with 42 abstentions.

Kerensky, as the new Prime Minister, also retained the Ministry of War, and Tereshchenko remained Minister of Foreign Affairs. The 'Second Coalition', unlike the first, could boast a majority of 'moderate' socialist ministers, most of them to the Right of their respective parties. As for its real political weight, Miliukov was right to say that it lay with 'the most convinced champions of bourgeois democracy'. Thus the new government included four Cadets, who while holding portfolios of secondary importance were nevertheless able to exert a disproportionately great influence and pressure on the government, especially as the latter had seen fit to dispense with any declaration of policy. After Lvov's resignation, Kerensky, as head of a temporary cabinet, showed that he intended to take full advantage of the setback the Left had suffered in July by sending some ninety thousand reluctant soldiers to the front. He also planned to evacuate a whole series of factories to the countryside. Even more significant—because this measure was long to remain a bone of contention between the Right and the Left—he re-introduced the death penalty for 'certain major crimes committed by men on military duty'. He also ordered the disarming of the militia, and passed a series of measures designed to improve labour discipline among railway workers.

The return of Cadet representatives into the government greatly strengthened his hand. One of the first declarations by the Minister of Finances was a promise to lower direct, and to increase indirect, taxation. Peshekhonov, the Minister of Food, had this to say: 'The more forces we attract from the Right, the fewer will remain of those who wish to attack the government.' The future was to prove the vanity of all such tactical subtleties.

The bourgeoisie was in fact increasingly determined not only to have final say over government policy but also to change the leading actors. The demands by members of the Old Duma, who despite the ban by the Provisional Government continued to meet in 'private conferences', were characteristic of this new mood. Thus a member of this institution declared quite openly, 'It is only thanks to the Duma that the Revolution took place; it is the greater pity that in these historic and tragic hours a handful of demented fanatics, adventurers and traitors, parading as the Executive Committee of the Soviet, should have usurped the Revolution.' And he concluded his somewhat questionable interpretation of the February events with this strange argument: 'We demand that the government present itself before us and accept what decisions we make on its conduct.' A few weeks later, at the Moscow State Conference,[1] Rodzianko, echoing these remarks, declared that the Duma was 'the only legal body representative of all the people of Russia'. At the same time business circles, in particular, launched a campaign for what they called a 'strong government'. This was a title to which the team round Kerensky could lay less and less claim. The Congress of Commerce and Industry which met in the month of August did not mince its words on this subject. 'The Provisional Government', it declared, 'has only the shadow of power ... At present, a gang of political charlatans is in control.'

In short, the conservatives were becoming more and more pressing, while the Provisional Government became more and more conservative. The Soviet, for its part, stayed meekly in the wings. After the failure of the July demonstrations, it had joined in the chorus about the Bolshevik plot, and Tseretelli, who was both Minister of the Interior and the extremely influential leader of the Soviet majority, had taken the responsibility for measures against

[1] See pp. 202 f.

the extreme Left. The rest of the Executive Committee had fallen into step by deciding that 'all persons inculpated by the legal authorities are expelled from the Executive Committee [of the Soviet] until such time as the Tribunal makes its decisions known.' The Mensheviks and the Social Revolutionaries, moreover, insisted that the Bolsheviks issue an 'immediate, categorical and clear repudiation' of their leaders. This demand was rejected by the entire Leninist faction of the Soviet, who saw it as a barely disguised attempt to divide their Party. But once again it revealed the capriciousness of its authors.

And this time they had good reason to hold back. Speaking at the end of July, the Menshevik Dan, while fulminating against the extreme Left, also admitted that the country was threatened by a 'military dictatorship' and that it was essential to 'wrest the bayonets from its hands'. This meant clearly that the moderate socialists had at last come to see that the greatest threat came from the Right—men who, no longer content with attacking the Bolsheviks, were bothering less and less to disguise their hostility to the entire Soviet and even to the Provisional Government. But despite this realization, these socialists, far from putting greater pressure on Kerensky and his ministers, continued to bear with their conservative convolutions, if sometimes with gritted teeth. Their subservience to the Provisional Government remained complete, their animosity to the Bolsheviks expressed itself in diatribes no less than in minor acts of harassment (they lacked the power, in any case, to proceed to sterner measures and were afraid to alienate the more radical Left completely—they might well have to seek their help against the extreme Right with its incessant clamour about 'Soviet interlopers').

Such, by and large, was the political situation of Russia in July and August 1917. The apparent weakness of those who had seemingly failed in July—the Bolsheviks—and the apparent strength of the victors—the conservatives—had a double consequence of decisive importance: it forced Lenin to make a fundamental revision of his revolutionary strategy, and it persuaded the extreme Right that the time was ripe to seize power.

The failure of the July Days had made a deep impact on Lenin. During the first months of the Revolution he had believed that its natural dynamic must impel the Soviet to make a stand against the bourgeoisie and take the first steps towards a democratic republic.

He had said and repeated that there was no reason why his Party should have recourse to violence and that, in Russia at least, the workers and peasants could seize power by relatively peaceful means. He had often declared that only if the bourgeoisie itself chose violence first would the workers have to reply in kind. The repressive measures against the Bolsheviks and the workers' militia and, more generally, the blusterings of the Right, egged on by the officers' corps—all these now convinced Lenin that the bourgeoisie was not prepared to accept a peaceful solution. More precisely, he saw them as the denial of democratic liberties—and especially of the freedom to propagate socialist ideas.

Thus, on July 8th, hardly four days after the July demonstrations and when the repression had started, he wrote, 'Recent events have ... shown quite plainly ... that [at this moment] Russia is lacking in both a proper government and proper tribunals.' And he concluded, 'Power now lies with a military dictatorship.' Lenin returned to this theme in an article he wrote on July 23rd and published ten days later in one of the Bolshevik papers that was replacing the banned *Pravda*. He began by saying that 'the counter-revolution has become organized and consolidated and has actually taken state power into its hands.' This may strike us as somewhat hasty and ill-considered judgment, for despite the sudden recovery of the conservatives, the counter-revolution had by no means seized power and indeed was quite incapable of doing so. The sudden threat from the Right may have assumed disquieting proportions, but the state nevertheless maintained the precarious equilibrium it owed to its dubious origins and mixed social composition.

More important, however, than this assessment of the facts was the lesson Lenin drew from them. 'All hopes for a peaceful development of the Russian Revolution have definitely vanished,' he wrote. 'The objective situation is this: either a victory of the military dictatorship with all it implies, or victory of the armed insurrection of the workers.'[1] And Lenin continued, 'The slogan of all power passing to the soviets was a slogan of a peaceful development of the Revolution, possible in April, May, June and up to July 5th–9th ... Now this slogan is no longer correct, as it does not

[1] In the published version, the term 'armed insurrection' was replaced by 'decisive struggle'. One wonders whether this was owing to caution on the part of the editors or to a new disagreement with their leader.

take into account the change in power that has taken place, nor the complete betrayal of the Revolution by the Social Revolutionaries and Mensheviks.' And the future builder of the Soviet state went on to warn against 'constitutional or republican illusions' and against 'illusions of a peaceful way'. The new slogan he gave out and the new task he defined for his party were, 'Gather the forces, reorganize them and steadfastly prepare for armed insurrection [decisive struggle], if the course of development permits it on a really massive, national scale.' Meanwhile, it was essential not to miss a single hour of legal work, but at the same time to 'organize immediately underground cells or nuclei'.

Profound though this change of attitude was, and decisive though it proved for the destiny of the Revolution, it did not imply that Lenin, having broken with his habitual prudence, had suddenly opted for adventurous or rash tactics. True, he now held that the peaceful struggle for revolutionary objectives had become impossible, but for all that he did not call for armed struggle there and then. Before an insurrectionary movement could succeed, the toiling masses must be won over. 'The victory [of the armed insurrection of the workers] is impossible unless the insurrection coincides with a profound revulsion on the part of the masses against the government and the bourgeoisie, following the economic disaster and the prolongation of the war.' While waiting for this to happen it was essential to be 'fully aware of the situation' and to practise 'self-control'.

When Lenin alleged that the counter-revolution was already in command, he was obviously so overwhelmed by the first serious setback the working class had suffered and the first savage repression to which his Party had become exposed that he mistook what was a mere threat for the reality. Apart from that, however, he continued to display a remarkable capacity for 'reading' the events, for sensing their impetus, and for distinguishing revolutionary ups and downs. With a firm grasp of the mood of the masses, a deep understanding of their capabilities and inhibitions, Lenin combined the conviction that no revolutionary party must run ahead of the proletariat. 'Adventurism' and 'Leftism' consisted precisely in calling the masses to revolutionary struggle at a time when they were discouraged or hesitant. 'Reformism', on the other hand, was the sin of holding back at a time when the masses themselves were ready for resolute action.

In July, prudence was what was needed. To the Bolshevik militants, strongly tempted to reply with force to repression and brutality, Lenin said that 'premature action and resistance on their part ... would simply serve the counter-revolution,' and he repeated that the 'decisive struggle is impossible unless there is a new revolutionary upsurge.'

That time had not yet come. Recalling the immediate aftermath of the July Days, Sukhanov wrote that the recent events had 'destroyed Bolshevism'. This, despite the Party's obvious disarray, was a gross exaggeration. In fact, it was not so very long before the Bolsheviks recovered their former strength. Paradoxically, this recovery was hastened by the first — and last — offensive the Right was able to launch before it was soundly trounced by the working class.

The Moscow State Conference

Though the failure of July had struck a blow at the Bolsheviks, it had done little to strengthen the hand of the Provisional Government or of the Soviet majority. Far from it — the weakness of the government had only become the more obvious. As for the Soviet, its authority had been overtly challenged by hundreds of thousands of workers and soldiers, and though this challenge had petered out, it had done so not because of firmness on the part of the Soviet, but simply because the masses themselves had been lacking in leadership and clear-cut objectives. No matter what boasts moderate socialists felt free to utter after the demonstrations, deep down they felt relieved at their timely rescue, and far from triumphant. Few objective observers thought otherwise. Bourgeois circles in particular, after watching the feeble attempts by the authorities to re-establish order, longed fervently for the replacement of these pusillanimous ministers and slippery socialists with men more deserving of their confidence. The news from the front only helped to increase the discontent and carpings of these men; to their simple minds it was only because the government lacked real authority over the working class at home that it was unable to stand up to the enemy in the field. It struck them as being still more deplorable that now that the revolutionary forces were licking their wounds the government still failed to press the rightful claims of the bourgeoisie with any measure of success. No wonder, then, that the Right began to call for a 'strong man', for a 'saviour from anarchy'

However, suitable candidates for this great mission were few and far between. The political inadequacy of the bourgeois class was a direct result of its social weakness. Not that the Constitutional Democratic Party—unlike the Social Revolutionaries and Mensheviks—had lost its campaigning zeal, but the party of Miliukov, Nekrassov and Rodzianko had thrown away most of its originality and was increasingly prepared to ditch its faith in bourgeois democracy and parliamentary government. Brought face to face with its own weakness it drew ever closer to the conservative Right and to the supporters of the old regime, so much so that it became increasingly difficult to distinguish between them. The Right had never bothered to disguise its hatred of the parliamentarian ideas so dear to the Cadets—their former support for the Tsar showed clearly that they preferred to live under an autocratic ruler. And as the impotent liberals drew nearer to the Right, they, too, began to evince a taste for personal dictatorship.

It remained to be seen, however, on whom the mantle of the dictator would descend: the liberals seemed singularly lacking in candidates; conservatives of the old school were even less eligible— the old regime was too discredited and too disgraced to produce a counter-revolutionary movement with pretensions to legitimacy. Hence the champions of the 'iron fist' were perforce thrown back on the army—though military talent did not abound in it, and political gifts were even rarer, it was a case of needs must when the devil drives. One of the few army commanders not to have forfeited all claims to popular respect was General Kornilov, a man who had time and again given clear proof of his personal courage and resolve: for example, he was greatly admired for his spectacular escape from an Austrian prisoner-of-war camp. As Commander of the Petrograd garrison in 1917 he had offered to reduce the revolutionary masses to silence, an offer the Provisional Government had declined. Finally, during the June offensive the troops under his command had done relatively well, possibly because he had restored the death penalty on his own initiative and had ordered all deserters to be shot out of hand. After the collapse of the offensive, Kornilov was made Supreme Commander.

Nor was his iron fist Kornilov's only strength; ever since the fall of Tsarism he had evinced republican sentiments that served as a guarantee of his democratic respectability. As for the rest, the man had nothing to recommend him, least of all in the political arena.

One of his fellow generals, Martynov, had this to say of him:
'Distinguished by a persevering love of work and great self-
confidence, he was, in his intellectual faculties, an ordinary and
mediocre man, not possessed of a broad outlook.' General Brussilov
was no more laudatory: 'The chief of a bold guerrilla band and
nothing more,' he said of him. Or listen to another witness: 'He
was very little acquainted with the interlacing interests of the
different strata of Russian society, knew nothing either of party
groups or of individual political leaders.' Perhaps General Alexeiev
summed it up best when he said that Kornilov was 'a man with a
lion's heart and the brain of a sheep.' This would certainly be the
verdict of history.

But before that verdict was finally given, the Right busied itself
with burnishing the general's image, turning him into 'the
standard-bearer of counter-revolution for some, and the saviour
of the fatherland for others' (General Denikin). Conservative
organizations and military groups rallied enthusiastically to his
support. Rodzianko put the final touches to the publicity campaign
when he sent Kornilov a fervent telegram: 'All thinking Russia
turns towards you, full of hope and faith.' The Soviet, meanwhile,
became increasingly filled with anxiety, and its Executive Committee, reflecting the growing disquiet, demanded that this over-
ambitious soldier be kept in his place. It was not only his growing
prestige that worried democratic Russians; they were even more
disturbed by the political and military programme that he intended
to implement without delay.

When he was proposed as Supreme Commander, Kornilov immediately informed the government that he would only accept the
new post if a series of laws were passed to strengthen military
discipline. In particular he demanded that the death sentence,
which had just been re-introduced at the front, come into force at
the rear as well. In addition, trade-union agitation, especially
among railwaymen, would have to be severely curtailed. Moreover,
the Supreme Commander wanted it to be known that he intended
to be responsible to no power other than 'his own conscience and
the nation'. In other words, he was not prepared to submit to the
authority of the Provisional Government.

This displeased the Soviet as much as it delighted the officer
corps and the bourgeoisie; they were now set on a collision course.
When the Central Executive Committee called for Kornilov's

dismissal, the Right struck back at once: soldiers, politicians and industrialists loudly proclaimed their loyalty to Kornilov, 'our hero and leader', 'our well-loved chief'. Cossack leaders threatened the government with armed rebellion if it gave way to the Soviet demands. And so Kornilov remained at his post.

For the rest, both camps held fast to their views: the Soviet continuing to oppose Kornilovism; the conservatives loudly protesting their complete faith—real or assumed—in their admirable figurehead; and the cabinet, led by Kerensky, trying to sit on both chairs at once. The Moscow State Conference brought all three together for a brief moment—the moment before the storm. Meeting from August 25th to 28th, its official object was to effect 'a rapprochement between the state power and all the organized forces of the country'. The proletarian part of these 'organized forces' was ostensibly protected by the Soviet, but there was apparently nobody representing the entire nation, and it was this gap the conveners of the Conference were anxious to fill—until the convocation of a Constituent Assembly. Only a body of that stature could hope to reconcile all trends of Russian public opinion and establish national concord in the place of division and civil war.

The venue of the State Conference was no less characteristic than its social composition: Moscow was chosen instead of Petrograd with its revolutionary atmosphere. As for the 2,500 or so delegates, they came from the State Duma (close on 500), the cooperatives (more than 300), the trade unions (some 170), trade and industry (150), municipalities (150), and the army (over 100). The soviets supplied a contingent of 329 delegates, so that the bourgeois and conservative elements were in a clear majority, and were left even freer because the Bolsheviks had decided to boycott the Conference and call a general strike in Moscow. And indeed on the first day of the Conference the city was paralysed when some 400,000 workers downed tools. Similar stoppages took place in other towns of the province.

The Conference assembled in the Bolshoi Theatre, whose great halls, brilliantly decorated, glittered under crystal chandeliers. The Soviet delegates were officially segregated from the rest by an aisle, but so crowded were the benches of the Right that a large number of the bourgeois and conservative delegates spilled over on to the other side. The boxes were crowded with officers in gala uniform. Kerensky sat symbolically in the precise centre of the stage, the incarnation of the national will, supposedly neutral and solely concerned with unity. Morgan Philips Price, the Russian correspondent of the *Manchester Guardian*, who was present at the Conference, was struck by the contrast between the appearance of the delegates of the Right, 'all respectable people with frock-coats and collars', and those of the Left, 'with unshaven chins and the working-day shirt'. Once more two worlds were confronting each other.

The debate was opened by Kerensky who, in a characteristic address, tried to curry favour with both sides, distributing his wise counsels, admonitions and threats evenly over all. 'May everyone know,' he declared, 'and may those know who have already attempted to raise their armed hand against the people's government, that these attempts will be crushed with iron and blood. Therefore let those beware who have already participated in an unsuccessful attempt and who think that the time has come to overthrow with the help of bayonets the revolutionary government!... Our patience has reached a limit and anybody who exceeds that limit will come up against a force whose repressive strength will remind these criminals of the old regime.'

But the greatest attraction by far of the Conference was not so much Kerensky as Kornilov, who had made his entry into Moscow on August 13th. Surrounded by his bodyguard, he was greeted by innumerable delegations before being led in triumphant procession from the station. The Cadet Rodichev ended his speech of welcome with this heart-felt cry, 'Save Russia and her grateful people will crown you!' After which Kornilov repaired to the Ivarsky shrine (where the Tsars worshipped on the eve of their coronation) and communed with a miraculous icon. Spiritually refreshed, he rested before addressing the State Conference next day. His speech was greeted with interminable hurrahs by the Right, while the Left, including the soldiers' delegates, stayed pointedly in their seats. For this failure to show proper respect to the 'first soldier of the Provisional Government' they were showered with cries of abuse by the officers in their boxes. The indignation of the latter and the cold hostility of the soldiers' delegates were, in fact, far more revealing than the uninspired speech of the great hero himself—all Kornilov did was to harp once again on the need for discipline as the sole assurance of military victory.

There followed rather insipid and necessarily restrained contributions by Chkheidze and Tseretelli, whose appeals for moderation fell on sceptical ears. The Conference was also treated to harangues by such revolutionary veterans as the anarchist Kropotkin, who inveighed against the dangers of revolutionary pacifism, and Plekhanov, who after recalling the 'unhappy memory of Lenin' invited the workers to 'reach an agreement with the representatives of the commercial and industrial class'. Such collaboration had by then become a Utopian dream.

The Church Council, represented by Archbishop Platon, threw its own weight behind these politicians: 'I have come here', the worthy cleric declared in terms that few of his listeners could have appreciated, 'to say from this platform to all Russia: "Have no fear, my own one ... If a miracle is needed for the salvation of Russia, God, thanks to the prayers of the Church, will accomplish this miracle." '

At the Conference itself, no such miracle was recorded. True, the champions of class collaboration had cause for fervent rejoicing when Bublikov, a leading industrialist, warmly embraced Tseretelli, but this mood of exaltation was fleeting in the extreme—a moment later Left and Right were back at each other's throats. Thus when the Cossack General, Kaledin, had finished an extremely reactionary speech, a young officer followed him on to the platform and declared that the General's views were by no means those of the men. He was acclaimed by the Left, while the boxes once more roared with indignation. One of the officers shouted, 'German gold!' whereupon fists started flying and a vast uproar ensued. And so the State Conference ended in dismal failure, a fact that no amount of pathos on the part of Kerensky could gloss over. 'May my heart turn to stone,' he shouted. 'I shall cast from me the key to my heart, beloved people. I will think only of the state.'

Alas, he was not the only one to think of that. Kornilov, too, had similar dreams and now that the government had once again given proof of its utter impotence he thought that the time for polite speeches was over.

Kornilov's Putsch

The State Conference had convinced General Kornilov that action against the Soviet—whose antagonism he had been able to judge at close quarters—had become a matter of urgency. The Bolsheviks were, of course, the chief obstacles to a national revival, but the rest were not very much better. Certain that all socialists were agitators and very often German spies to boot, he felt that they must be put down once and for all. 'It is high time we seized all these German agents and spies with Lenin at their head,' he confided to his chief aide, General Lukomsky. 'And for the rest, we shall hit this Soviet of workers and soldiers so hard that it will never dare to come out again.' And he decided to entrust his adjutant, General Krimov, with the noble task of shooting all members of the Petrograd Soviet.

With the Provisional Government he was somewhat more lenient. All that was needed there was a purge of the more unreliable elements, and the best way of ensuring this was to place himself at the head. His dealings with the ministers had served to convince him of their basic weakness. It was true that Kerensky and his friends had not opposed his demands for greater discipline and the militarization of the working class, but afraid of Soviet opposition, they had done little about it; so little, in fact, that the exasperated Kornilov had been forced to call for the resignation of the entire cabinet.

Before taking this fateful step, Kornilov had thought that his plans to subject the workers would be greeted with benevolent neutrality by the government as a whole and with acclaim by the Cadet ministers in it. Thanks to the good offices of the right-wing Social Revolutionary Savinkov — Kerensky's general administrator in the War Ministry and a keen supporter of Kornilov's programme — there existed a permanent link between Kornilov's army headquarters and the government in Petrograd. Thus Kerensky's confidant must have known of Kornilov's plan to invest the capital with counter-revolutionary forces, and that the troops in question had already been assembled at a spot not far from Petrograd. Kornilov, moreover, hoped to reinforce this contingent with some two thousand 'trusted patriots' inside the capital.

On August 21st, 1917, the Latvian city of Riga fell to the Germans despite a determined stand by the Russian garrison. It now looked as if the Germans might invade Russia herself, and this danger strengthened Kornilov's hand, for he had warned all along that lack of military discipline and revolutionary pacifism were bound to deliver Riga over to the enemy. According to Miliukov, too, who kept in close touch with the aspiring dictator, the fall of that city 'was certain to cause a flood of patriotic fervour'. While the claim by Trotsky and Sukhanov that Kornilov deliberately handed Riga to the Germans has not been proved, the fact remains that the surrender caused a veritable explosion of right-wing activity. Everything was made ready for the final assault, which was planned to take place just as soon as the Bolsheviks in the capital called the next demonstration. This seemed likely to happen at any moment, since the Party was bound to join in the widespread agitation against the re-introduction of the death penalty. The atmosphere in the capital was electrified further by the forthcoming celebrations of six months of revolutionary rule. The answer to any 'disturbances' would be immediate: 'Two regiments can easily crush the rebellion,' Savinkov declared.

Unfortunately for the conspirators, Petrograd remained calm. The Bolshevik Central Committee warned its members against calling or joining any demonstrations whatsoever. What meetings were held in celebration of February took place in complete calm. The counter-revolutionaries accordingly prepared to supply the missing impetus. As Miliukov explained, 'agitation in the factories was undoubtedly one of the tasks which officers' organizations were supposed to fulfil.' These officers had lost all authority in the barracks, and their influence on factory workers was even weaker. Moreover, as Chernov has explained, 'it was [later] discovered that the organization included young playboys who toyed at being conspirators, throwing money about and claiming that they were doing it for the cause.' And still the Petersburg proletariat stood firm, determined not to give Kornilov the least pretext for intervention. In the end, he had to move without one.

The whole Kornilov affair suddenly took a new turn, when the former Procurator of the Holy Synod, Prince Lvov—not to be confused with the first President of the Provisional Government—appeared before Kerensky with a proposal that he act as intermediary between him and Kornilov. As we have seen, Kerensky already had a direct link with the General through Savinkov, but in order to test the latter's reliability he agreed to make use of Lvov's services as well. On August 25th, Lvov returned with a report that Kornilov was determined to seize complete civil as well as military power. Kerensky knew full well that the Supreme Commander was planning to subdue the workers of Petrograd, but he had not realized that he was aiming to bring down the Provisional Government as well. This Kerensky was not prepared to tolerate.

A few days later, when the trial of strength between these two men began, many people had the mistaken idea that Kerensky was defending democracy against reaction. In reality, the struggle between Kerensky and Kornilov arose not so much out of political differences as out of political similarities. While the Right looked upon the Supreme Commander as a dictator who would save the country from anarchy, Kerensky simply thought that he himself was the better qualified candidate for that office. His shift to the Right had been accompanied by the adoption of an increasingly conservative programme (discipline, sacrifice, labour) and also by a growing taste for personal power. He no longer even bothered to disguise this fact. In July he declared, 'I, as head of the government ... consider that I have no right to hesitate if the changes [in the structure of the government] ... increase my responsibility in matters of supreme administration.' And at the Moscow State Conference he had seen fit to represent himself as 'your Minister of War and Supreme Commander'.

It is possible that he had all along intended to turn the Kornilov plot to his own advantage—in any case he admitted that he had known of it since the end of the Moscow Conference. Thus on August 23rd he sent Savinkov to army headquarters with the request for a cavalry detachment to enforce martial law in Petrograd. In other words, Kerensky was no less anxious than Kornilov to clamp down on the revolutionary workers of the capital. And so obvious was this fact that many 'well-disposed' politicians did their utmost to prevent what they considered a quite unnecessary breach between the two.

But while Kerensky was more than willing to make use of Kornilov's services and to include him in the cabinet, he was not at all disposed to take second place to him. That was why on August 26th, when Kornilov's true aims could no longer be mistaken, he ordered him to 'surrender your post to General Lukomsky who will act as temporary Supreme Commander' and to return to Petrograd forthwith. Kornilov was stunned by this telegram, for Prince Lvov and Boris Savinkov had given him to understand all along that Kerensky would be only too happy to hand over to him. As it was, Kornilov had not the least intention of submitting to an authority he no longer recognized and which he intended to supplant. He refused point blank to resign his post, and in so doing transformed his fight with the Soviet and the working class into open rebellion against the Provisional Government.

On the surface, it looked as if the General was in an unassailable position. To begin with, he enjoyed the confidence of the entire General Staff and of the operational chiefs on all fronts. Indeed, General Lukomsky refused to act as Kornilov's successor, and when Kerensky nominated General Klembovsky he met with a similar rebuff—Klembovsky simply observed that 'all changes in the army command would be extremely dangerous'. Worse still, all the Cadet ministers resigned from the government *en bloc*, thus openly declaring their support of Kornilov. The socialist ministers did likewise, but for quite different reasons. They had lost all confidence in Kerensky.

Kornilov, for his part, held yet another trump card: he enjoyed the confidence of the Allies. Trotsky alleged, in fact, that Britain supplied him with direct aid, notably in the form of equipment and military advisers. Be that as it may, there is little doubt that the Allies raised few objections against the pleas of a man who promised to stamp out defeatism at home and strengthen discipline at the front. Ambassador Buchanan, in any case, knew all about the plot but claims that he advised the conspirators to hold back until the Bolsheviks offered them cause for action. After the break between Kornilov and Kerensky, whose 'close co-operation' was 'Russia's best hope of salvation', Buchanan, on behalf of the Allied representatives in Petrograd, offered his good offices as mediator between the two rivals. Meanwhile Kornilov's supporters in Petrograd were apparently given free access to the British Embassy. One of them, 'an elegant young Cossack officer with blue eyes and perfect manners' was promised medical aid by Lady Buchanan and, according to the Ambassador's daughter, 'we drew up a long list of everything we could supply.'

The attitude of the Allies was, in any event, such as to weaken Kerensky in his stand against Kornilov. Hardly had he ordered Kornilov to hand over to Lukomsky when, on the advice of some of his closest colleagues, he decided to go back on this impulsive decision. He also asked the press to say nothing at all about the whole matter, but his request came too late—the papers came out with lengthy accounts of the recent events, and Kerensky was forced to continue a fight he would much rather have dropped. Even now he saw fit to entrust the defence of Petrograd to Savinkov, a man who, as he knew, was deeply implicated in the General's plot.

The counter-revolutionaries had further cause for satisfaction: the Provisional Government quite obviously lacked the forces needed to put up any measure of effective resistance. Kornilov and his supporters had good reason to feel confident. They not only believed that the 'whole commanding staff, an overwhelming majority of the officers and the best of the rank-and-file elements of the army' would rally to them, but according to the testimony of one of them, Prince Trubetskoy, they also thought that they would find among the 'lower orders ... an indifference which would submit to the least crack of the whip'. While they may have gauged correctly the mood of the commanding staff, of the officers' corps and of bourgeois and conservative circles, their calculations as to the 'lower orders' were grievously wrong. Far from succumbing at the first 'crack of the whip', the masses, repairing the deficiency of the government, rose up against the plotters in force and inflicted a decisive defeat upon them.

Kornilov made the first move when in answer to Kerensky's telegram he proclaimed, 'I, General Kornilov, declare that under the pressure of the Bolshevik majority of the soviets,[1] the Provisional Government acts in complete harmony with the plans of the German General Staff ... killing the army and undermining the very foundation of the country.' And when Kerensky replied with an order to 'the columns marching on Petrograd and the suburbs ... to return to their previous positions', Kornilov decided to launch his offensive.

The counter-revolutionary camp was in a state of euphoria. It was said at headquarters that 'nobody will defend Kerensky. This is a walk-over. Everything is ready.' On August 28th, Kornilov's Savage Division, renowned for its military feats, prepared to advance, but their progress was slowed down and then brought to a full stop by organized sabotage on the part of railway-men. In this the railway workers had scrupulously followed a general plan of the Trade Unions.

Next day, groups of workers from the capital made contact with the soldiers of the Kornilov divisions, and showed them that their commanders had deceived them. Some of them had been told that they were marching to the aid of Riga; others believed that they

---

[1] This was an error, deliberate or otherwise (and in the second case a clear sign of Kornilov's political ignorance) — at that time the Bolsheviks were, in fact, a minority in the soviets.

were needed to stop alleged Bolshevik massacres in the capital. The
workers quickly disabused them and explained that Kornilov had
but one aim: the destruction of the Revolution and the humiliation
of the 'lower orders'. Lack of supplies did the rest—without having
fired a single shot, the attacking army vanished just as suddenly as
it had appeared.

Meantime, the workers in Petrograd had not been idle. Convinced at last that Kornilov posed a threat to the entire Left, the
Mensheviks had called for the creation of a 'Committee of Struggle
against the Counter-Revolution'. At the same time, the Central
Committee of the Petrograd Soviet had called on all workers to stop
Kornilov's advance whatever the cost. No effective resistance
against the Kornilov threat could be organized without the participation of the Bolsheviks, so the leaders of the various moderate
socialist parties, reluctantly or otherwise, invited the latter to join
them in the 'Committee of Struggle'. The Bolsheviks readily
agreed, and though they formed no more than a tiny minority in
the Committee their real influence was incomparably greater. As
representatives of the most radical and militant workers in the
capital, it was they who, in the event, took charge of the entire
operation, galvanizing the Committee—which soon afterwards
changed its name to 'Committee of Revolutionary Defence'. Under
Bolshevik pressure it was decided to arm the workers and so to
resuscitate the 'Red Guard' which had been disbanded after July.
Within a few days, twenty-five thousand workers had joined in the
struggle. In addition, the Committee took over the city administration, and especially the distribution of supplies, which were expected to run short during a possible siege. Not afraid of courting
unpopularity, they immediately reduced the daily bread ration to
half a pound per person.

The Bolsheviks may therefore be said to have rallied wholeheartedly to the aid of a government they had always opposed, a
government, moreover, that continued to persecute them and to
keep their leaders in prison or exile. Thus, on August 18th Lenin
affirmed, 'Our workers and soldiers will fight the counter-
revolutionary armies if the latter should take the offensive against
the Provisional Government, but *not* in order to defend that
government ... it will be to defend the revolution and its true
objectives: the victory of the workers, the victory of the poor, the
victory of peace.'

Some of his supporters nevertheless remained sceptical. Even while the capital was mobilizing against Kornilov, Trotsky, still in prison, was visited by a delegation of Kronstadt sailors who asked him why on earth the Bolshevik leaders were expecting them to fight Kornilov on Kerensky's behalf. Trotsky found it difficult to convince them that the struggle against the Provisional Government had not been abandoned but only deferred, and that all accounts would be settled in due course.

On this topic the Bolsheviks and the leaders of the Soviet remained deeply divided. Social Revolutionaries and Mensheviks alike were, of course, fully aware that the government, and particularly its chief, had adopted a most ambiguous attitude towards Kornilov and his friends; so much so that several of them had made a secret pact with some of their liberal friends—even as the counter-revolution was collapsing—to discard both Kerensky and Kornilov in favour of General Alexeiev, whose ideas differed in no way from those of his Supreme Commander. The moderate socialists, however, refused to be party to any such plan. They made this clear both to Kerensky (who would obviously not agree to his own political overthrow) and to some of his ministers who, like Tereshchenko, were in close contact with the Allies and desired Kerensky's downfall. But what precisely were the aims of the Mensheviks and Social Revolutionaries? To them the answer seemed quite obvious: to keep the Kerensky government in power but to demand a more radical stand from it. The Mensheviks, in particular, wanted their Head of State to proclaim a republic, to put an end to the activities of the Old Duma and to proceed immediately to the long overdue agrarian reforms.

Kerensky, however, despite the weakness of his position, refused to make any concessions to the Soviet leaders, from whom he demanded 'unconditional support'. And the Soviet meekly agreed, and tried vainly to plaster up the ominous cracks that had appeared in the coalition. Its left wing was bitterly hostile to Kornilov and, with the Bolsheviks, had brought about his defeat; its centre, under Kerensky, was as spineless as ever; its right wing had never bothered to disguise its sympathy for the counter-revolutionary plotters, and some had even taken active steps to aid them—after all, it was in support of Kornilov that the Cadet ministers had tendered their resignation. Had not General Lukomsky declared shortly before that 'it would not be a bad idea to ask the Cadets to quit the Provisional Government on August 27th (September 9th)'?

Kerensky's own attitude is perhaps best gathered from the way he dealt with the defeated plotters. True, one of them, General Krimov, shot himself when he was summoned to Petrograd, but the rest were treated with the greatest kindness and consideration. Thus when a soldiers' delegation from among the defeated counter-revolutionary forces asked Kerensky to punish their former commanders with the utmost severity for having abused the nation's confidence and for having conspired against the Revolution, they were told haughtily, 'Your business is simply to obey your commanders; you can leave the rest to us.' This 'rest' was reduced to the strictest minimum: Alexeiev was appointed Supreme Commander in Kornilov's place and immediately let it be known that, in his view, 'the officers now decried as counter-revolutionaries are all of them true patriots.' Kornilov and his adjutant, General Lukomsky, were arrested on September 1st, and an Inquiry Commission was charged to look into their conspiracy. After the first hearing, Lukomsky was heard to say that 'all the members of the Commission were very well disposed towards us.' Kornilov himself was sentenced to house arrest in the south of Russia, where he enjoyed a most peaceful and comfortable existence until the Bolsheviks seized power. Then he immediately gave his guards the slip and took service with the White Army.

Since the government refused to take action against the counter-revolutionaries, the masses decided to take justice into their own hands. In Petrograd, the Red Guards arrested a number of Kornilov's officers, and there were even a few summary executions. Far more important than these isolated acts of retribution was the fact that the counter-revolution had collapsed even before it had joined battle—its leaders had proved as incompetent on the political front as they were in the trenches. Now this very failure demonstrated to all the world that the Russian upper class was politically bankrupt and quite incapable of swaying the balance of power against the proletariat. This was the meaning of their inability to govern and of their failure to establish a real and effective liberal democracy in the country. With the collapse of the Kornilov putsch, the upper classes —the aristocracy, the capitalists and the haute bourgeoisie—bore witness to their own impotence. And since the organized workers had been the only force to frustrate their ambitions, the labour movement gained greatly in prestige and strength. More precisely, the most revolutionary among them, defeated in July and driven underground, were given a new lease of life and a fresh and decisive impulse. In the circumstances, Kornilov's lamentable failure could only have one consequence: the victory and final triumph of the Bolshevik Party.

8

The Agony of the Provisional Government

THE summer of 1917 interrupted the steady growth of the revolutionary forces begun in February, and the bourgeoisie, anxious to take full advantage of this lull, was quick to attack both the Soviet and the socialist parties whom they blamed for all the country's ills. However, the Provisional Government had by then grown far too weak and discredited to reassert its authority. The relative improvement in the economic and social situation during the harvest season turned out to be of very short duration — in late autumn, the spectre of hunger and cold reappeared and caused social tremors so great that they could no longer be contained. As Sukhanov put it in his faithful record of the events, ' "disorders" were taking on absolutely unendurable, menacing proportions in Russia. Anarchy was really getting under way. The city and the countryside were both in revolt, the first demanding bread, the second land.' During the Kornilov putsch, the bread ration in Moscow and the capital was, as we saw, reduced to half a pound per day. Subsequently it was cut down further to 100 grammes per day, and finally to 500 grammes per week. Some districts had to go without bread altogether for an entire week. Sugar was no more plentiful; sweets and fruit had completely disappeared. According to the American journalist, John Reed, whose *Ten Days that Shook the World* is perhaps the most telling account of the atmosphere in Petrograd during the last weeks of the Provisional Government and the first days of the October Revolution, the city had only half the milk supply it needed to feed its babies.

In many other parts of the country, and especially in Moscow, the situation was no better. Fuel, too, was running short, and women everywhere organized protest marches that often culminated in riots. On August 30th, for instance, demonstrators smashed their way into the police commissariat in Astrakhan; on September 1st they sacked the headquarters of the Tashkent Soviet, which struck them as being too moderate and for which they substituted a Provisional Revolutionary Committee. On the

14th, Rostov erupted into violence and looting, and the next day the exasperated and famished population rioted in Kharkov. On September 22nd, prisoners in Saratov gaol were released by 'hunger marchers'. By the middle of autumn, the looting of supply trains had become a daily occurrence.

And while the cities rioted, the countryside was in the throes of rebellion. In its issue of September 3rd, the Social Revolutionary paper *Dyelo Naroda* pointed out that 'practically nothing has been done to stop the state of slavery that still reigns supreme in the countryside', and went on to complain that the Provisional Government had done nothing but take repressive measures against the peasants, thus proving that 'far from discarding the old habits of the Tsarist administrators' the revolutionary ministers preferred to rely on 'Stolypin's iron fist'.

But there was one important difference: whereas Stolypin had crushed the Revolution of 1905 with as much competence and efficiency as brutality, the 'revolutionary ministers' of 1917 were as feeble in organizing repression as they were in running the state. And so they sat by impotent as the riots assumed increasingly dangerous proportions. A statistical survey shows that the number of peasant raids on landed estates went up by 30 per cent from August—a relatively peaceful month—to September, and by a further 43 per cent in October. Of the 624 districts constituting Old Russia, 482 witnessed violent attacks on landlords; in Siberia, the proportion was much higher. Moreover, not only the number but also the intensity of these disturbances was constantly increasing—the peasants were clearly at the end of their tether. Thus October 1917 saw half as many acts of violence as the period February to September.

The peasants, not content with pilfering grain and other stores, increasingly set fire to manors, ejecting and sometimes killing their owners. This orgy of destruction was chiefly the work of the poorest strata. For example, a government commissar reported that though a local village assembly had decided to confiscate a number of estates in an orderly fashion and to avoid all wanton damage, 'the poor being in the majority', that night 'a sea of fire engulfed the estates of the entire district and everything in sight was razed to the ground, including a model plantation and a herd of prize cattle'.

Most of the ringleaders were apparently recruited from among deserters or soldiers home on leave. In some cases government troops sent in to restore order deserted their units, joined in the revolt, and turned with redoubled fury against those they were supposed to protect.

It should, however, be noted that these riots were not accompanied by any real growth in political consciousness. Thus the Social Revolutionaries maintained their electoral hold over the peasantry at large, while Bolshevik ideas barely began to take root. Nevertheless, it is true to say that many old prejudices against the Bolsheviks were fast disappearing. When a militant Social Revolutionary tried to incite the *moujiks* of Tver against the 'Leninist looters and traitors', his audience interrupted him with loud cries of: 'Stop lying to us! Where is our land? We've had quite enough of you, just bring us a Bolshevik!' And by the end of the autumn many villages had begun to call for the transfer of power to the soviets.

Thus the urban proletariat was on the point of gaining a most powerful ally. In fact, as the crisis grew daily more acute and it became clear that liberals and conservatives were too incompetent and weak to do anything about it, that Lenin and Miliukov were right to argue that there was no room for a compromise, the nation gradually realized that the only solution was another large step on the road to revolution.

The sad plight of the Russian army made this step even more inevitable. Any lingering doubts on this subject must have been dispelled by General Verkhovsky, the last Minister of War under the Provisional Government. In a report to a Joint Session of the Committees on Defence and Foreign Affairs on October 20th, he admitted quite frankly that according to a statement of the Minister of Food it was no longer possible to feed more than seven million soldiers, when the army needed a minimum of nine million.

The General went on to explain that in September the delivery of flour to all the fronts did not exceed 26 per cent of the requirements, and that the deliveries of meat had run 50 per cent short of the orders. The provision of footwear, which the approach of winter made essential, was also far behind the requirements, and general transport difficulties rendered the military situation most precarious. Addressing the Plenary Assembly of the Pre-Parliament[1] four days earlier, the Minister of Supplies had seen fit to read out the following laconic but eloquent telegram from the Commander

[1] See p. 227.

of the Northern Front: 'The most terrible autocrat—hunger—threatens the army.' And the Minister had added that a number of army bakeries had been forced to shut down for lack of flour, while the rest might have to follow suit within the next few days.

According to General Verkhovsky, the 'morale factors' in the army were even more discouraging. 'General disintegration has gained momentum, particularly under the influence of the Kornilov affair.' In fact, the soldiers, who for months had been voicing their objections to an offensive, had begun to desert from the trenches in growing numbers. Soldiers demonstrating in Moscow during September had brandished such banners as, 'We'll die on the barricades but not at the front!' On the Rumanian Front, the most disciplined of all, regimental delegates informed their commanders that 'the men have decided to go home at first snowfall.'

The Minister of War, forced to become a realist at last, expressed the view that Russia would have to start immediate peace talks, preferably in agreement with the Allies. 'We can no longer wage war,' he declared on October 20th. Two days later he was put on leave of absence by the Provisional Government. In another three days the Provisional Government itself was put on permanent leave by a nation that, as Verkhovsky had rightly gathered, neither could nor wanted to continue the war.

The impotence of the Provisional Government

The fall of the Provisional Government was, in many respects, reminiscent of the collapse of Tsarism. The latter, though, had taken centuries to lose its grip and degenerate finally into a lifeless body, whereas the Provisional Government, helped by the accelerating rhythm of history, took very much less time to reach the same degree of decomposition. It had never impressed anyone with its vigour, but its last weeks involved such a singular display of decrepitude that it was hard to tell pathos from farce.

Government incompetence tainted all levels of public life, and on so vast a scale that it reflected the bankruptcy of a whole class rather than the failure of individuals. That class was the petit bourgeoisie, which increasingly had become the mainspring of the coalition government. The liberals, who had at first held most of the important cabinet posts, had gradually made way for moderate socialists and, as champions of petit-bourgeois aspirations—however lukewarm—these men increasingly lost what bourgeois sym-

pathy they had originally enjoyed. Their loose alliance—for no
fixed purpose and with no clear programme—had been given a
further jolt by the Kornilov affair, which had enjoyed the barely
disguised support of the liberals. Yet, despite the increasing rift
and tension, everything was done to patch up the threadbare
coalition. And so on September 24th, 1917, after a month-long
crisis, a new government was formed, still under Kerensky, and
with the active participation of the Cadets. As a condition of their
co-operation they insisted on the presence in the cabinet of a
number of military and business leaders, and stipulated that any
steps taken against the Kornilov plotters must not be allowed to
undermine the unity of the army command—which meant, in
effect, that punitive measures were reduced to the absolute minimum. Though Kerensky was quick to accept all these conditions,
the alliance remained extremely shaky. The fiction of class collaboration was transformed into a system of government at a time
when class conflict had become acerbated to flash point. Hence it
was not at all surprising that what had started in a vacuum should
have ended in a void. Not in command of anybody or in control of
anything, the new ministerial team became the laughing-stock of
its adversaries and a mere straw in the storm of events.

Had it been able to implement any kind of policy, that policy
would certainly have been conservative in the extreme. As Sukhanov
has pointed out with justifiable bitterness, while the old cabinet included several of Kornilov's accomplices, the new one was almost
entirely in their hands. Kerensky, for his part, had all but completely severed his links with the Soviet. Receiving a delegation of
Cossacks, he had told them that 'the Provisional Government, far
from being answerable to the Soviet, regrets its very existence.'
Tereshchenko, his Minister of Foreign Affairs, fully shared this
sentiment; indeed, he saw fit to confide to the British Ambassador
that 'only a counter-revolution can now save this country.' As for
Konovalov, the Vice-Premier, a member of the Cadet Party and a
big industrialist, he was notorious for his threat to the starving
workers that unless they behaved he would have all the factories
closed. And this was the man whom Kerensky, now spending most
of his time at army headquarters, entrusted with the political
destiny of his unhappy country!

Pulled in opposite directions, the Provisional Government struck
out at Left and Right in turn. It ordered the closure of provincial

soviets in such trouble spots as Tashkent, Kaluga and Rostov. It broke strikes—in particular the one that had paralysed the industrial Donetz basin. But anxious to appease the Central Executive of the Petrograd Soviet, it also offered bribes to the moderate Left: it dropped Kornilov's plan to militarize industry, to which Kerensky had agreed in principle; it banned a number of extreme right-wing organizations implicated in the conspiracy; and it ordered the old Imperial Duma not to meet—not even in 'private conference'.

However, these measures did nothing to solve the most urgent problems: agrarian unrest and the clamour for peace. With regard to the first, even within the government it was beginning to be said that something must be done for the long-suffering peasants, and the Minister of Agriculture began to draft legislation for the overdue transfer of some of the larger estates to the agricultural councils. But on October 16th, when he presented his plan to the cabinet, the great majority of his colleagues rejected it out of hand.

On the question of peace, the Provisional Government did try to make a stand during the last four weeks of its existence. But this change of heart did not involve a real change in policy since, short of an agreement with the Allies, it could have no practical consequences. Although it did not go quite so far as the Minister of War, who had called for immediate peace negotiations, the government saw fit to make a number of statements likely to displease the Allies. Kerensky, for instance, when interviewed by Associated Press, had this to say: 'Why don't the Russians fight? I shall tell you why. Because the masses are economically exhausted and because they have been let down by the Allies.'[1] Moreover, under pressure from the Petrograd Soviet, whose attitude to the war was increasingly being swayed by the Bolsheviks, the Provisional Government had decided to present new peace proposals at the forthcoming Allied Conference in Paris. Menshevik and Social Revolutionary deputies had even asked Skobelev, the former Minister of Labour, to represent them at the Conference and to press their demand for a peace 'without annexation or indemnities'. If in so doing they showed their distrust of Tereshchenko, they also gave proof of their invincible political naivety. Several British ministers, including Arthur Balfour, the Foreign Secretary,

[1] The U.S. State Department sent the text of the interview to Kerensky asking him to rephrase it. Kerensky himself refused, but one of his secretaries did so.

declared quite bluntly that the Allies had not the least intention of talking peace at Paris—all they were concerned with was military victory in the shortest possible time.

In their foreign policy Kerensky and his collaborators were thus as impotent as they were in home affairs.

There was yet another sphere in which the Provisional Government aroused universal hostility, because its actions were considered either too conservative and timorous or else too radical. This was the problem of the nationalities, which made an already extremely complex and delicate situation even more confused. But if the new Russia was really intent on putting an end to autocratic oppression this was a problem it could ill afford to ignore. These subjects of the Tsar had not only been oppressed as such, but had been further discriminated against as members of the various national minorities. In 1913 the Empire counted 70 million Russians proper, together with 90 million 'allogeneous people'. Of these, 17 per cent were Ukrainians, 6 per cent Poles, 4·5 per cent White Russians, the rest Jews and Orientals. What was the Provisional Government going to do about the national claims of these people?

With the Jews, a group without a territory of their own, the new regime did, in fact, put an end to many acts of discrimination which the Tsarist regime had inflicted. Since these measures did not interfere with the territorial integrity of the country, they met with no official opposition. Anti-Semitism did not disappear, but on the political plane it became a monopoly of the most reactionary elements, and these were on the defensive. National minorities, however, who lived in distinct geographical boundaries, presented the new rulers with a much more serious problem. Here, as in so many other matters, they were torn in different directions: while national minorities demanded a large measure of autonomy, the Russian bourgeoisie was bitterly opposed to any measures that might threaten to split up the fatherland. Now while it was hard to reconcile the latter approach with the democratic ideology professed by the new regime, too much was apparently at stake to allow 'mere sentiment' to obscure the material realities.

The problem of Poland was obligingly solved by the German generals, who saved the Russian ministers the embarrassment of long and fruitless discussion. The claims, on the other hand, of the Finns, Ukrainians and to a lesser degree of the Balts and a number of Oriental subjects, continued to create conflicts. In Finland, for instance, where the socialists were determined to gain full independence, the bourgeoisie were equally resolved to retain the old links with Russia. On July 18th, the Helsingfors Seim (Diet), which had an overall socialist majority (103 to 97) declared in favour of internal autonomy, while granting Petrograd control over foreign and military policy. Kerensky immediately dissolved the Seim and called for new elections, in which the socialists lost their absolute majority. Long negotiations then ensued during which the Provisional Government dropped any liberal pretences it may have had in the face of Cadet determination to preserve the unity of the Russian Empire. It was not until after the seizure of power by the Bolsheviks that revolutionary Russia finally recognized the full independence of Finland.

Ukrainian claims for autonomy met with even greater opposition, no doubt because of economic considerations: the Ukraine was rich not only in grain but also in mineral resources, particularly in coal. No wonder, then, that the Petrograd government was in almost continuous conflict with the autonomous institutions appearing in Kiev soon after the February Revolution, and in particular with the Rada (Parliament) which, though of doubtful status, kept pressing for greater independence in accordance with what many Ukrainians believed was the spirit of the new Russia. Overriding Kerensky, the Rada had appointed an executive of its own, the Secretariat-General, and had set up special Ukrainian units in the Russian army. In October, Petrograd decided to move against the rebellious Ukrainian leaders, but since government authority was as tenuous in Kiev as it was on the banks of the Neva, nothing at all came of this. Last but not least, an Asian deputy was heard to assert a few weeks before the Bolshevik uprising that as far as the 'allogeneous' people were concerned, 'the February Revolution had brought no changes'. In short, the Provisional Government left the Bolsheviks with a Tsarist blot they had had neither the time nor the desire to eradicate.

This last failure of the Provisional Government was in keeping with the rest. After months of impassioned speeches and utter inactivity, completely out of breath, the ministers no longer inspired anything except the hatred of their enemies, the exasperation of their few remaining friends, and the contempt of the world at large. The ministers themselves were under no illusions. One of them declared that 'people everywhere are crossing themselves before turning their backs on us.' And Kerensky, in characteristic style, told the Pre-Parliament:[1] 'I am a condemned man. Everything leaves me cold ... ' And this was the politician whose declared object it was to stop the Bolsheviks, to assuage popular discontent, to oppose the revolutionary genius of Lenin! Much as in the first few months of the Revolution he had been the trumpeter of victory, so now he was the very symbol of collapse. According to Miliukov, 'He revealed all the signs of that pathological condition of the spirit which in medical language is called "psychic neurasthenia".' And the famous liberal historian added that the Cadet minister Kishkin, a professional psychiatrist, enjoyed a special influence in the cabinet thanks purely to his medical services to the Head of State.

On September 12th,[2] *The Times* declared that Russia had no government at all. Soon afterwards Sukhanov contended that his country was being run by a 'comic-opera team'. And, in fact, Kerensky, who had never had anything of the revolutionary about him and who relied entirely on bureaucratic methods, was quite incapable of mastering the explosive situation of Russia in 1917. True, several of his ministers, of whom he had a considerable turnover, looked upon themselves as champions of revolutionary democracy, but their actions invariably belied their noble declarations of intent.

From the start the Provisional Government had acted as a brake on revolutionary progress, and throughout its existence it had based its authority on conservative institutions whose social composition had not been changed by the fall of Tsarism—among them the courts, the Holy Synod of the Orthodox Church, and the Diplomatic Service. At a teachers' conference in June 1917, one delegate explained that during the first four months of the Revolution not a single change had been made in teaching methods or in the old curriculum. Worse still, the Senate, the Tsar's chief administrative machine, was left in office and as late as September refused to approve a government decision on relations between Russia and the Ukraine. In a Revolution that ought to have finished with old restraints, to have swept the rotten remains of Tsarism and of the past off the board, these old fogeys and blind reactionaries were left free to strut about in their ancient uniforms.

[1] See below.   [2] Western calendar.

On one occasion, when a new recruit to their august ranks had the temerity to appear before them in a mere frock coat, his outraged colleagues had him put out immediately. Such was the administration with which the Provisional Government intended to lead Russia into the future, to transform her into a modern democracy.

In these circumstances it is not at all surprising that the Provisional Government should have forfeited the confidence of the parties it was supposed to represent and of the Soviet majority, whose near-saintly forbearance and inexhaustible spirit of conciliation it had stretched beyond the limit. Thus on the eve of the Bolshevik Revolution (October 25th) the Pre-Parliament was asked to vote on two resolutions. The first, submitted by the conservative wing (the Constitutional Democrats and a number of right-wing socialist groups), gave firm support 'to the Provisional Government[1] in its struggle against the threat from the extreme Left'. The second resolution came from the Mensheviks, Social Revolutionaries and Internationalist Mensheviks. After denouncing 'revolutionary attempts aimed at seizing state power' it went on to explain that all these attempts were due to 'the delay in the implementation of urgent measures'. The Left resolution accordingly went on to call for the speedy 'transfer of the land to the agrarian committees' and for 'energetic intervention with the Allies ... aimed at immediate peace talks'.

While this was not an explicit rejection of the Provisional Government, it was nevertheless a call for the kind of policy Kerensky had opposed all along. The Left resolution was carried by 123 votes to 102 with 23 abstentions. Kerensky was briefly tempted to tender his resignation, but changed his mind. Destiny had accorded him a few hours' grace.

During that night (October 24th–25th), while the Bolsheviks ordered the Red Guard to occupy various strategic strong points in the capital, Kerensky received the two Menshevik leaders, Dan and Gotz, accompanied by the Social Revolutionary Avksentiev, President of the Pre-Parliament. His visitors asked him in view of the resolution that had just been carried to declare publicly that the government had decided to hasten the convocation of a Constituent Assembly, to transfer the large landed estates to the agricultural committees and to propose to the Allies an immediate cessation of

[1] The Bolsheviks had withdrawn from the assembly.

hostilities. Dan explained that this was the only means of 'cutting the ground from under the feet of the Bolsheviks', but Kerensky, 'who looked like a man at the end of his tether', refused to make the least concession even now. 'The government does not stand in need of your advice,' he told his visitors, and sent them away empty-handed.

This last show of obstinacy was yet another proof of his utter political blindness. Scorning the advice of his few remaining allies, Kerensky also forfeited what military help they might still have given him.

Failure of the Pre-Parliament and crisis in the Soviet

The torpor and inertia of the Provisional Government was shared by all the parties represented in it. While the Constitutional Democrats, betraying their own ideals, ceased to believe in the virtues of parliamentary or bourgeois democracy, the moderate socialists who dominated the soviets were in full disarray, fast losing support in the country at large and bitterly squabbling among themselves.

The Social Revolutionaries, in particular, who had been the most powerful party during the first months of the Revolution, went into a steep decline as the petit-bourgeoisie deserted them in force. Thus the Moscow municipal elections, which had given them 58 per cent of the votes cast in July, only gave them 14 per cent in October. And while the party majority remained bogged down in a political wilderness—supporting the Provisional Government yet becoming increasingly hostile to Kerensky—its leftist minority broke away and under the leadership of Kamkov and Maria Spiridonova drew ever closer to the Bolsheviks; so much so that Trotsky believed that it was 'becoming very much easier to reach an understanding with them'.

The right-wing Mensheviks—who supported the Provisional Government and participated in it—had for all practical purposes ceased to count as an organized force.[1] In Petrograd on the eve of the Bolshevik insurrection they were unable to attract more than twenty or thirty people to their meetings, while the Bolsheviks filled hall after hall to capacity. And though the Mensheviks preserved an appearance of unity to the outside world, their 'Internationalist'

[1] Maxim Gorky's *Novaia Zhizn* admitted that the Mensheviks had as good as disappeared from the capital.

8

faction, led by Martov, had nothing in common with the right wing except their label.

Mensheviks and Social Revolutionaries thus paid the price for their inertia and blindness. True, they could still attract votes at elections—though these continually dwindled—but they were completely cut off from the workers, soldiers and the more militant peasants. Quite often, delegations from the front in search of political guidance would call on Menshevik or Social Revolutionary deputies to the Petrograd Soviet, but when they failed to obtain an audience they turned increasingly to the Bolsheviks who welcomed them, listened to them, discussed their problems with great sympathy and explained their own policies at length. By then, most people had, in any case, had quite enough of calls for patience and greater discipline—the only remedies prescribed by the moderate Left. Thus *Izvestia*, the official organ of the Central Executive Committee of the Soviet, declared in its issue of September 17th, 'The government cannot possibly accede [to the popular demands] ... Its prime task is to protect the entire nation, to save it from utter ruin, and to that end it can only pursue one path: to deny these demands, however just and well-founded they may be, and impose sacrifices on all parties.' Thus even at this late stage the Soviet Executive failed to realize that by asking the famished masses to accept further sacrifices it was committing political suicide.

When this truth finally dawned on the moderate socialists it was, of course, much too late. Addressing the Pre-Parliament on October 24th, the last time it assembled, the Menshevik Dan exclaimed, 'It is the duty of everyone to satisfy the popular demand for a peaceful settlement of the conflict ... Further, we must raise the question of the land in such a way as to leave no one in any doubt as to our determination to meet the needs of the people.' In the Petrograd Soviet, where the Mensheviks were delivering similar speeches at about the same time, they were shouted down from all sides with, 'Too late! We have stood behind you for full eight months, and our patience is at an end.'

And so the Mensheviks awoke from their futile dreams of national and international conciliation at the very moment when the Bolsheviks were making ready to wipe them off the political map. Even then they continued to mix wild fantasies with short bursts of lucidity. Thus the British Ambassador was able to inform his government of a conversation on October 25th—the day the

Bolsheviks seized power!—with the former Minister of Labour, Skobelev, and the Social Revolutionary Tchaikovsky:

> They told me that a socialist government, exclusive of the Bolsheviks, was about to be formed, that it would include representatives of the Cossack democracy, and that it would be supported by the Cadets. On my asking how they proposed to put down the Bolsheviks, they replied—by force ... But if they were to succeed they must be authorized to tell the army that the Allies were preparing to discuss terms with a view to bringing the war to a speedy conclusion. Such an assurance, they said, would give them a great advantage over the Bolsheviks, with whom the Allied governments would not treat.

The last idea of these floundering politicians was hatched in September 1917. On the 14th of that month, a 'Democratic Conference' held in Petrograd brought together the 'flower' of Russia's political intelligentsia in a final attempt to exorcize the spectre of civil war. The whole thing was a copy of the Moscow State Conference, but this time the sights were set much higher: it was meant to act as a kind of buffer between the Provisional Government and the nation, pending the convocation of the Constituent Assembly in November. To that end, the 'Democratic Conference' was made to look far more representative of the nation than the Moscow Conference, to which the propertied classes had sent a quite disproportionate number of delegates—this time workers' and peasants' deputies were in a clear majority. The Right supplied a contingent of so-called 'Co-operators', a hybrid compounded of moderate socialists and bourgeois elements; the extreme Left was made up of the Bolsheviks, as intransigent as ever.

At one of its first sessions, the Democratic Conference decided to transform itself into the more sonorous 'Provisional Council of the Russian Republic', better known as the Pre-Parliament. It comprised 550 members, composed of 15 per cent of the members of the Democratic Conference, with an additional 120 seats for the institutions of the possessing classes, and 20 seats for the Cossacks. The result, by political parties, was 120 Social Revolutionaries, 66 Bolsheviks, some 60 moderate Mensheviks, 30 Internationalist Mensheviks and a sprinkling of socialists belonging to other factions—308 Leftists of various persuasions all told. Then there were some 75 or so Cadets, together with Rightist and business representatives. The moderate socialists, anxious to provide the government with the democratic framework it so badly needed, proposed that the Provisional Council be endowed with legislative powers and with a measure of control over the cabinet, a suggestion Kerensky was quick to veto. Sukhanov said that compared with it 'even the Stolypin Duma under Rasputin's boot seemed the ideal of an all-powerful parliament, filled with grandeur'. He added that for all that, if one compared it with the comic-opera government, it was at least some sort of power in the land. In fact, both were equally impotent and symbols of the same political void.

This impotence became particularly obvious from the debate and vote on the peace problem with which the Pre-Parliament concluded its deliberations. A motion by the Right that army morale must be strengthened by convincing the soldiers that Russia was fighting for democracy and freedom was rejected by 135 votes to 130, with one abstention. A Menshevik and Social Revolutionary resolution calling, *inter alia*, for 'the signing of a general democratic peace' with the minimum of delay, was also rejected — by 127 votes to 95 with 50 abstentions. The impasse of the Pre-Parliament fully reflected that of the regime.

From the creation of the Pre-Parliament, and even earlier during the Democratic Conference, Lenin had called for a boycott of this institution, but the Central Committee of the Bolshevik Party, though endorsing his view by 9 votes to 8, had decided that the majority was so small that the whole question would have to be referred back to a larger Party conference. The latter decided by 77 votes to 50 to override Lenin. Soon afterwards, however, the Bolshevik group in the 'Provisional Council' staged a spectacular walk-out, after Trotsky had read out the following declaration:

> We, the Bolshevik faction of the Social Democratic Party, announce that we have nothing whatever in common with this government of treason to the people and with this council of counter-revolutionary connivance. We have nothing in common with that murderous intrigue against the people which is being conducted behind the official scenes. We refuse to shield it either directly or indirectly for a single day.

Whereupon the 66 Bolshevik delegates rose and left the hall amidst general uproar and shouting.

Without the Bolsheviks, the Pre-Parliament became a mere sham of a representative body, an academy of sleepwalkers. Was there any other tribune to take its place? The workers, soldiers and peasants still had their Soviet, the only institution that, since February, had enjoyed some measure of stability. But here, too, the signs of decay had become unmistakable.

Born under the star of dual power, the Soviet had become resigned to leaving affairs of state in the hands of the Provisional Government, and merely intervened at moments of acute crisis when the lack of ministerial authority threatened to throw the country into chaos. The rivalry between Soviet and government was thus transformed into a kind of division of labour, reflected by the presence in the cabinet of a number of socialist ministers. Dual power became the single rule of the Provisional Government, that is, the absence of all real power. Then, in September, the Bolsheviks' growing strength put an end to this state of affairs.[1] As the Party became a majority in several important soviets, particularly those in Petrograd and Moscow, fresh clashes between Government and Soviet seemed likely and with them a return to the old dual power structure. However, this threat did not fully materialize. In June, the All-Russian Congress of Soviets had, in effect, elected a Central Executive Committee which was controlled by moderate socialists and these did their best to collaborate with Kerensky and his ministers. Moreover, fearing that the Bolsheviks would repeat their local successes at the Second National Congress of Soviets planned for October 15th and put an end to Menshevik and Social Revolutionary predominance, the Menshevik Dan moved a postponement of the Congress, and the soldiers' section, which was under the thumb of right-wing socialists, gave him their full support. The Executive Committee of the Soviet of Peasants declared, for its part, that it was dangerous and undesirable to hold the Congress. This attitude incensed the Bolsheviks. Trotsky declared that if the Central Executive Committee refused to summon the Soviet delegates by legal means, it would be called by revolutionary means. Under mounting pressure, the Mensheviks finally agreed to hold the Congress on October 25th (November 7th), though, until the end, they used all sorts of delaying tactics, and challenged the mandate of all delegates arriving in the capital.

Their vain manoeuvres were proof positive that they had abandoned what revolutionary aims they had pursued in the early days

[1] See below.

of the Revolution. The soviets had been created to pave the way for liberation from the yoke of Tsarism and exploitation, and as such they had enjoyed the trust of the working class. But this faith had slowly been shattered, and in July the workers of Petrograd had risen up against a Soviet that had turned conservative. When this happened, the Menshevik leaders, far from becoming more radical, had decided that the soviets had outlived their usefulness, the more so as some under Leninist control—for instance in Tsaritsyn (the future Stalingrad), Viatka, Kiev and also in the capital—had begun to play a more revolutionary part by tackling a growing number of social and political tasks. 'There was', reported one member of the Central Executive Committee, 'an appreciable cooling off towards the soviets ... The functions of the soviets are gradually being reduced.' Their financial sources, too, diminished rapidly, and the moderate socialist leaders, far from regretting this development, congratulated themselves on it quite blatantly and tried to accelerate it.

Thus on September 28th, 1917, *Izvestia* (which was controlled by the Soviet) wrote, 'The useful life of the soviets is coming to an end; the moment approaches where they, together with other organs of the revolutionary apparatus, must disappear from the political life of a free and victorious people that will henceforth struggle in peaceful ways.' And on October 23rd the same paper returned to the charge. 'When the autocracy and the bureaucratic regime collapsed, we created the soviets as a sort of shelter in which democracy could seek temporary refuge. Now we are about to build a more durable edifice to replace this shelter, and it is natural that the people should move into the more comfortable home.' But while these self-styled architects had done their utmost to void the soviets of their revolutionary content and were quite happy to let them go by the board now that the Bolsheviks were on the ascendant, the latter took quite a different view. Two days after *Izvestia* published its leader, the despised shelters were occupied by the forces of the Revolution. The Soviet Government was launched.

The Bolsheviks: *from recovery to predominance*

Recalling the political climate at the time, Sukhanov, as we saw, declared that the July days had 'destroyed' Bolshevism. Two months later he recorded an entirely different situation. The Bolsheviks 'were at one with the masses because they were always there, taking the lead in details as well as in the most important affairs of the factory or barracks. They had become the sole hope ... The masses lived and breathed together with the Bolsheviks. They were in the hands of the party of Lenin and Trotsky.' The history of the Russian Revolution is the history of this transformation: within three months, the Bolsheviks first captured the imagination of the people and then went on to seize the reins of state power.

After the reverses it had suffered in July, Lenin's Party began to show clear signs of revival in August. Addressing the Party Congress during that month, Volodarsky had felt free to declare: 'We have a colossal, an unlimited influence in the [Petrograd] factories.' At the same time, the Bolsheviks had made new headway in Moscow where, as we saw, they were able to call a general strike during the opening of the State Conference. From then on their progress was in the nature of a tidal wave. On all levels and sectors of public life they reaped the harvest of their own constancy and of the repeated failures of their adversaries.

On August 20th, the elections for the Central Petrograd Town Council provided the Bolsheviks with their first great triumph at the polls. True, the Social Revolutionaries, who obtained 37 per cent of the votes, remained the leading party, but they had suffered a considerable set-back. While the Cadets held their ground, the Mensheviks received a mere 5 per cent of the votes. The real victors, according to Sukhanov, were the Bolsheviks, 'so recently trampled in the mud, accused of treason and venality, utterly routed morally and materially, and filling till that day the prisons of the capital. People had almost ceased to notice them. Then where had they sprung up from again? What sort of strange, diabolical enchantment was this?' They collected just under 200,000 votes and this while working under semi-clandestine conditions. A third of the inhabitants of Petrograd had voted for them, for the revolutionary vanguard of the proletariat.

A month later, the Bolsheviks scored an even more brilliant victory in Moscow—their municipal candidates received 51 per cent of the total vote—and hence an absolute majority over the Cadets (20 per cent), the Social Revolutionaries (15 per cent) and the Mensheviks (4 per cent). In several provincial cities, notably in Kostroma and Tsarytsin, the results were similar, and the more remarkable in that the voters represented all classes of the population.

In the army, too, that recognized stronghold of the Social

Revolutionary Party, the Bolsheviks, whose propaganda had been banned after the July Days, made a striking recovery. The Fifth Army, renowned for its discipline and hence considered a sheet-anchor of the government, elected a new committee with a Bolshevik majority. Even the artillery, another reputed stronghold of loyalism, suddenly became 'open to defeatist propaganda'. And Boris Sokolov, the Social Revolutionary expert on military questions, contended a few weeks before the October insurrection that 'all regimental party organizations have become completely disorganized with the exception of the Bolshevik ones.' Things were even more favourable to Lenin's party among the sailors. The Baltic Fleet, meeting in congress, sent a message to the head of the Provisional Government which ended with this disagreeable salutation: 'To you, Napoleon Kerensky, traitor to the Revolution, we send our maledictions.'

The spread of Bolshevik propaganda in the countryside, electoral successes in the towns, the capture of a host of military committees —all this was significant enough. It was essential, however, that the Bolsheviks should capture the most influential Soviet of all. On August 31st, the Petrograd Soviet carried a motion calling for the transfer of power to the proletariat by an overwhelming majority. The moderate socialist leaders were so taken aback that they called for a second vote, which produced much the same result: despite a number of defections under obvious pressure, the Bolshevik resolution was once again carried by 279 votes to 115 with 51 abstentions. On September 9th there was a further test of strength between supporters and opponents of the Provisional Government. This time the Bolshevik forces were led by Trotsky, who had been released on bail a few days earlier after the Petrograd Trade Unions had been granted the great 'privilege of standing bail for this great leader of the revolutionary proletariat'. When the Menshevik and Social Revolutionary leaders of the Petrograd Soviet now staked the survival of the Presidium on a motion of confidence, Trotsky asked if Kerensky was still a member of that body. He was told that this was so, and immediately pointed out that in that case the vote of confidence in the Presidium was a vote of confidence in Kerensky. 'This threw over to our side another hundred or so of the delegates who had been vacillating,' Trotsky explained, and as a result the vote of confidence was rejected by 519 votes to 414 with 67 abstentions.

Tseretelli now mounted the tribune. 'We are conscious and proud of having borne aloft the banner of Revolution for six months. Now this banner has passed into your hands. We can only express the hope that you will keep it flying for at least half that time.' A fresh committee was elected, and since the old 'standard-bearers' refused the invitation of the Bolshevik majority to work with them, the new executive was made up exclusively of Bolsheviks, left-wing Social Revolutionaries and Internationalist Mensheviks.

On September 5th, the Moscow Soviet also passed into the hands of the Bolsheviks, and a vote of no confidence in the Provisional Government was passed by 335 votes to 254. Kiev, the capital of the Ukraine, followed suit a few days later and so did Kazan, Baku, Nikolaiev, Krasnoyarsk and a host of other industrial towns. Finnish soviets gave even more wholehearted support to Lenin's party, and the reason why the Central Executive of the All-Russian Congress of Soviets remained under right-wing control was simply that, having been elected in June, it no longer reflected the actual balance of power.

The failure of the July demonstrations and the anti-Bolshevik campaign of the moderate socialist leaders had convinced Lenin that calling for the transfer of power to the soviets was now an empty slogan—the soviets had clearly ceased to be revolutionary. What the Bolsheviks must aim at instead was the capture of the soviets themselves, as an indispensable step towards the seizure of state power. And when they achieved the first objective within a matter of weeks Lenin thought the time was ripe for tackling the second, and accordingly gave orders for the mounting of an armed insurrection.

Towards the armed insurrection

Lenin's paramount role in the Russian Revolution was due to two main achievements: immediately after his return to Russia, he had persuaded his Party not to be satisfied with the establishment of bourgeois democracy and to oppose the Provisional Government at all costs, and this at a time when many socialists were still full of hope in its great promises; moreover, before the October insurrection, he had not only convinced his sceptical comrades that an uprising was possible but had called for its preparation with all speed and energy. To do so he had been forced to clear a host of formidable obstacles. Consider the position of his party after the

failure of the July Days: government repression had forced many
of its leaders to go underground or into prison; the masses had
turned away from the Bolsheviks, had joined in the campaign of
vilification and were repeating the calumny that Lenin was a
'German-Bolshevik spy'; the militant working class had been disarmed and demoralized. True, their setback had been of short
duration—since August the forces of Revolution had made a
remarkable recovery. But how could the Bolshevik leaders forget
the experiences of July and the fatal threat they had posed to the
very survival of their Party? Hundreds of thousands of workers and
soldiers had risen up against the Provisional Government, and the
result had been the near-destruction not of that government but of
the Bolshevik movement. Was it reasonable, so soon after so foolhardy an enterprise, to take the risk of a new adventure?

But Lenin used all his powers of persuasion to impose his view,
and this at a time when the counter-revolutionary wave was still at
its crest. Small wonder therefore that his proposals were greeted
with so much scepticism, and that so many staunch Communists
put up a bitter fight against them. The noise of the July demonstrations had barely receded, government persecution had laid low the
Bolshevik leadership—indeed, many were still in prison—and
already their chief was calling for an end to the 'constitutional
illusions' and for an armed uprising. Though he kept his grip on
reality—for Lenin warned his comrades to keep a cool head in the
face of constant provocation—his call for insurrection nevertheless
seemed to be a great gamble, the more so as he himself was far
from the scene of the proposed action. Ever since July, Lenin had
been cooling his heels in Finland, cut off from events and from
most of his colleagues and supporters. After several months of
intense activity it looked as if he had escaped from a Swiss prison
only to serve in a Finnish one. Trotsky tells us that to break his
isolation he summoned 'various Bolsheviks, subjected them to
searching questions, supervised the speeches and actions of the
party leaders, and used the most devious channels to send his
instructions to the Central Committee'.

In August, the Bolsheviks had held their National Congress and
had elected a new Central Committee of twenty-one members and
eight stand-ins. Lenin, unable to be present at most of their
deliberations, was reduced to infusing them with the necessary
revolutionary ardour by writing them letter after letter, sending

them admonition after admonition, alternating warnings with threats. Physical contact with his friends was well-nigh impossible, and hence he had little chance of deploying his immense powers of personal persuasion. In his absence, though they continued to respect him as before, quite a few members of the Central Committee gained the impression that since he was so far from Petrograd Lenin had become a dreamer, and accordingly turned a deaf ear to many of his appeals.

A case in point was the letter Lenin wrote them some time between September 12th and 14th, 1917. In it he declared that 'having obtained a majority in the Soviets of Workers' and Soldiers' Deputies of both capitals, the Bolsheviks can and must take power into their own hands.' After justifying this conclusion by a brief analysis of the political situation, he went on to call on his comrades to 'place on the order of the day the armed uprising in Petrograd and Moscow'. In a second letter, written almost at the same date and addressed to the same body, he explained his reasons at greater length and came back to the same theme with even more insistence:

> We must at the same time, without losing a single moment, organize the staff of the insurrectionary detachments; designate the forces; move the loyal regiments to the most important points; surround the Alexandrinka Theatre,[1]; occupy Peter and Paul Fortress; arrest the general staff and the government; move against the military cadets, the Savage Division, etc., such detachments as will die rather than allow the enemy to move to the centre of the city.

The reaction to his letter has been recorded for us by Bukharin. 'We all gasped. Nobody had yet posed the question so abruptly ... At first all were bewildered. Afterwards, having talked it over, we made a decision. Perhaps that was the sole case in the history of our party when the Central Committee unanimously decided to burn a letter of Lenin.'

And so, Lenin was forced to send further messages, to issue new appeals against his own party's hesitations. On September 27th he wrote a voluminous letter to Smilga, President of the Finnish Regional Committee of Soviets. 'What are we doing?' he asked. 'We only pass resolutions. We are losing time, we are setting

[1] The meeting place of the Democratic Conference.

dates ... Isn't it ridiculous to put things off like this ... ?' And he went on to say: 'History has made the military question the fundamental political question now. I am afraid that the Bolsheviks forget this, being steeped in "day-to-day events", in petty current questions ... ' And, no doubt suspicious of his Central Committee, he asked Smilga to 'have this letter typed out and delivered to the Petrograd and Moscow comrades', thus by-passing the party leaders.

On September 29th, 1917, Lenin launched another appeal for an insurrection: 'What then is to be done? *Man muss aussprechen was ist*,[1] "say what is", admit the truth, that in our Central Committee and at the top of our party, there is a tendency in favour of *awaiting* the Congress of Soviets, *against* an immediate uprising. We must *overcome* this tendency or opinion. Otherwise the Bolsheviks will COVER THEMSELVES WITH SHAME FOR EVER; THEY WILL BE REDUCED TO NOTHING as a party. For to miss such a moment and to "await" the Congress of Soviets is either *absolute idiocy* or *complete betrayal*.' Clearly, if Lenin had been able to face his comrades in person at this point he would have picked them up by the scruff of their necks and shaken them hard until they saw his point of view. But in his exile he could do little more than repeat his vehement imprecations, followed by threats. 'To refrain from seizing power at present, to "wait", to chatter in the Central Executive Committee ... means to *ruin the revolution*.' As for the threat: 'Seeing that the Central Committee has left EVEN WITHOUT AN ANSWER my writings insisting on such a policy since the beginning of the Democratic Conference, that the Central Organ IS DELETING from my articles references to such glaring errors of the Bolsheviks as the shameful decision to participate in the Pre-Parliament ... I am compelled to recognize here a "gentle" hint as to the unwillingness of the Central Committee even to consider this question, a gentle hint at gagging me and a suggestion that I retire. I am compelled to *tender my resignation from the Central Committee*, which I hereby do, leaving myself the freedom of propaganda IN THE LOWER RANKS of the party and at the Party Congress.'

And on October 1st, 1917, Lenin once again addressed himself to the Central Committee but so as to reach a wider audience than the latter, in which he was fast losing confidence, he asked specifically that part of his letter be distributed among the members of

[1] In German in the original.

the Moscow and Petrograd Bolshevik committees and Bolshevik members of the soviets. To all of them Lenin declared that 'delay has become positively a *crime*' and that the Bolsheviks 'have no right to wait for the Congress of Soviets, they must seize power *here and now*, and so save the world revolution'. And Lenin ended his letter with an impassioned: 'To wait is a crime against the revolution.'

On October 8th, 1917, Lenin sent a letter to Bolshevik delegates to the Regional Congress of Northern Soviets. In it we twice find the phrase, 'Temporization is death.'

On October 10th, Lenin finally managed to attend a Central Committee meeting in person. According to Trotsky, he 'came in a wig and spectacles without a beard'. It was in this guise that the great professional revolutionary prepared to meet the day he had been instrumental in hastening by nearly twenty-five years of incessant activity, conspiracy, struggle, polemics and debates. Seeing him during one of these decisive hours, Antonov-Ovseënko, one of the leaders of the October insurrection, described him as 'a small, greying, meek man, wearing pince-nez and in the pink of health. One might have taken him for a musician, a teacher or a second-hand-bookseller.' There was indeed something of the teacher and even of the bookseller in one whom Malaparte has called that *bonhomme Lenin*. But despite the well-groomed disguise, it was the revolutionary in him who was uppermost at this hour.

The minutes of that historic meeting of the Bolshevik Central Committee on October 10th, 1917, are too dry to give us even the slightest hint of the tense atmosphere in which heated discussions were pursued for ten long hours. As for Lenin's contribution, the minutes merely note his remark that 'from the beginning of September there has been a kind of indifference to the question of the insurrection ... We must rather talk of the technical side. Now, by all appearances, we have wasted a considerable amount of time [when] ... politically the situation is ripe for the seizure of power.' Lenin then gave his reasons. He had already made them the subject of an important paper entitled 'The crisis has matured', part of which had appeared in the official party organ during October. In it he listed all the factors favouring an immediate insurrection. Chief among them were the international situation and the propitious political, economic and social climate in Russia at that moment. It was characteristic of Lenin's strategy that he should have begun by stressing the international factors: 'Mass arrests of [socialist] party

leaders in free Italy, and especially the beginnings of mutinies in
the German army, are undoubted symptoms of the great turning
point, the symptoms of the *eve of revolution* on a world scale.' And
he insisted on this point: 'There is no room for doubts. We are on
the threshold of a world proletarian revolution. And since we,
Russian Bolsheviks, alone out of all the proletarian internationalists
of all countries, enjoy comparatively great freedom ... since we
have on our side the *majority* of the masses of the people in revolutionary times, to us may and must truly apply the famous dictum:
he who has been given much shall have to account for more.'

As for Russia herself, Lenin thought that a number of indications
favoured the immediate seizure of power. In the first place there
was the uprising of the peasants. Then there was the inability of
the Provisional Government to solve the national problem, or to do
anything about the general social disturbances to which the massive
railway strike bore witness. Finally there were the sweeping electoral successes of the Bolsheviks in borough councils and soviets, all
of which were symptomatic of the impatience of the masses and of
their readiness to take revolutionary action.

By the time the Central Committee of the Bolshevik Party met
on October 10th, Lenin, though by no means unopposed, had
succeeded in swinging the leadership a long way to the Left. Thus
while some of the speakers still stressed the weakness of the Bolshevik organizations, notably in the matter of armaments, the
meeting rose after passing a resolution that by and large endorsed
Lenin's views. It ended on the following note: 'Recognizing ...
that the armed uprising is inevitable and fully ripe, the Central
Committee proposes to all organizations of the party that they be
guided by this, and from this point of view consider and decide all
practical questions ... '

One point, however, remained undecided: on what precise date
would the uprising take place? Many Bolshevik leaders, including
Trotsky, argued that it was technically and politically desirable that
the insurrection should coincide with the meeting of the All-
Russian Congress of Soviets. In this way the impression would be
given that the uprising had been ordered, in the name of that
workers' institution, by a broad section of the proletariat and not
simply by a political party, thus increasing the prestige and the
chances of success of the revolutionary movement. Lenin opposed
this argument. 'We must guard', he argued, 'against illusions and

constitutional hopes based on the Congress of Soviets.' Why this impatience? Was he afraid that the moderate socialists would try to postpone the Congress and so prevent the uprising? Or did he suspect that some of his own comrades used arguments about the precise date of the insurrection simply as a blind? In any case, the resolution of October 10th did not entirely remove his doubts, and he continued to condemn those Bolsheviks who thought the time was unpropitious for an uprising.

Such a faction did, in fact, exist within the party, and it was not by chance that it was headed by Kamenev, who during the first few weeks of the revolution had called for a conciliatory attitude towards the Provisional Government. Lenin opposed this line now just as he had opposed it before: his wish to overthrow Kerensky was based on the same arguments that had originally caused him to come out in intransigent opposition to the bourgeoisie and their moderate socialist allies. For while Lenin took the classical Marxist view that the socialist revolution must follow the bourgeois after the latter had inaugurated a series of profound economic, political and social transformations, he also believed in a 'permanent revolution', i.e. in the need for transcending the bourgeois phase and for moving forward, in a continuous historical sweep, to the proletarian phase. And the fact that in 1917 he failed to attach a label of origin to this doctrine—which was Trotskyist—changed nothing in the nature of this broad political perspective. His political view differed from that of the Mensheviks not only in matters of internal party organization but also in the firm conviction that the working class was called upon to perform a number of democratic and socialist tasks that would bring it into sharp conflict with the bourgeoisie.[1] For all that, the gap between Bolsheviks and Mensheviks was far narrower than one might be inclined to think in retrospect. In particular, the Menshevik Left and the Bolshevik Right were very close to each other: Kamenev's campaign against Lenin differed little from Menshevik attacks on all attempts to identify Marxism with insurrectionary action. In both cases, rejection of the violent path sprang from reluctance to break with the bourgeois revolution.

Now Kamenev was not alone. In particular, he enjoyed the support of Zinoviev, one of Lenin's closest associates, and one who had twice followed him into exile. Zinoviev and Kamenev formed a

[1] See Chapter 2.

redoubtable couple in their opposition not only to insurrectionary agitation but—far more fundamentally—to the 'permanent revolution'. Nor were they alone in warning against the risks of an uprising. Thus one day while taking a walk with a comrade in Moscow, Rykov, a leading member of the Bolshevik Right and later Chairman of the Council of People's Commissars, turned to his companion and said, 'Here, in the very centre of bourgeois Moscow, we really seem to be pygmies thinking of moving a mountain.' According to the witness of another Bolshevik militant, party members were saying quite openly that 'Lenin has gone crazy; he is pushing the working class to certain ruin. His armed insurrection will get us nothing; they will shatter us, exterminate the party of the working class and that will postpone the revolution for years and years to come.'

Similar views were also expressed by Nogin, Miliutin, Lunacharsky and Kalinin, to mention only a few of the most important Bolsheviks. In a number of local committees, Moscow among them, the majority was strongly opposed to an insurrection and remained so until the eve of the October Revolution. Moreover, quite a few Bolshevik organizations in the provinces continued to collaborate closely with the Mensheviks against what they called the 'forces of counter-revolution'.

The freedom of expression that still reigned in the Bolshevik Party at that time gave Lenin's opponents every chance to organize themselves and to propagate their views. Kamenev and Zinoviev used it to the full. On October 11th, they explained their attitude at length in a declaration meant for the Party leadership. Like Lenin they introduced international considerations, arguing that 'to call for insurrection at this stage is not only playing with the future of our party and the Revolution, but also with that of the world revolution.' An insurrection was not only risky but completely unnecessary since 'if we used the correct tactics we could obtain more than a third of the seats in the Constituent Assembly'. So strong a Bolshevik contingent could easily come to terms with the peasant delegates, whereas Lenin's radicalism was bound to push the peasants and the petit-bourgeoisie in general into the arms of the Right. Kamenev and Zinoviev went on to demonstrate that the conservatives were still very powerful in Petrograd, while the revolutionary forces, in Russia as in the rest of Europe, remained far too weak to 'declare war on the entire bourgeois world'.

What then did they want the Bolshevik Party to do? They argued that 'the party of the proletariat must be enlarged', that its 'programme must be made increasingly clear to the masses'. Was it not an old objective of social democracy to develop the political and economic organizations of the working class and to concentrate on the task of political propaganda and education? For the rest—and this was another old plank in the Social Democratic platform—it was essential while consolidating electoral successes to wait until external pressures favoured action by the revolutionary forces, or, indeed, made such action unavoidable. Such pressures could come either from 'our allies abroad'—the revolutionary proletariat of Europe—or from the inner enemy, the Russian bourgeoisie. According to Kamenev and Zinoviev, only two sets of circumstances could justify recourse to insurrection: a revolution by the workers of Western Europe blazing the trail for their 'Russian brethren', or else a counter-revolutionary attack against the soviets which would force the Bolsheviks to reply in kind. Save for these two contingencies—both equally improbable according to the Bolshevik Right—the only salvation lay in persistent organization and patience.

Lenin's reply was brief and to the point. His opponents preached patience, but 'hunger does not wait, the peasant uprising has not waited, the war does not wait.' He had nothing but disdain for the wait-and-see policy of Zinoviev and Kamenev. 'Under harsh and infernal conditions,' he exploded, 'with Liebknecht[1] *alone* (and he in prison), without newspapers or mass meetings, without soviets, facing the incredible hostility of *all* classes ... Germans, or rather the German international revolutionaries, workers in sailors' uniforms, have started a mutiny with one chance of success in a hundred. And we, with dozens of papers, freedom of meeting, we who hold the *majority* in the soviets, proletarian internationalists more solidly entrenched than all the rest, refuse to support the German revolutionaries by an insurrection of our own. We argue like the Scheidemanns and Renaudels.[2] We apparently believe that the wisest course is to do nothing at all, lest they start shooting at

[1] Karl Liebknecht, German Social-Democrat deputy sentenced to thirty months' imprisonment for his opposition to the war. With Rosa Luxemburg he founded the German Communist Party in December 1918. Both were assassinated in January 1919.

[2] A German and a French socialist who, in 1914, declared their support for the war and for class collaboration.

us and the world lose internationalists of the finest kidney, reasonable and most perfect. We want to show the world how sensible we really are. So we simply adopt a resolution of sympathy with the German insurgents, and call off the insurrection in Russia.'

But neither Lenin's fury nor his scorching irony was enough to convince his opponents or to reduce them to silence. True, Lenin's resolution of October 10th which stated, *inter alia*, that 'an insurrection is inevitable' and called upon the Party to prepare it, had been carried by ten votes to two—those of Kamenev and Zinoviev —but the latter were far less isolated than these figures suggest. Quite a few members of the Central Committee had voted for Lenin's motion with mental reservations—of the kind expressed by Kalinin a few days later during a meeting of the Petrograd Bolshevik Committee. He called the resolution of October 10th, 'one of the best the Central Committee had ever adopted ... We are practically approaching the armed insurrection. But when will it be possible? Perhaps a year from now—one can't really tell.'

On October 16th, 1917, the Central Committee held another meeting, attended by delegates from a number of important party organizations: the Petrograd Executive Committee; the Military Organization; the Bolshevik faction in the Petrograd Soviet; trade unions; factory committees, and so on. Lenin was present at this meeting as well and concluded his report on the political situation with the following remarks: 'An analysis of the class struggle in Russia and Europe will show the absolute need for a most resolute and active policy, in short for armed insurrection.' However, the chief importance of this meeting was that it heard reports from the Petrograd rank and file on the political and social climate in the capital and its suburbs.[1] Since the provinces were far less well represented, many of Lenin's opponents seized this opportunity and demanded a national conference before an insurrection was finally decided upon. Zinoviev and Kamenev returned to the charge as well. Zinoviev pointed out that if the resolution of October 10th had indeed been binding, Lenin would not now be offering it for discussion by a wider audience. In other words, the matter was far from settled. Kamenev, for his part, had this to say: 'A whole week has gone by since we have taken this resolution ... [and] nothing has been done ... This proves that the present conditions are not in the least propitious to an armed insurrection.' And he concluded,

See below.

'Two tactics are in conflict here: the tactic of conspiracy and the tactic of faith in the motive forces of the Russian Revolution.'

Miliutin, a member of the Central Committee, added his voice: 'We are not ready to strike the first blow. We are in no position to overthrow the government or stop its supporters in the days to come.' And he concluded that the perspective before the Party 'was not one of insurrection'. Moreover, a representative of the Petrograd Committee declared that 'we cannot come out but we ought to be ready.' And Sokolnikov, another member of the Central Committee, contended that only after the meeting of the Second All-Russian Congress of Soviets 'must we decide whether or not to appeal to the masses'. Joffé, another famous party leader, argued similarly when he said, 'It is not true that the question before us is a purely technical one; the moment of insurrection must be considered from the political point of view as well.' This came back to expressing doubt in the possibility of, and need for, an armed uprising.

Two resolutions were now put before the meeting. The first had been drafted by Lenin. It summoned 'all organizations and all workers and soldiers to a detailed and vigorous preparation of armed insurrection in support of the Centre which will be created for that express purpose'.[1] It went on to express 'confidence that the Central Committee and the soviets would in due course determine the propitious moment for, and the precise nature of, the attack'. The second resolution was penned by Zinoviev. It was brief, and simply called for 'unflagging study and preparation', adding that 'from now until the consultation of the Bolshevik faction in the Congress of Soviets, any demonstration is out of place'. Lenin's motion was carried by twenty votes to two, with three abstentions during its first reading. During a second reading and, after the rejection of a number of moderate amendments, it was carried again, though the number of those in favour had decreased to nineteen and the number of abstentions had increased to four. Combining opponents and abstainers, we thus find that six members out of a total of twenty-five did not support Lenin's policy in the Central Committee. In fact this result did not reflect

[1] The Revolutionary Military Centre was made up of Sverdlov, Stalin, Bubnov, Uritzky and Dzerzhinsky. It played no part at all in the October events, though Stalinist historiographers, great myth-makers that they are, gave it an imaginary role so as to turn Stalin into one of the chief architects of the Russian Revolution.

the true balance of forces. Thus when Zinoviev's resolution was put to the vote, six members of the Central Committee voted in favour, fifteen voted against and three abstained. This time the moderate wing included 9 Party leaders, i.e. more than a third of the executive.

Lenin himself had apparently gone back on his earlier stand when he agreed that 'the propitious moment and the precise nature of the attack' would be determined no longer by the Party alone but by the Party *and* the soviets. But in practice all he had done was to agree with Trotsky and other Bolshevik leaders to start the insurrection on the day the Congress of Soviets met, though several hours before it opened. By ratifying a *fait accompli* the Congress would give the impression of having been responsible for it, and in any case would strengthen its appeal.

On October 16th, however, though the political decision was taken, the practical means were not yet to hand. So Lenin's opponents within the Bolshevik Party were given a few days' grace to try one more manoeuvre before the Congress of Soviets was convoked. To that end, and in flagrant violation of the rules of Party discipline bordering on sabotage, *Novaia Zhizn* came out on October 18th with an article by Kamenev in which the secret plans of the Party leadership were made public. Kamenev explained that the 'problem of insurrection had been the subject of important discussions in the Bolshevik Party' and that he and Zinoviev had 'protested most strongly against an armed insurrection at the present moment'. And he went on to call for opposition to any attempt to start an uprising.

Kamenev's article earned him a swift rebuke from Lenin, who that same day wrote an indignant 'Letter to Members of the Bolshevik Party'. In it he declared that he could no longer think of Kamenev and Zinoviev as comrades, and that he would 'fight with all my powers, in the Central Committee and in the Congress, for their expulsion from the Party'. In a second letter, addressed to the Central Committee and published on October 19th, Lenin, while finding it 'painful to write these words about old comrades who were so close to me', nevertheless insisted that they must be taken severely to task for their 'shameless infamy and downright treachery'. *Pravda* published both letters but preceded them with an editorial note by Stalin, who contended that the 'sharp tone of Comrade Lenin's article notwithstanding, we all remain good comrades at heart'. Was this refusal to condemn Lenin's adversaries a sign of tolerance, or did it rather show that Stalin shared their attitude to the insurrection? We cannot tell; all we do know is that when the matter was brought up before the Central Committee, and when Kamenev repeated his earlier offer to resign rather than take responsibility for a decision he deplored, several members pleaded with him to change his mind. In the end his resignation was accepted 'provisionally' by five votes to three. Zinoviev's defection was not even discussed, nor was Lenin's demand that both 'rebels' be expelled.

By carrying the debate outside the Party, the leaders of the Bolshevik Right had clearly acknowledged the defeat that had been inflicted on them within it. Henceforth the Bolshevik path was clear: the Party had cut the umbilical cord that connected it to the February Revolution. All that remained was to organize the insurrection. The Revolution had ceased to be an idea—it had become a method.

The vigil of arms

It was only then that Trotsky came into his own. So far he had played a secondary and almost episodic role, at least compared to that of Lenin, the true architect of that great instrument of revolution which was the Bolshevik Party. Almost single-handed, Lenin had broken its links with all the other parties, had taught it to rely on none but the radicalized masses; he more than anyone else had instilled his followers with courage to fight for the proletariat and against the Provisional Government. Lenin had played a unique role in the birth and subsequent course of the Russian Revolution. But if Lenin was its father, if he alone gave a name to the aspirations of the anonymous mass of people who paved the way for and participated in the great October events, Trotsky was the organizer of the actual insurrection—and also its poet. It was he who at meeting after meeting, in proclamation after proclamation, gave voice to the enthusiasm and fury of the people; he who had his finger on the people's pulse; he who made it beat faster; he who showed the entire nation that their actions had a scope far beyond the narrow confines of Russia.

Life had fully prepared him for his double role of organizer and poet of revolution. To begin with he was an outstandingly talented writer and speaker; he had the temperament of an artist and the brain of a mathematician. As a writer he scaled the heights; as an orator he was peerless. Compared with his searing sarcasm and brilliant turns of phrase, Lenin's style seemed heavy and laboured. As a theorist, too, Trotsky was Lenin's superior—he had the keen intelligence, the cultivation and the powerful imagination needed for broad elaborations of doctrine. True, he lacked the more pedestrian, but for all that more profound, virtues that made Lenin the founder of Soviet Russia—if such personal labels can, indeed, be attached to great collective movements. He lacked the unfaltering determination, the inexhaustible patience and the political shrewdness that enabled Lenin to sense unfailingly which way the wind was blowing. It was this failure for which Trotsky had to pay so dearly in the 1920s when he tried to stem the rising tide of Stalinism. He also lacked the modesty that enabled Lenin to play the part of a political leader without imposing his own personality, to overcome opponents without crushing them, and of resolving the conflict of individuals and ideas that threatened the unity of the leading team. Lenin was the perfect militant, indeed, a militant of genius. Trotsky often wore the garb of the prophet[1] or of the artist and actor, and it is as such that he left his mark on Russian politics—in him, the poetic gift went hand in hand with exceptional administrative and strategic skills. With the prophet he shared his great eloquence; with the administrator and strategist a feeling for organization and a gift for leadership. Now, in October 1917, when Russia entered the final struggle for power, it was these qualities that helped to turn Trotsky into Lenin's chief collaborator—to couple their names in the imagination of the whole world. In their similarities and their differences both men symbolized for some the great hope of the Russian Revolution, and for others its evil machinations.

Subsequently, historical falsification would idealize Lenin, turning him into the incarnation of all human virtues and endowing him with the supernatural attribute of infallibility. The Stalinists deified Lenin and liquidated Trotsky. But not content with that, they tried to drag Trotsky's name through the mud: no distortion of historical truth was crude enough, no lie big enough, no slander

[1] It is as a prophet that Isaac Deutscher has treated him in his biography (see Bibliography). There are many biographies of Lenin, some of them excellent. Those of Trotsky are few and far between; Isaac Deutscher's has the exceptional merit of placing the man in his social and historical context, thus affording the reader a view of the whole Soviet experience.

wild enough, too fantastic or absurd. As a result, the official history of the Russian Revolution became a perversion of history, one that few people outside the Soviet Union take seriously today. In Russia herself, however, no one was brave enough to protest, with the result that calumny came to take the place of official truth, and lies attained the validity of a simplified but false catechism.

Trotsky, Sukhanov tells us, was everywhere at once. 'His influence, among both the masses and the revolutionary leadership, was immense; in those days he was the principal actor, the hero of that extraordinary page in history.' He harangued enormous crowds in overflowing halls in Petrograd, especially the *Cirque Moderne* which was packed day and night. His official job was to arm the people, and his oratory proved invaluable. Ever since the Bolsheviks had gained the majority in the Petrograd Soviet, Trotsky had been the leading spokesman of the extreme Left in the capital. He was once again President of the Soviet—twelve years after first holding that position during the Revolution of 1905. And this time Trotsky made sure that his office was turned into a command post and a centre of revolution. To that end, he made use of a resolution passed by the Mensheviks, but gave it a scope its sponsors had never intended.

On October 9th, 1917, the Mensheviks had called on the Petrograd Soviet to form a 'Committee of Revolutionary Defence' charged with solving military problems in the capital in close co-operation with the general staff of the local garrison. These problems had grown acute: the Provisional Government was determined to send troops from the capital to the front, and this at a time when the fall of Riga and the loss of the Moonsund Islands made a German offensive against Petrograd seem a military certainty, so much so that the government itself was preparing to move to Moscow. (It was only thanks to fierce opposition by the Left that this plan was dropped.) For the rest, Kerensky did succeed in sending some of the 'politically unreliable' regiments—ninety thousand men all told—to the front, ostensibly in answer to urgent requests from the commanders in the field. That this was merely a pretext may be gathered from a telegram the Commander of the Northern Front sent to the Minister of War in early October. It pointed out that the 'initiative of transferring troops from the Petrograd Garrison to the front has come from you and not from me ... When it became clear that these contingents did not want to go to the front, that is that they were incapable of fighting, I informed your representative that ... we have more than enough such contingents at the front, but seeing your determination to send them, I did not insist ... ' In any case, the transfer caused a furore in the Petrograd barracks.

This was but one of the acute problems the Committee of Revolutionary Defence was meant to tackle. But when instead of using it to soothe the incensed soldiers the Bolsheviks tried to turn the Committee into a revolutionary instrument, the Mensheviks decided to back out. The Committee now adopted a new name: the 'Military Revolutionary Committee of the Soviet of Petrograd', and as such it was to play an important role in the preparation and subsequent course of the October insurrection. In theory it included representatives from numerous workers' institutions in the capital, but in practice the main work was done by a smaller body, the Bureau, largely run by the Bolsheviks. Trotsky, the President, was ably assisted by Podvoisky (Vice-President), Antonov-Ovseënko (Secretary), Lashevich, Lazimir (a left-wing Social Revolutionary), Sadofsky and Mekhonoshin. Together they formed the staff of the insurrection.

The task of the Committee was a double and, to a large extent, contradictory one: it was meant to prepare the uprising while disguising it, and to keep up the enthusiasm of the workers and soldiers while telling them nothing about the precise insurrectionary plans. These tactical requirements forced the leaders of the Revolutionary Committee to lift a corner of the veil at one moment and to lower it at the next, to use thousands of artifices by which they could give their friends to understand that the plans for the attack were proceeding apace, while lulling the fears of their vigilant adversaries. In public, Trotsky insisted that the Petrograd Soviet was solely involved in defensive preparations against a possible attack by reactionary forces, and so skilful were his evasive tactics that he kept the moderate socialists guessing to the very end, all the while putting the finishing touches to his plan of campaign.

In this he was greatly helped by the support of a number of rebellious regiments and of the Baltic Fleet. But the Bolsheviks' main source of strength was the Red Guard. Its origins went back to February 1917, or at least to the first days of the new regime. During the events that had led up to the fall of Tsarism, workers in the capital had laid their hands on large quantities of arms and ammunition and most of these had remained in their possession. As a result, Petrograd could boast a strong workers' militia, and so could most other industrial centres—a fact that the bourgeoisie found highly disturbing. These were the men who had eventually banded together into the Red Guard, more or less spontaneously, arresting employers suspected of economic sabotage, acting as stewards at demonstrations, or training for combat. The Kornilov uprising gave the nascent Red Guard a tremendous boost, and the capture by the Bolsheviks of the majority in the Petrograd Soviet did the rest.

In the weeks immediately prior to the insurrection, thousands of factory workers received military instruction from highly trained men, and were issued with rifles by the Military Revolutionary Committee. As a result, the Red Guard increased its membership from some ten thousand men in July to twenty thousand in October. Each battalion—from four hundred to six hundred men —was divided into three companies; each company into three squads, and each squad into four tens. The Red Guard also included a number of special technical commands, machine-gun sections, stretcher-bearers and telegraphers. Enrolment was voluntary but collective—the decision to join was taken by a factory committee and not by individual workers. The Guards were paid for their service at the normal rate, and did, in fact, continue to work in the factories. The entire commanding staff was elected by the men themselves or by the factory committee. For the rest, discipline was strict, and all orders had to be carried out without discussion. The carrying of arms for unauthorized purposes was a punishable offence, and the number of infractions recorded during the insurrection was extremely small.

While the Military Revolutionary Committee and the Red Guard represented the armed staff and spearhead of the revolution, the Bolshevik party, the Petrograd Soviet, the factory committees and the Permanent Garrison Conference were its political executive. The factory committees had for a long time been under the control of the most politically conscious workers, so much so that for months they had formed the chief bastions of Bolshevism—even the repression following the July Days had been quite unable to dislodge them. The Permanent Garrison Conference, which emerged when preparations for the insurrection were in full swing, rapidly took the place of the Soviet of Soldiers' Deputies which, ever since its creation, had been controlled by the Mensheviks and above all by the Social Revolutionaries. The Garrison Conference, too, had been the scene of a brief struggle between the moderate socialists and the Bolsheviks, but in the electric atmosphere of Petrograd the latter easily carried the day—every Bolshevik speaker received a standing ovation while the Menshevik and Social Revolutionary delegates could not even make themselves heard. If the Petrograd garrison had by no means completely gone over to the Bolsheviks, the latter could at least count on its benevolent neutrality. In any case—and this was the decisive factor—no regiment was prepared to lift a finger in support of the Provisional Government.

Such then were the forces the Bolsheviks could muster or ignore. They had their weaknesses, and these were legion. Speaking of the Red Guard, Trotsky admitted that its members 'were in the majority badly trained, communications were badly organized, the supply system was lame'. But in political struggle no less than in military combat, what matters is not so much the relative strength or weakness of one of the adversaries as the relationship of forces between the two. What precisely were the arms the Provisional Government could muster in face of the assault the revolutionary proletariat was preparing to mount?

In the capital and its immediate vicinity, the Provisional Government could count on the support of a few thousand military cadets —the 'Junkers'—who were filled with blind hatred of the Bolsheviks and all they stood for. The government could also rely on three Cossack regiments, on a motorized battalion, and on an armoured division. In addition, they could bring up the Women's Battalion, which had made a poor showing during the June offensive. For the rest, the authorities were confident that the front-line troops could be relied upon to stop any disorders in Petrograd. In short, the government had no shortage of military forces; what was in doubt was its ability to command them. In the event, this turned out to be the crucial question, for the Bolshevik organization was so badly divided that a determined enemy would probably have carried the day.

But during the last weeks of October, bragging took the place of planning in the government, and when it came to bragging no one could outdo Kerensky. The head of the Provisional Government proclaimed to the world at large that the Bolsheviks had not the least chance of succeeding, and that if they dared to call for an insurrection Lenin would be finished for good. It was in the same vein that he informed Sir George Buchanan, 'I only wish that they would come out, and I will then put them down.' He told the Cadet Nabokov much the same thing, 'I hope to God that they start their uprising. I have more forces at my command than I need. They [the Bolsheviks] will be beaten once and for all.' And to General Dukhonin, 'That little matter can be settled without me, since everything is prepared.' And Kerensky saw fit to spend the last days of his reign at General Headquarters, while the fate of his regime was being decided in the capital where government authority had completely collapsed. His last public declarations were typical of the man no less than of the regime he represented. In the Pre-Parliament, summoned by deputies worried by the recent turn of events, he proclaimed solemnly, 'I can only say that the Provisional Government is fully informed of all the plans, and that it sees no reason for panic.' This view was shared by many conservatives. Prince Trubetskoy, for example, believed that 'the signs of recovery are already present. The very growth of Bolshevism is such a symptom. Everything that is in the middle fails; there remains only what is sound, and a lifeless, putrefying mass. Bolshevism is such a mass. And its death is inevitable.' This was on October 13th, 1917: two weeks later, the 'lifeless, putrefying mass' of Bolshevism was in power. Such optimism strikes us as blindness, but then the very idea that Lenin's Party could run a government caused nothing but amusement to all those who thought of it as a band of madmen or, at best, of extremist demagogues, incapable of concerted action. Here is how the Cadet paper *Rech* put it at the end of September 1917:

> ... Despite the passion of their proposals, despite their vain-glorious boasts, their show of assurance, the Bolsheviks, except for some fanatics, are courageous in words only. Hence they will never try to seize 'all the power' as their chief is urging them to do. Disrupters and destroyers *par excellence*, they are at heart nothing but poltroons, fully aware of their crass ignorance and of the evanescent nature of their current successes ... Irresponsible by nature, anarchistic by method and procedure, their platform can only be described as an aberration of political thought ...

Some left-wing Mensheviks—Sukhanov among them—had a
much clearer grasp of the meaning of the Bolshevik successes, and
realized to what extent Bolshevik propaganda and increasing activity in matters great and small had captured the imagination of the
masses. However, they, too, believed that despite their undoubted
organizational qualities the Bolsheviks were completely lacking in
political judgment. Lenin's followers were admittedly good at
making inflammatory speeches at public meetings, but when it
came to action they were sadly lacking—as the events of July had
shown. And it was their failure on that occasion that now convinced
the bourgeoisie that the Bolsheviks would once again collapse at the
slightest show of force. In Petrograd, rumour had it that the
Bolshevik insurrection was planned for October 17th, but nothing
at all happened on that day. Then there was a fresh rumour that the
uprising had been postponed to October 20th. But that day, too,
passed peaceably enough. The bourgeoisie began to breathe more
freely again, and some of them were even sorry to miss this opportunity of crossing swords with the Bolsheviks and giving them the
trouncing they so richly deserved.

The editorial from *Rech* we have already quoted went on to say
that the 'best way of getting rid of the Bolsheviks for many years to
come is to entrust their leaders with the destiny of our country'.
Four days before the outbreak of the insurrection, *Rech* still contended that 'if the Bolsheviks start their adventure, they will be
crushed without difficulty'. Other liberals expressed similar views
in private conversations. When John Reed, meeting a very influential member of the Cadet Party, asked him what he thought of the
much talked of Bolshevik insurrection, he was told with a shrug and
a sneer, 'They are cattle—*canaille*. They will not dare, or if they
dare, they will soon be sent flying.'

Mensheviks and Social Revolutionaries were less confident.
They realized that if the Bolsheviks tried to seize power their own
parties would be the losers, whatever the outcome. If the Bolsheviks
won, the moderate Left would be finally discredited; if they lost,
the counter-revolution would crush Chernov, Dan and Tseretelli
as ruthlessly as it would crush the insurrectionists. Their papers
accordingly published a stream of warnings to the proletariat,
repeating time and again that any hasty action now was bound to
unleash a civil war and end in misery and destruction. The left-
wing socialists round Maxim Gorky spoke in much the same vein,

and called on the Leninists to deny the rumours of a planned uprising.

Such in brief were the reactions of the various political groups on the eve of the October Revolution. Most were discredited and unpopular men whose waning strength precluded them from any real influence on the course of events, men whose fears or hopes had ceased to have any weight. But what was the attitude of the Petrograd masses, of the workers and soldiers whose active support or at least passive sympathy would be decisive in the coming struggle? Their reaction had been hardened by the social climate of Petrograd at the beginning of autumn—by the contrast between their own bitter misery and the insolent display of luxury by 'good' society.

While the queues outside bakeries and food stores grew longer and longer, while the rations were cut down further and further and the lack of fuel threatened yet another insupportable winter, the rich behaved as if nothing at all was amiss. John Reed tells us that 'the ladies of the minor bureaucratic set took tea with each other in the afternoon, each carrying her little gold or silver or jewelled sugar-box, and half a loaf of bread in her muff.' And these ladies looked almost poverty-stricken in comparison with the war profiteers who filled all the elegant restaurants of the town to capacity. Jules Destrée has left us a vivid description of them. He was a Belgian socialist who before the war had belonged to the 'impatient' wing of his Party, and had pleaded the cause of direct action by the masses. The war had transformed him into an ardent patriot, in which capacity he heaped abuse on all pacifists, ridiculing them as sexless wretches, and called for great sacrifices in the war for freedom. His government rewarded him with an ambassadorial post in Petrograd, where he arrived just in time to watch the death-throes of the Provisional Government. His aesthetic tastes and his new convictions made him seek out the 'best' society, and he had every opportunity of savouring the gastronomic delights the capital still had to offer. 'Young officers were dining with elegant ladies who laughed just a little too loudly. Under the bright lights, everyone revelled in a holiday atmosphere of unrestrained gaiety ... The war, the famine, the Revolution, were completely forgotten, and to chase away any lingering clouds a frenzied orchestra ... accompanied passionate songs of love and joy.'

Moreover, as John Reed tells us, 'young ladies from the

provinces came up to the capital to learn French and cultivate their voices.' In short, two worlds were living cheek by jowl, and did their best to ignore each other. But so many glaring contrasts and so many injustices—the careless abandon of a few, the crying misery of the vast majority; the inability of the politicians to offer the exasperated masses any way out of their pitiful condition— inevitably caused a disruption of social unity and a loss of discipline. This in turn led to the appearance of rowdy elements, and produced the first bloody clashes. Increasing anarchy was a sign not only of the utter collapse of the old but also of the birth-pangs of a new order. John Reed reports that 'hold-ups increased to such an extent that it was dangerous to walk down side streets ... On the Sadovaya one afternoon I saw a crowd of several hundred people beat and trample to death a soldier caught stealing ... Mysterious individuals circled round the shivering women who waited in queues long cold hours for bread and milk, whispering that the Jews had cornered the food supply—and that while people starved, the soviet members lived luxuriously.' And all this time 'gambling clubs functioned hectically from dusk to dawn, with champagne flowing and stakes of twenty thousand roubles. In the centre of the city at night, prostitutes in jewels and expensive furs walked up and down and crowded the cafés ... '

This was, of course, in the elegant quarters, which continued to attract young ladies preoccupied with their French accents and the refinement of their voices. But what did the workers' suburbs say and think? Were they determined once again to converge on the city centre to make their voices heard?

According to Sukhanov, a most attentive if not always completely objective observer, 'The atmosphere, by and large, was clearly favourable to the Bolsheviks; but when it came to insurrectionary activity, they, too, were rather weak and vague.' The Social Revolutionary Savinkov arrived at similar conclusions: 'The soldiers have begun to hold Bolshevik views. But their Bolshevism is passive— they have no inclination to intervene actively, with arms.' The Bolsheviks themselves, in order to gain a better idea of the mood of the masses, had summoned a large number of militants in close contact with the 'rank and file' to the Central Executive meeting on October 16th we have already mentioned. One by one these men reported on the political climate in the various parts of the capital. Their several observations left the leadership rather at a loss. 'Poor fighting spirit,' said some. 'If a campaign is started, the masses will support us,' said the others. Others again reported that 'The masses are too timid;' 'There is no will for action;' 'There will be a sudden swing towards the Bolsheviks;' 'Things are going badly for us;' 'There is a wait-and-see attitude;' 'The workers are full of doubts.' Reports from the barracks were no less confusing: 'Morale is low but the Bolshevik influence is strong;' 'The Kronstadt garrison will have no part of any insurrection.' The trade unions, too, were said to be afraid of joining the insurrectionary movement, lest they be disbanded by the government.

But there were more encouraging voices as well: 'The masses will take to arms with enthusiasm;' 'Had the Petrograd proletariat been armed, it would by now have come out in the streets;' 'If we do not seize power, the army and the navy will abandon us.' At the same time there was talk of a resurgence of the Anarchists and Anarcho-Syndicalists, groupings traditionally to the Left of the Bolsheviks.

All these reports would not, of course, be taken at face value— the sampling of public opinion is a highly unscientific business at the best of times. The enthusiasm and determination of the masses do not necessarily precede action; indeed, the converse is generally true: it is action that triggers off mass enthusiasm, particularly when the ground is well prepared. Workers on the eve of a strike, insurgents on the eve of an uprising, are filled by high hopes mixed with fears, by a desire for action mixed with doubts, by hesitation mixed with impatience. It is this conflict that forces them to face the fundamental issues—and this is precisely what the Russian working class did at the approach of the October battle.

But what conclusions did the Bolshevik leaders draw from these reports? Very prudently, Sverdlov, who was soon afterwards to exercise the functions of a head of state, said, 'We are not forced to conclude that the majority is against us; for the moment it is not with us, but it will not oppose us either.' Trotsky wrote later that 'the Petrograd proletariat had begun to feel rather dejected after so much waiting. They had even started to lose faith in the Bolsheviks. Were they going to turn out to be the same liars as the rest?' And Lenin, finally, 'There are symptoms of growing apathy and indifference. This is understandable. It is not a loss of faith in the Revolution, as the Cadets and their henchmen allege, but a loss of faith in resolutions and elections.'

Thus spoke the man who had led his party to the foothills of the mountain. Would the proletariat follow him? Would the Right put up a fierce resistance? There was much to argue about, to calculate and speculate on, while weighing up the chances and the risks. One could even ask Marxist questions about the rightness and strategy of a Russian Revolution. But the hour for questioning was past. 'Theory is grey, my friend,' Lenin said one day, quoting Goethe. 'But the tree of eternal life is green.' In Petrograd, at the onset of winter, on the eve of the insurrection, everyone forgot the grey theory. The tree of life caught fire.

9

The Seizure of Power

SUNDAY, October 22nd, was a strange day in Petrograd: it was not the mass demonstrations, which passed off calmly enough, but a series of minor events during the previous night — noticed by few — that proved to be the overture to an insurrection. Sunday itself had been proclaimed 'Day of the Soviet' by the extreme Left, and the impressive demonstrations called for that occasion had the double advantage of whipping up working-class enthusiasm and helping in the collection of urgently needed funds. Right-wing organizations, for their part, in association with religious groups, had called a religious procession through the centre of the city. Everyone expected trouble, and when there was none the bourgeoisie felt mightily relieved.

But with little reason. On Saturday night, a delegation from the Military Revolutionary Committee of the Petrograd Soviet had called on Colonel Polkovnikov, the District Commander, and had demanded the right to countersign all Staff orders to the garrison. If this were refused, the orders of the local commandant would no longer be followed. When the Colonel retorted that he did not recognize the authority of the Soviet, the latter — i.e. the Bolsheviks — sent a direct appeal to all units of the garrison. It took the form of a message on Sunday, October 22nd, and declared *inter alia* that the 'General Staff has broken with the revolutionary garrison and the Petrograd Soviet ... thus making itself the tool of counter-revolutionary forces.' The message went on to state that 'orders to the garrison, not signed by the Military Revolutionary Committee, are invalid', and ended with, 'The revolution is in danger!' Colonel Polkovnikov now tried to smooth matters over by calling for a meeting between his Staff and representatives of the Petrograd Soviet, at which the Bolshevik delegates simply repeated the earlier demand.

Now this conflict between the army — and hence the Provisional Government — and the Soviet was apparently not in itself a great cause of alarm to the authorities; it was all part and parcel of the familiar tug-of-war between the two partners sharing dual power and hence likely to be solved by yet another compromise. If they thought this they merely demonstrated their utter failure to grasp Lenin's policy, and it was that policy which now counted in the Soviet. On Monday, October 23rd, the moderate socialists did indeed promise a series of minor concessions if the Bolsheviks climbed down in their turn. When these negotiations dragged on, the Provisional Government stepped in and ordered the Military Revolutionary Committee to withdraw its message to the garrison. Then it took direct action.

The beginning of the insurrection

It did this in its own peculiar manner. On the night of October 23rd, it could still have ordered a full-scale raid on the Bolshevik leadership. But so much firmness was not in its style. Instead, the authorities contented themselves with issuing a ukase to the troops, prohibiting 'on pain of arrest for armed rebellion' the execution of any orders coming from 'various organizations'. It decided further to order the 'removal [from the garrison] of all Commissars of the Petrograd Soviet' and to hold an 'investigation into all illegal activities for possible submission to a court martial'. At the same time it alerted the Military Schools in Petrograd and also ordered troops on the outskirts of the capital to move into the centre. However, the latter had ceased to take orders from the Provisional Government; indeed, many regimental committees replied by passing resolutions of loyalty to the Petrograd Soviet. Railwaymen, too, repeated the disruptive tactics they had employed to such good effect during the Kornilov putsch. And so what action the government did take was finally reduced to an ineffectual minimum.

In fact, all it did do was to dispatch a few Junkers at 6 a.m. on October 24th to the offices of the Bolshevik papers *Rabochi Put* and *Soldat*, with orders to seal the printing presses and confiscate and destroy the copies already printed. Instead of aiming at the head of the insurrection, the Provisional Government thus struck at a minor offshoot. For all that, it had taken the initiative, and the fight was on.

When this happened, the 'head of the insurrection', i.e. the Bolshevik General Staff, was meeting at the Smolny Institute, an exclusive academy for the education of young noblewomen which the Petrograd Soviet had taken over in August 1917. Classrooms had been transformed into offices, and the great banqueting hall into a debating chamber for the moderate Central Executive Committee of the Soviet of Workers' and Soldiers' Deputies and the now Bolshevik-dominated Petrograd Soviet. And whereas the activities and influence of the former had sharply declined, those of the latter had grown increasingly important and hence took up more and more time. As John Reed put it, 'Delegates [were] falling down asleep on the floor and rising again to take part in debate.' Nor did they leave it at words—the leaders of the Military Revolutionary Committee were, in fact, putting the final touches to their plans for an uprising during the night of October 24th–25th, when revolutionary squads would occupy a number of strategic points in the capital, while sailors from the Baltic Fleet would arrive at the Finland Station to join forces with the Red Guards from the industrial quarters, march on the Winter Palace and arrest the members of the Provisional Government. (As the reader will see, this strategic plan had to be changed in two ways—because of the government attack on the Bolshevik press the insurrection started earlier and ended later than had been foreseen.)

One of the most important jobs of the Committee was to establish, maintain and improve contacts with the local regiments. In this sphere, the Bolsheviks concentrated chiefly on agitation, and their efforts demonstrated the close links between political propaganda and military insurrection. Thus, on October 23rd, when they learned that the Peter and Paul garrison, whose guns commanded the Winter Palace, had refused to recognize the Military Revolutionary Committee, thus threatening the outcome of the whole insurrection, Antonov-Ovseënko, the secretary of the Military Revolutionary Committee, proposed to disarm and oust the garrison by force. Trotsky said that the job could be done much better by political persuasion. He accordingly went to the fortress, called for a general meeting, and so fired those present with his own zeal that he swung them round completely. As a result the Bolsheviks gained not only the fortress itself, but also the near-by Kronverksky arsenal containing 100,000 rifles—all without firing a single shot.

This feat was typical not only of the October insurrection but of the entire Bolshevik Revolution. It involved no brilliant displays of military strategy, no spectacular show of force—the seizure of power was a *political* rather than a *military* achievement. It was compounded not of a tissue of dark, Machiavellian plots but of thousands of acts of persuasion and propaganda repeated with indefatigable patience. By refusing the temptation of a frontal attack, by going unarmed to the Peter and Paul Fortress to plead with the soldiers in person, Trotsky did the work of a true revolutionary: he chose conversion rather than conspiracy, argument rather than guns, agitation rather than bludgeoning.

A day later—on October 24th—when Trotsky and the other members of the Military Revolutionary Committee learned that the Bolshevik printing works had been closed down, he immediately sent out a Red Guard patrol who removed the seals, and in so doing advanced the planned insurrection by twenty-four hours. Soon afterwards, the Bolshevik papers reappeared in the street; at the same time the Military Revolutionary Committee announced a government plot and sent the following message to all army units: 'We order you to bring up a regiment in battle readiness and await further orders.'

What did the Provisional Government do in the meantime? They were meeting in the Winter Palace and heard Kerensky call for the immediate arrest of all Bolshevik leaders. When several of his colleagues argued that this step was unnecessarily provocative Kerensky gave way, and it was decided to repeat the call, first issued on the night before, for reinforcements from the Northern Front and from near-by garrisons. The government also ordered the cruiser *Aurora*, moored in the Neva, its crew favourable to the Bolsheviks, to return to base. Finally, they gave orders for the bridges between the centre of Petrograd and the working-class suburbs to be raised. This last step told the inhabitants that a new crisis was imminent: the raising of the bridges was the traditional Tsarist way of preventing the workers from 'descending' on the capital. The last time this had happened was in February, but then the Neva had been frozen over so that the workers had been able to storm across the hard ice. This time the Military Revolutionary Committee, unable to rely on the weather, ordered the Red Guard to intervene. Helped by the crew of the cruiser, which had ignored the government signal, they had little difficulty in restoring road contact between Vyborg in the north and the capital.

Meanwhile, Kerensky had set out for the Pre-Parliament to appeal for help, and finding the members in a state of deep gloom he decided to whip up their courage. 'I must inform you,' he declared, 'that a part of the Petrograd population is in a state of open insurgence ... I have proposed that judicial investigations be started immediately, and have also ordered arrests [protests from the Left]. Yes, yes, listen, because at the present time, when the state is imperilled by deliberate or unwitting betrayal and is on the brink of ruin, the Provisional Government, myself included, prefers to be killed and destroyed rather than betray the life, the honour and the independence of the state.' Whereupon all members of the Council, with the exception of the Internationalist Mensheviks, rose from their seats to accord their President a thunderous ovation. When the noise had abated Kerensky continued, and concluded on a firmer and much more optimistic note: 'All those elements of Russian society, all those groups and parties which have dared to raise a hand against the free will of the Russian people ... are subject to immediate, final and definite liquidation.' This fine turn of phrase was greeted with another standing ovation by the Right, the Centre, and part of the Left, and with laughter by the Internationalists. It was, in fact, Kerensky's swan-song.

After all this rousing rhetoric, the Provisional Government thought it was high time to take further action. But with the bridges up and the front-line troops as far away as ever, all it could do was to order the military cadets to occupy the railway stations, and to double the street patrols and the sentries posted outside public buildings. For the rest, the Provisonal Government could rely on the support of the Women's Battalion in the Winter Palace, a few more cadet companies and a handful of Cossacks. These were the remains of the vast army that had borne them to power a few months earlier. At one point during the afternoon it looked as if a motor-cycle battalion stationed in the Peter and Paul Fortress, and which had not attended the previous evening's meeting, would join 'the forces of law and order' as well, but a further meeting and a further speech by Trotsky quickly won them round, and the ministerial team continued vainly to scan the horizon for reinforcements.

The Smolny Institute, meanwhile, had begun to look like a besieged fortress, with armed soldiers and Red Guards posted thickly in the building and in the grounds. Guns, machine-guns and armoured cars had drawn up in the square and in the neighbouring streets. Orders were sent out, a stream of couriers was received and dispatched, in response to each new government step. Even at this late stage the battle was political rather than military.

The Plenary Assembly of the Petrograd Soviet and the Central

Executive Committee of the Soviet of Workers' and Soldiers' deputies continued their heated debates. Early in the afternoon, the Bolshevik faction heard a report by Trotsky. 'There can be no question of expounding before this caucus the whole plan of the insurrection. Whatever is said at a large meeting inevitably gets abroad.' Instead, the President of the Military Revolutionary Committee contented himself with demonstrating that a 'conspiracy does not contradict the principles of Marxism', and that 'the physical barrier on the road to power must be overcome by physical force'. Up till now, he went on, the Bolsheviks had not gone beyond self-defence, but 'this self-defence must be understood in a sufficiently broad sense'. That same morning, the Military Revolutionary Committee had still denied that it was planning an insurrection: 'Despite all sorts of rumours and gossip, the Committee ... declares that its business is not the seizure of power, but solely the defence of the interest of the Petrograd garrison and of democracy against counter-revolutionary attacks and disorders.' The semi-camouflage continued.

On the evening of October 24th, Trotsky addressed the Petrograd Soviet, which now had a Bolshevik majority but also included many opponents. Summing up the events of the day, he asked the following question, 'Is this insurrection?' And, for the last time, he gave an evasive reply: 'We have today a semi-government in which the people do not believe, and which does not believe in itself, because it is inwardly dead. This semi-government is awaiting that flick of the historic broom that will clear the space for an authentic government of the revolutionary people.' Was this a hint that an offensive was imminent? Not yet. Trotsky still kept up the fiction of self-defence. Recalling the impending convocation of the Second All-Russian Congress of Soviets, he went on to say that 'if the government attempts to employ the twenty-four or forty-eight hours remaining to it by plunging a knife into the back of the Revolution, then we declare once more: the vanguard of the Revolution will answer blow with blow and iron with steel.'

At about 11 p.m. he had to ward off an attack by Mensheviks and moderate socialists at a tumultuous meeting of the Central Executive Committee. Dan used the occasion to paint a frightening picture of a Russia being carried to the brink of civil war by the extreme Left. 'The hours in which we live have assumed the most tragic colours,' he declared. 'The enemy is at the gates of Petrograd ... and yet we await bloodshed in the streets of the capital, and famine threatens to destroy not only our homogeneous government but the Revolution itself.' And again: 'The Central Executive Committee has full powers to act and must be obeyed ... We are not afraid of bayonets ... The Central Executive Committee will defend the Revolution with its own body.'

'It's been a corpse for a long time,' somebody shouted, whereupon Gotz, the Menshevik Chairman, called, 'Silence, or I'll have you put out!' — 'Just try!' said a voice from the crowd.

After informing the meeting that the Pre-Parliament had that very day called for immediate peace negotiations and land reforms, Dan sat down and made way for Trotsky. 'His thin, pointed face was positively Mephistophelian in its expression of malicious irony,' Reed observed. Trotsky immediately launched a blistering attack on the Mensheviks and the Social Revolutionaries. For months they had done nothing at all, but now when things were not going their own way they suddenly saw fit to adopt the Bolshevik programme they had always condemned. 'Dan tells you that you have no right to make an insurrection. Insurrection is the right of all revolutionaries! When the downtrodden masses revolt, it is their right ... '

While Trotsky was making his speech, Lenin was still cooling his heels in the Vyborg apartment that served him as his last hiding-place. The hours crawled by and nothing seemed to be happening. Once again he was filled with suspicion. He dashed off a 'Letter to the Comrades' (of the Bolshevik Central Committee): 'I am writing these lines on the evening of the 24th. The situation is extremely critical. It is as clear as can be that delaying the uprising now really means death. With all my power I wish to persuade the comrades that now everything hangs on a hair ... We must at all costs this evening, tonight, arrest the ministers, having disarmed the military cadets (defeating them if they offer resistance) ... ' And by way of conclusion, the oft-repeated phrase: 'To delay action means death.'

In the event, it was the anaemic body of the government that died. During the night of October 24th, Kerensky, in his Winter Palace, made another desperate effort to summon his loyal troops to the relief of the capital. To that end he sent an urgent appeal to the Kornilovist General Krasnov. The desperate Menshevik and Social Revolutionary leaders took the same step. Kerensky also received a deputation of Cossack officers, who pledged their support, provided he promised in turn to take a much stronger line with the Bolsheviks. This Kerensky did most gladly. The officers next demanded infantry reinforcements, and that request was granted as well. In the event, no infantrymen ever materialized, and so the Cossack horses remained locked up in their stables.

That same night, Colonel Polkovnikov, Commander of what was now a phantom garrison, sent a telegram to General Dukhonin, Supreme Commander of the Army: 'The situation in Petrograd is menacing. There are no street disorders, but a systematic seizure of government buildings and railway stations is going on. Arrests continue. None of my orders is obeyed. The cadets surrender their posts almost without resistance.'

And, indeed, the insurrection, once started, spread with the speed of lightning. At 2 a.m. the Red Guard took over the Telegraph Station, the Post Office and the main railroad stations. By 7 a.m., the Telephone Exchange and the State Bank were in their hands as well. When Lenin, tired of waiting, emerged from his hiding-place on his way to Smolny, he crossed a town that unbeknown to him was already in the control of his Party. A few hours earlier the police had tried to arrest him; now, when only the ministers still eluded the grasp of the Revolution, a mere shadow stood between Lenin and power.

Before the final assault

Nothing more than a shadow. The dawn of October 25th witnessed the capture of the Winter Palace and the fall of the Provisional Government. But these two events were important merely as symbols. During the previous evening, the rapid and unopposed occupation of all strategic points in the capital had already sealed Kerensky's fate. On the morning of October 24th, the Military Revolutionary Committee had published an order that 'any attempt by disorderly elements to cause trouble in the streets of Petrograd ... will be ruthlessly suppressed.' This proclamation was quite unnecessary—there were no disorders. As Sukhanov has noted, the seizure of power by the Bolsheviks on the night of October 24th–25th, 1917, looked less like an insurrection than a changing of the guard.

Anticipating somewhat the actual course of events, the Military Revolutionary Committee published a solemn proclamation at

10 a.m.: 'The Provisional Government is deposed. All state authority has passed into the hands of the Military Revolutionary Committee, the organ of the Soviet of the Petrograd Soviet of Workers' and Soldiers' Deputies, acting in the name of the Petrograd proletariat and garrison. Long live the Revolution of Workers, Soldiers and Peasants!' Less than two hours later, Kerensky took leave of his ministers. Realizing that none of the Petrograd regiments had the least intention of coming to his defence, he had decided to appeal to the front-line troops in person. His departure was rather in the nature of an escape—according to Maliantovich, the Minister of Justice, Kerensky had to seek the help of the United States Embassy, which supplied him with a car flying the American flag. At this point—and for understandable reasons—'Kerensky's pale face was that of a man who had aged terribly ... he looked straight ahead without seeing anyone, his dull and blinking eyes betraying great anguish and secret fears.' This, at any rate, was how he appeared to Maliantovich. Kerensky himself was later to give a different version of his departure. He denied appealing to the American Embassy and insisted that he had crossed Petrograd in his open touring car: 'The whole street— both the passers-by and the soldiers—immediately recognized me. I saluted as always, a little carelessly and with an easy smile.' And, indeed, that morning the government had launched a 'counter-offensive' no less 'careless' than Kerensky's salute. The Chief Commissar of headquarters, Stankevich, at the head of a company of military engineering students, had decided to come to the defence of the Mariinsky Palace, the seat of the Pre-Parliament. However, when he realized that the Bolsheviks were too strongly entrenched in that part of the city, he prepared to flush them out of the Telephone Exchange instead. A few shots from a Red Guard armoured car sufficed to discourage the assailants. The whole incident passed off peacefully enough, except that it caused an outburst of hysteria among the telephone girls. According to an eye-witness, the deserted street outside the Exchange 'was suddenly enlivened with running and jumping skirts and hats'. As for the cadets, half of them vanished and the other half allowed themselves to be disarmed by the Red Guard.

In the early afternoon of October 25th, the deliberations of the Pre-Parliament were interrupted by the arrival of Red Guards who invited the deputies to leave the Mariinsky Palace forthwith. The

Pre-Parliament thereupon passed a motion of protest, but by fifty-nine votes against forty-seven decided not to offer any resistance to the Guards whose 'stupid, obtuse and malicious physiognomies' (the phrase used by the Liberal, Nabokov) filled the deputies with a mixture of scorn and fear. One of these 'malicious types' later told John Reed how off-handedly he had treated the leaders of that defunct institution: 'We walked in there, and filled all the doors with comrades. I went up to the counter-revolutionist Kornilovist who sat in the president's chair. "No more council," I says. "Run along home now." ' While this sort of procedure was, of course, quite unparliamentary, many members of the Pre-Parliament nevertheless shared Miliukov's sense of relief: 'We fully expected', he explained, 'that they would pick us up and place us under arrest, but luckily the revolutionary General Staff had other concerns.'

And, indeed, the Military Revolutionary Committee was far more perturbed by unexpected delays in their plan to storm the Winter Palace. Several thousand Kronstadt sailors and several warships were expected in Petrograd at 2 p.m. Time passed and no sailors appeared; every minute counted. The Second All-Russian Congress of Soviets was due to meet in the afternoon, and the Bolshevik leaders were determined to present the assembly with the *fait accompli* of the fall of the Provisional Government and the arrest of its members. The occupation of the Winter Palace was postponed until 3 p.m., and then 6 p.m., and in the end it was 7 p.m. when the Kronstadt sailors finally arrived. There were other setbacks as well: according to the plan, the *Aurora* was supposed to fire a blank volley to frighten the ministers. If this did not cause them to resign, the guns of the Peter and Paul Fortress would open up with live shells. However, the fortress gunners were rather half-hearted and kept muttering excuses—their guns were rusty, there was no oil in the compressors, and so on. In the end, Antonov-Ovseënko was forced to send a few gunners from the *Aurora* into the fortress to man the 'rusty' guns.

Lenin, too, was impatient. Still in disguise, he had reached the Smolny Institute where he greeted every new arrival with, 'Hasn't the palace been taken yet?' His anger mounted, and he turned his full fury on Podvoisky, the Vice-President of the Military Revolutionary Committee who was responsible for the final assault. 'The man ought to be shot, he ought to be shot,' Lenin kept repeating. Groups of angry workers, too, had begun to ask themselves whether 'the Bolsheviks had started playing diplomatic games like the rest'.

Throughout the afternoon, attention had been focused on two points: the Winter Palace, where the ministers were assembled in secret session, and the Smolny Institute, where Trotsky had opened an emergency meeting of the Petrograd Soviet at 2.35 p.m. 'In the name of the Military Revolutionary Committee,' he told the enthusiastic delegates, 'I declare that the Provisional Government has ceased to exist. Individual ministers are under arrest, the others will be arrested within the next few days or hours.[1] The revolutionary garrison has dispersed the Pre-Parliament.' And he went on to stress that despite dire Menshevik and Social Revolutionary warnings no blood had been shed—no casualties at all had been reported. He then gave a lengthy account of the last night's events and of the first reactions from the front. At this point, Lenin appeared in the congress hall.

Trotsky interrupted his speech: 'In our midst we have Vladimir Ilyich Lenin, who has been prevented by circumstances from appearing before us until this very moment.' According to a press report, Trotsky then gave a brief account of the remarkable part Lenin had played in the history of the Russian revolutionary movement and finished by crying, 'Long live Comrade Lenin!' Lenin replied with a brief speech. 'Comrades,' he began, 'the workers' and peasants' revolution has come to pass, that revolution which the Bolsheviks have constantly been showing to be necessary.' In a few telling phrases he went on to sum up the profound significance of the seizure of power, stressing the close links between the Russian workers and the 'world workers' movement which is beginning to develop in Italy, in England and in Germany'. And he concluded, 'In Russia, we must now devote ourselves to the construction of a proletarian socialist state. Long live the socialist world Revolution!' The assembly echoed these sentiments by passing the following resolution: 'The Soviet of Workers' and Soldiers' Deputies of Petrograd salutes the victorious Revolution of the workers and soldiers of Petrograd; it is convinced that the proletariat of Western Europe will aid us in leading the cause of socialism to a total and lasting victory.'

Before closing this brief meeting—which occupied a lull in the insurrection—Trotsky also announced that since troops were

[1] Two ministers who had not joined their colleagues in the Winter Palace had been arrested in the morning but had since been released.

advancing on Petrograd from the front it was essential to dispatch commissars who would be able 'to tell the broad masses of the people what has happened'. He was interrupted by a voice from the body of the hall, 'You're anticipating the will of the All-Russian Congress of Soviets!' To which Trotsky replied angrily, 'The will of the Congress has been anticipated by the tremendous fact of the insurrection of the Petrograd workers and soldiers, which has taken place. All we have to do now is to consolidate our victory.'

In the circumstances, this, as we saw, meant seizing the Winter Palace, where the ministers continued their august deliberations under the liberal Konovalov, Kerensky's Deputy Premier. They still had a direct line to Army Headquarters in Mohilev, and were sending appeal after appeal for reinforcements to General Dukhonin. The General supplied them with a list of the units he was dispatching to Petrograd, and from time to time informed the ministers of the expected time of their arrival. One advance battalion was due to arrive during the next few hours, the others to follow in quick succession. This news so bolstered the ministers' flagging spirits that they published a number of forceful proclamations against the 'madmen [who] have stirred up a rebellion against the only state power established by the people'. But the ministers' joy was very short-lived, for when the reinforcements finally arrived they turned out to be a few dozen Cavaliers of St George, members of a crack regiment, and a company of the Women's Battalion. The Petrograd Cossacks, far from heeding the ministers' plight, had decided to withdraw their two companies from the palace. The ministers now had to decide whether to capitulate there and then or to continue resisting in the hope that they could hold out until the arrival of troops from the front.

At 6.30 p.m., two cyclists presented the ministers with a message: they had twenty minutes—subsequently extended to thirty—in which to surrender. In case of refusal, the palace would be shelled and taken by storm. What were the ministers to do in the face of this threat? They had previously retired to an inner chamber, and as an additional precaution had put out all the lights except for a small lamp shaded by a newspaper. In this funereal atmosphere they now discussed their reply to the Bolshevik ultimatum. Maliantovich tells us that by then most of them no longer believed in General Dukhonin's promises of relief—they felt completely cut off. 'We wandered through the gigantic mousetrap,' the former

Minister of Justice wrote in his memoirs, 'meeting occasionally either all together or in small groups for brief conversations— condemned people, lonely, abandoned by all ... Around us, within us, a void.' A final appeal for a few hundred men had been sent to the Constitutional Democrats and Social Revolutionaries, but to no avail. Once again the ministers were faced with the apparent choice between immediate surrender or further resistance pending the arrival of reinforcements.

In fact, they did not even give the question of resistance a moment's consideration. All they were concerned with was saving face, declaring before all the world that they had yielded to brute force in the country's best interest. According to Maliantovich they could easily have issued a brief and concise military order. 'This would have been simple enough had it been a question of real combat and not of having to take a symbolic attitude.' Time and again, officers in charge of the few remaining detachments guarding the palace did, in fact, ask the ministers for instructions. The reply they received was highly illuminating: 'The cadet officers are not merely soldiers, they are also citizens and must therefore decide for themselves which side they want to take.' Maliantovich justified this attitude as follows: 'We cannot give orders to fight to the last man or the last drop of blood, because in this hour we may possibly be defending no one but ourselves.' In this correct assessment, this pathetic declaration, only the word 'possibly' was superfluous.

At 9 p.m., the cruiser *Aurora* fired its volley of blanks, and for the next hour there were confused skirmishes as the revolutionary forces began to occupy the square and the streets surrounding the Tsar's old residence. But the insurrectionists still hesitated to give orders for the first assault. A Red Guard was trying to hold back an impatient group of his men: 'No, comrades, we cannot possibly open fire. The Women's Battalion is inside. They will say that we have been shooting Russian women.' At 10 p.m., this battalion, having heard a rumour that General Alexeiev was surrounded in a building near Staff Headquarters, tried to break out and go to his rescue. As they emerged from the Winter Palace they were quickly disarmed by the Red Guard.[1]

---

[1] Subsequently, Petrograd was full of the most extraordinary rumours about the fate of these women. There was talk of a regular massacre and of mass rape. In reality, there were three rapes and one suicide, but no one was killed.

This abortive attempt was not the only one to thin the ranks of the besieged. The cadet officers of the artillery school, who had been manning the guns, also left the building and surrendered to the Red Guards. And while the palace was shedding its defenders, revolutionary soldiers and Red Guards crept in through undefended or badly guarded side gates. Inside, skirmishes were transformed into discussions, or discussions degenerated into brawls, but at no time was there a real clash of arms. At one point, the cadet officers, seeing a huge crowd approaching, opened a large gate to let them pass through. This was a mistake rather than an act of treachery: they thought that they were admitting a delegation of Municipal Duma deputies and other political leaders whom the ministers were expecting, and for whose personal safety and protection the cadets had been specially posted at the gate.

The Petrograd Municipal Duma was one of the last centres of anti-Bolshevik resistance—politically though not militarily speaking. Meeting during the evening and for part of the night, the councillors, who had been joined by delegates from the Soviet of Peasants' Deputies, had followed the course of events with increasing apprehension. Then one of them had a brilliant idea: by sacrificing their own lives, they, the duly elected representatives of the people, might yet be able to stem the insurrection. Their gesture would certainly be heroic, even if it failed in other respects. After all, the Bolsheviks themselves and the mass of workers and soldiers supporting them still respected the moral authority of the city councillors, and faced with the noble example of so much self-sacrifice they might abandon their criminal enterprise even at this late stage. With the exception of the Bolshevik members the entire Duma acclaimed this plan, and at dead of night a long procession led by old Schreider, the mayor, set out for the Winter Palace.

The ubiquitous John Reed saw them just as they were preparing to challenge a cordon of sailors drawn out across the Nevsky. 'There were about three or four hundred of them, men in frock-coats, well-dressed women, officers—all sorts and conditions of people.'

Mayor Schreider and Prokopovich, one of the ministers who had been arrested earlier and released, now asked the sailors to let them pass. When the man in command demurred, a cry went up from all sides:

'Shoot us, if you want to. We will pass! Forward! We are ready to die ... '

And still the sailors stood firm.

'What will you do if we go forward? Will you shoot?' asked one of the councillors.

'What will we do? We shall spank you,' cried one of the sailors. Was a blood-bath really necessary? Sobered by the cold night air, Minister Prokopovich thought not. Jumping up on a box and waving his umbrella, he harangued his companions, inviting them to keep their dignity but to recover their calm. 'Let us return to the Duma and discuss the best means of saving the country and the Revolution!'

The end of the Provisional Government

At this late hour of the night the Duma was deserted, but the Smolny Institute still echoed with tempestuous speeches and rousing appeals. The inaugural meeting of the Second All-Russian Congress of Soviets had been opened at 11.45 p.m. John Reed has described the scene as follows:

> In the row of seats, under the white chandeliers, packed immovably in the aisles and on the sides, perched on every windowsill and even the edge of the platform, the representatives of the workers and soldiers of all Russia waited in anxious silence or wild exaltation the ringing of the chairman's bell. There was no heat in the hall but the stifling heat of unwashed human bodies. A foul blue cloud of cigarette smoke rose from the mass and hung in the thick air. Occasionally someone in authority mounted the tribune and asked the comrades not to smoke. Then everybody, smokers and all, took up the cry, 'Don't smoke, comrades!' and went on smoking.

The Second All-Russian Congress of Soviets was in all respects quite unlike the First, which had been held in Petrograd in June. The differences were political no less than social. Whereas the Mensheviks and Social Revolutionaries had predominated in June, the majority of delegates had since fallen in behind the Bolsheviks. Precise figures are difficult to come by, and vary from source to source: some authorities claim that the Bolsheviks held 300 seats out of a total of 670; others speak of 390 Bolsheviks out of a total of 650. The strength of the Social Revolutionaries was given variously as from 160 to 190 seats, but this figure is misleading since that Party had long been divided by internal conflict, and at a meeting in the morning of October 25th it had officially split into two factions, the pro-Bolshevik one being the stronger. The Mensheviks, who in June 1917 had accounted for more than 200 delegates, were now reduced to a mere 60–70. One fact was in no doubt whatsoever: a very large majority of the delegates favoured the seizure of power by the soviets and the overthrow of the Provisional Government.

This political shift had gone hand in hand with a social transformation. The earlier Congress had been made up chiefly of petit-bourgeois elements, embodying the first revolutionary hopes and vaguely democratic aspirations of the masses. Intellectuals had been prominent and so had officers. The October Congress was both younger and much more proletarian, a fact on which many observers in the press gallery were quick to remark.

On behalf of the old Executive Committee, the Menshevik Dan presided over the first part of the meeting. He stressed the exceptional circumstances in which the Congress was being held: 'At this very moment ... our comrades in the Winter Palace are under fire.' And, indeed, the noise of gunfire could be heard from afar. A new executive was elected: it consisted of 14 Bolsheviks, 7 Social Revolutionaries, 3 Mensheviks and 1 left-wing socialist from the Maxim Gorky group. The right-wing Social Revolutionaries and Mensheviks declared at once that they would refuse to share executive power with the Bolsheviks.

Martov now mounted the rostrum and declared that the most urgent problem facing the Congress was the 'liquidation of the current crisis'. Despite the anti-Bolshevik tenor of his speech, despite his insistence that public order must be restored and that all political trends must have a say in the Soviet, he received the support of the Bolsheviks. The right-wing Mensheviks and Social Revolutionaries, on the other hand, opposed him, and bluntly rejected collaboration with the 'Party of insurrection', and so did the Bundists. Moreover, not content with that declaration of intent, the entire Right marched out of the meeting, after proclaiming their loss of confidence in the new Soviet Executive. Their departure emptied the hall of 20 per cent or so of the delegates.

This walk-out, received with cat-calls, proved to be of decisive importance in the subsequent course of events. It meant a definite break between the Bolsheviks and a large section of their socialist adversaries. Henceforth the two camps would be set apart not merely by ideological differences and by personal quarrels but also by profound constitutional differences—during the night of October 25th, 1917, the Bolsheviks had established a new legal order, and by refusing to accept it the Social Revolutionaries and right-wing Mensheviks deliberately disqualified themselves from playing the part of the official opposition. Worse still, they carried the dispute between Russian Bolsheviks and Social Democrats far beyond the old divisions—they challenged the very basis and character of the new Soviet regime during the first hours of its life. From the very start, therefore, these men did not act as *opponents* but as *rebels*, and inasmuch as the October insurrection was the logical and revolutionary extension of February—at least in the eyes of the Bolsheviks and the broad masses—the socialist Right became transformed into an agent of *counter-revolution*.

Such is the remorseless dynamic and strict logic of revolution—by sharpening the class conflict, or rather by bringing its existence into the open, revolution forces the propertied classes to cling ever more desperately to their old privileges, and to oppose even the slightest concessions as so many nails in their coffin. At the same time it prompts the disinherited classes to consolidate their early successes and no longer to accept half-measures and promises for the future. The resistance of the former increases the insistence of the latter, while those in between try to close what has become an unbridgeable gap—steeped in dreams of social peace, they try desperately to keep these dreams alive, the more so as the latter correspond to their own best interests. The dialectic of revolution rides roughshod over all such attempts. That is why the Mensheviks—just like the Girondins—were swept from the political scene as soon as the Revolution gathered momentum. Caught between the hammer of Revolution and the anvil of reaction, they would occasionally make common cause with the extreme Right, thus causing the Left to lump them together with the worst reactionaries. It has often been said that 'the revolution devours its own children', when, in fact, what violence it displays is imposed upon it by the broader historical process.

It was this process that the Mensheviks and Social Revolutionaries challenged when they walked out of the Soviet on the night of October 25th, 1917. It was true that at that moment they could still delude themselves with the hope that the Bolshevik triumph would be a fleeting one. However, even when the Revolution had consolidated its early successes, many of them continued to treat it with haughty disdain. In so doing, they not only destroyed Menshevism but also contributed to the increasing political isolation of the Bolsheviks, and so gave the history of modern Russia its characteristic look.

After the walk-out, Martov continued his speech as if nothing had happened, when, in fact, his proposal of a coalition between all parties represented in the Soviet was no longer relevant. Nevertheless he repeated it, inviting the searing irony of Trotsky, who had been under relentless pressure during the past few days — the night before he had fainted in the Soviet from sheer exhaustion. Lunacharsky would later recall that during the October days 'Trotsky walked about like an electric battery, and each contact with him brought forth a discharge.'

Trotsky now rounded on Martov: 'The masses of the people have followed our banner, and our insurrection was victorious. And now we are told: Renounce your victory, make concessions, compromise. With whom? I ask with whom ought we to compromise? With those wretched groups who have left us ... ? But we have seen through them completely. No one in Russia is with them any longer. Should those millions of workers and peasants represented in this Congress make a compromise, as between equals, with men who are ready, not for the first time, to leave us at the mercy of the bourgeoisie? No, here no compromise is possible. To those who have left, and to those who suggest it to us, we must say: You are miserable bankrupts, your role is over; go where you ought to be—into the dustbin of history.'

Incensed by this outburst, Martov shouted from the platform, 'Then we'll leave, as well.' When his decision was endorsed by the left-wing Mensheviks after an emergency discussion on the floor (fourteen votes to twelve), the Bolsheviks were isolated even further. The left-wing Social Revolutionaries, while condemning the conduct of the absent deputies, now pleaded for a coalition of all but the bourgeois parties. But their proposals lacked a sense of reality; indeed, the whole long debate was being held in a sort of historical vacuum, about to be filled by the capture of the Winter Palace and the collapse of the Provisional Government. At 2 a.m. on October 26th, the All-Russian Congress of Soviets interrupted its labours.

At the same moment, the Provisional Government was in its final throes. For the past hour, the Winter Palace had been the scene of utter confusion. As the first Red Guards filtered into what Minister Maliantovich had called 'that mousetrap', they were easily disarmed by the military cadets. But soon afterwards the infiltrators outnumbered the defenders, and the roles were quickly reversed. However, the palace was an immense building, a maze through which the workers and soldiers could only grope their way. At 2.10 a.m. they finally reached the hall outside the chamber in which the ministers had taken refuge. A cadet officer burst into the chamber to announce the arrival of Antonov-Ovseënko and his men.

'We are ready to defend ourselves to the last man,' he shouted. 'What are the Provisional Government's orders?'

'It's no use,' he was told. 'We give up. No bloodshed! We yield to force.'

But the correct form had still to be observed—after all, a government cannot surrender like a group of deserters. Even *in extremis* it must observe some decorum, must stick to the rules of propriety. The result was so comical that it could not have been improved upon even by some stage director who, hidden in the wings, was determined to put the finishing touches on his play with a stroke of the grotesque. For hours, the ministers had been sitting in the dark, in a state of the deepest despair. Some had been pacing the chamber nervously, others had peeled off their coats and had dropped into armchairs or were lounging on divans. Then, as the revolutionary soldiers were about to burst in, one of them cried, 'Let's all sit round the table.' And so they did—the loungers quickly put on their frock-coats, and it was with due solemnity, reflecting the seriousness of their deliberations and the high dignity of their office, that they prepared to receive the Red Guards.

The fall of a government, when it is the result of a popular uprising rather than of the vagaries of parliamentary life, is often beset with quaint incidents, and of these the October Revolution did not have the monopoly. Thus in February the fall of the last Tsarist cabinet was accompanied by a number of hilarious scenes. For example, when the ministers of Nicholas II were afraid that the masses might take it into their heads to rush into their solemn meeting-place, they had all the lights put out. Soon afterwards, when the danger had passed and the room was once more brightly lit, one of the ministers was found squatting underneath the table, ostensibly engaged in picking up sheets of scattered paper. In October, the new ministers, anxious to demonstrate the superiority of democratic institutions, were clearly determined to behave with greater dignity lest they give the victors reason for laughing at their expense as well.

And, indeed, their arrest caused no one any embarrassment. 'In the name of the Military Revolutionary Committee, I declare you under arrest,' Antonov-Ovseënko informed them. 'The members of the Provisional Government yield to force, and surrender in order to avoid bloodshed,' was the solemn reply of Konovalov, the Vice-Premier. A list of prisoners was drawn up, they were given an escort, and after passing an angry crowd in the Winter Palace they were taken to the Peter and Paul Fortress. Despite the hostility of the masses, despite the excitement of the moment and the fury with which the Red Guard and the revolutionary soldiers heard the news that Kerensky was not among his colleagues, not a single minister was harmed. True, individual soldiers tried to seize them and even threatened to lynch them, but the Red Guard escort was quick to warn them off.

'Get back,' cried one of them. 'What can you be thinking of, comrades? Don't you realize that these prisoners are human beings too? What infamy, what uncivilized behaviour!'

It was 2.30 a.m., and the Soviet had just resumed its session. Kamenev mounted the platform to break the great news that the Provisional Government had ceased to exist, that the Soviet regime was born.

All power to the soviets

In comparison to the stormy events of the previous night, the first day of the Soviet era, October 26th, was completely peaceful, at least in Petrograd. Nothing at all spectacular happened. The Military Revolutionary Committee took control of all the police commissariats and began to tackle the task of organizing the economic life of the capital. Luckily for them, the economy had not been greatly upset by the insurrection. The shops were open, the trams running, and the cinemas and theatres continued to draw crowds. The evening before, while the Provisional Government had been besieged, music-lovers had, as always, flocked to the opera, to applaud their beloved Chaliapin in *Don Carlos*. It had been a brilliant success, and the connoisseurs had gone home delighted at about the same time as the Red Guard—another society, another world—had begun to pour into the Winter Palace.

And so Petrograd remained calm throughout October 26th—it was not until the evening that the next great event took place: the presentation of the new government and of its programme to the All-Russian Congress of Soviets. The precise composition of that government set the new rulers a grave problem. The walk-out of the right-wing Social Revolutionaries and Mensheviks had strengthened Lenin's and Trotsky's determination to seek their allies exclusively among the Left factions of these groups, but the latter had not yet abandoned their belief in a broader coalition and refused to serve on the new team. Hence Lenin, this time without too many regrets, resigned himself once again to seeing his party isolated from the rest. He accordingly turned his attention to a somewhat less crucial problem, which Trotsky has described for us in *My Life*:

'What shall we call them?' asks Lenin, thinking aloud. 'Anything but ministers—that's such a vile, hackneyed word.'

'We might call them commissars,' I suggest, 'but there are too many commissars just now. Perhaps "supreme commissars"? No, supreme commissars does not sound well, either. What about "people's commissars"?'

'People's commissars? Well that might do,' Lenin agrees. 'And the government as a whole?'

'A Soviet, of course … the Soviet of People's Commissars, eh?'

And so the Soviet Government received its official name.[1]

Next came the selection of the commissars and the allocation of their functions. According to Trotsky, Lenin himself did not wish to become head of the government—he would have much preferred to devote all his energies to the job of organizing and leading the Bolshevik Party. Hence he contended that Trotsky, as President of the Petrograd Soviet, was the natural candidate for the highest office in the state. It was only when Trotsky himself moved to reject this proposal, and his motion was carried, that Lenin finally agreed to step into the breach. He now proposed that Trotsky be put in charge of internal affairs, in which capacity he would be able to consolidate the Bolshevik gains and ward off any possible

[1] It was not until 1946 that members of the Soviet Government adopted the title of minister.

counter-revolutionary threats. Again, Trotsky refused. He explained that in a country where the nationality question was far from being solved and where anti-Semitic prejudices remained acute, it would be unwise to entrust so important a commissariat to one of Jewish origin. In the end he accepted the Commissariat of Foreign Affairs, which, at a period when diplomatic affairs struck all true revolutionaries as a waste of time and moreover as doomed to an early demise, was thought to be a very minor post indeed. Trotsky himself told one of his comrades what he thought the work would consist of: 'I will issue a few revolutionary proclamations to the peoples of the world, publish a few secret treaties, and then shut up shop.' He was, of course, exaggerating, but there is no doubt that he, too, was profoundly convinced that international relations would soon cease to be governed by legal conventions and international negotiations—the victorious world proletariat would see to that. Clearly, the Bolshevik mind was much more naive than Machiavellian.

Military affairs were entrusted to a trio of 'specialists': Antonov-Ovseënko was chosen because of his recent experiences as leader of the insurrectionary forces; Krylenko because he had been a subaltern in the Tsarist army; and Dybenko because he had been an ensign in the Baltic Fleet. Few Bolsheviks could boast of equivalent titles. Joseph Stalin was given the Commissariat of Nationalities by virtue of a double qualification—he was a Georgian, and as such a natural defender of the interests of the allogeneous people, and he had written a work dealing with the delicate nationality problem.

In general, Bolshevik leaders when asked to join the government would plead lack of experience and of the requisite technical qualifications, but Lenin told them that such objections had little weight since everybody else was in the same boat. And so those serving in the government often combined improvisation with the maximum deployment of the minimum of competence. The story of one of the highest Soviet officials of the time—Stanislav Pestkovsky—bears witness to this. During the last days of October, he went to Smolny in search of work. He called on Lenin and Trotsky, and on his way out found the People's Commissar for Finances, Menzhinsky, stretched out on a divan in a corridor. Menzhinsky hailed him and asked him if he had ever done any studies.

'I did a bit at London University,' replied Pestkovsky, 'finance, among other things.' At this, Menzhinsky leapt up from his divan.

'Finance!' he cried. 'Magnificent. In that case we shall make you director of the State Bank.'

'I was alarmed,' Pestkovsky recounted later, 'and told him that banking was entirely outside my province. But Menzhinsky's only reply was to ask me to wait. He was gone for a few minutes, and then returned with a piece of paper bearing Lenin's signature. It was the decree appointing me Director of the State Bank.'

It is not difficult to imagine the reaction of orthodox political circles, in the capital no less than in the provinces, to this sort of ministerial team. The journalist Philips Price echoed this feeling when he wrote, 'I tried to imagine a committee of common soldiers and workmen setting themselves up in London and declaring that they were the government and that no order from Whitehall was to be obeyed unless it was countersigned by them.' This, indeed, involved a tremendous strain on the imagination. In Petrograd, however, you had but to open your eyes to see such fancies turned into reality.

And so the Provisional Workers' and Peasants' Government presented itself to the Congress of Soviets on the evening of October 26th to ask — and obtain — its 'investiture'. John Reed was present at the session:

> It was just 8.40 when a thundering wave of cheers announced the entrance of the Presidium, with Lenin — great Lenin — among them. A short, stocky figure with a big head set down on his shoulders; broad and bulging. Little eyes, a snubbish nose, wide, generous mouth and heavy chin, clean-shaven now but already beginning to bristle with the well-known beard of his past and future. Dressed in shabby clothes, his trousers much too long for him.

After some brisk exchanges between the Bolshevik deputies and some Mensheviks whose continued presence was the object of ironic remarks from their adversaries, several soldiers arrived from the front, with the fraternal greetings of their regiments. Then Lenin rose. 'Gripping the edge of the reading stand,' Reed tells us, 'letting his little winking eyes travel over the crowd as he stood there waiting, apparently oblivious of the long-rolling ovation which lasted for several minutes.' When the applause had finally died down, Lenin said quite simply, no doubt choking back the emotion that must have welled up within him, 'We shall now proceed to construct the socialist order.' Reporting another eye-witness, Jules Destreé tells us that at this moment Lenin looked like 'an accountant giving the result of an addition sum'. However, what he had to say was nothing so mundane—his first speech as head of the new government was devoted to the problem of peace. Unfortunately we lack a stenographic transcript of that address and, for that matter, of the debate that followed—the systematic sabotage with which most of Russia's civil servants greeted the October Revolution[1] also emptied the Soviet of its stenographers. All we have to go by, therefore, are what accounts the press published next day.

According to them, Lenin began by declaring that 'the question of peace is a burning question, the most pressing question of the present day.' He then went on to read the famous 'Peace Declaration to the Peoples of All the Belligerent Countries' in which he explained how his government intended to do what it could towards ending the war. Reduced to its bare bones, the Declaration was a proposal 'to all the belligerent people and to their governments to begin immediately negotiations for a just and democratic peace'. Lenin went on to explain precisely what the Bolsheviks meant by the last phrase: a just and democratic peace was one without annexations and without the national or colonial domination of one people by another. And he was careful to add, 'The government ... does not regard these conditions of peace as an ultimatum, that is, it is ready to consider any other conditions, insisting, however, that such be proposed by any of the belligerents as soon as possible.' In the debate that followed, he had to reply to left-wing accusations that he was making unwarranted concessions to the imperialist powers and calling for negotiations that were bound to weaken the democratic nature of the Bolshevik peace programme. 'We address ourselves to the governments *and* to the peoples,' Lenin told them, 'since an appeal to the peoples alone might involve a postponement of the peace.' And he added, 'We shall of course defend our peace programme in every way, but we must make it impossible for our enemies to say that their conditions are different and that there is therefore no reason to start negotiations with us.' He finally proposed a three-month armistice and an end to secret diplomacy. There was nothing very revolutionary about the last proposal. Various statesmen of moderate opinion,

[1] See Chapter 10.

President Wilson chief among them, had made similar suggestions to end the underhand dealings that went by the name of international negotiations and that democrats everywhere blamed for the outbreak of the war. But the Bolshevik approach was original in that not content with calling for the abolition of secret diplomacy they went one step further: Lenin declared that his government would forthwith order 'the complete publication of all the secret treaties'.[1] This breach of diplomatic custom aroused both enthusiasm and deep indignation. But it proved, in any case, that the Russian Revolution had no intention of being shackled by 'international usage' or by consular traditions.

While raising no objections to Lenin's proposals as such, the left-wing Mensheviks declared that in their view the peace programme had little chance of success unless the Bolshevik Government made way for a coalition representing every shade of Russian democratic opinion. However, when the 'Peace Declaration' was put to the vote, it was carried almost unanimously—there was only one abstention.

> Suddenly, by common impulse [John Reed tells us] we found ourselves on our feet, mumbling together into the smooth lifting unison of the 'International'. A grizzled old soldier was sobbing like a child. Alexandra Kollontai[2] rapidly winked the tears back. The immense sound rolled through the hall, burst windows and doors and soared into the quiet sky. 'The war is ended! The war is ended!' said a young workman near me, his face shining. And when it was over, as we stood there in a kind of awkward hush, someone in the back of the room shouted, 'Comrades! Let us remember those who have died for liberty!' So we began to sing the Funeral March, that slow, melancholy and yet triumphant chant, so Russian and so moving ...

The Congress now passed on to the next point on the agenda—the Land Decree. As the wording had been scribbled on a piece of paper Lenin had some difficulty in deciphering it, although the decree itself was his own work.

[1] They were, in fact, published in *Pravda* soon afterwards, and the Russian people first learned of the precise territorial increases the Allies had promised them.

[2] Member of the Central Committee of the Bolshevik Party.

'All private ownership of land is abolished immediately, without compensation,' Lenin read out, and 'all land-owners' estates and all lands belonging to the Crown, to monasteries, and the Church ... are transferred to the Township and Land Committees and the district Soviets of Peasants' Deputies, until the Constituent Assembly meets.' Moreover, 'the lands of peasants and of Cossacks serving in the army shall not be confiscated'. The decree itself was followed by a special section entitled 'Concerning the Land', which incorporated all the instructions the peasant electors had given their representatives at the first Congress of Peasants' Soviets. The special section was thus a Bolshevik endorsement of the *moujik* call for land. Hence, though article 1 laid down that 'the landlord's right to land is hereby abolished', and article 6 that 'hired labour is not permitted', it could not be called a Marxist solution of the agrarian question. In fact, it called for the sharing out of the land among the peasants and not for nationalization—'the distribution of the alienated land among the toilers is in charge of the local and central self-governing bodies.' In other words, for all that 'land cannot be sold, leased, mortgaged or alienated in any manner whatsoever', its ownership remained in the hands of individuals. Lenin's agrarian programme was in fact Social Revolutionary rather than socialist.

According to the Marxist doctrine, to which the Bolsheviks sub-scribed, it was the nationalization and not the sharing out of the land that would carry the premises of Communism into the countryside. Marxists had always looked upon the individual peasant's land-hunger as a petit-bourgeois aberration, characteris-tic of the social and cultural backwardness of the countryside. Marxists were convinced that the existence of small, individual allotments ran counter to the best interests of modern agriculture, which called for the kind of technical improvement large agri-cultural collectives alone could provide. Lenin, for one, had always held this point of view, if somewhat less rigidly than Menshevik champions of the 'municipalization' of the big estates, but anxious as he was to adapt his platform to Russian conditions and to avoid a head-on clash with the peasants, he had been careful not to commit himself to too narrow a formula. Nevertheless, after the February Revolution he had on several occasions opposed the division of the land into smallholdings: 'Small-scale agriculture', he had declared, 'is *unable* to emancipate humanity ... we must think of passing over to large-scale agriculture working for the benefit of society at large ... '

In May, when addressing the All-Russian Soviet of Peasants' Congress, he had still been quite unequivocal on this point. 'We do not call for the individual appropriation of these lands [the big estates]—we are in favour of a different type of sharing', i.e. 'the collective cultivation of land by land-workers provided with modern equipment ... ' Now the Land Decree not only failed to introduce the nationalization of the existing smallholdings, but called explicitly for the sharing out of the big estates among the peasants. This idea had come to Lenin in August when, in his Finnish exile, he had read the list of peasant claims in *Izvestia* and their endorsement by the Social Revolutionary party. Realizing that the overthrow of the bourgeoisie and of the Provisional Government was impossible without the assistance of the revolutionary (but in no way socialist) peasantry, he made up his mind to pay the indispensable price for the alliance between the urban proletariat and the countryside: he adopted the *moujik* claim for the re-allocation of the big estates. He had developed this point of view in an article that did not attract much attention at the time although, in fact, it marked a milestone on the Leninist road: 'The peasants want to keep their small properties, standardize them on a basis of equality ... Let them do it. No reasonable socialist will break with the peasant poor on that ground ... The rest ... will be suggested by practice.'

Many Marxists called this change of attitude rank opportunism, and it was to them that Lenin addressed himself when he declared during the debate of October 26th, 'In a democratic government, we cannot ignore the resolutions of the lower strata of the people, even though we may not be in sympathy with them. In actual practice, the peasants will find out for themselves where the truth lies.' And that truth, Lenin had no doubt, was the superiority of large-scale socialized agriculture over small-scale, individual cultivation.

The Social Revolutionaries now accused Lenin of stealing their programme. His reply was that they only had themselves to blame for not implementing it when they were in power. This rebuff closed the debate on the agricultural question, though it by no means resolved it. In fact, the Bolsheviks never dropped their own ideas on the subject of land reform, as witness the 'Fundamental

Law of Socialization' they passed in February 1918. This law set out the objectives the new regime intended to pursue, among them the encouragement of 'the collective system of agriculture at the expense of individual farming, the former being more economical and leading to a socialist economy'. This programme, as we know, was to get the Soviet regime into serious difficulties, but was it not the inevitable price it had to pay for leading a backward agricultural country forward to proletarian revolution?

During the night of October 26th–27th, 1917, the new rulers contented themselves with adopting the Land Decree by an over-whelming majority—there were eight abstentions and only one vote in opposition. Thus barely twenty-four hours after the seizure of power, the Bolsheviks had demonstrated their determination to fulfil their two major promises to the people: the land was handed over to the clamorous peasants and the first step had been taken on the path that culminated in the signing of a peace treaty.

Before disbanding, this historic session of the All-Russian Congress of Soviets still had to give official recognition to the new government—for the first time, the soviets found themselves in a position of real authority, exercising control over the work of the executive: the All-Russian Congress of Soviets had become the highest power in the land. This represented a radical change, a complete innovation—the Provisional Government had never had to account to any representative institution. The precise composition of the Council of People's Commissars became the subject of a fierce debate that continued to rage in the Soviet for weeks to come: while the Bolsheviks declared that they had no objections to the co-option of members from all the Parties still represented at the All-Russian Congress (which excluded the Social Revolutionaries), other delegates demanded a much broader coalition involving all socialist Parties.

The meeting ended with the election of a new Central Executive Committee of the Soviet. Apart from ten delegates without precise political affiliations, it was made up of sixty-two Bolsheviks and twenty-nine left-wing Social Revolutionaries.[1] It was 5.15 a.m. when Kamenev closed the meeting. Lenin retired to his room in the

---

[1] On November 15th, following an agreement between the Soviet of Workers' and Soldiers' Deputies and the Soviet of Peasants' Deputies, the Central Executive Committee was enlarged by the addition of peasant, soldier, and trade-union delegates.

Smolny Institute where, bedding down on the floor beside Trotsky, he finally took a few hours of well-deserved rest. *'Es schwindelt,'* he whispered to his companion.[1] Within twenty-four hours, the most subversive revolutionary of modern times had been transformed into the head of a major country.

The paradox of October

Among the many paradoxes October presents to the historian, none is more remarkable than this: while the Petrograd insurrection was one of the most important turning-points in modern history — changing the world more radically than any war, than all the treaties, more radically even than all the scientific discoveries — no other event in a century full of social upheavals was less spectacular. True, few historical upheavals looked at in isolation reflect the full importance of the broad current of which they form an essential part. Thus none of the ups and downs that marked the French Revolution, not even the storming of the Bastille, an event that has captured the imagination of many generations, tells us about the overall historical significance of 1789. Yet July 14th, 1789, in Paris was incomparably more dramatic than October 25th and 26th in Petrograd. In Russia, these two days set the seal upon a long period of mounting agitation, of troubles, street demonstrations, violence, class conflict, political crises and violent scenes. But when the final signal was sounded, the signal that ushered in a new era, it was barely audible. A whole society had crumbled while Chaliapin was delighting enthusiastic crowds with his rendering of *Don Carlos*.

In his *History of the Russian Revolution*, Trotsky put it like this: 'The first act of the Revolution seems, after all this, too brief, too dry, too businesslike — somehow inconsonant with the historic scope of the events. The reader experiences a kind of disappointment. He is like a mountain climber who, thinking the main difficulties are still ahead, suddenly discovers that he is already on the summit or almost there.' And Victor Serge, in his moving account of the Revolution, speaks of the same phenomenon with a measure of disappointment: 'Everything happened so simply and so naturally ... It was all quite unlike any of the revolutionary scenes we knew from history.' Or as Sukhanov put it: 'In some ways, it was like the changing of the guard.'

Compared with the classical revolutionary scheme, October was

[1] 'It makes one giddy.'

quite unique. There were no great street processions in Petrograd that day, no mass demonstrations, no baton charges—not even any marked rise in popular agitation, and barely any victims.[1] This is one of the reasons why so many of Lenin's socialist adversaries refused to recognize the revolutionary nature of the Bolshevik seizure of power. They spoke of a coup d'état, or of a conspiracy—according to them, the overthrow of the Provisional Government was the work of a few plotters working behind the scenes regardless of popular sentiment or of the dire consequences of their action. And while historians have at long last agreed to speak of a Russian *Revolution*, many still continue to apply the term 'subversion' to the most far-reaching of social movements, a movement that had nothing to do with spying or conspiracy. In other words, though no serious person today can deny that the transformation begun in Russia in 1917 ushered in an irreversible political, economic and social Revolution, many people still argue that the 'incident' which triggered it off was a sinister plot hatched by a handful of professional revolutionaries.

Sukhanov, who always refused to join the Bolsheviks, even in their hour of triumph, was quite explicit in his rejection of this view. 'To call it [the October Revolution] a military conspiracy rather than a national uprising is utterly absurd since the [Bolshevik] Party was already the *de facto* power in the land, and since it enjoyed the support of the enormous majority of the people.'

L'Entente, a conservative French paper published in Petrograd, said much the same thing when it wrote on November 2nd, 1917:

> While the Kerensky government discusses and vacillates, the government of Lenin and Trotsky attacks and acts. To call it a government of conspirators is quite wrong ... No, there is no conspiracy; on the contrary, quite boldly, without mincing their words, without disguising their intentions, they have stepped up their agitation, intensified their propaganda, in the factories, in the barracks, at the front, in the countryside, everywhere, going so far as to proclaim in advance the precise day on which they will take up arms, the day on which they will seize power.

[1] The only casualties in the whole of Petrograd fell during the capture of the Winter Palace on the night of October 25th–26th; *all five came from the ranks of the insurrectionists.*

Nothing further needs to be said, except that this truthful assessment of the facts leaves the paradox of October unexplained. There was no conspiracy, but the Revolution was unlike any other in that the vast majority of the masses stayed in their factories and barracks. The contrast between October and February, when the streets of Petrograd had run with blood, was glaring. During the overthrow of the Tsarist regime hundreds of thousands of people had come out into the streets of Petrograd, and it was under the pressure of this great human tide that the old system had crumbled. In October, on the other hand, the organized revolutionary forces numbered no more than thirty thousand in the capital, and of these a half at most were actively involved in the insurrection. The Bolshevik organization was, moreover, found wanting in a great many ways—which explains, for example, why Kerensky was able to escape so easily from a city controlled by men who set great store by his capture.

But how could a force numerically so small score such a resounding victory and usher in a Revolution that was to prove so far-reaching and so durable? The answer must be sought in the events preceding the actual insurrection; in the slow maturing of the spirit of revolt from February to October; in the 'April Days', in the 'Spring Storms', in the 'June Days' and the 'July Days'; in the growing dissatisfaction of the workers; in the impotence of the bourgeoisie and the clamour of the peasants. Throughout this time, the Bolsheviks had remained steadfast and had gradually earned the trust of the masses, whose continued distress had given rise to an unprecedented upsurge of class consciousness. The zeal of the Party militants, the constancy and lucidity of many Bolshevik leaders, had done the rest—they had channelled the rising revolutionary tide. While the history of revolutions, victorious and unsuccessful alike, is studded with thousands of missed opportunities, wasted efforts and ill-timed attacks, the Bolsheviks, for one, succeeded in keeping these so often wasted efforts to a minimum, and so gave their own Revolution the maximum effect. Hence if anything at all was unique about the Bolshevik uprising it was this: unlike all its precursors, it was a *directed* Revolution.

Most other revolutions started spontaneously and brought on to the scene vast crowds who came we know not whence, and who did not know where they were going. As a result, their achievements fell far short of their vague aspirations. Take for example France in

1789: the people came out into the streets and the village squares;
but if the heart of the Revolution beat in them, its brain was elsewhere. It was vested in a much smaller group, one with a much
clearer certainty of purpose, with a riper political experience, with
more clearly discerned interests—the bourgeoisie. This class
shared some enemies but few other interests with the masses; it felt
nothing for its plebeian troops except a mixture of fear, disdain and
suspicion. In the Russian Revolution of 1917 things happened
quite differently. True, here too February had the violence and
suddenness of a volcanic eruption, but thereafter Russia witnessed
the parallel and smooth progress of the proletariat and its Party.
When this double growth reached full maturity in the autumn, its
two branches quickly fused: the working class became at one with
the Bolshevik movement. There are few other examples in history
of so close a union, of so intimate a contact, of so great a com-
munion, so complete an identification between millions of workers
and tens of thousands of militants. And when, at long last, there
was a headlong clash between the established authority—already
badly eroded—and the new candidates for state power, the latter,
unlike all other revolutionary forces, could already boast an army of
its own, and that army its own general staff. In all previous revolutions, the people had been nothing but a mass of willing pawns
manipulated by strategists who shared neither their condition nor
their interests. The Bolshevik Party in 1917 was the Party of the
Russian working class; it expressed its sorrows, its hopes and its
angers better than any other Party had been able to express the
aspirations of any other class. It was this characteristic that enabled
the Bolsheviks to take the initiative in the October insurrection, the
more so as the social and political weaknesses of the Russian
bourgeoisie were such as to preclude the latter from playing a
decisive, or even an independent, part in the subsequent course
of events.

So many witnesses have spoken of the close link between the
Russian working class and Lenin's Party that there is no need to
dwell on it here at greater length.[1] But to suppose that this alone

[1] This remarkable identification between a class and a Party is also borne out
by the rapid numerical growth of the latter. Party membership was 23,000 in
February; on the eve of the insurrection, Sverdlov was able to inform the
Central Committee that the number had gone up to more than 400,000 members.
This figure has been challenged, but it should also be remembered that, at the
time, the Bolshevik organization was still too rough and ready to launch a fully

explains the Bolshevik triumph of October is to ignore the fact that the Russian industrial proletariat, of which the Bolshevik Party was the political mainstay, only represented a small fraction of the nation. The bulk was made up of peasants. The rural peasant population has always posed difficult and sometimes dramatic problems to modern revolutionaries. Thus in June 1848, when the workers of Paris rose up against the bourgeoisie, the army which shot them down was an army of peasants in uniform, frightened of the Red Flag. A quarter of a century later the Paris Commune, which may be called the first proletarian state in modern Europe, also came up against the hostility of the countryside. True, the Commune was welcomed in a number of provincial centres, but the mass of the peasants provided the forces of reaction with their shock troops and with a basis for the 'moral order' they built on the ruins of the Commune. In Russia, too, the *moujiks* took up arms against the rebellious working class in 1905, but by 1917 when the Tsar needed them more than ever they had defected *en masse*. They lacked the cohesion, unity, political consciousness and dynamic force without which there can be no revolutionary advance, but they had finally severed their links with a regime that had kept them in misery for centuries. And once the peasants became neutral, they ceased to be a conservative counterweight to the revolutionary energy of the modern proletariat. And so Tsarism had to fall by the wayside.

Had the Provisional Government had any foresight at all, it would have bent over backwards to gain and retain the confidence of the peasants. But all it did was to issue appeals for patience and send out punitive expeditions whenever the peasants gave active expression to their hunger for land. And when it failed so miserably on the agrarian front, the Provisional Government sealed its own fate. Those in the cabinet who ought to have known the peasantry better—the Social Revolutionaries—had become so much part of the regime that they turned their backs on their main supporters. The Bolsheviks, by contrast, urged on by Lenin and sometimes doing violence to their own principles, but in any case putting dogmatic scruple behind them, made the peasants' demands their own. Throughout the spring and the summer they pressed

effective recruiting campaign. Many workers followed the Bolshevik line without taking out membership cards. Moreover, the industrial proletariat of Russia did not exceed 2,500,000 workers at the time.

unceasingly for immediate land reforms and, while not actually welcoming excesses, gave overt approval to the general peasant revolt. Their enemies accused them of demagogy, when in fact the Bolsheviks took their promises to the peasants very seriously—so much so that hardly had they seized power when they set about fulfilling them. What was true of the land problem was equally true of the peace question. In this sphere, too, their speeches were bold, but no more so than the programme and policy they pursued after the fall of the Provisional Government. And so, thanks to Lenin, the urban proletariat found a staunch ally in the countryside. The peasants did not 'make' October, but if the anti-Bolshevik forces counted on them to 'unmake' it, they were cruelly deceived. The peasants may have stood prudently on the sidelines but at no time —then or in the months that followed—did they dream of rising up against those who had 'given' them peace and land.

The support of the peasants, or rather their benevolent neutrality, also meant the support or neutrality of the army. In the October insurrection the army played a much more unobtrusive part than it had in February, when a mutiny in the ranks had helped to seal the Tsar's fate. Eight months later, the number of soldiers— the sailors were a special case—who intervened in the overthrow of the Provisional Government was very small indeed, and when they did intervene it was more often than not under the leadership of Red Guards recruited from among the civilian population. In any case, the Bolsheviks had no need of the *active* support of the army —the Military Revolutionary Committee even ordered a number of regiments to stay in barracks. It was the old ministers who wanted to bring them out against the workers' militia, and in this they were spectacularly unsuccessful. If the Bolshevik Revolution had forged an unusual alliance between the working class and the peasants, it had also sealed a no less unusual alliance between the workers in revolt and the soldiers who were meant to put them down. In October, the people did not come out in the streets—they did not need to, for there was no armed resistance to overcome. Once the insurrection had started, the working class already held the upper hand.

The sense of security with which this double alliance filled the fighters of October was another specific feature of the Petrograd uprising. It was good-humoured and serene, and its magnanimity in victory has been vouched for by many independent observers.

On several occasions, military cadets arrested during the actual operation were immediately set free, as soon as they signified that they would not again take arms against the Revolution. They promised, but many of them broke their word. The socialist ministers, too, were quickly released; the members of the Pre-Parliament were not even bothered—much to the surprise of some of them. In his memoirs, the former Minister of Justice, Malian-tovich, tells us how Antonov-Ovseënko dissuaded some of his men from locking up the military cadets they had captured in the Winter Palace:

'The facts of the matter are these, comrades. Three cadets have been caught in the Winter Palace. For the rest of the time they have stayed peacefully enough in our armoured car, too afraid to start anything. The other comrades will bear me out. And so I have ordered their release after removal of their epaulettes.'

'Let them go? But what for? They must be judged,' someone said.

'Why do that, comrade? Judged? What have they done? We must be generous. Let them go.' And go they did.

A few days later, the Kornilovist General Krasnov, whom Kerensky had ordered to recapture Petrograd,[1] also fell into the hands of the Bolsheviks. He was immediately released on giving a promise not to engage in any further counter-revolutionary activities. Once at liberty, he departed immediately for the south of Russia where he became one of the founders of the White Army.

The Bolsheviks' benevolence during the first days in power did much to revive the flagging spirits of the bourgeoisie. John Reed witnessed several scenes in which Red Guards were insulted by emboldened passers-by. Thus on October 26th, walking down the Nevsky a little after midday, he saw Red Guards and sailors with bayoneted rifles, 'each one surrounded by about a hundred men— clerks, students, shopkeepers, *chinovniks*[2]—shaking their fists and bawling insults and menaces ... Nothing like this, I imagine, ever occurred in history'. A few days later, after an attempted putsch by the Junkers,[3] the workers' militia seized the Telephone Exchange occupied by the rebels. Hardly had news of this reached the rest of the city when hundreds of good bourgeois citizens appeared outside to voice their displeasure: 'Fools! Rabble! How long do you think

[1] See Chapter 10.   [2] Civil servants.   [3] See Chapter 10.

you will last? Wait till the Cossacks come!' and the Red Guards let them be.

It was not until the bourgeoisie had gone beyond hurling abuse, not until they had enlisted the support of foreign troops and unleashed a bitter civil war, that the Russian Revolution, forced to abandon its good nature and tolerance, began to answer assassination with repression, came down on the rebels with a heavy hand and, fighting for its very survival, resorted to terror. Petrograd in October was still very far from that. The Bolsheviks, abandoning the peaceful methods Lenin had preached only a few months earlier, had just succeeded in launching the most peaceful of all insurrections.

10

The Beginning of Soviet Rule

O N October 25th, the Provisional Government fell without a struggle and Petrograd was in Bolshevik hands. Next day, the capital was completely at peace. All observers are agreed on this point. Captain Sadoul, a French military attaché in Petrograd who later turned Communist, noted that 'with the exception of a few individual lapses, public order is far better maintained than it was before the insurrection. The number of burglaries has dropped considerably.' The French journalist Claude Anet said much the same: 'The city is more orderly than it has been at any stage since the beginning of the [February] Revolution.' And the Petrograd military authorities sent the following message to Army Headquarters: 'The insurgents are maintaining order and discipline. There is no looting and there are no pogroms; on the contrary, insurgent patrols have been arresting drunken soldiers.'

The consolidation of Bolshevik power

All this confirmed, if confirmation were needed, the ease with which the Bolsheviks had seized power. But if, looking back, we find that their insurrection was to revolutionary strategy what the *blitzkrieg* is to the art of war, the Bolsheviks themselves did not think so. Zinoviev, who was admittedly a notorious pessimist, gave the new regime no more than a fortnight, and the Petersburg bourgeoisie could not believe that the bungling Leninists could stave off collapse for even that length of time—their own incompetence and the efforts of their enemies would see to that. True, the capital was in the hands of the revolutionaries, but the conservatives and moderate socialists were firmly convinced that the expected reinforcements from the front would quickly restore order. Moreover, they knew that the Bolsheviks counted numerous enemies within the city gates, and that these would make common cause with the troops Kerensky had promised. The 'Generalissimo' had arrived at Northern Front Headquarters in Pskov late on

October 25th, where he had learned to his dismay from the Commander-in-Chief General Kheremissov that the men were in no mood to march upon the capital. However, Kerensky had received a more sympathetic hearing from General Krasnov—not that this former collaborator of Kornilov had a particular liking for the head of the late Provisional Government; it was just that he hated the Bolsheviks even more and was itching to lead his seven hundred Cossack horsemen into battle against them. General Dukhonin, the Chief-of-Staff, was of much the same persuasion.

On October 27th they accordingly ordered a 'March on Petrograd', and had little difficulty in capturing Gatchina, some twenty-seven miles from the centre of the capital. Soon afterwards, Tsarskoe Selo fell to Krasnov as well. Petrograd was now only some fifteen miles away, and pamphlets bearing Krasnov's signature had already begun to circulate in the city. 'I call upon you to save Petrograd from anarchy, from tyranny and famine, and to save Russia from the indelible shame to which a handful of ignorant men, bought by Kaiser Wilhelm's gold, are trying to subject her,' the General proclaimed. 'The active army looks upon these criminals with horror and contempt. Their acts of vandalism and pillage, their crimes, the German mentality with which they regard Russia—stricken down but not yet surrendered—have alienated them from the entire people.'

Meantime the 'criminals', too, continued to appeal to the soldiers at meeting after packed meeting. Next day, on October 28th, the Bolshevik Government declared a state of siege in Petrograd, and ordered the war soviets and factory shop committees to move out the greatest possible number of workers for the digging of trenches, the erection of barricades and the reinforcement of barbed-wire entanglements. And the masses were quick to heed their call.

> By tens of thousands [John Reed tells us], the working people poured out, men and women; by tens of thousands the humming slums belched out their dumb and miserable hordes. Red Petrograd was in danger! Cossacks! South and south-west they poured through the shabby streets towards the Moscovsky Gate, men, women and children, with rifles, picks, spades, barbed wire, cartridge belts over their working clothes ... Such an immense outpouring of a city was never seen!

In the elegant quarters, the rich took courage as well, and openly rejoiced at the Bolsheviks' discomfiture—when an aeroplane dropped pamphlets bearing Kerensky's signature they felt sure that the end of Lenin's government was only a matter of hours. The 'Generalissimo' himself sent General Dukhonin a most optimistic telegram. 'Bolshevism', he declared, 'is collapsing and no longer exists as an organized force even in Petrograd.' A reception committee was preparing to give the 'saviour' a hero's welcome.

The anti-Bolsheviks resistance had rallied round the 'Committee to Save the Country and the Revolution'. The latter, founded on October 26th, included delegates from the City Duma, the Pre-Parliament, the Central Executive Committee of the First All-Russian Congress of Soviets, the moderate socialist parties and the Cadets. They set it up as an interim government with headquarters in the offices of the City Duma, whence they launched proclamation after proclamation denouncing the new regime as an illegal upstart. Their bill-posters waged a running battle with the Bolsheviks for the best hoardings. On October 27th, the Committee held a public meeting during which one of the speakers was heard to declare that the Bolsheviks must be 'crushed without mercy'.

Nor did it rest at speeches. Next day the military cadets, whom the Bolsheviks had trustingly released on parole, betrayed the trust and staged an uprising. During the night of October 28th they seized the Telephone Exchange and arrested Antonov-Ovseënko who happened to be inside. Sporadic fighting continued throughout the next day, until the Red Guard eventually forced them out with field guns. By then some two hundred people had been wounded or killed.

The Committee to Save the Country and the Revolution also tried to cripple the soviets by organizing a strike of civil servants—with financial help from the big banks. As a result of their obstruction the ministries ground to a halt, and so did the Petrograd and Moscow municipal services. When Shliapnikov, the Commissar of Labour, arrived at his ministry, what few officials had stayed behind refused to show him to his office. Alexandra Kollontai, Commissar of Public Welfare, found herself with a staff of only forty, while her ministry was besieged by a vast crowd of crippled and starving people with pinched faces.

> With tears streaming down her face [John Reed says],
> Kollontai arrested the strikers until they should deliver the

keys of the office and the safe; when she got the keys, however, it was discovered that the former minister, Countess Panina, had gone off with all the funds, which she refused to surrender except on the orders of the Constituent Assembly.

Trotsky, too, was put in a most humiliating position when he tried to take over the former Ministry of Foreign Affairs. This is how the right-wing Social Revolutionary *Dielo Naroda* described the affair in its issue of October 28th:

> Yesterday the new 'Minister' Trotsky presented himself at the Ministry of Foreign Affairs. After summoning all the officials he declared, 'I am the new Minister of Foreign Affairs, Trotsky.' He was received with ironic laughter. He paid no attention and ordered everybody to return to work. The employees then ... went home and decided not to return while Trotsky remained head of the Ministry.

The situation was much the same in the State Bank: when Lenin's government asked for thirty-five million roubles the cashiers locked the vaults and declared that they would make no payment to anyone except the Provisional Government.

Since the officials refused to work the Bolsheviks were forced to find replacements at a moment's notice, and it was these – workers, soldiers, sailors, with dazed looks and lolling tongues – whom John Reed watched sweating blood as they laboured over gigantic ledgers. Even the attempt to sabotage the telegraph agency, which would have had the effect of cutting Petrograd off from the outside, was thwarted by volunteers. Meanwhile, the strikers themselves did not go short of anything – they had been paid a whole month's salary by various bankers and industrialists. Their resistance ended only with Kerensky's defeat.

It came on October 30th, at Pulkovaia Gora (Pulkovo Heights) on the outskirts of Petrograd, where for lack of reinforcements Krasnov had been forced to halt his advance during the previous night. Next morning he was attacked by the Red Guard and pro-Soviet artillery, who inflicted heavy losses on the 'Whites' and forced him to retire to Gatchina. The Revolution had scored its first military victory. True, General Dukhonin had not yet given up hope of restoring the Provisional Government by force of arms, but when most of the divisions he 'called up' refused to obey orders he, too, had to concede victory to the enemy. On October 31st the 'Generalissimo', who only two days before had entered Gatchina triumphantly on a white charger, gave the order to suspend military operations against the Bolsheviks. For once he was obeyed, and to the letter.

On November 1st a truce was arranged, and General Krasnov promised People's Commissar Dybenko to have Kerensky arrested by the Cossacks and to hand him over to the Military Revolutionary Committee. In return, Dybenko undertook to write into the treaty a clause 'barring Lenin and Trotsky from holding any ministerial post or from participating in political life until such time as they had been cleared of the charge of treason against the homeland'. It goes without saying that Dybenko, good Bolshevik that he was, put his name to this clause tongue-in-cheek. But while sanctions against Lenin and Trotsky had not the least chance of being implemented, those against Kerensky were thwarted only by the action of a soldier who helped the former head of the Provisional Government to escape moments before the Cossacks came to arrest him. A little earlier, Kerensky had submitted his resignation to the Social Revolutionary Avksentiev, President of the Pre-Parliament. So ended the career of one who for many months had worn the mantle of the Russian Revolution. Abandoned by all, he was unable to play even the smallest part in his country's coming struggle and destiny.

The first phase in the counter-revolutionary campaign came officially to an end on November 2nd, with the arrest of General Krasnov. Soon afterwards, however, he was released on parole and immediately hastened to southern Russia where, as we saw, he organized the White Army and played a leading part in fostering the rebellion of the Don and Kuban Cossacks.

On the day of Krasnov's arrest, Moscow witnessed the last round of a week-long battle between the two camps. In Moscow, unlike Petrograd, the bourgeoisie had put up fierce resistance to the new regime. On October 25th, when the Moscow Soviet decided by 394 votes to 106 with 23 abstentions to support the Petrograd Military Revolutionary Committee, bourgeois and right-wing socialist leaders immediately joined forces in a Committee of Public Safety. They could muster more than ten thousand armed supporters, many of them seasoned soldiers, against a Bolshevik force that though much larger in number (some fifty thousand men) was poorly equipped and badly trained.

On the evening of October 27th, the anti-Bolsheviks took the offensive and succeeded in capturing a number of public buildings. Early on October 28th, they called on the revolutionary forces in the Kremlin to surrender, promising that there would be no reprisals. This promise was immediately broken: within minutes of the surrender, the Junkers threw themselves on the disarmed Red Guards and killed a large number of them. Such acts of blind violence were repeated in other parts of the city as well—many Bolsheviks were executed on the orders of self-appointed courts martial.

Having captured the Kremlin, the 'Whites' were in control of the centre of the city, while the 'Reds' were entrenched in the industrial suburbs. After a truce, hardly observed by either side, fighting broke out again on October 31st, when thanks to their numerical superiority the revolutionary forces, strengthened by Red Guards from Petrograd, quickly gained the upper hand. On November 1st, 'Red' gunners bombarded the Kremlin, which suffered some damage. Next day they took it by storm, dissolved the Committee of Public Safety and disarmed the Junkers. This time there were no reprisals.

While the events in Moscow did not affect the course of the Revolution, they nevertheless threw an unexpected light on the behaviour and spirit of some Bolshevik leaders at the moment of their greatest victory. When the Council of People's Commissars heard the news that the Kremlin had been seriously damaged, Lunacharsky, the chief of the Department of Education, burst into sobs: 'I cannot stand it,' he cried, 'I cannot bear this monstrous destruction of beauty and tradition.' Deeply conscious of his duty as educationalist and protector of the arts, he immediately tendered his resignation and published the following rather pathetic declaration: 'Comrades, you are the new masters of this country, and although you now have many other things to reflect upon, you must also defend your artistic and scientific heritage.' Recalling the shelling of historic buildings in Moscow, he went on to say: 'It is frightful to be a Commissar of Education in these days of savage war, so pitiless and so full of blind destruction. In these painful days, faith in the final victory of socialism, of the new and higher culture which will recompense us for everything, is our only consolation. But I am responsible for the protection of the people's artistic treasures. I cannot remain at a post while I am impotent to discharge that responsibility and accordingly have tendered my resignation.[1] But, comrades, I implore you to stand by me, to help me preserve for yourself and for your descendants the great monuments of our country. Be the guardians of the people's heritage. Soon even the most uncultured among us, those whom oppression has kept in ignorance for so long, will be educated and will understand what source of joy, of strength and wisdom, are the great works of art ... '

Though Lunacharsky was not the only Bolshevik to have this passionate concern with culture, with him it sometimes took the most curious forms. Thus in August 1917 he had taken time off from his pressing revolutionary preoccupations to treat a vast audience of workers to a brilliant series of lectures on Greek art in a packed Cirque Moderne. This love of learning, this determination to join social emancipation to cultural progress, has also been remarked upon by John Reed: when he was visiting the front shortly before the October insurrection, he came across 'gaunt and bootless men, sickened in the mud of desperate trenches. When they saw us, they started up with their pinched faces and the flesh showing blue through their torn clothing, demanding eagerly, "Did you bring anything to read?" '

For the time being, however, demonstrators throughout Russia were clamouring not so much for culture as for the transfer of all power to the soviets. Generally they achieved their ends by peaceful means — in most industrial cities the Bolshevik victory was often no more than a simple formality; in other parts they were forced to follow the example of Petrograd, and forming Military Revolutionary Committees they quickly subdued what sporadic resistance the bourgeoisie was able to put up. True, the weakness of the new government was exploited by several local councils who set up as states within the state, but as the revolutionary 'contagion' gradually spread, the Bolsheviks were able to impose their will over the greater part of Russia. They proved far less successful with some of the national minorities. In Georgia, where the Mensheviks remained strong, a number of regions rejected Bolshevik rule; in the Ukraine, nationalist forces took over the western areas, but here,

---

[1] Lunacharsky soon afterwards returned to his old post. In fact, the Kremlin had suffered far less damage than was believed at first.

too, the more highly industrialized eastern part rallied to the Bolsheviks. Much the same thing happened in Baku.

In south-eastern Russia, again, the Don and Kuban Cossacks were exposed to all sorts of counter-revolutionary influences, and the Bolsheviks could not extend their influence beyond such industrial cities as Rostov and Taganrog. The Cossacks found a leader in General Kaledin, who in late November assembled an anti-Bolshevik force numbering several thousands. They were joined soon afterwards by a host of generals and liberal politicians. Among the former were Generals Alexeiev, Denikin, Krasnov and Lukomsky, all of whom had held important positions under the Provisional Government; the latter included such Cadet stalwarts as Miliukov and Rodzianko. Alexeiev quickly founded a 'Volunteer Army' of some three to four thousand men, a relatively small but socially homogeneous and highly trained striking force—most of them were former Tsarist officers.

Thus while the north, the centre and the east of Russia passed rapidly into the hands of the new leaders, the south became a hotbed of reaction. The Bolsheviks paid little heed to what was still a small band of dissidents squabbling among themselves, and made full use of the lull in the fighting to consolidate their own forces.

The peace of Brest-Litovsk

During their first weeks in power, the Bolsheviks were, in any case, far less concerned with clamping down on deposed politicians and die-hard officers than with fulfilling the hopes of millions of Russians by putting an end to the war. The Bolsheviks themselves had always remained true to the old slogan of international socialism: that the world war must be transformed into a world revolution as the only guarantee of lasting peace.[1]

Events in Russia had gone a long way towards justifying their steadfast adherence to these tenets: the Russian Revolution was the answer of an entire nation exhausted by bloody sacrifice, first to the Tsar, and then to a system that according to socialist doctrines was the fundamental cause of all modern wars: capitalism. And now that the overthrow of the capitalist puppet government had cleared this obstacle out of the way peace seemed just round the corner, particularly since the Germans, anxious to concentrate all their forces on the Western Front, were as keen as the Bolsheviks them-

[1] See Chapter 3.

selves to put an end to the fighting in the east. The Bolsheviks, moreover, would not bother about such niceties as obtaining Allied agreement first.

However, the situation was not as simple for the Bolsheviks as it appeared. Their strategy was not, in fact, based on national considerations alone; they looked upon themselves as just one column in a large army, and upon their Revolution as just one figure on a vast canvas. To them, the Russian uprising was part and parcel of the world socialist revolution and its every step was aimed at encouraging the rest of Europe's proletariat which, in its turn, would ensure the future safety and progress of their Russian comrades. By signing a separate peace with Germany and Austria-Hungary, would not Lenin's government have hindered rather than helped international solidarity? What would the workers of Europe think of a revolutionary state, barely born, that came to terms with one side in the imperialist struggle for power and so enabled it to continue the massacre with redoubled strength? For that very reason the Bolsheviks, while still in opposition, had bitterly opposed the signing of a separate peace with Germany, and had let it be known that once in power they would appeal to *all* the belligerent countries to put an end to the conflict. The governments involved would be staking their very future on the response they made to this appeal: if they rejected it—as they were likely to do—they would unleash the fury of their own proletariat and hence start a revolution; if they accepted it, the world would be indebted to the Bolsheviks for having put a stop to the slaughter, and the world proletariat, encouraged by their example, would take to the path of revolution.

And so within hours of its formation the new regime published a Peace Decree, appealing to all nations and all governments to stop the war. On November 8th, Trotsky, as People's Commissar for Foreign Affairs, returned to the charge when he handed a note to the Allied ambassadors. In it he drew their attention to the terms of the 'Peace Decree' and asked them to 'regard this document as an official proposal for an immediate armistice on all fronts and for the immediate opening of peace negotiations'. His note remained unanswered—the only response it evoked was an Allied warning to General Dukhonin, still the Chief-of-Staff of the Russian Army, that the signing of a separate peace would have the gravest consequences for Russia. In acting as they did, the Western governments not only demonstrated their refusal to recognize the new regime, but also their determination to fight the war to its bitter end.

Their attitude did not really surprise the Bolsheviks; it simply confirmed their belief that Western capitalism was not interested in a truly democratic peace. The next move would come from the workers themselves. Many Bolsheviks were convinced that an up-rising was imminent, and that is precisely what Trotsky had meant when he said that he would soon be shutting up shop in the Ministry of Foreign Affairs. Diplomacy would surely make way for revolution — the only problem was when. But as time dragged on and nothing happened, the Bolsheviks, heavy-hearted, felt that they had no option but to make a unilateral approach to the Central Powers. On November 13th, Russian plenipotentiaries accordingly crossed over to the German lines and arranged for preliminary peace parleys to be held at Brest-Litovsk on November 19th. These parleys had no equal in the entire history of diplomacy.

To begin with, diplomatic negotiations usually involve statesmen and soldiers, and while Germany and Austria-Hungary did, in fact, send men of such standing to Brest-Litovsk, the Soviet representatives were men of much less refined metal. The result was a strange confrontation between stiff diplomats and officers of the old school and revolutionaries with straggly beards, many of whom had only just come out of hiding. Moreover, the Bolsheviks, mindful of thei revolutionary mission, had co-opted to their delegation, led by Joffé and Kamenev, a simple soldier, a simple sailor and a work-man. Then on their way to the station, one of the Bolshevik plenipotentiaries had remarked that without a true representative of the Russian peasantry their delegation was incomplete. To fill this gap they asked a *moujik* passer-by to join them on their official excursion to Brest-Litovsk. Taken by surprise, the peasant accepted and was in fact present at all the parleys. Though this was his sole contribution to the peace treaty, he certainly made a strong im-pression on the Austrian and German representatives, some of whom never ceased wondering at the enormous quantities of alcohol this strange diplomat used to put away during diplomatic dinners. And what surprised them even more was that, as one of the Ger-mans explained, this Russian spokesman was completely indifferent to the finer distinctions between white wine and red wine, however carefully selected.

This anecdote is more significant than one might think, for it highlights the paradoxical character of the Bolshevik presence in Brest-Litovsk: forced to play the part of negotiators, the Soviet representatives were determined to conduct themselves as revolutionary militants. Thus Trotsky, who led the Soviet delegation during the decisive phase of the parleys, told the German Foreign Secretary, 'We members of the Russian delegation do not belong to the diplomatic school, but consider ourselves rather as soldiers of the Revolution and as such prefer the rough language of the soldier.' And Trotsky went on to remind the Germans that he, the head of the Russian delegation, was still under the prison sentence which the Kaiser's court had passed on him for his revolutionary activities.

Trotsky's words did not simply introduce a new style into diplomatic usage, they bore witness to an entirely new approach, as did the actions of Russia's other delegates. One of these was Karl Radek, a hardened militant who had played an important part in German and Polish left-wing politics before the war. He travelled with Trotsky to Brest-Litovsk, and as soon as the train stopped, and while the Russian delegation was still exchanging greetings with the cream of Germany's and Austria's diplomatic corps, he turned his back on the august assembly and in the most natural way possible began to distribute revolutionary pamphlets among the German soldiers forming the guard of honour.[1]

During the negotiations, technical discussions often turned into political debates in which representatives of two social systems remorselessly attacked the shortcomings of their adversaries. Trotsky, in particular, excelled in digressions of a sociological and philosophical kind, to which most of the German and Austrian officers listened with utter stupefaction. For Trotsky, these debates, in which only Kühlmann had the wit to make the occasional rejoinder, had the double advantage of giving him the chance of attacking the enemy on familiar ground, and also of dragging on the negotiations as long as he possibly could. In these oratorical bouts, the negotiators were quick to score points. Thus when a German fancied he could attack Bolshevik press censorship, Trotsky

---

[1] In his *Russia and the West under Lenin and Stalin*, the American diplomat G. F. Kennan alleges that Radek amused himself blowing pipe-smoke into the face of the German Commander, Major-General Max Hoffmann, and that he stared at him in an insulting way. However, such behaviour was too extreme even for Radek, so that this story must be treated with some reserve.

rounded on him with, 'I shall be happy to learn that socialist papers in Germany enjoy as much freedom as the opposition press does in Russia.' Major-General Hoffmann, unaccustomed to tolerating such impudence, indignantly remarked that Trotsky was speaking 'as if he represented a victorious invader of our country', when all the facts seemed to prove the contrary.

On this point, too, there was a profound difference between the two delegations. For despite the collapse of the Russian Army and the military supremacy of the Germans, the Bolsheviks had not the least intention of playing the role of the vanquished. On the contrary, Lenin's party looked upon itself as one that had just scored a decisive victory at home, and considered itself not so much the mouthpiece of one nation as of the international proletariat, and in that capacity was not facing the delegates of a hostile *people* but of a hostile *class*, which was responsible for the war and hence guilty of slaughter on a vast scale. It was this fact Trotsky had referred to when, shortly before leaving for Brest-Litovsk, he had told the Petrograd Soviet:

'Sitting at one table with them [the German negotiators] we shall ask them explicit questions, which do not allow of any evasions, and the entire course of the negotiations, every word they or we utter, will be taken down and reported by radio-telegraph to all nations, who shall be the judges of our negotiations. Under the influence of the masses, the German and Austrian Governments have already accepted to put themselves in the dock. You may rest assured, comrades, that the prosecutor, in the person of the Russian revolutionary delegation, will be in his place and in due time will make a thunderous speech for the prosecution on the diplomacy of all the imperialists.' To make such speeches and to hold such views called for enormous self-assurance. This was not so much justified by Russia's internal situation as by the belief that the enemies of the Revolution would soon be facing not just the depleted ranks of the Russian Army, or the newly formed Red Guard, but also the much more massive and more experienced forces of the Western proletariat.

If this faith in world revolution explained the strong language of the Russians at the conference table—which the Germans mistook for natural arrogance—it also explained their tactics. The longer the negotiations continued, the more obvious it would become to the Western proletariat that the imperialists did not want true

peace and that the workers must rise up against them. The Bolsheviks accordingly played for time, raising all sorts of questions
directly or indirectly related to the peace problem.

However, weeks passed and still there was no response from the
German working class. True, in January 1918 Berlin, Vienna and
many other German cities witnessed a series of major strikes, but
the authorities were able to put them down before they got out of
hand. And when that happened the Bolsheviks were forced to conclude that no immediate help would come from those on whom
they had counted so confidently.

By then, they had already signed an armistice with the Central
Powers. It gave them great satisfaction in at least two respects: the
Germans undertook not to transfer troops to the Western Front[1]
while the peace negotiations continued; and they also agreed not to
interfere with the fraternization between German and Russian
soldiers at the front which, in the circumstances, meant that the
Bolsheviks had a free hand to make revolutionary propaganda
among the German troops. The Petrograd presses had begun to
pour out an unending stream of German papers and pamphlets and
the Russians had not the least doubt that this 'subversive' literature
would make its mark.[2]

The actual peace negotiations were not started until December
9th, when at the request of the Russians they were immediately
prorogued to enable the Western Powers to join in. They were
resumed on December 22nd, but once again cut short on January
5th to enable Trotsky to convey the German demands to his
government. These demands were harsh in the extreme; tired of
the interminable wrangles that had caused so much vexation and
indignation, the Germans in the person of General Hoffmann had
produced a list of precise territorial claims against the Russians.
When Trotsky objected that these demands ran counter to the
original German declaration about a peace without annexations or
indemnities, he was told that German goodwill had been strained

[1] When the Germans gave this undertaking on December 2nd, 1917, they had
already transferred part of their army to the West. The mere fact, however, that
the Bolsheviks made this stipulation demonstrated their determination not to
favour one side to the detriment of the other.

[2] When General Hoffmann protested against this Bolshevik propaganda,
Trotsky replied that the armistice terms gave the Germans the right to engage
in counter-propaganda among the Russian soldiers and that the Bolsheviks
would do nothing to stop them.

beyond endurance by the continued refusal of the Western Allies to
join in the negotiations.

Whatever the truth of this explanation, the Bolsheviks were now
facing an entirely new situation—so far they had apparently held
most of the aces, but now the enemy had decided to overtrump.
Previously, they had been fighting enemies much weaker than
themselves; now they were up against so strong a force, so solid a
barrier, that their revolutionary courage ceased to be effective and
its limitations were revealed. For the first time in its history, the
Bolshevik Party was forced to temporize in the international arena,
and to do so it had to undergo a crisis of conscience that imperilled
its unity and nearly cost it its life.

When they were faced with the treaty of Brest-Litovsk, the
Bolsheviks split into three factions: the 'left-wing communists'
who wanted to wage revolutionary war on the German imperialists;
the 'peace group' led by Lenin; and a third faction led by Trotsky,
which fought under the slogan of 'neither peace nor war'. The
'left-wing communists' represented a considerable force. They
could count on the support not only of a large number of influential
Bolshevik leaders but also of the most important Bolshevik
organizations in Petrograd and Moscow. They claimed to represent
the revolutionary consciousness in its purest and most intransigent
form, and as such they had a strong appeal to all those Party
militants whom the October victory had taught the toughest line is
often the most effective. According to them, Bolshevism, the implacable foe of imperialism, could not possibly treat with its sworn
enemies, let alone make peace with them. Without doubt the
struggle of Russia against Germany was an uneven fight between a
country that had been bled white and one that had remained
powerful, but the left-wing communists, headed by Bukharin,
remained convinced that a revolutionary appeal to the German
masses would not go unheeded for long. And even if their struggle
were to end in disaster, it was far better 'to perish for the cause of
socialism than in abject submission to Wilhelm II'. The honour of
the Revolution was at stake, and any other solution was a betrayal
of the international proletariat. Lenin, for his part, declared that
'such a policy may perhaps answer the human yearning for the
beautiful, dramatic and striking, but it absolutely ignores the objective relation of class forces and material factors in the present stage
of the socialist revolution.'

And for Lenin, it was the latter that mattered most of all. He, too, had believed that the longing for peace would quickly cause workers throughout the world to rise up against their masters. He, too, had believed that the parleys in Brest-Litovsk would lead to a growth of revolutionary sentiment among European workers in general and the German proletariat in particular—but nothing of the kind had happened. The head of the Soviet Government did not surrender his deep faith in the revolutionary response of the Western masses, but he also believed that while waiting for Western imperialism to be attacked from within the Bolsheviks must come to terms with its continued existence. Revolutionary optimism had led Lenin to seize state power; a keen sense of reality now persuaded him to revise his former calculations. There was no choice; the Bolsheviks must sign the peace the Germans were determined to impose upon them.

Lenin appreciated the sentimental appeal of the leftist position, but the only moral imperative he recognized was that no sacrifice was great enough to safeguard Bolshevik power, now the spearhead of the world revolutionary movement. Since the German peace conditions, however harsh, did not threaten the survival of the Soviet regime, they would simply have to be swallowed. To wage a revolutionary war against Germany was, in any case, out of the question in view of the parlous state of the Russian Army. When Lenin's opponents objected that the Bolsheviks had pledged themselves to a remorseless fight against imperialism, he replied, 'We never gave any pledge to start a revolutionary war without taking into account how far it is possible to wage it at any given moment. Unquestionably, even at this juncture we must *prepare* for a revolutionary war.' Such preparation demanded a respite, and hence a truce. The Russian revolutionaries would resume the offensive again as soon as their Western comrades had established a second front in the international class war.

'We must hold back until at last the time of rebirth does come'—such, according to Lenin, was the slogan dictated by the temporary isolation of the Russian Revolution. A few weeks earlier, he had constantly repeated, 'It is death to wait;' now it was vigorous action that apparently imperilled the Revolution. Unfortunately for Lenin, not all the Bolsheviks were prepared to endorse this sudden change of tactics, to adapt themselves to this sudden change of circumstances. Quite apart from the 'purist' followers of

Bukharin, there were other Party members who tried to escape Lenin's implacable logic and who refused to see that there were only two alternatives: 'to accept the annexionist peace or to launch a revolutionary war here and now. All halfway solutions are quite impracticable.' Trotsky, for one, was not convinced by this argument. The head of the new Soviet 'Diplomatic Corps', while holding that the left-wing-communist position was romantic in the extreme, was nevertheless unwilling to renounce the intransigence which had swept the Bolsheviks into power. He was also concerned to refute the current lies that the Bolsheviks were the conscious or unwitting tools of German imperialism, lies that were bound to find wide credence once Soviet Russia signed a separate peace with the Central Powers. All his attacks on the German and Austrian representatives at Brest-Litovsk had been designed to demonstrate the complete independence of the Bolsheviks—their refusal to support one group of belligerents against the other. He now felt that such declarations were not enough, that they had to be supported by actions.

'We cannot continue the war', he admitted, 'for we lack the means to do so. But nothing forces us to sign a peace. If the Germans impose over-harsh conditions, we shall tell them that we shall stop fighting but that we shall refuse to endorse their imperialist aims and that we shall withhold our signatures from the peace treaty.' What would the Germans do then? It was quite possible, Trotsky thought, that for fear of offending public opinion they would hesitate to resume operations against an elusive and defenceless enemy. In that case, the Bolsheviks would have lost nothing, but would have been able to give proof of their revolutionary integrity. But it was equally possible that the German Army might advance further into Russia and threaten the existence of the new regime. In that case, there was time enough to bow to the invader's dictates. It was a risk that must be run, and it offered the German proletariat yet another chance to come to the aid of the Russian proletariat.

From January 5th, when the negotiations in Brest-Litovsk were cut short, until their resumption on January 17th, the three Bolshevik factions remained at loggerheads. A meeting of leading Party officials ended in a non-binding vote that revealed the relative strength of the three groups: thirty-two delegates voted in favour of the revolutionary war, fifteen in favour of Lenin's peace, and sixteen for Trotsky's slogan of 'neither war nor peace'. When the Bolshevik Central Committee re-examined the problem a few days later, it rejected Bukharin's solution by eleven votes to two with one abstention, and approved Trotsky's by nine votes to seven, after Lenin had decided to give his support to a position he considered far less obnoxious than that of the left-wing communists.

On January 17th, 1918, Trotsky was back at the conference table in Brest-Litovsk. This time he had to contend not only with the German and Austro-Hungarian delegations but also with representatives of the *Rada*, which had profited from the overthrow of the Provisional Government to proclaim the independence of the Ukraine. The credentials of these delegates were somewhat questionable since many Ukrainian soviets had voted in favour of an alliance with revolutionary Petrograd and had, in fact, succeeded in ousting the *Rada* from Kiev. By signing a separate agreement with the Ukrainians, the Germans hoped to face the Bolsheviks with a *fait accompli*, and to tie them down completely. Imagine their surprise, therefore, when on January 28th, Trotsky told them in ringing tones: 'We no longer wish to take part in this purely imperialist war in which the claims of the possessing classes are openly paid for in human blood ... In expectation of the approaching hour when the working classes of all countries seize power ... we are withdrawing our army and our people from the war ... ' Up to this point in Trotsky's address, the assembled generals and diplomats still believed that their opponents would make passionate protests, meant for home consumption, before meekly putting their signature to all the German demands. But the end of the Bolshevik declaration forced them to revise their opinion. 'We are issuing an order for the full demobilization of our army ... [but] we refuse to sanction those conditions which the sword of German and Austro-Hungarian imperialists is ready to inscribe on the flesh of living nations. We cannot enter the signature of the Russian Revolution under conditions that carry oppression, sorrow and suffering to millions of people ... ' The audience sat dumbfounded, and their silence was only broken when General Hoffmann exclaimed: 'Unerhört!'[1] Soon afterwards the Soviet delegation walked out in a body.

The Germans were utterly taken aback by an attitude that, according to their historical experts who busily consulted their

[1] 'Incredible!'

manuals, had only one precedent in the annals of diplomatic history
—the conflict between ancient Athens and Persia. Their embarrassment proved clearly that Trotsky's solution, though fraught with
grave risks, was not nearly as far-fetched as his detractors had
affirmed. The Austrian leaders, for instance, now argued that it was
best to keep to the present lines and not to continue hostilities on
the Eastern Front. Many German statesmen—including Kühlmann—shared this view. The German generals, on the other hand,
were determined to press their advantage home and to crush the
remains of the Russian Army. The issue was finally settled at a
'summit meeting' in Bad Homburg chaired by Kaiser Wilhelm in
person. The general staff won: on February 17th[1] General Hoffmann announced that the German Army would continue its
advance, and a day later the Kaiser's divisions did in fact move
forward without meeting the slightest resistance. Reval, Dvinsk
and Minsk fell to them in quick succession and the Ukraine lay
open before the German host. The Soviet Government was faced
with the very situation Lenin had warned them against: now,
clearly, they could delay no longer but must choose between
capitulation and war.

On February 17th and 18th, the Central Committee of the
Bolshevik Party was in almost continuous session, during which it
became obvious that despite the overwhelming superiority of the
German Army, the champions of revolutionary war were still as
intransigent as ever. On February 17th, Trotsky still had high
hopes that the Germans would not launch their threatened offensive, and Lenin's proposal that new peace talks be requested
immediately was rejected by seven votes to six. On the 18th, a
further meeting of the Central Committee arrived at the same conclusion, Trotsky maintaining his wait-and-see position. However,
when the debate was resumed in the evening, the issue was no
longer in doubt: the Germans had decided to exploit their advantage and were advancing at speed. Lenin now declared that 'if the
Germans should demand the overthrow of the Bolshevik Government, then, of course, we would have to fight,' but since this was
not the case it was far better to sign their peace treaty. Trotsky still
held that it was too early for that, but when the matter was put to

[1] On January 31st, 1918, a decree of the Soviet Government abolished the
Julian calendar and adopted the Western (Gregorian) calendar. February 1st
(Julian calendar) thus became February 14th.

the vote, he decided for the sake of party unity to throw his weight behind Lenin's motion, which was then carried by seven votes to five with one abstention. While not convinced by Lenin's argu- ments, Trotsky had come to realize that continued divisions within the Party threatened its very survival. In any case, he felt certain that revolutionary war could only be waged by a firmly united movement. Later that night the whole question was thrown open for further discussion, since the Social Revolutionary Commissars, who had joined the government in December, were not bound by the decision of the Bolshevik Central Committee. Opposed to the signing of a peace but in a minority, they, too, were outvoted in the end. On February 19th, the Russians informed the Germans that they were ready to sign a peace treaty.

But Germany and Austria had meanwhile decided to step up their demands, and the new peace terms were harsh in the extreme: in a note communicated on February 23rd to the Russian Govern- ment the Central Powers demanded that Russia cede Latvia and Estonia, evacuate Finland and the Ukraine, order the total de- mobilization of her army and pay a vast war indemnity. The Russians were given twenty-four hours to reply, and when the Central Committee of the Bolshevik Party met that day, it did so under more dramatic conditions than ever before. In order to silence the continued opposition of the left-wing communists, Lenin threatened to resign from the government and from the Central Committee if the German conditions were rejected. He once again explained the reasons for his stand: 'If you do not sign the treaty, you will be signing the death-warrant of the Soviet Government in less than three weeks.' Trotsky, convinced that the Soviet regime could not survive without Lenin, voted for the acceptance of the German ultimatum, but not everyone else fol- lowed his example. Thus Lomov, speaking for the Left, declared that 'If Lenin threatens to resign, there is nothing to be afraid of. We shall hold power without Vladimir Ilyich.'[1] Other members of the Central Committee, too, called for revolutionary war, but

---

[1] In his excellent work on the Brest-Litovsk peace, the British historian, J. Wheeler-Bennett, reports that at a meeting of the Central Bolshevik Com- mittee in January 1918 Radek, another left-wing communist, told Lenin that if there were 500 brave men in Petrograd they would have thrown him into gaol; to which Lenin replied that if Radek calculated the probabilities, he would probably find that it was not him (Lenin) but Radek they would have locked up.

during the vote seven delegates sided with Lenin, four voted against signing the peace treaty and four others abstained.

The Party having decided, the whole question was referred to the Central Executive Committee of the Soviets,[1] which endorsed the Bolshevik resolution by 116 votes to 84. A telegram was immediately dispatched to the Germans who at once halted their advance. A fresh Soviet delegation made for Brest-Litovsk, and on March 3rd, 1918, signed what turned out to be a catastrophic treaty. Russia ceded large territories of great economic importance, including the Baltic States, part of White Russia, Courland and the Ukraine. She also had to surrender the districts of Kars, Ardahan and Batum to Turkey. As a result, she lost 34 per cent of the population of Old Russia and 32 per cent of her arable land. This, according to Lenin, was a necessary sacrifice: 'I am yielding space in order to gain time,' he declared.

But Russia not only yielded space, she also lost a large fraction of her economic potential: 85 per cent of her beet crops, 54 per cent of her industries, and 89 per cent of her coalfields. In short, she was made to pay an extortionate indemnity for having dared to withhold her signature for a few short weeks. The country, already exhausted by war, was now despoiled after negotiations Russia had entered for the express purpose of dictating terms to the Austrian and German imperialists in the name of the world proletarian revolution. Let down by the Western working class, paying the price for its illusions, Soviet Russia suffered the first of that long series of defeats which forced her to revise her entire strategy and to reduce to very modest dimensions the immense hopes her first victories had kindled everywhere. For all that, many years were still to pass before this fateful revision took place. Meanwhile, the All-Russian Congress of Soviets, having ratified the peace of Brest-Litovsk by 784 votes to 261, gave Lenin the respite he so badly needed. Three years and seven months after the outbreak of a war that had cost Russia two and a half million dead, a nation had found peace. At the price of a major retreat, accused by its enemies of treason, the Bolshevik Party had carried out an essential part of its revolutionary programme.

[1] The Central Executive Committee had sovereign legislative powers when the All-Russian Congress of Soviets was not in session.

The 'Soviet Republic'

After more than three years of war and many months of social turmoil under a weak government, was Russia, now led by a strong and popular team, to enjoy the fruits of peace and reconstruction? Would a regime swayed by entirely different motives succeed in giving the whole country a new face, now that hostilities had come to an end? Foreign observers, preoccupied as they were with the great war drama that was being played out in the West, had by and large lost interest in Russia; to most of them the Bolsheviks were nothing but traitors and profligates who would disappear as ignominiously as they had appeared, when Russia would once again be able to participate in the comity of civilized nations. Military leaders, less given to patience, would have liked to recapture this vast territory and turn it into a huge base. For the time being, however, they had not yet managed to convince the politicians of the need for an anti-Bolshevik crusade.

And so Russia was left to her own devices, and tried to set her house in order, while waiting for the world proletariat to rally round the Red banner. Alas, the proletariat was given very little time, for soon afterwards foreign interventionists and local counter-revolutionaries threw Russia into the horrors and massive destruction of the Civil War. Meanwhile, what was the course along which her new leaders, some of the most determined social experimenters of all time, were trying to steer the new Russia? What did the country stand for in political, economic and social terms during the first month of the Soviet regime?

From the very outset, the Council of People's Commissars described itself as a 'Provisional Government of Workers and Peasants'. In January 1918 Lenin published a 'Declaration of the Rights of the Toiling and Exploited Peoples', in which the new regime was described as a 'Soviet Republic of Workers', Soldiers' and Peasants' Deputies'. A few months later the name was changed to 'Russian Federal Soviet Socialist Republic'. But no matter what the label, the new rulers were clearly determined to make theirs a soviet system, i.e. to vest full sovereignty in the All-Russian Congress of Soviets, thus solving a dilemma that had faced them throughout 1917. For months they had been forced to ask themselves what path revolutionary Russia must embark upon: the parliamentary path or another more original one, better adapted to the circumstance and the character of their country. Forced to solve a host of less theoretical problems, and swallowing a hefty dose of pragmatism, they had avoided a clear choice, leaving it to the events themselves to bring the correct solution.

All along they had been calling for a Constituent Assembly, and had bitterly attacked the Provisional Government for its failure to hold national elections. At the same time, however, they had also demanded the transfer of all power to the soviets, and these two demands were, of course, incompatible with each other. Thus while the Constituent Assembly would be elected by universal suffrage, the soviets were elected by the workers only. To opt for a Constituent Assembly meant opting for parliamentary, bourgeois democracy. Moderate socialists and even some Bolsheviks had been quite resigned to this, since they thought Russia was not yet ready for socialist rule. However, Lenin's strategy had given history a sudden impetus: in October, the bourgeois phase of the Revolution was transcended, and power fell to the industrial proletariat and its peasant allies—to the soviets, in short. In that case, what was the function of a Constituent Assembly, a body whose authority would clash with that of the Soviet? The Bolsheviks themselves hesitated to answer this question—before they could do so they had first to shed the heavy burden of old ideas and antiquated concepts. For they, too, had been convinced all along that the collapse of Tsarism would open up an era of liberal democracy and capitalist progress.

When they first came into power they were still evading the issue. Thus, though Lenin declared at the opening session of the Second All-Russian Congress of Soviets of October 25th, 1917, 'We shall have a government of soviets ... without the least participation of the bourgeoisie ... the old state machine will be completely destroyed and make way for the leadership of the soviets,' the Peace Declaration he published at almost the same hour laid down that the terms of the settlement with Germany would be submitted to the Constituent Assembly 'which will then decide, officially, what can and what cannot be granted'. As for the Land Decree, it was presented as a provisional measure pending a 'final solution by the Constituent Assembly'. In the debate that followed Lenin still saw fit to declare, 'And even if the peasants ... give to this party [the Social Revolutionaries] the majority in the Constituent Assembly, we shall still say: so be it. Life is the best teacher, and it will show who is right. Let the peasants starting from one end, and we ourselves from the other, settle this question.'

Here was a flagrant contradiction, which 'life' in fact helped to solve, but not at all in the manner Lenin had suggested. On October 27th, the Council of People's Commissars announced a national election for November 13th, thus fulfilling a promise the Provisional Government had made but never kept. It seems certain that a few days later Lenin still intended to allow the Constituent Assembly to function normally, provided only it agreed to bow to certain demands of the new democratic spirit. Thus, on November 19th Lenin drafted a decree demanding that the principle of revocability be applied to the future assembly no less than to the soviets—if public control was to have any real meaning, the electors must have the right to withdraw their mandate at any moment. On November 21st, the Central Executive Committee of the Soviet endorsed Lenin's draft. The elections had previously taken place on the appointed date and had been carried out in an atmosphere of considerable freedom, though it is true that the Constitutional-Democratic Party was subjected to a number of restrictions. The results (in the whole of Russia) were as follows:

> Social Revolutionaries: 20,900,000 votes, representing 58
> per cent of the electorate;
> Bolsheviks: 9 million votes, or 25 per cent;
> Bourgeois parties (Cadets, etc.): 4,600,000 votes, or 13
> per cent;
> Mensheviks: 1,700,000 votes, or 4 per cent.

Thus the Social Revolutionaries, left and right wings combined, emerged as the most powerful Party in Russia. However, these figures call for some amplification. In particular, they did not reflect the relative strength of the Parties in the major cities, and it was here that political life was at its most intense. Thus Petrograd and Moscow together produced the following results:

> Bolsheviks: 837,000 votes;
> Cadets: 515,000 votes;
> Social Revolutionaries: 218,000 votes.

In Petrograd alone the Bolsheviks collected some 415,000 votes, the Cadets 245,000 and the Social Revolutionaries 150,000, and all the other Parties combined 117,000. Another important fact was that while the Bolsheviks received 43 per cent of the votes in the

Petrograd civilian wards, they obtained 77 per cent in the military wards.[1] In the army at large, the Bolsheviks (1,791,000 votes) came second to the Social Revolutionaries (1,885,000 votes) with the Cadets lagging far behind (51,000 votes). Among units stationed near the capital, however, the Bolsheviks collected a million votes while the Social Revolutionaries could muster no more than 420,000. In short, the countryside voted for the old Party of the peasants and the urban workers and urbanized soldiers for the Bolsheviks. The Mensheviks, for their part, clung to a few of their traditional 'fiefs', such as the Caucasus, but the industrial proletariat had deserted them almost to a man.

For all that, the Bolsheviks were going to be a minority in the Constituent Assembly: the Social Revolutionaries had 410 seats (out of a total of 707) of which 370 went to their right wing; the Bolsheviks had 175; the Cadets 17 and the Mensheviks 16. The national minorities accounted for a further 86 seats. On November 26th, the government announced that the Constituent Assembly would be opened as soon as the first 400 deputies had arrived in the capital.

Meanwhile various anti-Bolshevik organizations, chief among them the Committee for the Defence of the Constituent Assembly, decided to take matters into their own hands and with the help of Boris Savinkov, leader of the military organization of the Social Revolutionary Party, tried to bring out a number of Petrograd regiments in support of their call for the immediate convocation of the Constituent Assembly. Not content with that, Savinkov further instructed a gang of strong-arm men to kidnap Lenin and Trotsky. These harebrained schemes came to nothing, though Lenin's car was, in fact, fired on by terrorists. Savinkov's zeal, moreover, struck many members of the Committee for the Defence of the Constituent Assembly as quite unnecessary. When he proposed a military coup in defence of democracy, these men told him not to be silly — the great Russian people would make sure that the Bolsheviks did not profane the greatest idea engendered by the Revolution. And Chernov, who had just returned to Petrograd from army headquarters in Mohilev, agreed with them: the Bolsheviks would never dare to lay hands on the representatives of the people.

So much assurance simply proved that the former Minister of Agriculture and his friends had not learned the lesson of October.

---

[1] The military wards were those with a high proportion of barracks.

For Lenin had meanwhile decided against the Assembly. He explained his reasons at length in a series of theses which *Pravda* published on December 13th, 1917. Here he argued that the Constituent Assembly was a purely bourgeois institution and as such of questionable democratic character, while the soviets 'which the people themselves have created, are a form of democracy of which there is no equal in any other country'. Moreover, Lenin questioned the circumstances in which the recent elections had been held – the voters had not been offered an honest choice. Thus the Social Revolutionaries had appeared on a single list when in fact their right and left wings had very little in common, and the final allocation of seats no longer corresponded to the interrelation of forces after the October Revolution.[1] Last, but not least, 'the Civil War started by the counter-revolutionary uprising of the Cadets and the Kaledinists against the Soviet, against the workers' and peasants' government, has plainly sharpened the class struggle and has vitiated any hopes that a formal democracy might solve the most burning questions history has posed to the people of Russia.' And judging that the slogan 'All power to the Constituent Assembly' had been usurped by the bourgeoisie and the counter-revolution, Lenin believed that it must be opposed.

All Bolsheviks did not share this view, and the differences between the 'hard-liners' and the rest were buried in a compromise that was rather illogical but had the advantage of settling the issue to Lenin's own satisfaction. It was decided to convoke the Assembly on January 18th, 1918, but to make its continued existence dependent on its endorsement of the Bolshevik 'Declaration of Rights of the Toiling and Exploited Peoples'. This stated, *inter alia*, that 'the Constituent Assembly unreservedly rallies to the policy of the Soviet authorities and feels that it would be quite wrong, even technically, to set itself up in opposition to ... that power.' Overriding the basic principles of parliamentary democracy, the declaration went on to say that 'power must belong entirely and exclusively to the working masses and their elected representatives, the Soviets of Workers', Soldiers' and Peasants' Deputies.' In these circumstances, what was the role of the Constituent Assembly?

[1] This argument was pertinent. The actual allocation of seats (370 to the right wing of the Social Revolutionaries and a mere 40 to the left wing) no longer reflected their relative strength in the country. Elections to the Soviet of Peasant Deputies in December 1917 gave a decisive majority to the left wing.

If it acknowledged that it had 'no power beyond working out some of the problems of reorganizing society on a socialist basis', it could at best act as a rubber stamp for the Soviet. It should, however, be added that had sovereignty been genuinely shared between the Congress of Soviets and the Constituent Assembly, Russia would have re-established dual power at the very moment when she had declared the primacy of her soviet institutions. As a result there would have reappeared, in a political situation at last cleared of ambiguity, an element of uncertainty that would have been unable to resist the pressure of events for long.

On January 18th, the Constituent Assembly met in Petrograd. After electing Chernov President (he received 244 votes, while Maria Spiridonova, the left-wing Social Revolutionary candidate supported by the Bolsheviks, collected 153), the deputies rejected the motion Sverdlov had tabled on behalf of the new regime. At the end of a long debate that continued deep into the night and gave the delegates ample opportunity to express their hostility to Bolshevism while taking full credit for the substance of the Peace Decree and the Land Decree, a sailor approached the President and remarked that, the guard being tired, the session might perhaps be suspended. The deliberations were due to be resumed a few hours later. But on the morning of January 19th, the Central Executive Committee of the Soviet published a decree disbanding the Constituent Assembly.[1]

And so the brief parliamentary episode in the long history of Russia came to a sudden end. It had lasted less than twenty-four hours. The Soviet decree was described as a frontal attack on democracy and denounced as such by various sectors of Western public opinion. Even today, many authors still see it as a criminal onslaught on the liberty and sovereignty of the people. And there is, in fact, no doubt that it was a flagrant violation of the principles of parliamentary democracy. But having said this, we hasten to add that Western indignation would have sounded more convincing had these principles ever been applied in Russia or had they had the least chance of being established there. As it was, the first storm clouds of the impending civil war militated against the inauguration of parliamentary rule. Beyond that, Russian society was badly suited to liberal experiments, so badly, in fact, that in the months preceding the October insurrection the liberals themselves had

---

[1] The decree was opposed by a minority of the Bolshevik delegates.

turned their backs on them to rally behind the idea of a military dictatorship, seeking an alliance with the conservatives, who had never had anything but contempt for constitutional and democratic theories.

The only genuine champions of parliamentary democracy were the moderate socialists, and these had proved their utter impotence under the Provisional Government. If Lenin and the Bolsheviks had recognized the authority of the Constituent Assembly in January 1918, they would surely have been trampled underfoot by the Chernovs, Tseretellis and Dans, by the very men, that is, whose vacillations had cost the moderates the support of the disappointed masses. A civil war is never propitious to political systems founded on the equilibrium of groups or classes. But in Russia, it was not the Civil War or its prelude that destroyed democracy; stillborn, it had no place in a country lacking the social basis needed for its growth. Here an anaemic bourgeoisie was keen to grasp the hand of a reactionary Right that was neither able nor willing to introduce the liberal ideas so dear to the West, and it seemed most unlikely that its timid, vacillating and dependent socialist allies would do very much better. Nor was there a much greater chance that the Bolsheviks, having just seized power, would renounce it in favour of politicians and classes that had given such signal proof of their incompetence. In the twentieth century, no new regime anywhere chose the path of parliamentary democracy, and even the older democracies shed much of their democratic substance. There is no reason at all for thinking that Russia could have proved the exception to this general rule.[1]

Thus, from January 1918, the Russian Revolution presented itself as a *Soviet* democracy, with sovereign powers vested in the All-Russian Congress of Soviets, and between sessions in its Central Executive Committee. The government was wholly responsible to these two bodies. For all that, the precise relationship between the various political institutions remained very elastic, the Bolsheviks having no taste for 'legalistic subtleties' and believing, moreover, that the new system represented a transitional stage on the road to world socialism.

[1] It is significant that the dissolution of the Constituent Assembly caused no public reaction in Russia herself. The right-wing socialist, Stankevich, said in this connection that so much weakness and so much timidity caused even supporters of the Constituent Assembly to blame the defeat on the moderate deputies rather than on the Bolsheviks.

Having said this, we must add that the Council of People's Commissars wielded considerable powers, and used its initiative in all spheres of public life. The reader will remember that immediately after the seizure of power it consisted exclusively of members of the Bolshevik Party—the moderate socialists had walked out of the Second All-Russian Congress of Soviets and refused to participate in the new government. As for the left-wing Social Revolutionaries, they too rejected the Bolshevik offer of a coalition government. They were hoping instead to form an alternative bloc with various political organizations and particularly with the important railway union which, under its moderate leaders, had refused to recognize the Bolshevik Government. During the week following Kerensky's overthrow, manoeuvres, negotiations and parleys proceeded apace, but because of deep differences between the would-be partners they all came to nothing.

Right-wing Social Revolutionaries and Mensheviks had divided into two factions, both equally hostile to the Bolsheviks, but while one was opposed to any form of collaboration with either Lenin's party or with the Cadets, the other was prepared to join the Bolshevik Government provided only that Lenin and Trotsky played no part in it. This was a blatant attempt to divide the Bolsheviks. Though left-wing Mensheviks refrained from pressing these demands, the Bolsheviks found it difficult to make common cause with them. The only alliance Lenin and Trotsky wanted was one that would unite them with the representatives of the small peasants, that is with the left-wing Social Revolutionaries. Any other combination struck them as an attempt to whittle away the achievements of the Revolution. The more moderate current in the Bolshevik Party, on the other hand, called for a cabinet embracing all socialist parties, and some of them were so afraid of isolation that they were even prepared to sacrifice their leader. It was only the continued refusal of the socialist Right to recognize the sovereignty of the soviets, together with Lenin's intransigence, that caused the collapse of a project, hastily improvised and in any case irreconcilable with what had by then become a deep split in the ranks of the Left.[1] And so, in December, the left-wing Social Revolutionaries alone made their entry into the Council of People's

[1] In the Bolshevik ranks the conflict between the Leninists and the Right, once again led by Kamenev, was so violent that it ended in the resignation of several members of the Central Committee and of several People's Commissars.

Commissars, where they took a number of important posts, including the Commissariats of Agriculture and of Justice.

The coalition was, however, extremely short-lived—the Social Revolutionaries, no less than the left-wing communists, were bitterly opposed to the signing of a separate peace, and one day after the ratification of that treaty by the All-Russian Congress of Soviets, they tendered their resignation *en bloc*. When they did so, they simply drove revolutionary Russia one step farther along the road to single-party rule. At that time, however, the socialist opposition was still represented in the Congress of Soviets—the sovereign body of the new regime—and in its Central Executive Committee. Thus at the Congress held in July 1918, there were 678 or 773 Bolsheviks (depending on which statistics we go by) and 352 or 382 left-wing Social Revolutionaries. Other socialist groups accounted for a further 35 deputies.

While the preliminary skirmishes of the Civil War were already drawing blood, the July Congress still enjoyed so much freedom of expression that its deliberations quickly degenerated into mudslinging. 'You are nothing but a band of savages, fools and bandits!' the Bolsheviks were told. A right-wing Social Revolutionary deputy contented himself more modestly with saying that Lenin was out of his mind. Lenin himself had a great deal of trouble in making himself heard over the constant interruptions and catcalls of his adversaries. This, it is true, was the last episode of this kind in Soviet history—the summer of 1918 was to prove so critical for the new regime[1] that it felt compelled to clamp down on its opponents. The active support many Social Revolutionaries gave to the counter-revolution, the inexorable law of intransigence which extends and multiplies its effects, the dynamics of the struggle between parties and factions, and the new militant alliances between former partisans of the Soviet and genuinely conservative or reactionary politicians and generals—all these militated against further co-operation or even coexistence between the deeply divided branches of the old socialist trunk. And so, at the All-Russian Congress of Soviets which met in November 1918, non-Bolshevik delegates found themselves reduced to a bare minimum.

Later, when the Civil War had begun to abate, the Soviet Government made several attempts to bring their former allies back into the fold—the Mensheviks were, in any case, allowed to

[1] See Chapter 11.

continue their existence as an organized and officially recognized party until the beginning of 1921. The Social Revolutionaries had by then split into rival factions, some of which had joined the Bolsheviks. Still, by the time the Civil War was over, the single-party system was firmly implanted—the party of the working class had become *the* party of Soviet Russia and this sociological phenomenon was turned into a political principle and inscribed in the statutes as such.

The Revolution after October

During the eight months of its existence, the Provisional Government had acted as if all eternity lay before it. The Bolsheviks, on the contrary, behaved as if time was extremely precious, as if every hour counted and had to be used to full advantage. In the economic sphere and in various fields of social life they were anxious to demonstrate that the inauguration of the Soviet regime signified a profound change, a fundamental transformation in the life not only of public institutions but also in everyday relations between men. The Council of People's Commissars, almost totally deprived of administrative assistants, met daily for sessions that continued uninterrupted for five, six hours and more. Decree followed upon decree, each making a new impact on the economy, the administration and the organization of public life.

While this is not the place to look at this spate of legislative activity in detail, it is nevertheless important to examine it in broad outline, for it will give us some idea of the spirit that inspired the Soviet Revolution during the first months of its existence. As far as the economy was concerned, it is important to remember that the Bolsheviks had no intention of establishing a socialist system straight away—they realized that backward Russia was not yet ready for so radical a solution. True, Lenin presented the new regime as a Socialist Republic, and the term 'socialist' figured prominently in the constitution adopted in July 1918, but the head of the Soviet Government took great care to make clear that this label was not so much 'intended to describe the socialist nature of the new economic structure, as to give proof of our determination to effect the transition towards socialism'.

Now to all good Marxists, socialism called for the nationalization and centralization of all the means of production and distribution. The new regime, however, did nothing of the sort. To begin with, it deliberately refrained from collectivizing the land, or at least deferred this measure, which it recognized as essential. As a result of the Land Decree and its application during the winter of 1917 and the spring of 1918, the big landed estates were carved up and there was a large increase in the number of smallholdings. This was not socialism, but simply the fulfilment of the old peasant dreams and the abolition of the last vestiges of a semi-feudal system.

In the industrial field, too, the Soviet regime failed to take systematic steps towards nationalization, or even to make serious attempts at centralization. In other words, in the industrial no less than in the agricultural sector, the Bolsheviks failed to implement a socialist programme. One of their earliest decrees, indeed, published in *Pravda* on November 3rd, 1917, sanctioned the idea of 'workers' control', a term that smacks of anarchism. In passing it, the Bolsheviks endorsed a principle by which the Russian workers themselves had in 1917 evinced their determination to forge a better life for themselves. Workers' control was now officially extended to all industrial, commercial and agricultural enterprises employing at least five workers and having a turnover in excess of ten thousand roubles per year. Henceforth production could not be interrupted without the consent of the workers or their elected representatives, who, moreover, were given the right to check all account books and all stocks. The decree did not, however, create an entirely new situation—throughout 1917, many workers had been doing just that on their own initiative. For the rest, the ownership of all businesses and factories was left in the hands of their old proprietors.

Workers' control, by its very nature, eluded the long arm of the central authorities. As a concession to the initiative of the masses and to the spirit of the times, it opened wide the path to anarchist trends whose origins went back well before the October uprising. In many cases, the workers exceeded the terms of the decree, looking upon their places of work as their own and running them without bothering about the general interests of the economy. Quite often, their 'excesses' were simply a reply to the employers' industrial sabotage. But no matter what the motives, these attempts simply added to the general disruption of the Russian economy which was daily becoming more intolerable. The creation of a 'Supreme Council of the National Economy' on December 2nd, 1917, aimed at eliminating the worst effects of this situation by subordinating the activities of the different industrial sectors to a central authority.

During the same period, the government ordered the nationalization of a number of individual enterprises without, however, evincing any desire to extend this measure to the entire economy. In each case, they were motivated by the departure or the hostile attitude of the proprietors, or by the particular importance of these enterprises. Thus all Russian banks were nationalized by decree on December 14th, by which time it had become clear that their directors were engaging in systematic sabotage. Altogether, no more than a few hundred businesses were nationalized, but soon afterwards the Bolshevik Government was forced to reconsider its relatively moderate policy which depended on some measure of co-operation by the industrialists, who became more obstructive as the Civil War drew nearer. Others, as we saw, simply took to their heels, with the result that the country lost a large section of its former ruling class. And when the Civil War could no longer be averted, and the production of arms had to be stepped up, centralization became a matter of life and death for the new regime, the more so as it was hampered by the fact that anarchy on the shop floor increased to an alarming extent as the most class-conscious and disciplined workers began to leave the factories for the ranks of the Red Army. On June 29th, 1918, the Council of People's Commissars accordingly ordered the nationalization of a wide range of industries (mines, metallurgy, textiles, cement, transport, etc.) and, in so doing, took an important step towards 'war Communism', which was to remain a characteristic feature of the Soviet economy until the introduction of the New Economic Policy (N.E.P.) in 1921.

Lenin's government passed yet another far-reaching decree during the first months of its existence, and this merits special attention if only because it caused a great stir in Western Europe. On February 10th, 1918, Soviet Russia annulled all debts contracted by the 'Governments of the Russian landlords and Russian bourgeoisie'; only small bond-holders were to be indemnified with subscriptions to a new loan whose value, however, was extremely problematical. This measure aroused the fury of all those who had subscribed to the numerous state loans that had helped Tsarism to survive after the 1905 Revolution. At that time, the Petrograd Soviet let it be known that the new Russia born out of the ashes of

Tsarism would not repay what sums the deluded West saw fit to contribute to the coffers of Nicholas II. Hence, when Lenin's government made good this old promise the West had little reason to complain, though it protested bitterly for all that.

Nor did the People's Commissars restrict themselves to purely economic reforms. At a time when one might have expected them to focus their attention on the sorry economic aftermath of Brest-Litovsk, they spared no efforts to revolutionize every branch of public life, thus demonstrating their unflinching will to give full expression to the values they wished to impress upon society. We could mention scores of decrees dealing with social insurance, labour relations, the equality of women, the abolition of titles and class distinctions, the nationalization of living accommodation and the remuneration of officials. Thus the pay of People's Commissars was fixed at five hundred roubles per month (plus one hundred roubles for each dependent child) which put them on the same wage level as qualified workers. Civil marriages were sanctioned by law, natural children were accorded the same rights as legitimate children, and divorce was made much easier. Finland was granted independence and all national minorities were given the right to determine their own fate and, if they so desired, to secede from Russia.[1] Church and state were officially separated.

The last measure was widely interpreted as a Bolshevik plot to eradicate what Marx had called the opium of the people. And, indeed, in a country where the Orthodox Church was completely identified with the old regime, had espoused the most reactionary ideas and engaged in the most questionable arguments, strong anti-religious measures were only to be expected. It is, however, wrong to associate the nascent Soviet regime with the crude utterances and brutal manners that were characteristic of the sub-sequent activities of a number of atheist organizations. True, religious teaching was banished from state schools, and during the Civil War quite a few churches and monasteries were turned into hospitals, prisons, barracks or schools. True, also, the relationship between the Soviet Government and the Church authorities be-came increasingly strained as the Orthodox clergy as a whole sided

[1] Lenin had always declared that there could be no self-determination without the right of secession. Though this principle was reaffirmed after the creation of the Soviet regime, it often conflicted with the strategic needs of the struggle for the survival of the Revolution. In these circumstances, it had sometimes to be sacrificed.

openly with the counter-revolution, and the Patriarch Tikon took it upon himself to anathematize all Communists and to consign them to the fires of hell. But for all that Lenin was most anxious not to hurt the religious susceptibilities of the masses by violent measures that would only have served to aggravate social tensions. In an address to the First 'Congress of Russian Workers' held in November, 1918, he declared: 'We must fight religious prejudices with extreme prudence. Those who upset religious feelings cause a great deal of harm.' And in March 1919, when the Bolshevik Party, known since 1918 as the 'Communist (Bolshevik) Party of Russia', adopted a new programme, it took care to define its attitude to religion as follows:

> The Communist Party will sever the links between the exploiting classes and the organization of religious propaganda, and will rid the proletariat of religious prejudice, by means of massive scientific and anti-religious propaganda. In so doing it will guard against hurting the feelings of the believers, who might otherwise be driven to religious fanaticism.

In spite of all its good intentions, though, the Soviet Government could not prevent all clashes between the forces of religion and the triumphant revolutionary movement.

In general, it is true to say that the liberation from old constraints caused an explosion that shook all established ideas and institutions to their very foundations, causing an outburst of passion in which the best was mixed with the worst. While the sense of human dignity was riding high, old feuds were still far too often settled by hideous acts of retribution. Their brutality reflected not only the bottled-up resentment of the oppressed classes but also the persistent refusal of their former rulers to give them even the rudiments of education. In the Russian Revolution, as in all great social upheavals and in all great historical movements, deeds of heroism, sacrifice and unselfish devotion to the cause of emancipation vied with the most detestable outbursts revealing man at his most bestial and society at its most inhuman.

Russia was no exception to this rule, and had her share of ugly excesses which the authorities were quite unable to stop: both sides of the barricade were responsible for bloody murders, and witnessed scenes of drunkenness, almost of collective frenzy. Thus

December 1917 brought Petrograd a 'wine pogrom'—the mass looting of the cellars of the Winter Palace and of innumerable private houses. 'Drink is the joy of all Russians,' as an old proverb has it. And, indeed, the capital was the scene of so vast a drunken orgy that the government had to call in the Red Guard. There were other ugly scenes as well, in which popular justice, summarily dispensed at sham trials, often ended in barbarous executions.

Against these evils, of which no single nation or social movement has the monopoly, we must set the immense sense of liberation and hope the revolution inspired. Domestic servants suddenly refused to humble themselves before their masters; coachmen scorned tips, which they now saw as an affront to their dignity; large assemblies of workers and soldiers cut short their weighty deliberations to listen to lectures on the history of art or the principles of modern physics. It was the same burst of democratic enthusiasm which caused the proliferation of committees at all levels. For during the first exalted weeks, committees sprang up throughout the length and breadth of the land. There were workers' committees, peasants' committees, housewives' committees, factory committees and district committees, housing committees—all of which discussed a thousand and one details of collective life. Jules Destrée tells us that while travelling from Petrograd to Moscow—a long journey at the slow speed the train was making—the people sharing his compartment had formed a travelling committee before they reached their destination.

What has remained of all this boundless enthusiasm? Its ups and downs are writ large in Soviet history, as the country and its government were tossed to and fro by the jolts of an arduous journey that, in a matter of two generations, took it from the Dark Ages to the atomic era. There was, however, one sector of public life in which the new rulers proved remarkably consistent from the very outset: education and culture.

In November 1917, when nothing had yet been settled, when the power structure and the peace still lay in the balance, when the Bolshevik Party itself was deeply divided, when civil servants engaged in systematic sabotage, when everything had to be organized afresh and the enemy had to be kept at bay, Lenin nevertheless found the time to submit a draft for the 'Reorganization of the Petrograd Public Library' to the directors of that institution. In it he called for regular book exchanges between Russian and foreign libraries, and insisted that the lecture halls and reading rooms be kept open until 11 p.m., Sundays included, to allow the workers free access to them. On December 29th, 1917, the Soviet Central Executive published a decree on the printing of cheap books, the detailed proposals including a plan to publish all the great masters in full or, in some cases, in abridged form. The decree went on to state that, as far as possible, books ought to be supplied to the public free of charge. The Russian countryside, still barbarous in so many other respects, was quick to respond to this immense cultural drive: 'reading *isbas*' were set up in a host of small villages.

We could go on for a long time listing similar achievements. All of them attested to the great importance the leaders of the Soviet Revolution attached to educational and cultural progress. During the first years of its existence, the Soviet regime, despite grinding poverty and despite the crippling struggle against the 'Whites', established 1,500 new schools. No doubt many of them were run under deplorable conditions and quickly disappeared again when, after the end of the Civil War, the whole educational system was reorganized. But for all their shortcomings, they bore witness to a firm determination to foster science and art, and to the profound desire for intellectual emancipation which has been a characteristic feature of Soviet rule and which, despite the thousands of setbacks and errors, has weathered all storms and has stood firm under the blows of all those who have tried to destroy its roots.

II

The Fate of the Russian Revolution

W E ARE leaving our story at the moment when Soviet
power had become a reality. In front of it lay a Civil War,
foreign intervention, and a long period of unexpected
isolation, all of which must be taken into account by anyone who
wishes to grasp the complex features of modern Russia: the heavy
burden of the Tsarist past, the aspiration of the Bolsheviks, the
onslaught of the counter-revolution and foreign troops, and the
withdrawal of Russian Communists into the inhospitable soil of a
backward country.

Soviet democracy

Though the 'philosophy' of Bolshevism merits a far more systematic analysis than the slender frame of this work allows, we must
nevertheless take a brief look at its most distinctive characteristics.
Starting with a trenchant critique of liberal democracy, Russian
Marxists went on to build a political system in which democracy
would rest not on a precarious balance of political power, but on
complete equality. True, the principle of equality had previously
been inscribed on the banner of the French Revolution, but
Russian revolutionaries went much further than their French precursors: they maintained that under bourgeois rule the notion of
equality must remain an empty legalistic phrase, and liberty the
monopoly of the dominant class, however cunningly it tried to
disguise this fact or to temper its worst effects. And though many
socialists had come to terms with their bourgeois enemies of the
past, revolutionary Marxists not only refused to do so, but extended
their hostility to all those who did.

Russia's political institutions in the period between February
and October 1917 were by and large those associated with bourgeois
and liberal democracy, except that the government was too weak to
put its loud professions of democratic faith to the test of a popular
election. Social Revolutionaries and Mensheviks lived in high
hopes that this minor deficiency would soon be cured and that

Russia could fall into step with the West, a prerequisite of progress towards a truly socialist society. Lenin, whose arguments swayed the Bolsheviks and directed their strategy, lacked the virtue of patience which the Mensheviks, like Social Democrats in the West, had in such abundance. Thus when his hopes that Russia's peculiar situation might help to consolidate the achievements of the February Revolution by peaceful means were dashed by the July Days, he was quick to revise his former position—he now took the view that only an armed uprising could give the soviets real power and so safeguard the interests of the dispossessed. He accordingly prescribed a political and social alternative to parliamentary rule, namely *Soviet democracy* plus *the dictatorship of the proletariat*. The two may strike us today as quite incompatible, but to the disciples of Marx and Engels the dictatorship of the proletariat was only a phase in a process that would culminate in the complete withering away of the state. To them, bourgeois democracy was simply the dictatorship of the bourgeoisie over the working class, a type of domination that could only be terminated by the establishment of a state in which the old relationship of forces was reversed. Only by establishing their own class supremacy could the workers lay down the law to the bourgeoisie, abolish capitalism and install socialism. Marx and Engels had been rather vague on the precise methods by which these ends might be achieved, thus allowing for the most varied interpretations. Some followers passed the whole idea of the dictatorship of the proletariat over in tactful silence; others, like Bernstein, denounced it as a harmful doctrine. 'Orthodox' Marxists, for their part, led by Karl Kautsky, while not rejecting the revolutionary teachings of the 'masters', emptied them of their explosive content by 'adapting' them to the 'democratic spirit' of their own day.

Lenin was the first modern Marxist to resurrect the doctrine without equivocation, and to devote innumerable articles and papers to it. He also dealt with it in his *The State and Revolution*, a major theoretical treatise which he wrote in Finland prior to the October uprising. In it he not only laid down that the dictatorship of the proletariat was a *sine qua non* of the overthrow of capitalism, but also called it an 'expansion of democracy ... which *for the first time* becomes democracy for the poor, democracy for the people, and not democracy for the rich folk ... democracy for the vast majority of the people and suppression by force, i.e. exclusion from democracy, of the exploiters and oppressors of the people.'[1]

Hence Lenin's choice of dictatorship *and* democracy, a choice on which he based his revolutionary theory and his entire strategy. The dictatorship of the proletariat would replace the rule of the bourgeoisie by which a minority imposes its will on the majority of people. Henceforth the roles would be reversed, but this would not, in itself, strip the state of its repressive or violent characteristics — 'during the transition from capitalism to Communism, suppression is still necessary, but it is now the suppression of the exploiting minority by the exploited majority.'

To justify the change, Lenin pointed to the immense tasks before the victorious Revolution. The mere expropriation of the capitalists did not solve everything, let alone ensure equality:

> There can be no equality between the exploiters who, for many generations, have enjoyed education and the advantages and habits of prosperity, and the exploited, the majority of whom ... are cowed, frightened, ignorant, unorganized. It is inevitable that the exploiters should still enjoy a large number of great practical advantages for a considerable period after the revolution. They still have money (since it is impossible to abolish money at once); some moveable property (often of a considerable extent); social connections, habits of organization and management; knowledge of all the secrets of administration ... higher education, closeness to the higher technical experts (who live and think after the bourgeois style), incomparably higher knowledge and experience in military affairs ... and enormous international connections.

Hence it was not simply armed resistance by counter-revolutionary forces that made a dictatorship imperative; equally noxious was the continued hegemony, albeit legally abolished, of the old ruling class. The dictatorship of the proletariat, violent and repressive though it was, was 'democratic' in that it organized and

---

[1] Lenin set no store by democracy as such. According to him, 'democracy is a form of the state — one of its varieties. Consequently, like every state, it consists of the organized and systematic application of force against human beings.' And he added, 'The more complete the democracy the nearer the moment when it begins to be unnecessary.' *Lenin's ideal — and that of Marxists in general — was therefore not a democracy imposed upon the minority by the majority, but the elimination of all forms of coercion, i.e. the abolition of all — even democratic — state power.*

protected the rule of the people, and above all in that, not content with giving the people a monopoly of political power, it completed and authenticated that power, by entrusting the people themselves with the running of public affairs. According to Lenin, democracy was a sham if all it did was to grant the people the right of casting their votes periodically at election time but prevented them from *'playing an active part in the daily life of the administration'*.

Lenin developed this idea at length in his *The State and Revolution*, where he tried to show that the running of public affairs is an infinitely less complex affair than is commonly thought; that, to a large extent, it is well within the reach of ordinary men and women: *'All* citizens become employees and workers of *one* national state syndicate.' And he went on to show that in so doing they will quickly learn that the chief skills of civil servants—accountancy and control—are nothing like the great mysteries they have been made out to be. Not that Lenin was naive enough to imagine that the proletarian state could dispense completely with the services of bourgeois specialists and technicians—all he wanted was to make these subject to workers' supervision, since only in this way could the proletariat speed the demise of a bureaucratic caste whose very existence voided democracy of its substance.

According to Lenin, the bourgeois state is built on the twin pillars of administrative coercion and military violence—the first restraining, the second compelling. The dictatorship of the proletariat—as the guardian of democracy—must therefore not only endeavour to reduce the grip of the bureaucracy, but must also replace the old army with a popular militia, thus transforming an instrument of naked repression into an instrument of popular liberation. Once counter-revolutionary resistance is finally crushed, even the militia will be disbanded, and the people will be able to devote their entire energy to the far nobler task of building and managing a new society. A few months after the seizure of power, Lenin repeated that 'our aim is to enlist the practical participation of *all the dispossessed without exception*, in the government of the country.' And again, 'Our aim is to fill all government jobs with workers volunteering for this task after they have done their eight hours of "productive work".' And though his few months in office had taught him that 'this was a singularly difficult process', he nevertheless insisted that 'only here do we have a guarantee of the definitive consolidation of socialism'.

Despite the setbacks this project suffered, Lenin remained faithful to it. In January 1919, he still wrote, 'We shall find that we can ... teach the vast masses of workers to administer the state and industry, to develop practical skills, to extirpate the noxious and age-old prejudice that the administration of the state is the business of privileged men ... ' And he concluded, 'Such is the new psychology of the working class, such the gigantic historical mission of the proletariat.' Of all the mass of legislation intended to translate this 'new psychology' into reality, we only have space to mention a decree published in April 1921 by the Council of People's Commissars. Its declared object was to 'maintain close links between Soviet institutions and the labouring masses and to encourage the Soviet administration to rid itself of bureaucratic elements'. The decree proposed, *inter alia*, that women workers should be taken out of their factories for periods of two months, and be put in charge of the administrative work of various Soviet departments. This type of participation in government was not only one of the main objects of *Soviet democracy*, but also its chief distinguishing mark. And by vesting full sovereign powers in the soviets, it differed from liberal parliamentarianism in yet another characteristic way: as assemblies of producers, the soviets were elected by the proletariat alone so that the bourgeoisie was completely eliminated from the body politic. Now this was a feature that had never before been considered a necessary condition of the dictatorship of the proletariat. The new system also tried to eliminate the old distinction between the legislative and the executive by turning the soviets into deliberative-*cum*-administrative institutions, in which the people not only took decisions but also saw to their implementation.[1] Finally, it was laid down that all Soviet deputies were subject to immediate recall, and that elections would be held often enough to give the masses quasi-permanent control of the soviets.

All this caused Lenin to say that proletarian democracy (i.e. the dictatorship of the proletariat)[2] 'is a *million times more* democratic than any type of bourgeois democracy', or that 'the Soviet government is a million times more democratic than the most democratic

[1] In this the Bolsheviks were anticipated by the Jacobins and French Communards.

[2] In the early phases of the revolution, Lenin changed the Marxist formula of the 'dictatorship of the proletariat' to the 'dictatorship of the workers and peasants', which, he felt, was in better accord with Russian conditions. In this alliance, however, the leadership fell clearly to the industrial proletariat.

of bourgeois republics.' His claim could not, of course, be reconciled with the parliamentary definition of democracy, but by
transferring state power to the proletariat, the Russian Revolution
had, in fact, established an entirely new type of society—a direct,
popular and tangible democracy.

Its enemies were quick to decry these ideals as so many Utopian
pipedreams.[1] This was a pointless and quite superficial attack: no
revolution can do without great ideals, which are its mainsprings
and ensure its triumph. Realists have all the leisure they need to
stake out the distance between dream and reality, but it is not from
them that the great historical figures and the builders of new
societies take their inspiration. The Bolshevik ideal bore witness to
a most original and bold faith, one that resolutely turned its back
on resignation and mere routine. Not content with transforming
yesterday's slaves into today's rebels, it had perforce to turn
them into tomorrow's masters and administrators.[2]

The effects of the Civil War

Such an ideology could not have emerged outside an exceptional
social context. This context was the Revolution itself. The spectacle of vast masses shaking off their apathy, destroying the

---

[1] Coupled with a vast educational programme and the organization of leisure
activities, the Bolshevik attempt to associate all citizens with the administration
was, however, far less unrealistic than it might have seemed.

[2] The determination to transform the new Russia into a true democracy, in
which administrative powers would complete and give full meaning to political
powers, one in which the people would be masters of their own fate and not
simply delegate powers to remote officials, was voiced by Lenin time and again.
Let us quote only a few of his pronouncements on this subject: 'One of the most
important tasks, if not *the* most important task, of our time, is to give the greatest
possible encouragement to the spontaneous initiative of the workers, of all the
toilers and exploited masses in general, in their fruitful labour of *organization*.
We must destroy at all costs the old, *absurd*, barbarous, infamous and odious
prejudice that only the so-called "ruling classes", only the rich or those who have
attended schools for the rich, can administer the state, supervise the building
of a socialist society.' (December 1917.) 'All citizens without exception must
participate in the running of the country ... This is an extremely difficult task,
but socialism cannot be built by a minority, by a party, it can only be built by
tens of millions of people ... Our task is to help the masses put their shoulders
to the wheel straight away, and not to wait until they have learned all these
things from books and lectures.' (March 1918.) 'We shall find that we can ...
teach the vast masses of workers to administer the state and industry, to develop
practical skills, to extirpate the noxious and age-old prejudice that the administration of the state is the business of privileged men, that it is a special art ... '
(January 1919.) Many further examples could be quoted.

established power of the state, taking their fate into their own hands and pressing their claims with great vigour, outstripping even their own leaders in the determination to achieve complete emancipation —here lies the explanation for the optimistic philosophy of the Bolsheviks, here and in the Marxist vision of the great future of mankind. Before the war, Lenin himself had evinced some scepticism about the 'spontaneity' of the masses, arguing that their actions must needs be directed from the outside. In this he had differed radically from Rosa Luxemburg to whom confidence in the spontaneous creative powers of the masses was almost an act of faith. Now the events of 1917 had brought Lenin closer to her viewpoint, one that he had previously decried as naive and dangerous. Speaking in August 1918 of the work accomplished by the 'true masses', by 'the immense majority of the workers who are building a new life for themselves', he declared, 'Every error committed in the course of this task by tens of millions of simple workers and peasants determined to transform their entire existence, each one of their failures is worth thousands of millions of "infallible" successes by the exploiting minority … '

The revolutionary fervour and enthusiasm of the workers had opened up hitherto undreamed of possibilities. And since the workers, without heeding the counsels of prudence freely bestowed upon them by all sorts of organizations, Parties and committees, had succeeded in smashing the obstacles in their path and had destroyed the old world, would they not be equally capable of building the new without the guidance of self-appointed mentors? For some time, the Civil War gave encouragement to this hope— the new regime was forced to improvise its defences and those who manned them most willingly were, in fact, the industrial workers.

Of this frightful war which followed so close on the carnage of 1914–17 we shall say nothing here, except to stress the obvious: it demanded a total commitment on the part of the Russian people. The country had only just emerged exhausted from world war, under disastrous conditions and at an extremely heavy price. Less than three months later, Czechoslovak troops stationed in Russia who should have been transferred to Western Europe, made common cause with Russian counter-revolutionaries and so precipitated the country into a new blood-bath. To make things even worse for the new regime, some of its former allies turned against it as well. In July, the left-wing Social Revolutionaries, as champions of revolutionary war, assassinated the German ambassador in Moscow,[1] in the hope that this might lead to a resumption of hostilities. At the same time they organized an insurrection in Moscow which the Bolsheviks quickly put down. Soon afterwards, the Communist leaders became the targets of terrorist attacks by Social Revolutionaries and others. Volodarsky and Uritzky fell to the assassins, and on the day Uritzky died a Social Revolutionary fired on Lenin, who owed his survival to his exceptionally strong constitution.

Then the Western powers struck. They had always been bitterly hostile to the Bolsheviks, and had obstinately refused to recognize their government. In November 1917, Britain and France had already encouraged the Ukrainians to rise up against Petrograd, supplying them with limited military aid and considerable sums of money; but when Russia signed the Brest-Litovsk treaty, the Allies decided to make an all-out effort against the Bolsheviks, a bunch of utterly evil men who, not satisfied with ruining their own country, were aiding and abetting the Germans as well.[2]

The attempts by a handful of more enlightened Allied diplomats to make their governments realize that the Russians had been forced to sign the peace despite themselves, was met with total incomprehension. Plans were drawn up to send large military contingents into Russia with the double task of compelling the Germans to transfer considerable forces to the Eastern Front and of overthrowing the Soviet government. As a result, Europe witnessed the paradoxical situation of two warring camps joining forces in an attempt to destroy a nation that had opted out of the war. For it was the Germans who drove the Bolsheviks from the Ukraine and helped the *Rada* to establish their puppet government. Moreover, it was German support of General Mannerheim's White Army that led to the defeat of the Finnish revolutionary troops. The Western Allies, for their part, established and extended bridgeheads in the north of Russia and in Siberia in August 1918, while the Japanese disembarked seventy thousand men in Vladivostock.

Until the very end, the Civil War saw the Bolsheviks ranged against an alliance between Russian counter-revolutionary forces and foreign armies, while the blockade of Russia brought them

[1] The Soviet Government had moved to Moscow in March 1918, when a German attack on Petrograd seemed imminent.

[2] In fact, the Bolsheviks, by making peace propaganda and fostering a revolutionary spirit among German workers, had done much to undermine German army morale, as many German generals have never tired of repeating.

famine and the complete disruption of industry. In these circumstances, it is not at all surprising that passions should have been raised to boiling point and that terror should have gained the upper hand—two classes were locked in mortal combat. Both sides knew full well that if the other won, it would give no quarter. And the Russian workers, having only just discovered that they were more than mere slaves or cogs in a machine, that the masters of yesterday were not invincible, that humiliation and subservience were not the only lot reserved for them, and that the bourgeoisie would never resign itself to the disappearance of the old order, were determined not to give way. The concrete message the Revolution had spelled out to them—freedom and dignity—and also the realization that these were hanging in the balance, drove the Russian proletariat to fight remorselessly against all odds. On either side the stakes were extremely high, so high in fact that cruelty was only to be expected. When institutions are based on brute force, they do not disappear meekly or without violence—peaceful social transitions, when they can be accomplished, will be the rewards reaped by societies founded on liberty.

The human sacrifices demanded by the Civil War were monumental. It has been shown that from 1918 to the end of 1920, seven and a half million Russians perished from famine, exposure and epidemics. As for the victims of the Terror, it is impossible to establish their exact number. Millions of soldiers, workers and peasants were involved in the struggle, and many used the opportunity to settle old accounts with their former masters who, in their turn, defended their privileges with brutality born of desperation. The Soviet Government waited several months before it ordered the systematic repression of all counter-revolutionary activities—at the beginning of the Civil War, it went out of its way to stop and punish all excesses. And though the *Cheka* (All-Russian Extraordinary Commission for the Struggle against Sabotage and the Counter-Revolution) was established in December 1917, it was not until June 18th, 1918, that a revolutionary tribunal passed a death sentence. This does not mean that summary executions—in both camps—were unknown before that date, but the real Terror, officially proclaimed in defence of the 'threatened socialist fatherland' did not start before the summer of 1918.[1]

[1] It was in July 1918 that Nicholas II, the ex-Empress Alexandra and their five children were executed in Ekaterinburg. The Soviet Government had fully

Russian revolutionaries had never opposed violence on principle. Believing as they did that the old ruling classes would fight remorselessly against the Revolution, they felt that the revolutionaries were entitled to use all available means to defend themselves. Nor were the Bolsheviks alone in this view—recalling the violence of the Jacobin terror which, incidentally, was more than equalled by their enemies both during and after the French Revolution, Thomas Jefferson wrote, 'These I deplore as much as anybody, and shall deplore some of them to the day of my death. But I deplore them as I should have done had they fallen in battle. It was necessary to use the arm of the people, a machine not quite so blind as balls and bombs, but blind to a certain degree.' The Bolsheviks could only have applauded these sentiments, as did generations of revolutionaries who admired the determination of Robespierre, of Marat and Saint-Just to defend the Republic against all her enemies.

It is useful to compare the Russian 'Red Terror' with the Jacobin terror of 1793-4. According to the careful computation of W. H. Chamberlin,[1] some fifty thousand persons were put to death by the Red Terror, in addition to insurgents shot down with arms in their hands or people killed by mobs or uncontrolled groups of soldiers and sailors. The Bolshevik authorities (the *Cheka*) themselves put the figure at some 12,700 executions, while certain anti-Communist sources went so far as to speak of 1,700,000 victims of the 'Red Terror'. According to Albert Soboul, who based himself on the historian Green, the revolutionary tribunals and special courts of the Jacobins passed more than 16,000 death sentences, once again over and above the innumerable summary executions that occurred in France at the time. The full significance of these figures only becomes clear when we recall that the population of Russia in 1917 was approximately eight times that of France in 1792.

The number of deaths caused by the 'White Terror' is far more difficult to establish, because the counter-revolutionaries did not bother about compiling statistics. But in Finland alone, a small country in which the Civil War raged for only a few months,

intended to put the Tsar on trial, but in view of the rapid advance of the Czech troops (who soon afterwards occupied the town in which the imperial family had been detained) the local soviet, having just discovered a rescue plot, ordered their execution. The Council of People's Commissars approved this action after the event.

[1] *The Russian Revolution*, Vol. 2, p. 74.

reliable estimates show that the 'Whites' massacred from ten to twenty thousand workers, and we have good reason to suppose that the enemies of Bolshevism were no less implacable in Russia herself. The difference between the 'Red' and the 'White' terror was not so much the *number* as the *status* of the victims they respectively claimed. Thus while workers, soldiers and peasants organized systematic attacks on the aristocracy, the bourgeoisie, speculators, saboteurs and corrupt officials,[1] the 'Whites' gave their enemies no quarter either. As they advanced into 'Red' territory, they organized mass killings of workers in whom they saw, not without reason, the chief supporters of Bolshevism; in addition, they rounded on the Jewish population, whose blood they spilled freely for the greater glory of Mother Russia.

In short, the differences between the two camps reflected the old social divisions. The former ruling classes were the main enemies and chief victims of the Revolution. The industrial proletariat, despite certain defections due to sheer starvation, remained loyal to the Soviet cause throughout the struggle. The peasants, for their part, had a less clear-cut attitude and wavered between prudent hostility and cautious sympathy. If at first they had been won over to the Revolution by the Bolshevik land reforms, they later became estranged from the Revolution by such unavoidable measures as the systematic requisitioning of produce and livestock. Hence the sporadic peasant uprisings against the new regime. But while the 'Reds' failed to retain the allegiance of the countryside, the 'Whites' often filled the peasants with bitter hatred—the *moujiks* realized that if the 'White' generals won, the land the Revolution had given them would revert to its former owners. Moreover, social anarchy and misfortunes of all kinds (famine, speculation, disease) were much more prevalent in the 'White' camp than among the Bolsheviks, who made desperate efforts to contain them. Lenin once again proved his grasp of the mood of the countryside when, in June 1921, he put the following words into the mouth of a peasant: 'Yes,' he had him say, 'the Bolsheviks are very disagreeable. We have no love for them, but, for all that, they are better than the White Guard and the Constituent Assembly.' And with the Soviet Government firmly entrenched in Moscow and the working class determined to see the struggle through, it was the passive support

[1] P. Sorlin: *La société soviétique, 1917–1964*, p. 75, puts the number killed at some 350,000.

of the *moujiks* that eventually turned the tables on the counter-revolution, and helped to carry the Communists to victory.

But that victory was bought at a heavy price. The Civil War had, in fact, completely destroyed the economy of Russia, with the gravest political consequences. In his biography of Trotsky,[1] Isaac Deutscher gives us a devastating account of Russia's situation at the moment when the counter-revolution was finally crushed. 'At the end of the Civil War Russia's national income amounted to only one-third of her income in 1913; industry produced less than one-fifth of the goods produced before the war; the coal mines turned out less than one-tenth and the iron foundries less than one-fortieth of their normal output; the railways were destroyed; all stocks and reserves were utterly exhausted ... ' Cases of cannibalism were reported, as hunger seized the whole country. The cities counted eight million inhabitants less than in 1914—the population of Petrograd alone had dropped from 2,000,000 to 600,000; that of Moscow, the new capital, from 1,500,000 to 900,000. Industry, which had employed three million workers at the beginning of 1917, employed no more than 1,200,000 in January 1921.

This last figure is particularly revealing, not only of the parlous state of Soviet industry but of the fact that the urban proletariat, which had provided Soviet democracy with its social base and spearhead and the Red Army with its finest soldiers, had been decimated by Civil War no less than by unemployment, which had caused a mass exodus from the towns. The political consequences were dramatic. What was the meaning of a 'dictatorship of the proletariat' when the proletariat had suffered such terrible losses? The most class-conscious workers had been killed in the fighting or absorbed by the state machine, and those left behind were too few in number to provide the regime with a genuinely popular basis. Here lies one of the fundamental causes of the decline of Soviet democracy. Its backbone had been the existence, the political consciousness, the revolutionary activity and enthusiasm of the working class, and when that class was wiped out in large numbers the spirit of the Revolution itself began to shrivel.

The enthusiasm that had greeted the birth of Soviet democracy seemed to have exhausted itself. The soviets had lost their former independence to become branches of government, non-Communist

[1] Deutscher: *The Prophet Unarmed*, p. 4.

parties had ceased to exist—the price they had to pay for their participation in the counter-revolution. Power became concentrated in the hands of a single organization, and it, too, underwent a crisis of dramatic proportions. The Bolshevik Party had for years been brimming over with life; it had enjoyed a degree of internal freedom that, as the great historian Edward H. Carr so rightly remarked, has rarely been equalled by any other party. Here the various factions could speak up without fear or favour, fight hard, but at the end of the day remain comrades in arms. And even when power became increasingly concentrated in the hands of the Central Committee, intellectual life remained intense, not only because of the vision of the Party leaders but also because the breadth of the problems to be resolved called for considerable efforts of imagination. Finally, the Bolshevik Party, which had been built up by Lenin before the First World War, had been given a spectacular boost during the Revolution: new blood had flowed in to revitalize it, and as the clandestine practices and rigid discipline needed under the Tsarist regime could be discarded, the Bolsheviks were filled with a new spirit, born of the feeling that they were at one with the masses, could take their pulse, receive their enthusiastic support and defend their vital interests.

But the Civil War put a stop to all that. During the Bolshevik Party Congress of 1921 Lenin was able to force through a resolution banning the continued existence of organized factions. This measure was in no way peculiar to the Bolsheviks— no Party can permit closed groups to weaken its discipline and to imperil its unity. But the ban on factions and a ban on all freedom of discussion were only a few steps apart, and these were quickly taken. The result was Stalin's monolithic party in which all differences, however slight, were mercilessly stamped out. Lenin, for his part, had presented the decision of 1921 as a temporary measure demanded by the particularly difficult circumstances of Russia at the time. The workers and sailors of Kronstadt had just staged a revolt, facing the Communists with their first threat from the Left and for that very reason throwing them into complete disarray. The year 1921 also saw the beginning of the N.E.P. (New Economic Policy) which introduced a series of concessions—the first since 1917—to capitalism. In these circumstances doubts might have proved disastrous, lack of discipline might have led to panic, and panic to catastrophe. Lenin openly called it a retreat, and drew the following conclusions: 'When an army retreats, discipline must be ten times greater than during an offensive, when everyone is moving forward. But if, now, everyone were to pull back, that would be the end—swift and unavoidable.'

This was a far cry from his professions of confidence in the masses, and a far cry also from Soviet democracy: having disappeared from the soviets, democracy was about to vanish from the Party as well. It took a few years to disappear completely, or rather to be expelled, but even by the end of 1920 Lenin had to admit publicly that Soviet Russia was 'a workers' state with a bureaucratic deformity'. Soon afterwards the 'dictatorship of the proletariat' was turned into a dictatorship over the proletariat, though Lenin, physically exhausted and in poor health,[1] struggled on manfully against a 'deformity' that robbed the regime of its democratic content. Writing in *Pravda* in March 1922, he called the bureaucrats 'our worst enemies'. He fought on, but his was a losing battle, as he himself knew only too well. During the Party Congress of 1922, the last one he attended, he said, 'What is needed [to reach Communism] is more culture for the leading Communists. In fact, if we consider Moscow—4,700 responsible Communists—if we consider the bureaucratic machine, that enormous mass, can we really tell who leads and who is led? I doubt very much if the Communists are leading. To tell the truth, it is not they who lead, it is they who are being led.' He suggested all sorts of remedies against this evil, but for all that the 'bureaucratic deformity' persisted and grew. It gripped the entire Party and state, and in a thousand and one ways eroded the ideal of October: a Soviet democracy pledged to involve the humblest citizens— workers, peasants, soldiers, and housewives—in political decisions, in the administration of public affairs, and the building of a new society.

Socialism in one country

Was this pure Utopianism? We might be tempted to say so, though only if we measure Bolshevik achievement by the standard of their

---

[1] On May 26th, 1922, Lenin suffered his first stroke and could not return to Moscow until October. On December 16th, a second stroke left him with a paralysed right arm and leg. In March 1923, he lost the faculty of speech, and it was during that month that he wrote and published his last article. He died on January 21st, 1924.

early ambitions. But before relegating the greatest and most realistic of revolutionaries in contemporary history to the role of dreamers or demagogues, we ought to ask ourselves what Lenin and his comrades really had in mind when they spoke of Soviet democracy. As Marxists of the old school, could they really have believed that by setting up a proletarian dictatorship in a backward country they could pave the way for a truly democratic society? To do so, they would have had to turn their back not only on common sense but on all the teachings of Karl Marx, according to whom socialism could only take root in highly industrialized societies.

In reality, when the Bolsheviks propounded their ideals, they were setting their sights not so much on Russia as on world revolution, which the entire European socialist movement thought was just round the corner. Thus, Kautsky himself, before 1914 the high priest of German social democracy and the leader of the Second International, declared in 1909 that all talk of a 'premature' revolution in Europe was utterly absurd. The West was ready for socialism and, according to the declared opinion of socialists, the outbreak of war would only hasten its advent. True, it was generally admitted that the decisive work would fall to the more highly organized working class of the West, but the Bolsheviks—and Lenin and Trotsky in particular—judged that the first blow against international capitalism and imperialism must be struck at its weakest point. Once this was done, the main body of the proletarian army would step into the breach and finish off what its outriders had started.

Now the Russia of the Tsars, and later the Provisional Government with its precarious institutions and widespread misery, was one such weak point. And so the Bolsheviks struck there, in the firm conviction that they would not remain alone, and that the Russian workers would soon cede pride of place to workers in countries more qualified to lead the struggle to its successful conclusion—of implementing the great ideals expressed in Lenin's *State and Revolution*. We have followed Lenin on his return to Russia, watched his reconquest of his party, his struggle against the Provisional Government and against the hesitation of his own friends, and his preparation for armed insurrection. At each of these stages he insisted on the close links between the Russian uprising and world revolution. 'The Russian worker has begun,' he wrote in 1918, 'the German, French and English workers will carry on and socialism will triumph.' And again: 'The Russian Revolution is only one detachment in the world socialist army, and the success and triumph of the Revolution we have just accomplished will depend on the actions of the larger army.'

The Russian detachment led by Lenin was, moreover, less important to its leader than the German which, as Lenin declared in 1918, held the fate of the world revolution in its hands. In March of that year he added, 'It is absolutely true that without a German revolution we will perish.' Stalinists have tried to make out that it was Trotsky alone who established such close links between the Russian uprising and world revolution, who made the success of one dependent on the triumph of the other. Nothing could be falser. In November 1920 Lenin still contended that 'we only began our work because we counted unreservedly on the world revolution.'

True, it was Trotsky who, on October 26th, 1917, told the All-Russian Congress of Soviets, then meeting to approve the Bolshevik seizure of power, 'We place all our hopes in the fact that our Revolution will trigger off a European revolution. If the people of Europe do not rise and crush imperialism, we will be crushed — that is indubitable. Either the Russian Revolution will raise the whirlwind of struggle in the West, or the capitalists of all countries will strangle our Revolution ... ' But it was Lenin himself who declared in July 1921, 'When we began ... the Revolution ... we did this not with the conviction that we could anticipate its development, but because a whole series of circumstances impelled us to begin this Revolution. Our thought was: either the international revolution will come to our aid, and in that case our victories are wholly assured, or we will do our modest revolutionary work in the consciousness that in case of defeat we have nevertheless served the cause of revolution and our experiment will be of help to other revolutions. It was clear to us that without the support of the international world revolution, a victory of the proletarian uprising was impossible. Even before the Revolution, and likewise after it, our thought was: immediately, or at any rate very quickly, a revolution will begin in the other countries, in capitalistically more developed countries — or in the contrary case we will have to perish.'

Even Stalin, the man who a few years later elaborated the doctrine of 'socialism in one country', told a meeting of the Central

Bolshevik Committee in February 1918, 'The question is posed as follows: either our Revolution will be defeated and with it the revolution in Europe or else we shall have a breathing space and grow stronger.' The close ties between the Russian and European Revolutions could not have been stressed more forcefully. True, not a single Bolshevik was foolhardy enough to predict the precise date on which the Western proletariat would rise up, but everyone was quite convinced that it was only a matter of months at the most. And so the Bolsheviks kept hoping and playing for time—to 'manoeuvre, retreat, and lie low' as Lenin put it.

It was the same tactical consideration that had persuaded the Bolsheviks to accept the heavy sacrifices of the treaty of Brest-Litovsk, to withdraw into their besieged fortress while the world proletariat made up its mind to come to the rescue.

In November 1918, when the German workers overthrew the Kaiser, the Bolsheviks thought their hopes were at long last nearing fulfilment. Like the Tsarist, so the Hohenzollern Empire was over-turned by the spontaneous action of the masses: the Russian February had been resurrected in the streets of Berlin, and October could not be far behind. No good Marxist could have doubted this; Marxists had always placed their faith in the German working class whose strength had been an inspiration to the entire socialist International. But Germany was not to have her October. Revolu-tionaries led by Karl Liebknecht and Rosa Luxemburg did try to establish a proletarian regime and abolish capitalism, but the German bourgeoisie proved much more powerful than its Russian counterpart. Moreover, remnants of the Kaiser's defeated army rallied to the support of the counter-revolution. The German socialists, finally, were no less divided than their Russian comrades, and in Germany the right wing proved much stronger than the left. The former, from which most of the leaders of the German Social Democrat Party were drawn, decided not to run the risk of a civil war and to do nothing that would endanger the young Republic. Seeing that conservative and influential army circles had agreed to support the Republic, provided only that it did not change the economic system and the established social order, they thought it best to make common cause with these men against the revolu-tionary proletariat. One of these Social Democratic leaders, Gustav Noske, even agreed to play the part of what he himself described as '*Bluthund*' (bloodhound) of the counter-revolution.

And so, at the head of the old imperial army and the volunteer corps which a few years later supplied the growing Nazi party with its military staff, Noske, on behalf of his Party, made himself responsible for drowning the uprising of the revolutionary proletariat in blood. The German Left never recovered from the blow he dealt them in January 1919, and the Russian Revolution stayed as isolated as ever.

The Bolsheviks did not easily resign themselves to this situation, the less so as it upset some of their most cherished dogmas. For years to come they clung to the slogan Lenin had coined during the Brest-Litovsk epoch: Russian Communists must play for time at all costs and 'hold on'. They realized that they had overestimated the energy and impatience of the Western proletariat, and that they had underestimated the ability and resilience of capitalism. They protested loudly that they and the workers of Europe had been betrayed by right-wing socialists, men who refused to run the least risk on behalf of the working class but were loud in calling for sacrifices on behalf of the fatherland, men who had turned their back on socialism to rush to the aid of capitalism. For all that, the Russians never doubted the basic correctness of their original argument: the world revolution might take longer than they had thought, but come in the end it would. Moreover, if the workers of Europe delayed too long,[1] the colonial people would rise up in their stead, thus facing world capitalism with a new danger and giving the Russian Revolution new grounds for hope.

And in 1918 the Bolsheviks did gain a breathing space. In June 1921, Lenin still told the Congress of the Communist International that 'we are gaining time, and to gain time is to gain everything.' In March 1923, he published his last article. It was entitled 'Better Fewer but Better', and in it he took stock with almost brutal realism of what revolutionary Russia had achieved and what remained to be done. The problem was much the same as it had been in 1917, 1918 or in 1921: 'Can we hold on until the socialist revolution is victorious in the more developed countries?' But, as he went on to point out, we imagine rather sadly, waiting was not very easy, because in Russia 'the small and very small peasant is

---

[1] Lenin himself insisted on several occasions that the action of the Western proletariat had been of a real help to Soviet Russia. Thus he thought that it was thanks to the workers that the capitalists had been unable to wage an all-out war on Russia, a war that would inevitably have led to the defeat of the Red Army.

compelled by economic necessity to remain on an extremely low level of productivity of labour.' This problem had existed for a long time, and Lenin, at the end of a long career of protracted struggles and triumphs achieved with great bravery, did not apparently dare to offer the solution.

What mattered most to him, in any case, was to safeguard Soviet power. To foster world revolution was an impossibility—Russian Communists had never wanted to do more than encourage it and had all along made it clear that the decisive contribution could only come from the proletariat of Europe and America. Their own mission was limited to encouraging others, to leading them by example. It was with that end in view that in 1919 they set up the Communist International (Comintern) for the purpose of uniting all socialists who had rejected the reformist policies of the Second International. For the first time in history, a revolutionary movement could call on the resources of a state that did not stint it material and moral support. For all that, the Comintern was not meant to foster revolutions artificially by armed intervention, especially since by 1921 Russian Communists had come to recognize that capitalism was enjoying a new lease of life, and that the heirs of October would have to resign themselves a little longer to the discomforts of the backward country in which they were the sole masters.

This situation, as we saw, was one that took all good Marxists by surprise. To them, economic conditions were overriding, the infrastructure on which all social and political relationships were based and which had a decisive influence on the degree of social consciousness, culture and civilization. In Russia, however, politics dominated over economics: here the proletariat had seized the reins of power while a socialist system of production and distribution was still a long way off. To confuse matters even further, the Russian proletariat was relatively small and badly fitted to the task of socialist construction. Its links with the countryside had remained close, its productivity low and its capacity for work diminished by physical suffering. When industrial reconstruction once again attracted peasants to the cities, they lacked the sense of collective purpose and labour discipline without which modern production is impossible. Such was the 'human material' with which the Russian Communists had to launch and accomplish the gigantic task of building a new civilization in which power would be wielded by the working class, in which collective wealth would render the use of force unnecessary and which would create a new human type freed from wage slavery, alienation and constraint.

But when against all expectations they found themselves cut off from the rest of the world, could the Bolshevik leaders really be expected to maintain these great ideals intact? They never abandoned their socialist aspirations or their hope in world Communism, but Lenin and his colleagues realized that Soviet Russia was in no position to achieve them unaided. Thus when Lenin spoke of the need to 'hold on', what he had in mind was the preservation and consolidation of the Russian base from which, with the help of world revolution, it would be possible to make the decisive leap to socialism. But while she waited, Russia herself had to forge ahead, to reconstruct, to learn the best techniques from the bourgeoisie. The Russian proletariat would remain in the saddle, preventing the restoration of capitalism or the exploitation of Russia by foreigners. At the same time, it would help to reform agriculture by encouraging the gradual introduction of large-scale collective farming methods and by fostering a socialist outlook. But all this would take time, and was, in any case, a far cry from socialism. Socialism also demanded a higher degree of productivity than that attained by the capitalist world, the organization of labour relations based on collective principles, a fairer distribution of incomes, the gradual reduction of state power, and the participation of everyone in the task of economic and social management. Surrounded by enemies, poverty-stricken, Soviet Russia was in no position to implement these objectives.

Later, Stalin was to declare that his country was capable of building socialism within its own frontiers. Lenin had never even dreamed of this possibility. 'The complete victory of the socialist Revolution in a single country is unthinkable,' he declared in November 1918, and added, 'It calls for the most active collaboration of at least some of the developed countries of which Russia does not happen to be one.' At the end of his life, Lenin still called it an 'incontestable' fact that 'Russia has not yet reached the degree of development of her productive forces needed for the introduction of socialism.' And he was even more explicit in his 'Better Fewer but Better', which, as we saw, was the last article he published. In it he declared that 'the situation in regard to our state apparatus is ... deplorable, not to say outrageous.' And he inveighed against the boastful claims that 'we possess any considerable quantity of the elements necessary for building a really new apparatus that would deserve the name of socialist, Soviet, etc. ... No,' Lenin countered, 'we have no such apparatus and even the quantity of elements that we have is ridiculously small ... ' And he concluded, 'We lack enough culture to pass directly to socialism.'[1]

Until 1924, Stalin, like all Bolsheviks, took much the same line. In his *Foundations of Leninism* published during that year, the future dictator wrote that the 'efforts of a single country, especially of an agricultural one like Russia, cannot ensure the victory of socialism, nor the organization of socialist production'. But in the same year, a second edition of the same work carefully replaced this with a completely different idea—one that was soon afterwards to become a creed; namely, that a truly socialist society can be built in one country, no matter what happens in the rest of the world. The new ideology sprang not only from the continued isolation of Soviet Russia but also from her determination to temper some of its worst effects.

For Soviet Russia had good reason to feel abandoned by the Western working class, which was apparently determined to ensure that nothing must be allowed to mar the brief burst of prosperity Europe had begun to enjoy in the early 1920s. After much progress, the revolutionary movement had entered a period of stagnation. In these circumstances it was difficult to persuade the Russians not to lose faith in world revolution, or to argue that without it their efforts could not possibly bear fruit. And so, under the slogan of 'Socialism in One Country', Soviet citizens were invited to stand on their own feet and to build a new socialist society in the face of world hostility. By adopting this slogan they turned their backs on Marxist doctrine, on everything the Russian working class had been taught in the past. However, the new creed was not only of un-doubted psychological value but had the additional advantage of

---

[1] Stalinists have tried to saddle Lenin with one of their chief dogmas: that of socialism in one country. In support of this claim they have had to suppress innumerable declarations by Lenin and rely on a single remark he made in 1915, namely that socialism can achieve its first victory in a small number of capitalist countries, and even in a single capitalist country. However, nothing in this phrase suggests that Lenin had in mind so notoriously backward a country as Tsarist Russia or that his reference to the early victory of socialism implied the construction of a full-fledged socialist economic system.

offering Stalin ammunition in his fight against Trotskyist internationalism.

In 1935, Stalin declared that the Soviet Union had achieved
socialism. By then, bureaucracy was riding high, Marxism had
been perverted into a cult, the state had acquired altogether
excessive powers, police terror was growing apace, and social distinctions, far from receding, had grown to ominous proportions.
At the same time, Stalin's regime had become extremely cautious
in the international arena, so much so that the Comintern would
often go out of its way to hold back revolutions it deemed risky or
premature. All this had little to do with socialism: indeed, it was its
exact opposite. But while Stalinism was undoubtedly a perversion
of the spirit of October, it nevertheless had a number of undoubted
achievements to its credit. Thus, abandoning the N.E.P. in 1928, it
inaugurated the era of five-year plans and succeeded in modernizing the country at an exceedingly fast pace. In the most unfavourable
circumstance—for which it bore much of the blame itself—the
regime also proceeded to the collectivization of farms, thus achieving what has been called the 'second revolution'—albeit at the cost
of unspeakable excesses and crimes.

At the same time, the U.S.S.R. launched a cultural drive the
scope of which was quite out of proportion to the country's
severely restricted resources. Science and culture spread more
rapidly than anywhere else in the world, and though poverty was
not eradicated, it was nevertheless on the decrease. The regime
could take credit for a host of further social achievements. No
doubt it would have done still more had not preparations for a war
the Soviet Union never wanted involved the wasting of tremendous
resources. The cost of this terrible holocaust was, perhaps, best
summarized by President Kennedy when he said, 'At least twenty
million Soviet citizens lost their lives. Countless millions of homes
and farms were burned or sacked. A third of the nation's [Euro-
pean] territory, including nearly two-thirds of its industrial base,
were turned into waste-land.' No other country suffered as much
as the Soviet Union. But this time the result was military victory
over Germany, though victory at what cost! This is what Ernest
Bevin, Britain's Foreign Secretary and one of the signatories of the
Atlantic Pact, was thinking of when he said, 'All the aid we have
been able to give has been small compared with the tremendous
efforts of the Soviet people. Our children's children will look back,

through their history books, with admiration and thanks for the heroism of the great Russian people.'

After the defeat of Hitlerism, in which the U.S.S.R. played a decisive part and for which she paid a heavier tribute than all the other Allied countries combined, growing hopes that the regime might become more liberal were quickly disappointed. Russia entered a new phase of intense economic reconstruction and adopted an implacable political line. Stalin's personal dictatorship assumed almost demented proportions as he drove the Soviet people into super-human, if not inhuman, efforts to repair the ravages of war and to catch up with the United States, whose immense resources had grown even vaster during the war. But for all that—despite the new sacrifices, despite all the crimes, despite her detractors and often flying in the face of her enemies—the Soviet Union refused resolutely to re-establish capitalism and so kept open the Marxist road to the eventual emancipation of mankind. The bureaucracy had seized important privileges, and held on to them by the most violent means, by means, let it be said, that made a mockery of socialist morality. Nevertheless, it identified its own interests with those of a planned economy in which collective needs form the very basis of and reason for all national activity. Such, in broad outline, was the harvest Russia reaped from the revolutionary seeds she had sown in October 1917.

The international class struggle

It would be a simple matter to demonstrate the differences and contradictions between the social edifice planned by the Leninist architects of Revolution and the actual structures built by their successors; to show that social injustice, inequality, alienation and servitude continue to be rife in Soviet Russia; that the dreams of democracy of the early revolutionaries, though they remain ideals in the U.S.S.R., show no signs of being turned into reality. But can we really expect men to build an entirely new civilization within a few decades, beset, moreover, by the most terrible trials and tribulations? As Lenin put it in 1918, 'The working class is not cut off from the old bourgeois order by a Chinese wall. And when the Revolution starts it is not as if someone had died and his body was carted away. When the old society dies, the corpse cannot be nailed up in a coffin and lowered into a grave. It will decompose right among us to putrefy and contaminate us all.' And, indeed, fifty years after the October Revolution the Soviet Union remains a tangled skein of old repressions and bright promises for the future. It suffers from the conservatism of its bureaucratic leaders, from the inertia of its institutions and from indifference and scepticism, but it has never renounced its original hopes in Soviet democracy. Half a century is not enough to decide which are uppermost: the old forces of servitude or the new forces of liberation. Meanwhile the two remain locked in battle and the desire for progress continues to be nourished by the hopes of October.

Nor is it in Russia alone that the historical impact of the Soviet Revolution has made itself felt. The dynamism of the Russian Revolution was such as to send its ripples into the furthermost corners of the world. Without it, without the spell it cast on the imagination of mankind and the fears and hatreds it inspired, modern society would not have become what it is today. From whatever angle we look at political and social developments in the twentieth century, we must expect to meet the 'Communist presence', the all-pervading influence of the Russian Revolution. It is no exaggeration to say that international relations have been turned topsyturvy since 1917. The emergence of a state whose social and economic features differ radically from those of all other states has never ceased to produce its effect. In particular, the birth of Soviet Russia has taken the class struggle into the field of international politics.

Thus while international alliances and rivalries before 1917 involved parties with identical interests, the Bolshevik Revolution introduced an entirely novel and perturbing element into the diplomatic game. Henceforth, the manoeuvres of the chancelleries and military leaders were swayed by such considerations as the particular economic system of their partners or adversaries, and their adherence or non-adherence to the socialist camp. No doubt these ideological considerations were not the only ones to determine confrontations and alignments in the international field, but no one can deny their importance. Let us take but one example. Faced as they were with the growing threat of Nazi imperialism, Great Britain and France ought obviously to have made common cause with Russia against Hitler, but the economic and social structure of the Russian state not only prevented the British ruling class from accepting the need for such an alliance until 1941, almost two years

after Britain had declared war on Germany,[1] but also caused it to
show an almost inexhaustible forbearance towards German aggression. For despite the undoubted threat Hitler posed, the British
ruling class could never forget that, at the end of the day, Germany
still constituted a 'Western bastion against Bolshevism'.

More generally and far more fundamentally, capitalism as a
whole has had to meet a new challenge—ever since 1917. No longer
were the dissatisfied proletariat or the colonial people clamouring
for emancipation the only threats it had to face; now it also
came up against the policy, indeed the very existence, of Soviet
Russia, isolated at first but later surrounded by allies. The action
of the U.S.S.R. has sometimes been both direct, and more often
indirect, but it has always been a power with which the capitalist
states have had to reckon. Who would argue, for instance, that
U.S. policy towards her Latin American neighbours would have
been the present unwholesome mixture of selfish and liberal
motives, had not the shadow, however distant, of Soviet Russia and
of the 'socialist camp' permanently darkened the horizon of
American statesmanship? As late as 1954, the United States was
still able to silence moderate reformist attempts in Guatemala that
ran counter to the economic interests of a few big trusts, but less
than ten years later the increased strength of the Soviet Union was
a major factor in preventing the U.S. Government from bringing
Cuba back into the American 'sphere of influence' by force of arms.

We could quote a host of similar examples. Suffice it to say that
despite Soviet love for the cardinal virtues of peaceful coexistence,
despite Russia's diplomacy of extreme caution and her obstinate
determination to do nothing that might jeopardize the economic
development of the 'socialist camp', bourgeois diplomats, economists and soldiers still have to reckon with the Soviet presence at
almost every step they take. It may be argued that this presence
differs in no way from that of other great Powers pursuing their
own interests. But nothing could be more mistaken—the foreign
policy of the Soviet Union is anything but a faithful copy, or auto-
matic extension, of Tsarist diplomatic practices. True, the U.S.S.R.
is defending the same geographical boundaries as Old Russia, and
hence its foreign policy is bound to resemble that of the Tsars in a

---

[1] A Franco-Soviet alliance was signed in 1935, but French politicians did their
utmost to ensure that it remained a dead letter. This was one of the causes of the
Franco-British capitulation to Hitler at Munich.

great many respects. But in several ways it has been quite original. To ignore this fact is to rob an important phenomenon of one of its essential components. Thus when people dismiss Russia's post-war encroachments on Eastern Europe as rank imperialism, they tend to forget that this intervention was accompanied by profound social and economic changes, and that it put an end to capitalism and to domination by a privileged class. It is impossible to separate the two aspects of this composite process, and it is sheer blindness to ignore the fact that the foreign policy of the Soviet Union cannot but be 'coloured' by the special nature of her socialized economy.

That the Russian Revolution has, moreover, had a considerable impact on the colonial freedom movement is a truism on which we need not expand. Underprivileged people everywhere see it as proof that a backward nation can, in the face of bitter opposition by the big Powers, modernize its economy by a path other than that of 'free enterprise', which is, in any case, closed to the Third World. Hence, Communism has been able to spread its wings far afield, whereas social democracy, which flourished in an earlier phase of historical development, remained an almost exclusively Western movement. It is no coincidence that the Congress of Tours, which in 1920 presided over the birth of the French Communist Party, included an Indo-Chinese delegate who had never before found a place in the international labour movement, and whose subsequent political career was to make him a leader of the national and social liberation movement of the people of the Third World. His name was Ho Chi Minh.

It is true that in this sphere the Russian Revolution has handed over to the Chinese Revolution, whose dynamic may well appeal more strongly to a number of 'underdeveloped' nations. The difference between the two is not one of race or geography, but of policy. This fact has suggested to some observers that the class struggle has made way for a conflict between 'poor nations' and 'rich nations'. But while the gulf between the developed and dis-inherited countries is deep, and the injustices springing from it may lead to considerable upheavals, this interpretation strikes me as exceedingly far-fetched. If poverty and suffering were indeed the mainsprings of revolution, no country would be more revolu-tionary than modern India. Her case demonstrates clearly that the prevailing economic and social system continues to have a decisive effect on the choice of internal policies and of international relations. This remark applies to the Soviet Union as well.

True, the policy of peaceful coexistence advocated by its leaders tends to obscure the full force of this observation. In seeking a *modus vivendi* with the United States, the Soviet Union can be accused of class collaboration and hence of betraying the Third World and of going back on her former attitudes. In fact it would be quite wrong to think that Russia's current moderation is a complete *volte face*. Lenin's foreign policy was, essentially, dictated by the hostility with which the Western powers tried to isolate the Bolshevik 'pestilence', and tried to destroy it by military intervention or economic strangulation. The relationship between revolutionary Russia and the German Weimar Republic showed clearly that, even while waiting impatiently for the outbreak of a German uprising, the Soviet Union never dreamt of exporting its own brand of revolution, of practising 'subversion' abroad. As for Stalinism, it is only by a gross distortion of the facts that anyone can describe it as a champion of world revolution, or even of territorial expansion.

No statesman could have been more cautious than Stalin. Armed with the might of the Revolution, he nevertheless did his utmost to restrain the ebullience of foreign communists. For if Russia's continued isolation had taught him one thing in particular it was that the Soviet Union, as the sole bastion of revolution, must be defended at all costs, and that the prevailing relationship of international forces did not justify Russia or the world Communist movement, which he controlled with an iron fist, running the slightest risk. Stalin avoided making new enemies and sought desperately for new allies, at all times ready to repay them with even greater moderation. Thus when he tried to enlist Western support against the German menace, his foreign disciples quickly dropped their opposition to liberal democracy and bourgeois parliamentarianism, and readily sacrificed some of their most sacred principles (among them the refusal to fight in defence of capitalist countries) on the altar of the Popular Front. No signs of goodwill must be discouraged;[1] far from it, the petit-bourgeoisie and the middle classes must be shown that their fears of the Communists were quite groundless. During the Spanish Civil War, moreover, the Communists dissuaded the Republican regime from socializing its economic sector lest they imperil the unity of the anti-Franco forces.

[1] In France, Maurice Thorêz called for the 'sacred' union of the whole nation.

Stalinists at home and abroad showed no less moderation at the end of the Second World War. True, the satellization of Eastern Europe horrified Western Europe, and suggested that Russia was embarked on a systematic campaign of expansion and conquest, but Russia's advance was not prepared by a series of military coups. The new spheres of influence she acquired had in fact been more or less agreed between Stalin, Roosevelt and Churchill as 'recompense' for the great sacrifices the Soviet Union and the Communist-led resistance movements had made during the war. The Soviet Union, for her part, agreed to keep her hands off Greece, where the extreme Left, having played a most valiant part in the anti-Fascist struggle, was in a position to seize power. Communists behaved no differently in Italy and France, where they rallied to the cause of 'national reconstruction' and never tried to cash in on the great advantages their massive participation in the Resistance had brought them. The collapse of Fascism might have rebounded upon those conservative elements who had supported its rise, and the resulting crisis might have shaken European capitalism to its very foundations. But the leaders of the Soviet Union and of the Communist Parties once again refused to exploit the situation. Their caution was perhaps a sign of realism rather than of timidity —they may have thought that the West, under the leadership of the United States, was more powerful than ever, while the Soviet Union had just been bled white by the German juggernaut. Their temperance nevertheless demanded miracles of discipline and self-abnegation on the part of tens of thousands of Communist militants and sympathizers, ready for battle and still under arms.

Here we must stop our digression on Soviet restraint, which, incidentally, explains Stalin's somewhat lukewarm support for the Chinese Revolution. In any case, we have seen that in its fashion Stalinism, too, was a policy of peaceful coexistence; that notwithstanding its verbal broadsides, in which invective was often the dominant ingredient, it evinced a degree of mildness and circumspection that were anything but revolutionary. Does this mean that Trotskyist and other left-wing critics are right to accuse the Communist movement of suppressing the international class struggle? To affirm this calls for a great deal of assurance and a fair dose of prejudice. The struggle against Nazism and Fascism was a major phase in this class struggle, and who can forget the crucial role the Communists played in it? The 'conquest' of Eastern Europe by the

Red Army did not, admittedly, introduce socialism—a product that, in any case, does not travel well—but it nevertheless led to the abolition of the appallingly reactionary social regimes that plagued Hungary, Poland and Rumania before the war. In the final analysis, the foreign policy of the U.S.S.R. during and after Stalin's reign was and remains a mixture of opportunism and pragmatism. Fundamentally it reflects the contradictory and transitory nature of a regime in which totalitarian elements exist side by side with the spirit of socialism and progress.

Today this remains as true as in the recent past. Hence it would be extremely foolhardy to draw final conclusions from current Soviet attempts to reach an accommodation with the United States, attempts that only the war in Vietnam seems to be frustrating. If this policy were stepped up further, we might have good reason to wonder whether the new Soviet line was not a major change of the Stalinist, let alone the Leninist, one. Such a transformation, however, does not depend only, or even chiefly, on the will of politicians. Too many interests are involved, and forces far beyond the control or intention of mere individuals. Thus while the Soviet Union preserves its economic structures it must always pose an open or latent threat to capitalist states. The Krushchevs, Kosygins and Brezhnevs may nurture projects and philosophies that the Chinese are not entirely wrong in calling 'revisionist'. But they are and remain—perhaps despite themselves—heirs to October and to the Bolshevik Revolution. No leader of the Soviet Union, no matter what policies he advocates, can ever afford to disavow so compelling a heritage.

Socialism and communism

It is no wonder that the Russian Revolution has left its mark on every sphere of Soviet life and even on many aspects of the capitalist world. Willy-nilly, capitalism itself has been forced to make some adjustment to the Soviet challenge. To give just one example, the very idea of economic planning which rides rough-shod over the sacred principle of 'free enterprise' has become the chief hallmark of most countries.

In the political and intellectual spheres, too, the Russian Revolution has had a profound effect on the Western world in general and the world socialist movement in particular. It is often alleged that the Revolution was responsible for splitting the world labour movement, but does this claim have any substance in fact? To say that it has means ignoring all those cracks in the socialist front that, even before 1917, set revolutionaries against reformists in almost daily conflict. The First World War only served to increase these dissensions, and when some socialists chose to follow the national flag, conveniently forgetting their professions of international brotherhood, while others continued as passionately as ever to 'wage war on war', then all talk of unity was so much idle chatter. It did not need the Bolshevik Revolution to drive this point home: in April 1917, the German Social Democratic Party, the most powerful and renowned of its day, broke officially apart. The October Revolution and its sequel may have perpetuated the rift and rendered the divisions more rigid, but it did not create them.

Faced with the victory of a truly proletarian Revolution, and with the first successful Marxist attempt to overthrow the old social order, Western socialists divided once again. While some rallied unreservedly to Lenin's cause, the rest attacked the short-comings of the Bolshevik edifice—which were real enough—and passed over its merits in complete silence. Among the broad masses, too, the Russian Revolution evoked the admiration and solidarity of some, and the hatred and vilification of others. At the end of a war that had sacrificed millions of men to the glory of the various fatherlands, with the connivance and support of socialist leaders, these same leaders suddenly saw fit to blame the Bolsheviks for using violence as a political method. This accusation alone was enough to convict them of bad faith and to widen the rift in the workers' camp.

This was not surprising. The existence within one and the same movement of a conformist faction prepared to fit into the capitalist framework, and a revolutionary faction anxious to destroy that framework at the earliest possible opportunity, could only be tolerated during a relatively peaceful period in the history of the working-class movement. And when this period made way for one of sharp crises and social upheavals it was inevitable that reformists and revolutionaries should go their separate ways.[1] This happened during and immediately after the First World War. The reformists

[1] In her extremely well-documented *Aux Origines du communisme français (1914–1920)*, (Paris, 1964), the French historian Annie Kriegel alleges that in France the split of the socialist movement was an accident of history. Her argu-ment is rather unconvincing, for she ignores the world-wide nature of the rift and its underlying causes.

believed that the essential job of the working class was to participate—even at the price of further sacrifices—in the task of national
reconstruction within the existing economic system. The spirit of
'sacred union' of all classes, which had appeared in 1914, had
given some of them a first taste of political power, and they had no
wish to return to the 'negative' attitudes of yesterday. Having
known the blessings of patriotism and 'statesmanship', they were
determined not to renounce them for the less respectable virtues of
class warfare and systematic opposition.

Western revolutionaries, on the other hand, eclipsed or crushed
by the events of 1914 when international brotherhood went by
the board, began to realize in 1917 that their defeat was not
irreversible and that class solidarity must be restored at all costs.
Their disgust with the war and the social injustices it brought in its
wake infused them with new courage. The example of the Russian
Revolution, its repercussions in Europe and particularly in Germany followed by Hungary—the revolutionary effervescence for
which they had been waiting for so many years—did the rest: they
decided to break completely with the reformists, men who were
lukewarm whenever it came to social struggle and fully in favour
of wars between nations. The revolutionary faction, joined by a
few anarchists, accordingly founded the Third International and so
laid the cornerstone of the world Communist movement.

As estranged brothers, socialists and Communists would henceforth find reasons for opposing each other despite the similarity of
some of their ideals and despite—or rather because of—the identity
of their 'clients'. Their quarrels were not really doctrinal. In
Germany, for instance, an uprising by the workers, impatient to
follow the Russian path, was crushed by an incongruous coalition
of petty squires, capitalists—and right-wing socialists. The cracks
thus widened were never to be closed again, as those who have tried
have discovered to their sorrow. Although deeply divided among
themselves, most Western socialists now lend their support to the
self-same capitalist regime which they so bitterly denounced in the
past, and are content to restrict their efforts to the amelioration
of some of its worst features. On the political plane they have come
to accept the continued existence of monarchies, believing their
influence to be negligible if not beneficial. They have warmly
embraced the ideal of parliamentary democracy, which Marx never
tired of calling a sham. The distinction between liberal, bourgeois

democracy and socialist, proletarian democracy has evaporated completely, so much so that they have consigned the very idea of the dictatorship of the proletariat to the Chamber of Horrors.[1] Their support for ideals and institutions established by nineteenth-century liberal and bourgeois society without the co-operation of the working class, and very often in conflict with it, was greatly favoured by circumstance. The 1920s witnessed a temporary consolidation of capitalism and so helped to strengthen their conviction that far from rushing into foolhardy revolutionary adventures they ought to remain faithful to what Léon Blum has called the 'old house'. The Fascist threat served to rally them still more strongly to parliamentary democracy, to which they have clung ever since despite all setbacks and disillusions. This unconditional support for parliamentarianism is the clearest possible sign that the reformist wing of the Western labour movement has completely identified itself with bourgeois society.

The Communists took an entirely different line. Their movement had been born under, and bore the marks of, the double sign of solidarity with the Russian October Revolution and faith in a European revolution. But whether it was because Western capitalism itself was strong enough to surmount its inner difficulties, or whether it survived thanks only to the support of right-wing socialists, the Communists, in any case, failed to make revolutionary headway anywhere outside the Soviet Union. In Germany, Rosa Luxemburg and Karl Liebknecht were murdered; in Hungary, Bela Kun, the founder and leader of the short-lived Soviet Magyar Republic, was driven into exile, and while Russian Communists barricaded themselves in their beleaguered fortress, Western Communists became isolated as well. Such failures almost inevitably lead to demoralization and sectarianism, and the Communists were no exception: the collapse of their immense hopes caused them to withdraw into themselves. No one in the West tried to stop this development. Right-wing socialists often adopted the same attitude towards Soviet Russia as the most hidebound conservatives, and invariably treated the Communists in their own country with icy hostility. Meanwhile, the bourgeoisie did its utmost to pillory the Communist Party as a subversive organization in the pay of the foreigner, one that had best be immured in a political ghetto.

[1] Fascism and Stalinism merely served to foster this aversion.

How did European Communists react under these circumstances?
They had planned for offensive action but found themselves continuously on the defensive. Their movement was born at a time
when the general enthusiasm aroused by the Russian Revolution
attracted a vast number of young and fervent followers to their
ranks, but soon afterwards this swell dwindled into a mere trickle,
and the Communist movement began to suffer from the impossible
contradiction of being a revolutionary organization in a conservative social climate. Born out of the conviction that capitalism was
reaching its end, it had to witness the resurgence of capitalism in
the 1920s. And having failed to profit from the crisis of the 1930s,
it remained a lone wolf even in the 1950s. To its setbacks it reacted
in two ways: by intransigent hostility to Western ways and by
uncritical and unreserved adulation of the Soviet Union. In order
to resist the temptations of a society that was growing more
prosperous and seemed to be surmounting some of its most glaring
contradictions, Communists now had to display a degree of steadfastness that often bordered on heroism. But it also bordered on
blindness, for they not only refused the crumbs from the feast to
which capitalism had invited the workers, but denied its very
existence. Instead of looking inside the pots in which the feast was
being prepared—when they might have discovered its true in-
gredients—they preferred to turn their backs on the whole devil's
kitchen, blithely repeating the outworn dictum that capitalism must
needs lead to the progressive pauperization of the working class.

And while they failed to subject Western society to a trenchant
Marxist critique, using invective as a substitute, they were un-
stinting in their eulogies of the Soviet Union, turning a blind eye
to all her countless faults. The achievements of the regime were
glorified but their price never mentioned; failures were passed over
in decorous silence; crimes were called inventions and calumnies
by the anti-Communist propaganda machine, which, in fact, was
very active. And so there arose the incongruous situation in which
Communists who, in the West, struggled more vigorously than
anyone else in defence of democratic liberties, swallowed the most
vicious assaults on these liberties in the Soviet Union. They could
have declared their complete solidarity with the 'socialist fatherland', defended it against slanderous attacks—and there was certainly no lack of these—and could yet have tried to analyse the
causes of some of the shortcomings and by so doing have helped the

U.S.S.R. to correct some of her worst mistakes. But this intellectual approach—which calls for a degree of objectivity to which even intellectuals rarely rise—is not easily reconciled with the needs of the political struggle. As a result, the dogmatism which in Russia herself reached such alarming proportions and was widely attributed to the obscurantist mentality the Soviet Union was said to have inherited from her Tsarist precursors, found a ready echo in Western Europe, where the disciples of Marx repeated every Stalinist lie and oversimplification.

Admittedly this grave failure went hand in hand with absolute devotion to the cause of the working class, and was underpinned by the persecution of Western Communists. The bourgeoisie, having discovered that there were 'good' and 'bad' socialists, reserved its venom for the latter, thus strengthening Communist determination to have no truck with capitalism and to act as uncritical apologists for Russia. As a result, the Communist movement, born of *revolt*, increasingly followed the path of strict discipline. Discipline was of course indispensable to it, as the history of the workers' struggle had made perfectly clear, but it was only with the 'Russification' of the world Communist movement that discipline was turned into the cardinal virtue it has since become.

'Russification' was the last thing Lenin, Trotsky or the other founders of the Third International would have wanted, but the gradual withdrawal of the Revolution behind its Russian bastion made it almost unavoidable. The consequences were profound and lasting: the circumstances that had governed the transformation of the Communist Party in Russia now produced similar effects in an entirely different context. At first the Communist was a critic and a rebel. In the Soviet Union he had to change his outlook, an extremely difficult and dangerous operation that threatens to transform the revolutionary militant into an inveterate bureaucrat. Western political parties and trade unions have known less spectacular but no less profound transformation. This metamorphosis was successful in the case of only one man: Lenin.

Let us return to him once more and look at the part he played before October 1917: no revolutionary was more intransigent, no militant more determined to bring down a society whose injustices he never ceased to decry. His detractors speak of him as a mere nihilist, a destroyer, but these epithets do not stand up to even casual examination. Long before the seizure of power, Lenin gave proof of great organizational skills, of a methodical approach, and a concern for detail that are not normally associated with the typical revolutionary. The creation of the Soviet state helped him to develop these gifts to the full. Thus he was heard to declare in the spring of 1918, when Russia was in the kind of chaos that her enemies like to confuse with revolution, 'The chief task before the proletariat and the poor peasants ... is the positive and creative effort of perfecting an extremely complex and delicate system ... ' And realizing full well how painful this boring task would prove for the revolutionary militants of yesterday, he went on to say, 'It is infinitely easier to win in an insurrection. It is a million times easier to be victorious over the counter-revolution than to win in the field of organization.' This was a theme to which he was to return incessantly during the five years he continued to lead Russia.

In this field the workers were singularly inexperienced; all of them had to learn the humdrum tasks of the administrator almost from scratch. In his last article, Lenin repeated something he had said many times before: 'To improve our state apparatus we must set ourselves the following tasks: education, more education and still more education.' The Communists were the first revolutionaries in modern history to tackle the business of running a large country for any length of time. This unavoidably called for a transformation of their philosophy, of their outlook and of their mentality. This transformation has been completed, and today the Communist spirit is a mixture of *revolutionary ardour and discipline*, the latter gaining in importance over the former to the extent that the Russian Revolution and the revolutionary struggle in the West become separated in time. This is the difference between orthodox Communists and ultra-leftists whose impatience and doctrinal purity often strike the former as childish aberrations.

The transformation of 'rebels' into 'Communists' has set its seal on Soviet man. While no one can doubt the deep attachment of the Soviet people to the heritage of October, it remains a fact that Russian Communism owes more to the organizational tasks it was forced to tackle over a long period than to the living truth of the relatively brief insurrection. This is yet another difference between the Soviet Communist and his Chinese counterpart, whose armed struggle continued for close on twenty years, and it also explains the difference of mood, though not of interest, between Russian Communism and Castroism.

Now what is true of the Soviet Communist applies equally well to his Western comrades. There is not a country in which the Communist Party does not, in some way, constitute a state within a state. Ostracized everywhere, the European Communist has turned his Party into his castle, from which he continues to fire broadsides at the capitalist system. In this respect, too, the Soviet Union has been slavishly copied. The Soviet Communist Party is not only an immense organization linking the citizen to the state, it also harnesses him to the gigantic task of social construction. Its power derives from the wide variety of its functions, and like all social organisms it has tended to become an end unto itself. It is encouraged to do so by the role it played during the Revolution. For is it not the only political organization that has defended that Revolution and has identified itself with it? And, in fact, the identification of the Russian working class with the Bolshevik party in 1917 made possible the victory of the proletariat. However, even when the links between the Party and the working class were relaxed, the Party continued to look upon itself as the incarnation of the proletarian will. As such it has justified all its actions—the most necessary and the most legitimate as well as the most detestable. Nowhere have excesses of 'Party chauvinism' been more blatant than in the Soviet Union—and once again the world Communist movement has aped these outrages.

We could go on listing Communist shortcomings at length—historians have a marked tendency to set themselves up as judges. This role does not become them, but if they give in to its temptation they cannot really refuse to admit that the Bolshevik enterprise in Russia and outside had the grandeur of an immense collective epic. To embark on this adventure called for a measure of faith that few people have been able to express with so much courage and steadfastness; it demanded the unshakeable conviction that the improbable could be turned into the possible, that the great dream of mankind freed from the shackles of misery and injustice could yet be realized. Revolutionary prophets and heroes are by the very nature of things condemned to be judges and sometimes executioners. Socialism in Jaurès's day was admittedly purer and more humane than it became later—it was full of great ideals and dreams of peaceful conquests and fraternal victories. After the Russian Revolution, socialism has become, for some, the mere wish to manage society, but for others it remains the implacable determination to fight and to build. The Russian Revolution has not only destroyed a society but also a myth, reminding men that there is no work more perilous than the attempt to bring them happiness and freedom.

The serene attitude of those who, surveying human failure and social imperfections, judge them inevitable and withdraw into resignation and social conformism is admittedly far more comfortable. At most they will admit that the pioneers of a new world, men who have deserted the 'old house' and who have ventured on to uncharted paths, may have something to teach the world; but their own passivity makes them convinced that the game is not worth the candle. The revolutionary runs interminable risks—he may err, fail or even lose his life. It was Robespierre who at the end of his brief existence set up the bitter cry of the misunderstood apostle and the defeated warrior: 'Alas, the time for doing good has not yet come.'

It is, however, by such sacrifices, setbacks and sufferings that mankind alone makes progress. The moralist may condemn violence, but the sociologist meets its traces everywhere and records its ravages. Man has the choice between blind rejection and a more open mind. In the latter case he will measure the results of violence against the sacrifices it brings in its wake, and the motives and ends of those who strode on to the stage of history.

In the case of the Russian Revolution, this action still continues, so that we must perforce suspend final judgment. For all that, we are entitled to say that its dimensions and effects make it one of the greatest events in history. It has helped to shape the modern world and largely determines its future. For whenever men take the path of revolt in order to put an end to their misery and servitude, they will find in the Russian Revolution, in its bravery, in its victory and even in its mistakes and failures, in the fervour of its leaders and the enthusiasm of the masses, an inexhaustible source of inspiration.

Chronology of the Russian Revolution

(FEBRUARY 1917–JULY 1918)

The dates are given according to the old-style Russian (Julian) calendar which was in use in Russia until February 1st, 1918, and which was thirteen days behind the Western (Gregorian) calendar.

1917

February 22nd	Mass demonstrations in Petrograd.
February 24th	General strike and bloody clashes in the capital.
February 27th	Triumph of Petrograd insurrection. Provisional Committee of Duma appoints special commissars in charge of the ministries. Petrograd Soviet of Workers' Deputies formed.
February 28th	Moscow Soviet formed.
March 2nd	Abdication of Nicholas II.
March 3rd	Official inauguration of Provisional Government.
March 12th	Abolition of the death sentence.
March 14th	Petrograd Soviet calls for a peace without annexation or indemnities.
March 15th	General strike in Moscow in support of an eight-hour day.
March 29th	All-Russian Conference of Soviets in Petrograd.
April 3rd	Lenin arrives in Petrograd.
April 7th	*Pravda* publishes Lenin's April theses.
April 18th	P. N. Miliukov, Minister of Foreign Affairs, publishes note stating that Provisional Government will adhere to agreements with the Allies and that it will not make a separate peace.
April 20th–21st	Violent mass demonstrations in Petrograd against foreign policy of Provisional Government.
April 24th–27th	All-Russian Conference of Bolshevik Party: Lenin's theses are approved.
April 30th	A. I. Guchkov, Minister of War and Navy, resigns.

May 2nd	Miliukov resigns.
May 4th	All-Russian Soviet of Peasant Deputies established. Trotsky returns to Russia.
May 5th	First Coalition Government formed. Prince Lvov remains President; Kerensky Minister of War; the socialists obtain six ministerial posts.
June 3rd	First All-Russian Congress of Soviets of Workers' and Soldiers' Deputies opens.
June 9th	Bolsheviks call off anti-government demonstration in Petrograd.
June 18th	Russian offensive in Galicia begins. Mass meetings in Petrograd organized by the Soviet turn into pro-Bolshevik demonstrations.
July 3rd–4th	Violent anti-government demonstrations in Petrograd.
July 5th	Arrest of Bolshevik leaders ordered.
July 7th	Lenin goes into hiding.
July 8th	Prince Lvov resigns; Kerensky appointed head of an interim government.
July 12th	Provisional Government re-establishes death sentence at the front.
July 16th	General Kornilov appointed Commander-in-Chief of the Russian Army.
July 23rd	Trotsky arrested by Provisional Government.
July 24th	Kerensky forms a new Coalition Government.
August 12th–15th	State Conference in Moscow, and general protest strike.
August 20th	Bolshevik success in Petrograd municipal elections.
August 21st	Germans occupy Riga.
August 27th–30th	Abortive counter-revolutionary putsch led by General Kornilov.
September 1st	Petrograd Soviet carries a Bolshevik resolution.
September 4th	Trotsky freed on bail.
September 5th	Moscow Soviet carries a Bolshevik motion.
September 9th	Leaders of Petrograd Soviet go over to the Bolsheviks.
September 14th–21st	'Democratic Conference' meets in Petrograd.
September 24th	Kerensky forms third and last Coalition

Government. Bolshevik victory in the Moscow municipal elections.

October 7th	Opening of Pre-Parliament; Bolsheviks refuse to participate.
October 9th	Formation of Military Revolutionary Committee of the Petrograd Soviet.
October 10th	Central Committee of the Bolshevik Party declares for an armed insurrection.
October 22nd	Conflict between staff of the Petrograd garrison and the Military Revolutionary Committee.
October 23rd	Peter and Paul Fortress goes over to the Bolsheviks.
October 24th–25th	Overthrow of Provisional Government by Bolshevik forces in Petrograd.
October 26th	Inauguration of Soviet regime: Second All-Russian Congress of Soviets issues peace and land decrees.
October 27th	Fighting breaks out in Moscow.
October 29th	Bolsheviks defeat counter-revolutionary uprising in Petrograd.
October 30th	Kerensky's forces defeated at Pulkovo.
November 2nd	Bolshevik victories in Moscow; General Alexeiev begins organizing counter-revolutionary army in Southern Russia.
November 9th	*Pravda* publishes secret treaties.
November 12th–14th	Elections to Constituent Assembly.
November 14th	Decree establishing 'workers' control'.
November 19th	Peace negotiations opened at Brest-Litovsk.
December 1st	Formation of the Supreme Council of National Economy.
December 2nd	Armistice between Russia and the Central Powers.
December 7th	Cheka (All-Russia Extraordinary Commission) formed.
December 9th	Left-wing Social Revolutionaries agree to enter the government.
December 13th	Lenin publishes his 'Theses on the Constituent Assembly' in *Pravda*.
December 14th	Nationalization of banks.
December 18th	Soviet Government recognizes the independence of Finland.

1918

January 2nd	Unsuccessful attempt on Lenin's life.
January 9th	*Rada* proclaims the independence of the Ukraine.
January 18th	Meeting of Constituent Assembly.
January 19th	Dissolution of Constituent Assembly.
January 28th	Negotiations in Brest-Litovsk broken off: Russia stops the war but refuses to sign the peace.
February 5th	Separation of Church and State.
February 10th	Soviet Government repudiates Tsarist debts.
February 18th	German forces launch an offensive in Russia.
February 19th	Soviet Government agrees to resumption of peace negotiations.
February 23rd	Central Powers publish their peace terms.
February 23rd	Central Executive Committee of Congress of Soviets accepts German peace conditions.
March 3rd	Brest-Litovsk Peace Treaty signed.
March 5th	Allied forces land at Murmansk.
March 12th	Soviet Government leaves Petrograd for Moscow.
March 15th–16th	All-Russian Congress of Soviets ratifies the Brest-Litovsk peace treaty.
March 16th	German troops occupy Kiev.
April 6th	Japanese forces land at Vladivostok.
April 13th	German troops occupy Odessa.
April 20th	Germans occupy Crimea.
May 25th	Czechoslovak legions launch anti-Bolshevik offensive.
June 8th	Social Revolutionaries supported by the Czechoslovak legions form anti-Bolshevik Government at Samara.
July 6th	German Ambassador assassinated by Social Revolutionaries in preparation for uprising against the Soviet government.

Bibliography

From the wealth of books devoted to the Russian Revolution, I have chosen a number of works that strike me as the most likely to supplement the information contained in this volume. Most of these are general accounts of the events and the chief actors in them. In the main, I have kept to works written in, or translated into, French and English. The list does not include general histories of Russia, which the reader may nevertheless find extremely useful.

I OFFICIAL DOCUMENTS

Browden, R. and Kerensky, A., *The Russian Provisional Government (1917). Selected documents,* 3 vols. (Stanford, 1961).

Bunyan, J., *Intervention, Civil War and Communism in Russia. Documents and Materials* (Baltimore, 1936).

Bunyan, J. and Fisher, H., *The Bolshevik Revolution (1917-1918)* (Stanford, 1934).

Central Committee of the Bolshevik Party, *Bolsheviks and the October Revolution; Proceedings of the Central Committee of the Bolshevik Party (August 1917-February 1918)* (Moscow, 1964).

Degras, J., *Soviet Documents on Foreign Policy,* vol. i, 1917-24 (New York, 1951).

Gankin, O. and Fisher, H., *The Bolsheviks and the World War* (Stanford, 1940).

Marguerite, V., *Les Alliés contre la Russie pendant et après la guerre mondiale; faits et documents* (Paris, 1926).

Oldenbourg, S., *Le coup d'État bolchevik (20 octobre-3 décembre 1917); recueil de documents* (Paris, 1919).

Zeman, Z. A. B., *Germany and the Revolution in Russia (1915-1918); Documents from the Archives of the German Foreign Ministry* (New York, 1958).

II THE OLD REGIME

See also general works on the history of Russia, and books on special problems connected with the fall of Tsarism.

Gille, B., *Histoire économique et sociale de la Russie du Moyen age au XXe siècle* (Paris 1949).

Owen, A., *The Russian Peasant Movement (1906-1917)* (London, 1937).

Robinson, G., *Rural Russia under the Old Regime* (New York, 1949).

Seton-Watson, H., *The Decline of Imperial Russia* (New York, 1952).
Troyat, H., *La vie quotidienne en Russie au temps du dernier tsar* (Paris, 1959).

III SOCIALISM BEFORE THE REVOLUTION

Badaev, N., *Les bolcheviks au parlement tsariste* (Paris, 1932).
Berdiaev, N., *The origins of Russian Communism* (Ann Arbor, 1960).
Cole, G. D. H., *A History of Socialist Thought*, vol. 2 (New York, 1954), deals with the period 1850–90; vol. 3, (New York, 1956) with 1889–1914.
Dan, T., *Die Sozialdemokratie Russlands nach dem Jahre 1908* (Berlin, 1925).
    The origins of Bolshevism (New York, 1964).
Levin, A., *The Second Duma; a Study of the Social-Democratic Party and the Russian Constitutional Experience* (New Haven, 1940).
Lydin, M., *Material zur Erläuterung der Parteikrise in der Sozialdemokratischen Arbeiterpartei Russlands* (Geneva, 1904).
Martov, J., *Geschichte der russischen Sozialdemokratie* (Berlin, 1925).
Wolfe, B., *Three who Made a Revolution* (New York, 1948). (Excellent work on the beginnings of Bolshevism.)

IV BOLSHEVIK DOCTRINE AT THE TIME OF THE REVOLUTION

Bukharin, N. and Preobrazhensky, E., *The ABC of Communism* (Ann Arbor, 1966).
Kamenev, L., *The Dictatorship of the Proletariat* (Detroit, 1922).
Kautsky, K., *The Dictatorship of the Proletariat* (Ann Arbor, 1964).
    Terrorisme et Communisme (Paris, n.d.).
Lefebvre, H., *Pour connaître la pensée de Lénine* (Paris, 1957).
Lenin, V. I., *Collected Works. Completely revised, edited and annotated*, 23 vols. (London and New York, 1927–45). For doctrine, see particularly, *What is to be done?* (New York, 1929); *Imperialism: the Highest Stage of Capitalism* (New York, 1939); *The State and Revolution* (New York, 1921); *The Proletarian Revolution and Kautsky the Renegade* (New York, 1934); *'Left-wing' Communism: an Infantile Disorder* (Detroit, 1921).
Luxemburg, R., *The Russian Revolution* (Ann Arbor, 1961).
Mayer, A., *Lénine et le léninisme* (Paris, 1966).
Radek, K., *Proletarische Diktatur und Terrorismus* (Hamburg, 1919).
Russell, B., *The Practice and Theory of Bolshevism* (London, 1920).
Trotsky, L., *The Permanent Revolution* (New York, 1931).
    Terrorism and Communism (Reply to Karl Kautsky) (Ann Arbor, 1961).
Varga, E., *La dictature du prolétariat* (Paris, 1922).

V BIOGRAPHIES

Of Lenin

Bruhat, J., *Lénine* (Paris, 1960).

Fischer, L., *The Life of Lenin* (New York, 1964).

Gorky, M., *Lénine et le paysan russe* (Paris, 1924).

Gourfinkel, N., *Lénine* (Paris, 1959).

Guilbeaux, H., *Le portrait authentique de V. I. Lénine* (Paris, 1924).

Krupskaia, N., *Ma vie avec Lénine* (Paris, 1933).

Levine, I., *Lénine* (Paris, 1924).

Malaparte, C., *Le bonhomme Lénine* (Paris, 1932).

Pospelov, P., *V. I. Lenin; biography* (Moscow, 1960).

Shub, D., *Lenin* (New York, 1948).

Trotsky, L., *Lenin* (New York, 1921).

Walter, G., *Lénine* (Verviers, 1963).

Of Trotsky

Deutscher, I., *Trotsky;* vol. 1, *The prophet armed (1879–1921)* (New York, 1954); vol. 2, *The prophet unarmed (1921–1929)* (New York, 1959); vol. 3, *The prophet outcast (1929–1940)* (London, 1963). (These works are far more than biography; they constitute a remarkable history of Soviet Russia from its origins to 1940.)

Eastman, M., *Leon Trotsky: The Portrait of a Youth* (New York, 1925).

Serge, V., *Vie et mort de Trotsky* (Paris, 1951).

Of Stalin

Deutscher, I., *Stalin* (New York, 1967).

Marie, J. J., *Staline* (1879–1953), (Paris, 1967).

Souvarine, B., *Staline, aperçu historique de bolshevisme* (Paris, 1935).

Trotsky, L., *Staline* (Paris, 1948).

VI THE RUSSIAN REVOLUTION

Abramovitch, R., *The Soviet Revolution (1917–1939)*, (New York, 1962). (Menshevik approach.)

Alexinsky, G., *Du tsarisme au communisme; La Révolution russe: ses causes, ses effets* (Paris, 1923).

Bach, L., *Histoire de la Révolution russe; la révolution prolétarienne* (Paris, 1930).

Bettelheim, C., *L'économie soviétique* (Paris, 1950).

Bezemer, J. W., *De Russische revolutie in westerse ogen* (Amsterdam 1956). (Collection of Western press reports.)

Broué, P., *Le Parti bolchevik* (Paris, 1963).

Carmichael, J., *Short History of the Russian Revolution* (New York, 1964).

Carr, E. H., *The Bolshevik Revolution (1917–1923)*, 3 vols. (Baltimore, 1966). (Outstanding contribution in which maximum objectivity is coupled to extremely wide documentation and searching analysis.)

Chamberlin, W. H., *The Russian Revolution (1917–1921)*, 2 vols. (New York, 1965). (Most useful classic.)

Coquin, F., *La Révolution russe* (Paris, 1962).

Danilov, Y., *La Russie dans la guerre mondiale (1914–1917)* (Paris, 1927).

De Grunwald, C., *Le tsar Nicolas II* (Paris, 1965).

Dobb, M., *Soviet economic development since 1917* (London, 1956).

Ferro, M., *La Révolution de 1917* (Paris, 1967).

Fischer, L., *The Soviets in World Affairs (1917–1929)* (London, 1930). (Excellent work on foreign policy of revolutionary Russia.)

Florinsky, T., *The End of the Russian Empire* (New Haven, 1931).

Footman, D., *Civil War in Russia* (London, 1961).

Gorky, M., Molotov, V., Voroshilov, K., Kirov, S., Zhdanov, A., Stalin, J., *History of the Russian Revolution*, 4 vols. (Moscow, 1946).

Golikov, G., *The October Revolution* (Moscow, 1966).

Golovin, N., *The Russian Army in the World War* (New Haven, 1931).

Grenard, F., *La Révolution russe* (Paris, 1933).

Kennan, G., *Russia and the West under Lenin and Stalin* (Boston, 1961).

Kerensky, A., *La Révolution russe* (Paris, 1928).

Koghan, L., *Russia in Revolution (1890–1918)* (London, 1966).

Liebman, M., *La politique en U.R.S.S.*, in 'Le dossier Russie', 2 vols. (Verviers, 1966).

Miliukov, P., *Histoire de la Révolution russe* (Paris, 1932).

Nolde, B., *L'Ancien régime et la Révolution russe* (Paris, 1948).

Ollivier, J. P., *Quand fera-t-il jour, camarade?* (Paris, 1967).

Pares, B., *The Fall of the Russian Monarchy* (London, 1939).

Pipes, R., *The Formation of the Soviet Union: Communism and Nationalism* (Cambridge, Mass., 1954).

Rollin, H., *La Révolution russe: ses origines, ses résultats*, 2 vols. (Paris, 1931).

Rosenberg, A., *Histoire du bolchevisme* (Paris, 1936).

Serge, V., *L'An I de la Révolution russe* (Paris, 1965).

Schapiro, L. B., *The Communist Party of the Soviet Union* (New York, 1960).

    Origin of the Communist Autocracy (Cambridge, Mass., 1955). (Despite the author's hostility, a most useful work on the history of the Russian Communist Party since its origins.)

Sorlin, P., *La société soviétique (1917–1964)* (Paris, 1964).

Tchernov (Chernov), V., *The Great Russian Revolution* (New Haven, 1936).

Trotsky, L., *De la Révolution d'octobre à la paix de Brest-Litovsk* (Geneva, 1918).

    History of the Russian Revolution, 3 vols. (Ann Arbor, 1967).

(Fundamental to any serious understanding of the Russian Revolution; the author's political commitment in no way detracts from the historical importance of this work.)

Voline, *The unknown revolution* (*1917–1921*) (New York, 1956). (Anarchist approach.)

Welter, G., *La guerre civile en Russie* (*1918–1920*) (Paris, 1936).

Wheeler-Bennet, J., *Brest-Litovsk, the Forgotten Peace* (New York, 1939).

see also: *History of the October Revolution* (Moscow, 1966).

> *History of the Communist Party of the Soviet Union* (Moscow, 1960).

VII MEMOIRS AND CONTEMPORARY ACCOUNTS

Anet, C., *La Révolution russe*, 3 vols. (Paris, 1917–19).

Balabanoff, A., *My Life as a Rebel* (London–New York, 1938).

Bryant, L., *Six Red Months in Russia* (New York, 1918).

Buchanan, G., *My Mission to Russia*, 2 vols. (Boston, 1923).

Buchanan, M., *Dissolution of an Empire* (London, 1932).

Comte, G., *La Révolution russe par ses témoins* (Paris, 1963).

Denikin, A., *The Russian Turmoil* (London, 1932).

De Robien, L., *Journal d'un diplomate en Russie* (*1917–1918*) (Paris, 1967).

Destrée, J., *Les fondeurs de neige, Notes sur la révolution bolchevique. À Pétrograd pendant l'hiver 1917–1918* (Paris–Brussels, 1920).

Eddallin, A., *La Révolution russe par un témoin* (Paris, 1920).

Ehrenburg, I., *Men, Years—Life.* 5 vols. (London, 1961–4).

Finger, V., *Mémoires d'une révolutionnaire* (Paris, 1930).

Francis, D., *Russia from the American Embassy* (*April 1916–November 1918*), (New York, 1921).

Gorky, M., *The Petrograd Insurrection* (Moscow, 1958).

—— *Fragments from my Diary* (New York, 1924).

Kachowskaia, I., *Souvenirs d'une révolutionnaire* (Paris, 1926).

Kerensky, A., *The Catastrophe: Kerensky's own story of the Russian Revolution* (New York, 1927).

—— *La Russie au tournant de l'histoire* (Paris, 1967).

Kleinmichel, Comtesse, *Souvenirs d'un monde englouti* (Paris, 1927).

Knox, A., *With the Russian Army, 1914–1917* (London, 1921).

Kritchewsky, B., *Vers la catastrophe russe. Lettres de Pétrograd* (*octobre 1917–février 1919*), (Paris, 1919).

Lockhart, Bruce R., *Memoirs of a British Agent* (New York–London, 1933).

Loukomsky, A., *Memoirs of the Russian Revolution* (London, 1922).

Marischkine-Witte, V., *À Pétrograd pendant la Révolution; Notes et Souvenirs* (Paris, 1925).

Markovitch, M., *La Révolution russe vue par une Française* (Paris, 1918).

Morizet, A., *Chez Lénine et Trotsky* (Paris, 1922).

Nicholas II, *Journal intime* (Paris, 1925).

Niessel, A., *Le triomphe des Bolcheviks et la paix de Brest-Litovsk; Souvenirs (1917–1918)*, (Paris, 1939).

Noulens, J., *Mon ambassade en Russie soviétique (1917–1919)* (Paris, 1933).

Paléologue, M., *La Russie des Tsars pendant la guerre*, 3 vols. (Paris, 1922).

Paley, Princess, *Souvenirs de Russie* (Paris, 1923).

Pax, P., *Journal d'une comédienne française sous la terreur bolchevique* (Paris, 1919).

Pethybridge, R., *Witnesses of the Russian Revolution* (London, 1964).

Piatnitsky, O., *Souvenirs d'un bolchevik (1886–1917)* (Paris, 1931).

Price, M. Philips, *My Reminiscences of the Russian Revolution* (London, 1921).

Ransome, A., *Six Weeks in Russia* (London, 1919).

Reed, J., *Ten Days that Shook the World* (New York, 1935). (Extremely valuable eye-witness account of the atmosphere in Petrograd during the October insurrection by an American journalist sympathetic to the Revolution.)

Rodzianko, M., *The Reign of Rasputin: an Empire's Collapse; Memoirs* (New York, 1927.)

Sadoul, J., *Notes sur la Révolution bolchevique (octobre 1917–janvier 1919)*, (Paris, 1920).

Savinkov, B., *Memoirs of a Terrorist* (New York, 1931).

Sergevitch, L., *Aux premiers souffles de l'anarchie; Souvenirs d'un étudiant sur la Révolution russe de 1917 à 1919* (Paris, 1932).

Shulgin, V., *Memoiren aus der russischen Revolution (1905–1917)* (Berlin, 1928).

Steinberg, J., *Souvenirs d'un commissaire du Peuple (1917–1918)*, (Paris 1930).

Sukhanov, N., *The Russian Revolution (1917)* (New York, 1955). (Extremely interesting observations by a shrewd Menshevik observer.)

Tchernov (Chernov), V., *Mes tribulations en Russie soviétique* (Paris, 1921).

Trotsky, L., *My Life* (New York, 1930).

Vandervelde, E., *Trois aspects de la Révolution russe (7 mai–15 juin, 1917)* (Paris, 1918).

Verstraete, M., *Mes cahiers russes. L'ancien régime; le gouvernement provisoire, le pouvoir des Soviets* (Paris, 1920).

Williams, A. R., *Through the Russian Revolution* (New York, 1921).

Witte, S., *Mémoires* (Paris, n.d.).

Wrangel, Baron, *Mémoires du général Wrangel* (Paris, 1930).

Index

ABOUT THE AUTHOR

MARCEL LIEBMAN was born in 1929, and teaches political history and sociology at the Free University of Brussels. He took his D.Sc. (Political Science) with his thesis on the ideological origins of Belgian Communism. The author of numerous studies of modern Socialist and Communist trends, he is a regular contributor to Jean-Paul Sartre's *Temps Modernes*.